Cells at Work!

はたらく細胞

CELL

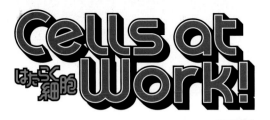

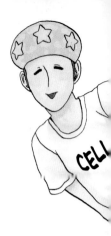

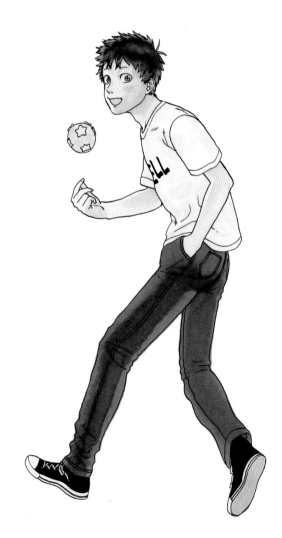

03

AKANE SHIMIZU

CONTENTS

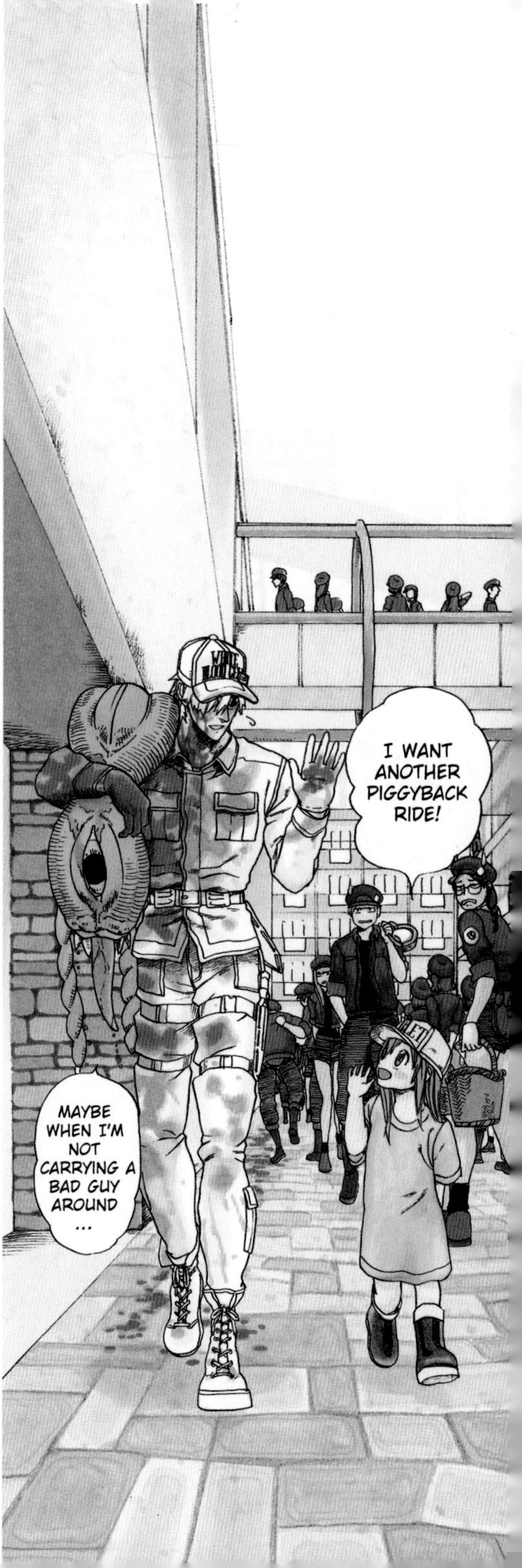

I WANT ANOTHER PIGGYBACK RIDE!
MAYBE WHEN I'M NOT CARRYING A BAD GUY AROUND...

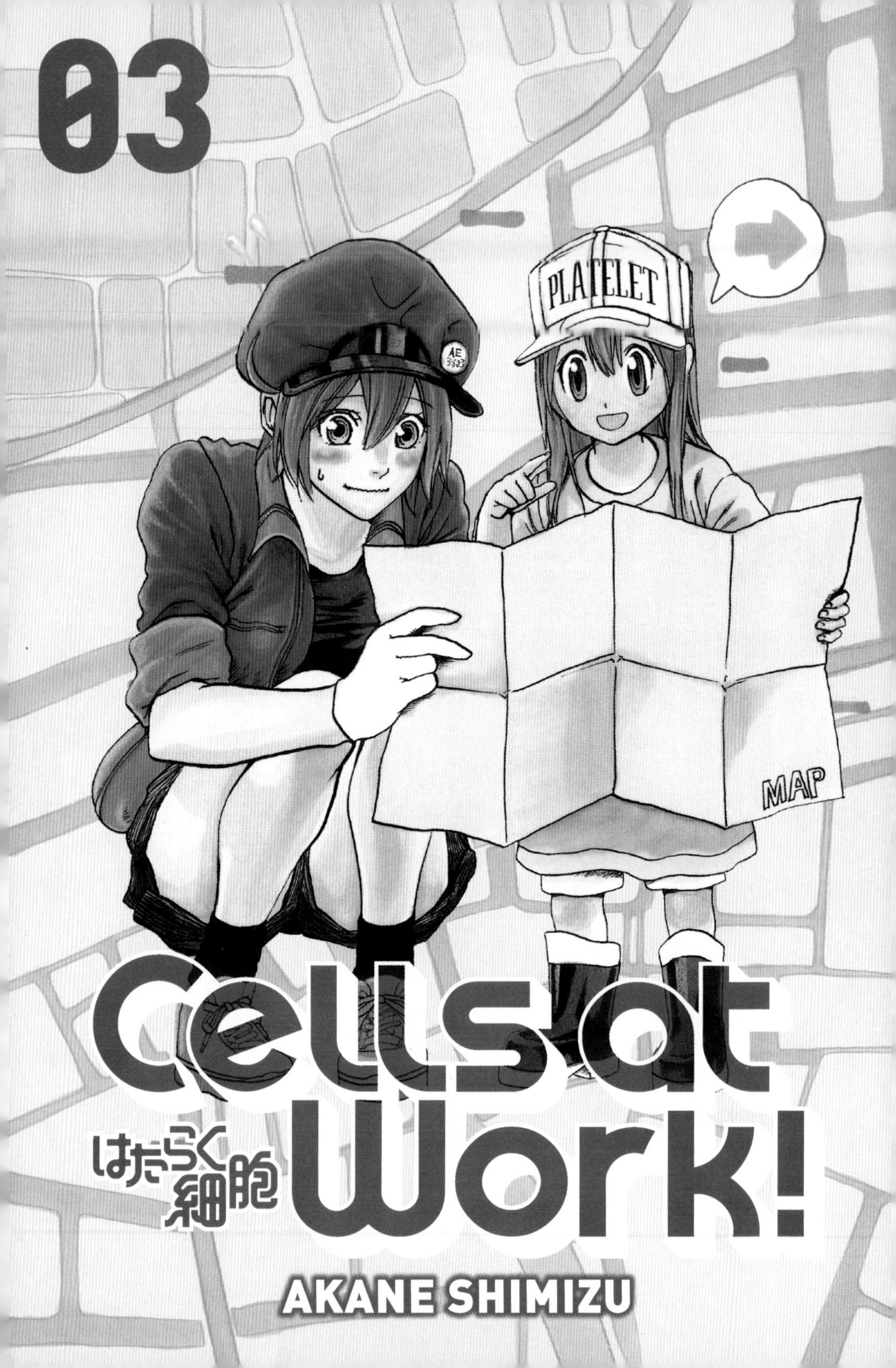
03
PLATELET
MAP
Cells at Work!
はたらく細胞
AKANE SHIMIZU

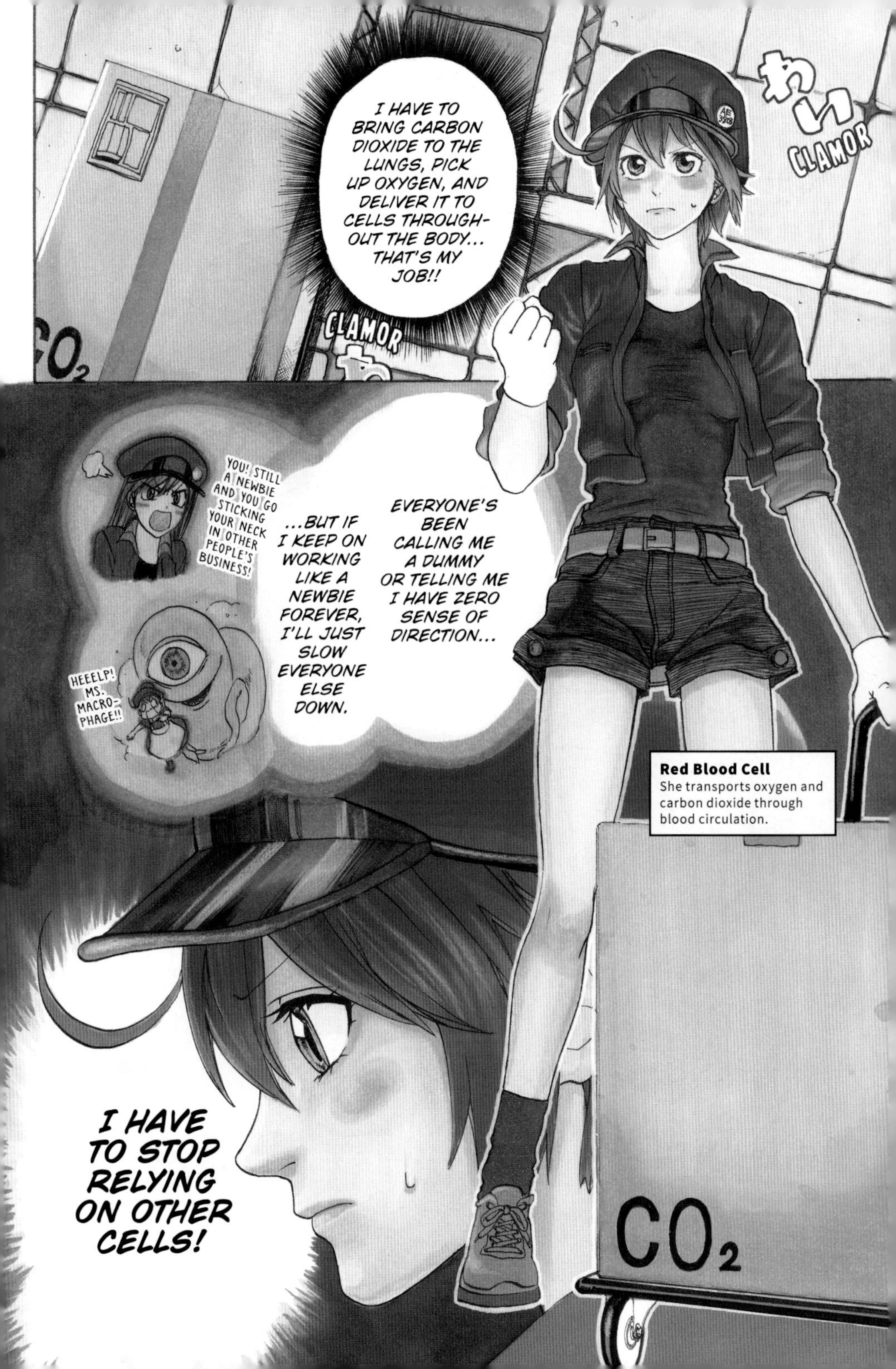
わい
CLAMOR
I HAVE TO BRING CARBON DIOXIDE TO THE LUNGS, PICK UP OXYGEN, AND DELIVER IT TO CELLS THROUGH-OUT THE BODY... THAT'S MY JOB!!
CLAMOR
CO_2
Red Blood Cell
She transports oxygen and carbon dioxide through blood circulation.
EVERYONE'S BEEN CALLING ME A DUMMY OR TELLING ME I HAVE ZERO SENSE OF DIRECTION...
...BUT IF I KEEP ON WORKING LIKE A NEWBIE FOREVER, I'LL JUST SLOW EVERYONE ELSE DOWN.
YOU! STILL A NEWBIE AND YOU GO STICKING YOUR NECK IN OTHER PEOPLE'S BUSINESS!
HEEELP! MS. MACRO-PHAGE!!
I HAVE TO STOP RELYING ON OTHER CELLS!
CO_2

CHAPTER 10: THE CIRCULATORY SYSTEM

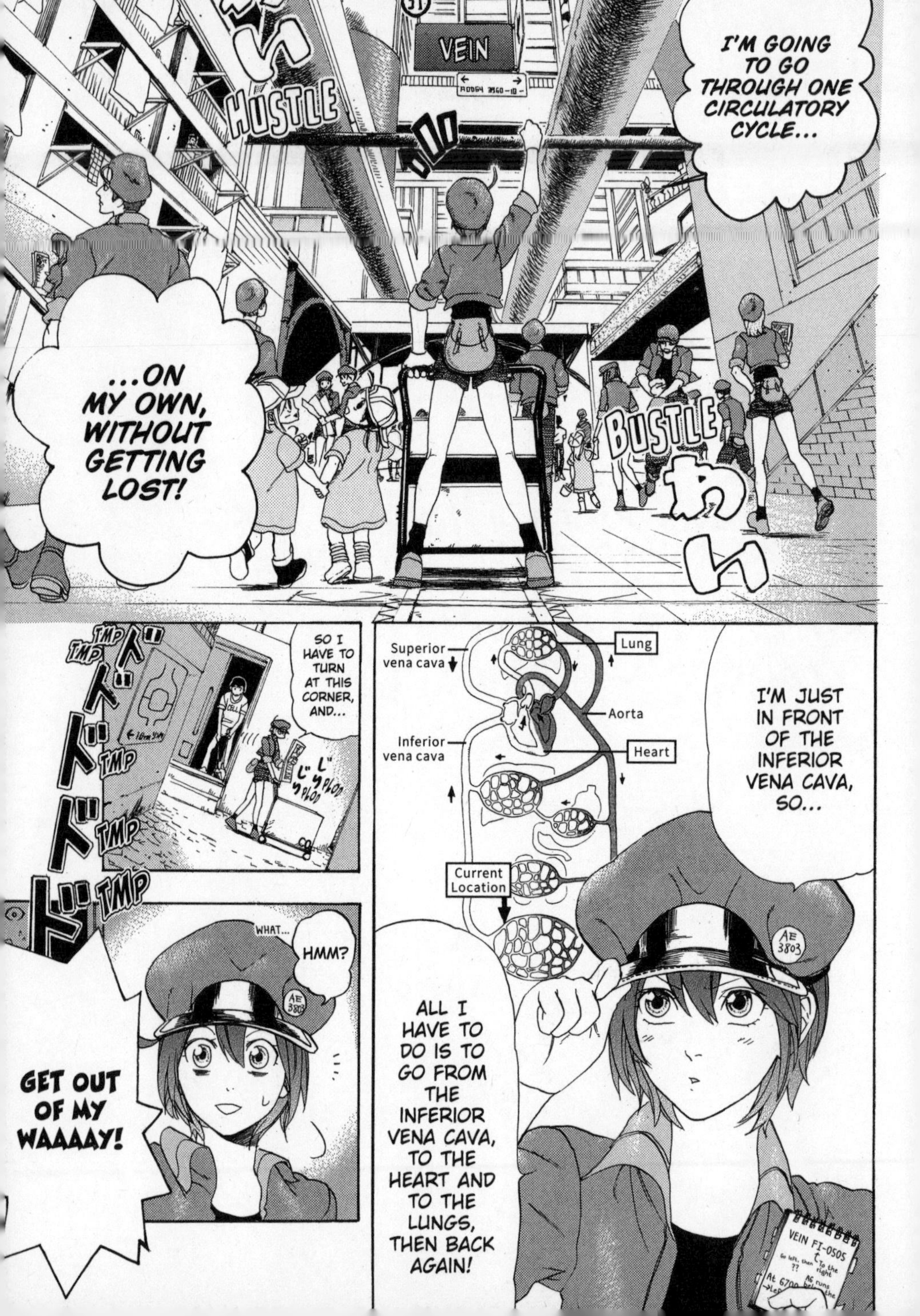
VEIN
I'M GOING TO GO THROUGH ONE CIRCULATORY CYCLE...
HUSTLE
BUSTLE
...ON MY OWN, WITHOUT GETTING LOST!
Superior vena cava
Lung
Aorta
Inferior vena cava
Heart
Current Location
AE 3803
I'M JUST IN FRONT OF THE INFERIOR VENA CAVA, SO...
ALL I HAVE TO DO IS TO GO FROM THE INFERIOR VENA CAVA, TO THE HEART AND TO THE LUNGS, THEN BACK AGAIN!
VEIN FI-0505
SO I HAVE TO TURN AT THIS CORNER, AND...
PLOD PLOD
TMP TMP TMP TMP TMP
WHAT...
HMM?
GET OUT OF MY WAAAAY!

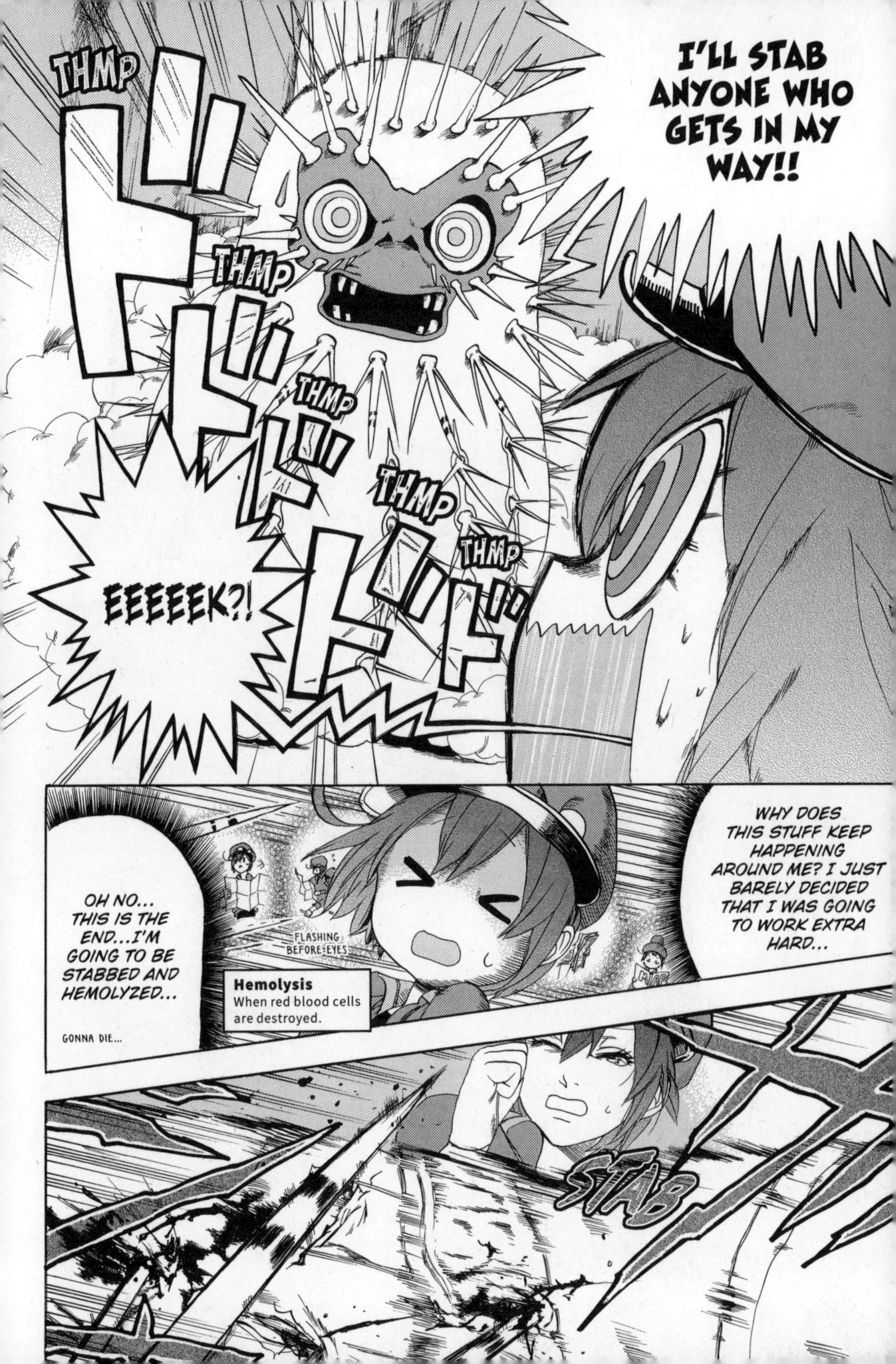

I'LL STAB ANYONE WHO GETS IN MY WAY!!
THMP
THMP
THMP
THMP
THMP
EEEEEK?!
WHY DOES THIS STUFF KEEP HAPPENING AROUND ME? I JUST BARELY DECIDED THAT I WAS GOING TO WORK EXTRA HARD...
OH NO... THIS IS THE END...I'M GOING TO BE STABBED AND HEMOLYZED...
FLASHING BEFORE EYES
Hemolysis
When red blood cells are destroyed.
GONNA DIE...
STAB

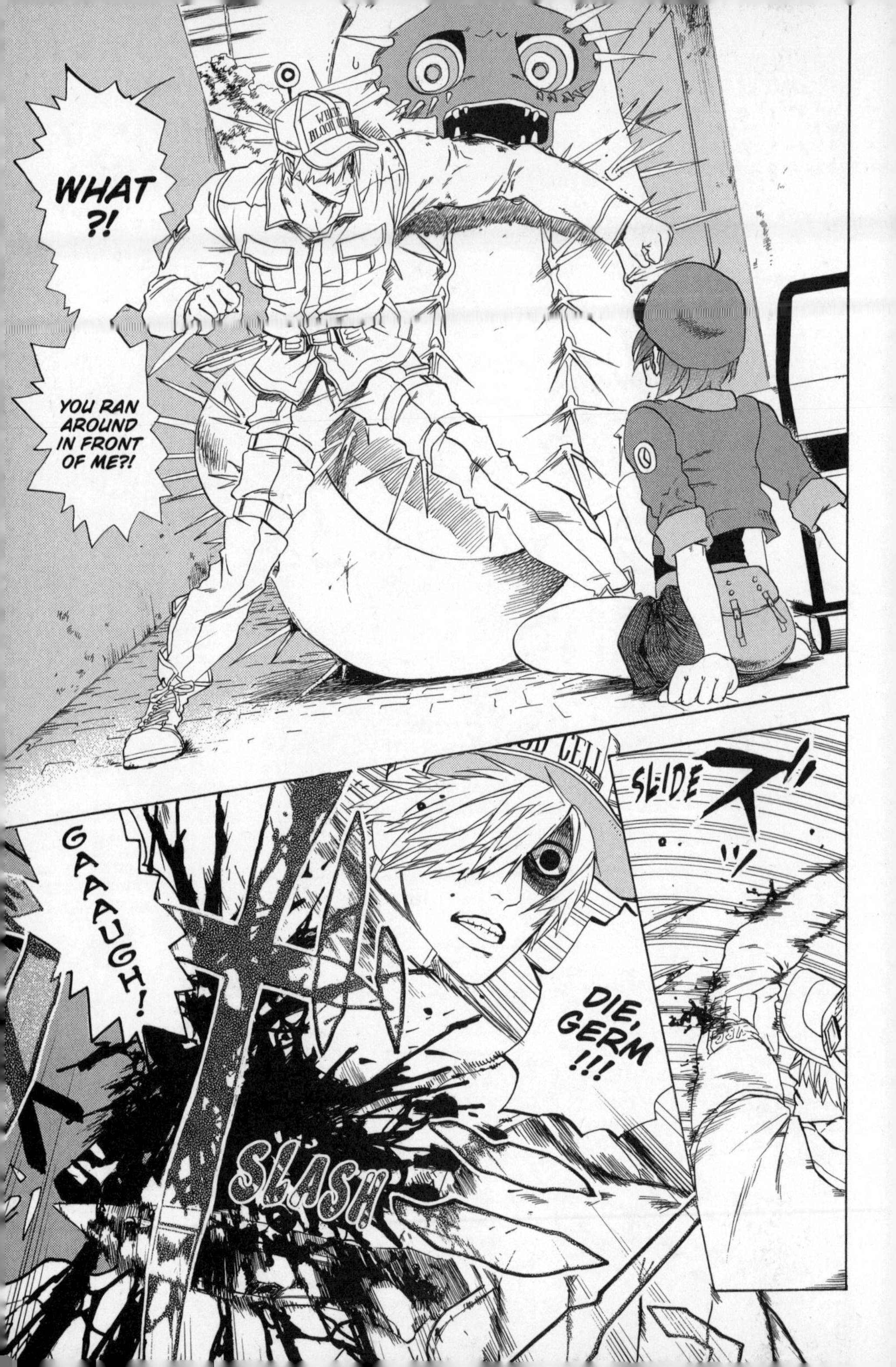
WHAT?!
YOU RAN AROUND IN FRONT OF ME?!
SLIDE
DIE, GERM!!!
GAAAUGH!
SLASH

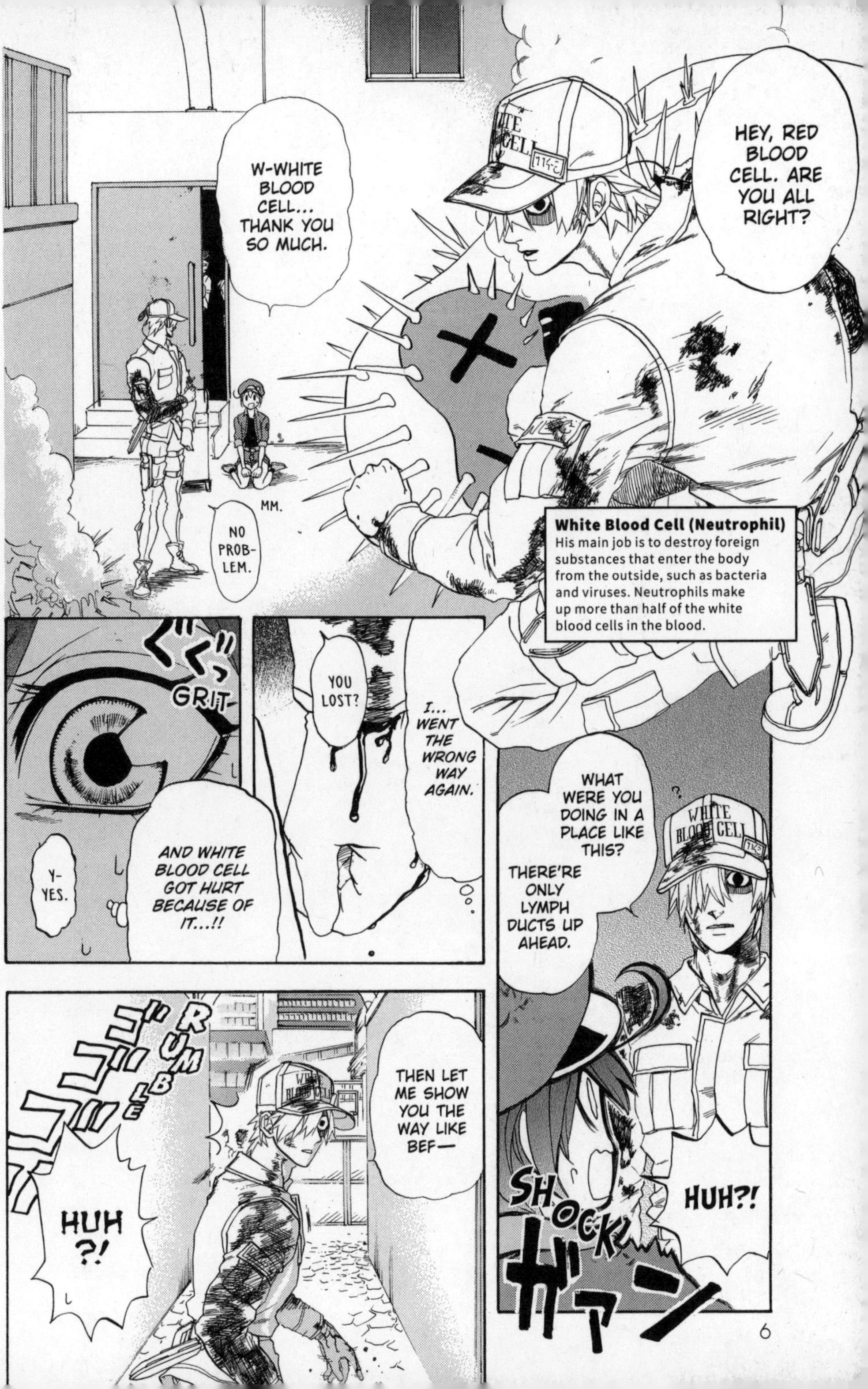
HEY, RED BLOOD CELL. ARE YOU ALL RIGHT?
W-WHITE BLOOD CELL... THANK YOU SO MUCH.
White Blood Cell (Neutrophil)
His main job is to destroy foreign substances that enter the body from the outside, such as bacteria and viruses. Neutrophils make up more than half of the white blood cells in the blood.
MM.
NO PROB-LEM.
WHAT WERE YOU DOING IN A PLACE LIKE THIS?
THERE'RE ONLY LYMPH DUCTS UP AHEAD.
HUH?!
SHOCK!
ガァン
YOU LOST?
I... WENT THE WRONG WAY AGAIN.
ぐぐ
GRIT
AND WHITE BLOOD CELL GOT HURT BECAUSE OF IT...!!
Y-YES.
THEN LET ME SHOW YOU THE WAY LIKE BEF—
RUMBLE
HUH ?!

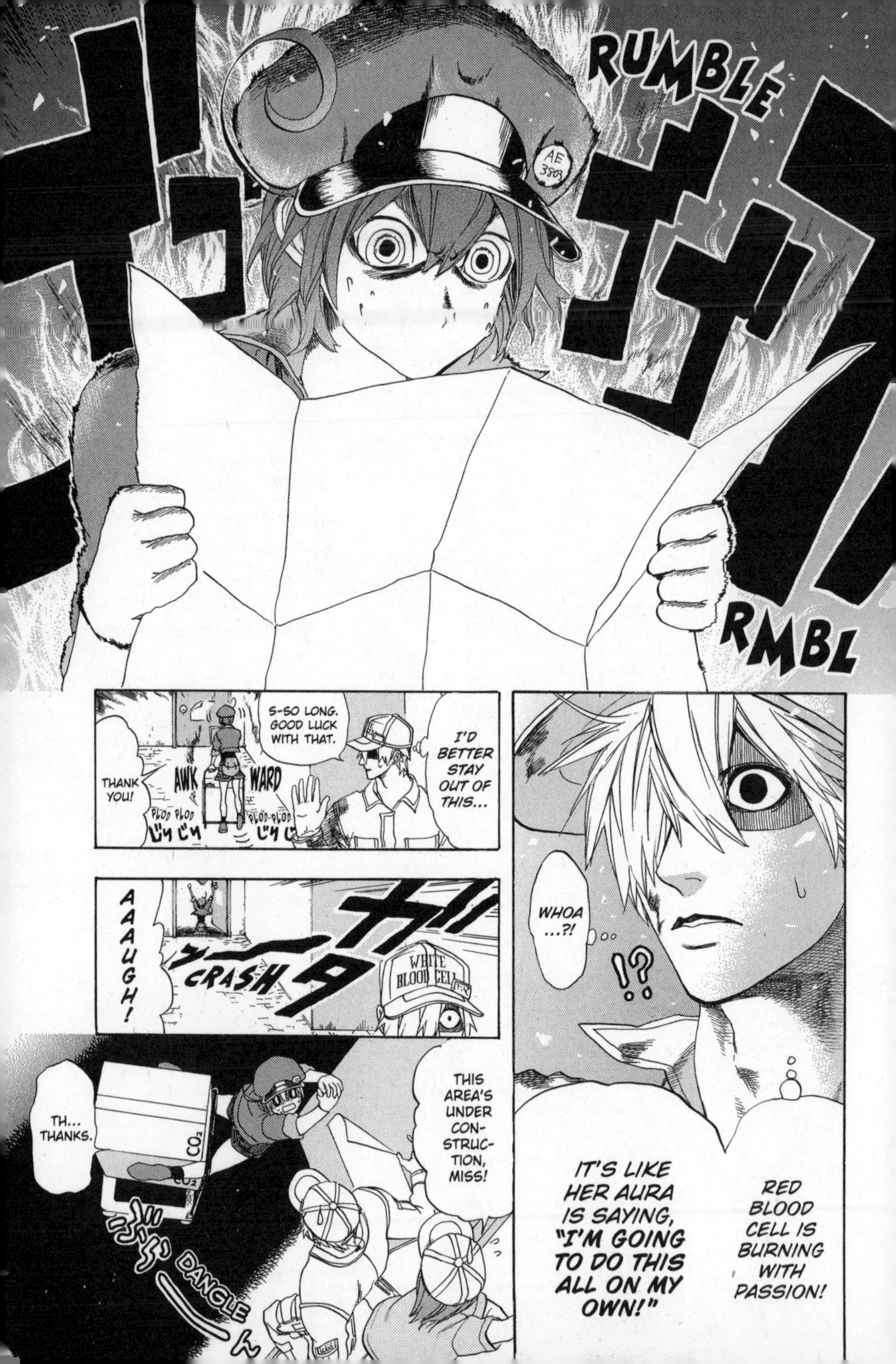
RUMBLE
RMBL
WHOA ...?!
!?
RED BLOOD CELL IS BURNING WITH PASSION!
IT'S LIKE HER AURA IS SAYING, "I'M GOING TO DO THIS ALL ON MY OWN!"
I'D BETTER STAY OUT OF THIS...
S-SO LONG. GOOD LUCK WITH THAT.
AWK WARD
THANK YOU!
PLOD PLOD
PLOD PLOD
CRASH
AAAAUGH!
THIS AREA'S UNDER CON-STRUC-TION, MISS!
TH... THANKS.
CO_2
DANGLE

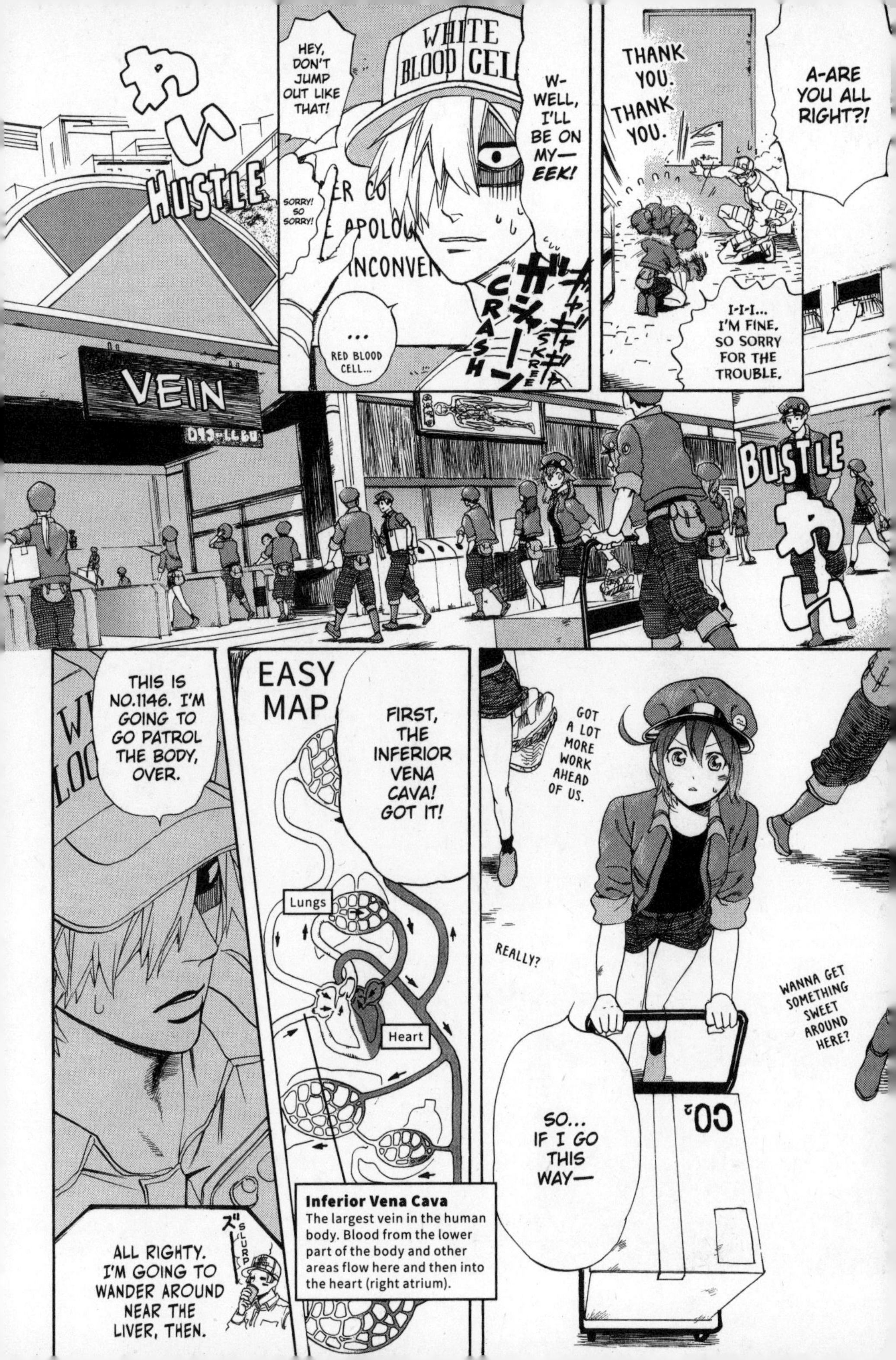
A-ARE YOU ALL RIGHT?!
THANK YOU. THANK YOU.
I-I-I... I'M FINE, SO SORRY FOR THE TROUBLE.
W-WELL, I'LL BE ON MY— EEK!
HEY, DON'T JUMP OUT LIKE THAT!
WHITE BLOOD CELL
SORRY! SO SORRY!
CRASH
SKREE
...
RED BLOOD CELL...
HUSTLE
VEIN
BUSTLE
WANNA GET SOMETHING SWEET AROUND HERE?
GOT A LOT MORE WORK AHEAD OF US.
REALLY?
SO... IF I GO THIS WAY—
CO_2
EASY MAP
FIRST, THE INFERIOR VENA CAVA! GOT IT!
Lungs
Heart
Inferior Vena Cava
The largest vein in the human body. Blood from the lower part of the body and other areas flow here and then into the heart (right atrium).
THIS IS NO.1146. I'M GOING TO GO PATROL THE BODY, OVER.
SLURP
ALL RIGHTY. I'M GOING TO WANDER AROUND NEAR THE LIVER, THEN.

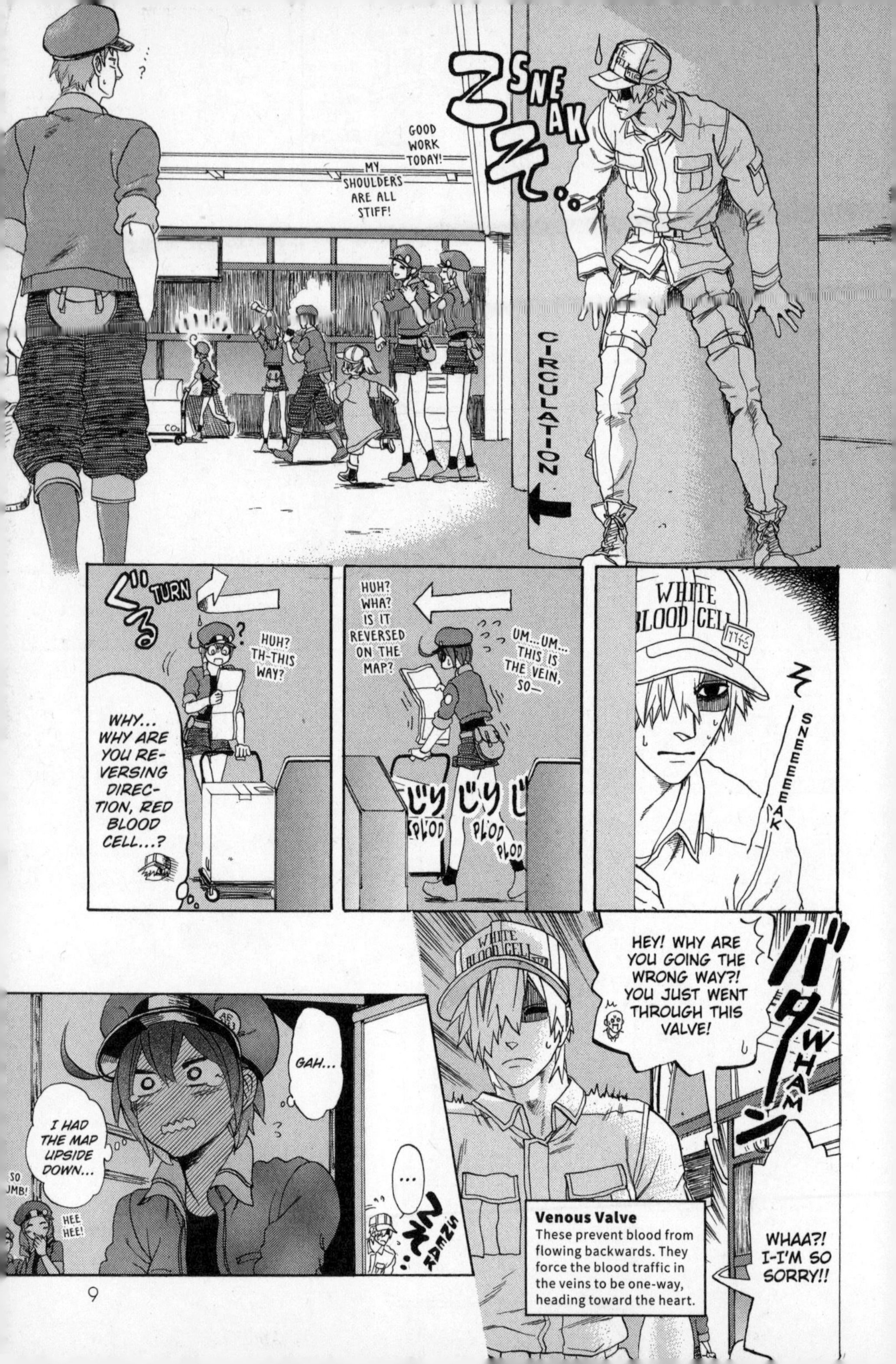
SNEAK
CIRCULATION
GOOD WORK TODAY!
MY SHOULDERS ARE ALL STIFF!
...?
WHITE BLOOD CELL
SNEEEEEAK
HUH? WHA? IS IT REVERSED ON THE MAP?
UM... UM... THIS IS THE VEIN, SO—
PLOD PLOD PLOD
TURN
HUH? TH-THIS WAY?
WHY... WHY ARE YOU RE-VERSING DIREC-TION, RED BLOOD CELL...?
HEY! WHY ARE YOU GOING THE WRONG WAY?! YOU JUST WENT THROUGH THIS VALVE!
WHAM
WHAA?! I-I'M SO SORRY!!
GAH...
I HAD THE MAP UPSIDE DOWN...
...
HEE HEE!

Venous Valve
These prevent blood from flowing backwards. They force the blood traffic in the veins to be one-way, heading toward the heart.

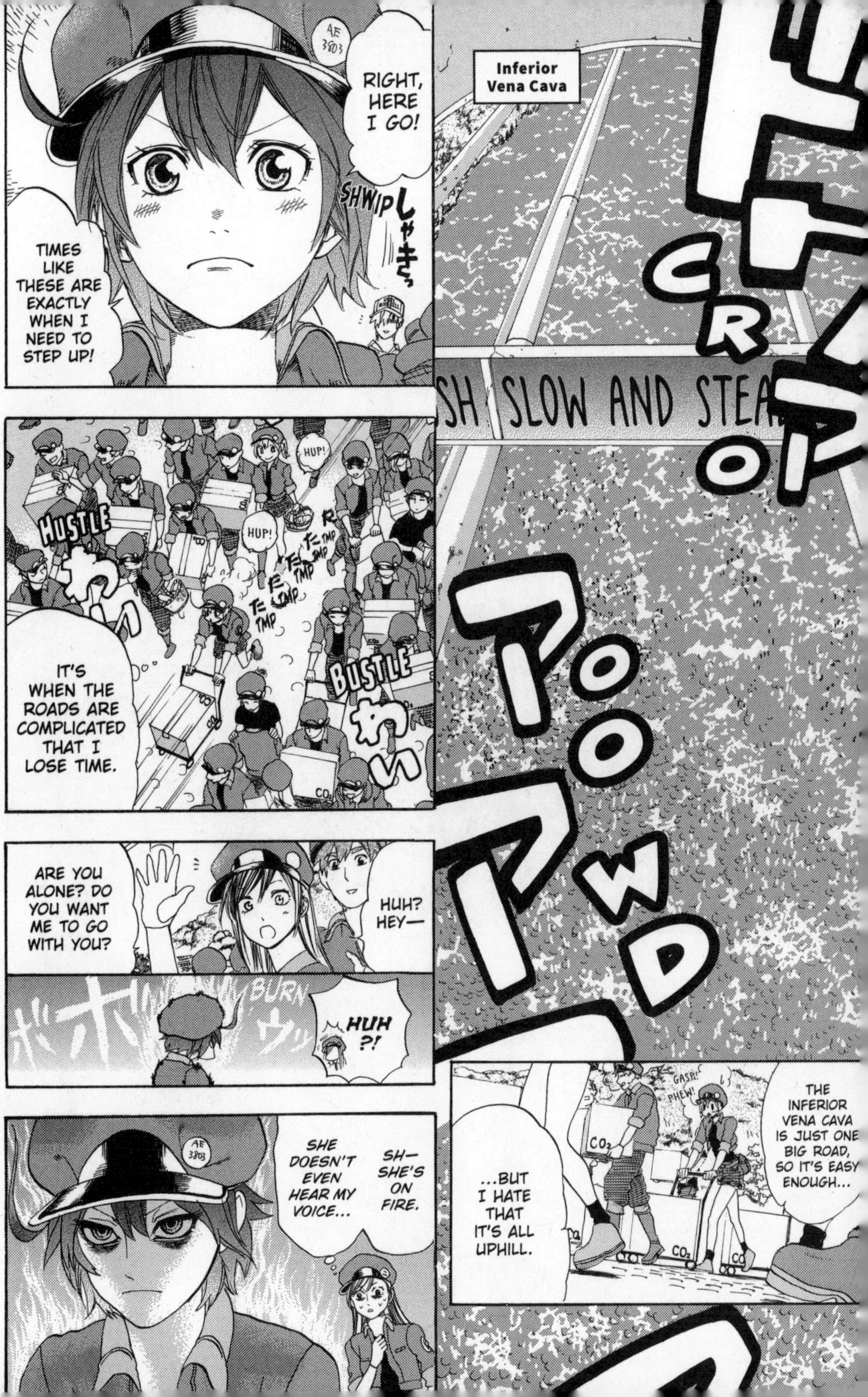

Inferior Vena Cava
SH SLOW AND STEA
CROOOWD
GASP! PHEW!
THE INFERIOR VENA CAVA IS JUST ONE BIG ROAD, SO IT'S EASY ENOUGH...
...BUT I HATE THAT IT'S ALL UPHILL.
AE 3803
RIGHT, HERE I GO!
SHWIP
TIMES LIKE THESE ARE EXACTLY WHEN I NEED TO STEP UP!
HUP!
HUP!
TMP TMP TMP TMP TMP
HUSTLE
BUSTLE
IT'S WHEN THE ROADS ARE COMPLICATED THAT I LOSE TIME.
HUH? HEY—
ARE YOU ALONE? DO YOU WANT ME TO GO WITH YOU?
HUH ?!
BURN
SH— SHE'S ON FIRE.
SHE DOESN'T EVEN HEAR MY VOICE...
AE 3803

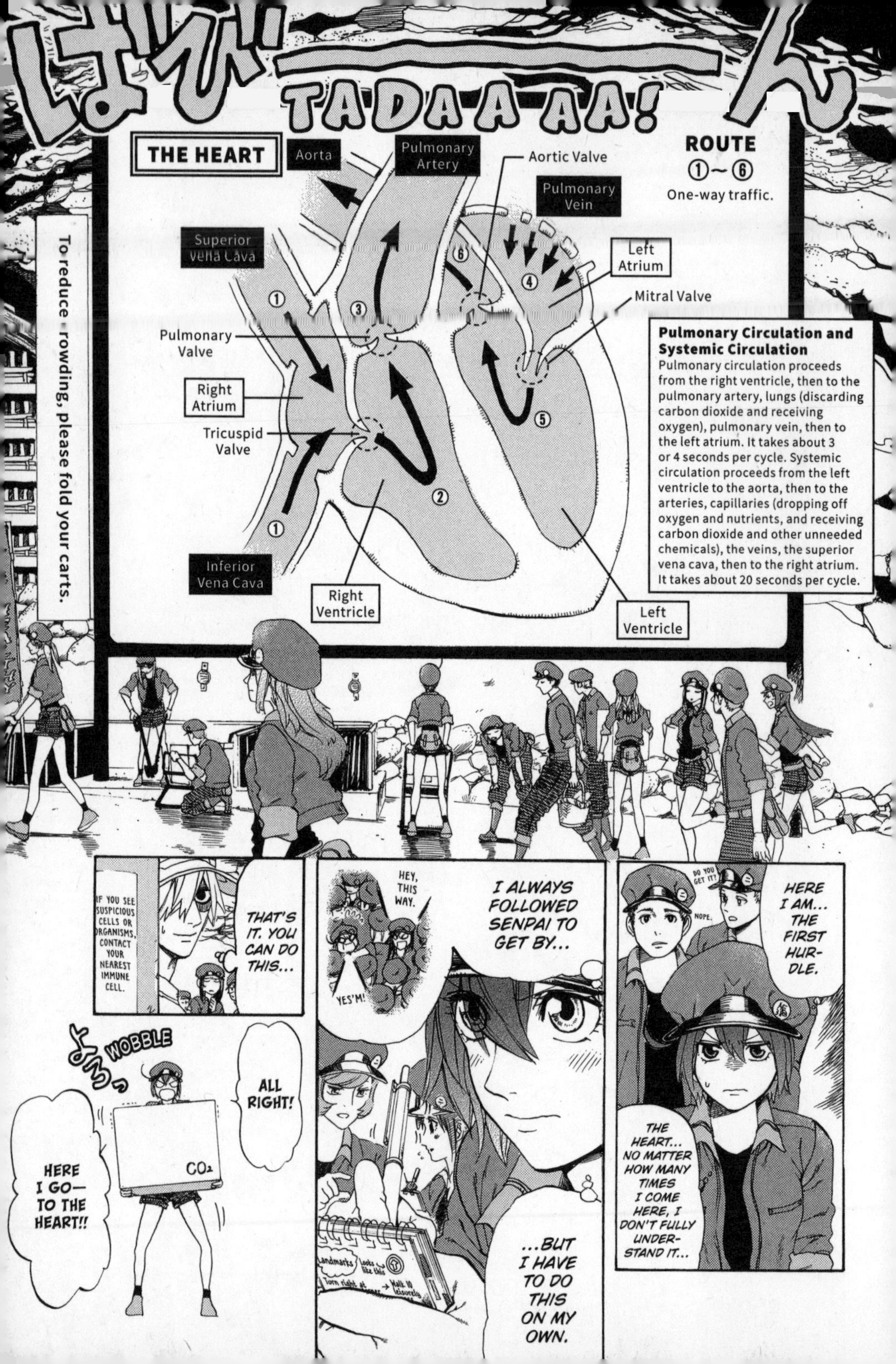
ばびーーーん
TADAAAAA!
THE HEART
Aorta
Pulmonary Artery
Aortic Valve
Pulmonary Vein
ROUTE ①~⑥
One-way traffic.
Superior Vena Cava
Left Atrium
Mitral Valve
Pulmonary Valve
Right Atrium
Tricuspid Valve
Inferior Vena Cava
Right Ventricle
Left Ventricle
Pulmonary Circulation and Systemic Circulation
Pulmonary circulation proceeds from the right ventricle, then to the pulmonary artery, lungs (discarding carbon dioxide and receiving oxygen), pulmonary vein, then to the left atrium. It takes about 3 or 4 seconds per cycle. Systemic circulation proceeds from the left ventricle to the aorta, then to the arteries, capillaries (dropping off oxygen and nutrients, and receiving carbon dioxide and other unneeded chemicals), the veins, the superior vena cava, then to the right atrium. It takes about 20 seconds per cycle.
To reduce rowding, please fold your carts.
DO YOU GET IT?
NOPE.
HERE I AM... THE FIRST HURDLE.
THE HEART... NO MATTER HOW MANY TIMES I COME HERE, I DON'T FULLY UNDERSTAND IT...
I ALWAYS FOLLOWED SENPAI TO GET BY...
HEY, THIS WAY.
YES'M!
...BUT I HAVE TO DO THIS ON MY OWN.
IF YOU SEE SUSPICIOUS CELLS OR ORGANISMS, CONTACT YOUR NEAREST IMMUNE CELL.
THAT'S IT. YOU CAN DO THIS...
ALL RIGHT!
よろっ WOBBLE
CO2
HERE I GO— TO THE HEART!!

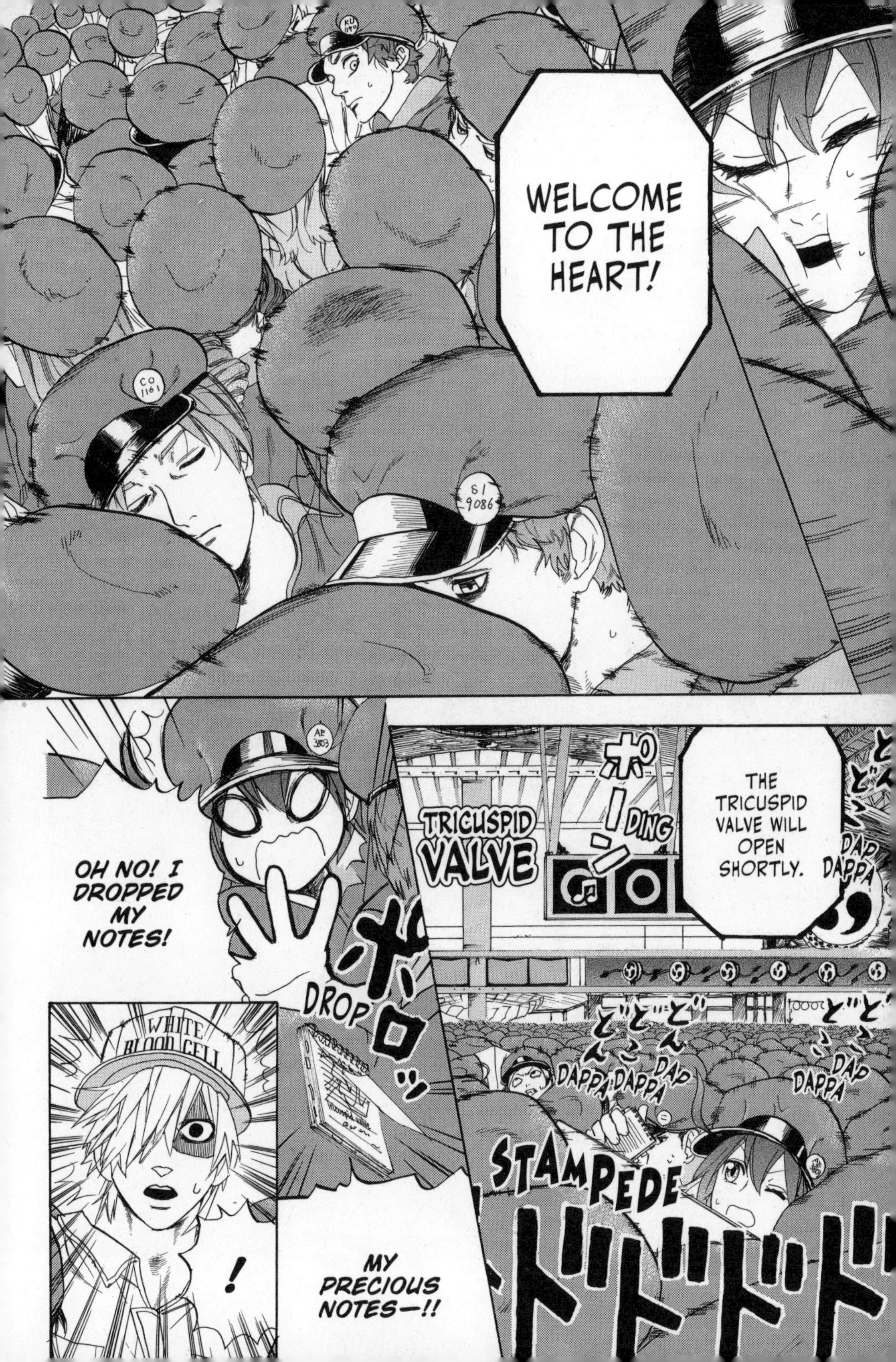

WELCOME TO THE HEART!
THE TRICUSPID VALVE WILL OPEN SHORTLY.
TRICUSPID VALVE
DING
DAP DAPPA
DAP DAPPA
DAP DAPPA
DAPPA
STAMPEDE
OH NO! I DROPPED MY NOTES!
DROP
WHITE BLOOD CELL
MY PRECIOUS NOTES—!!
!

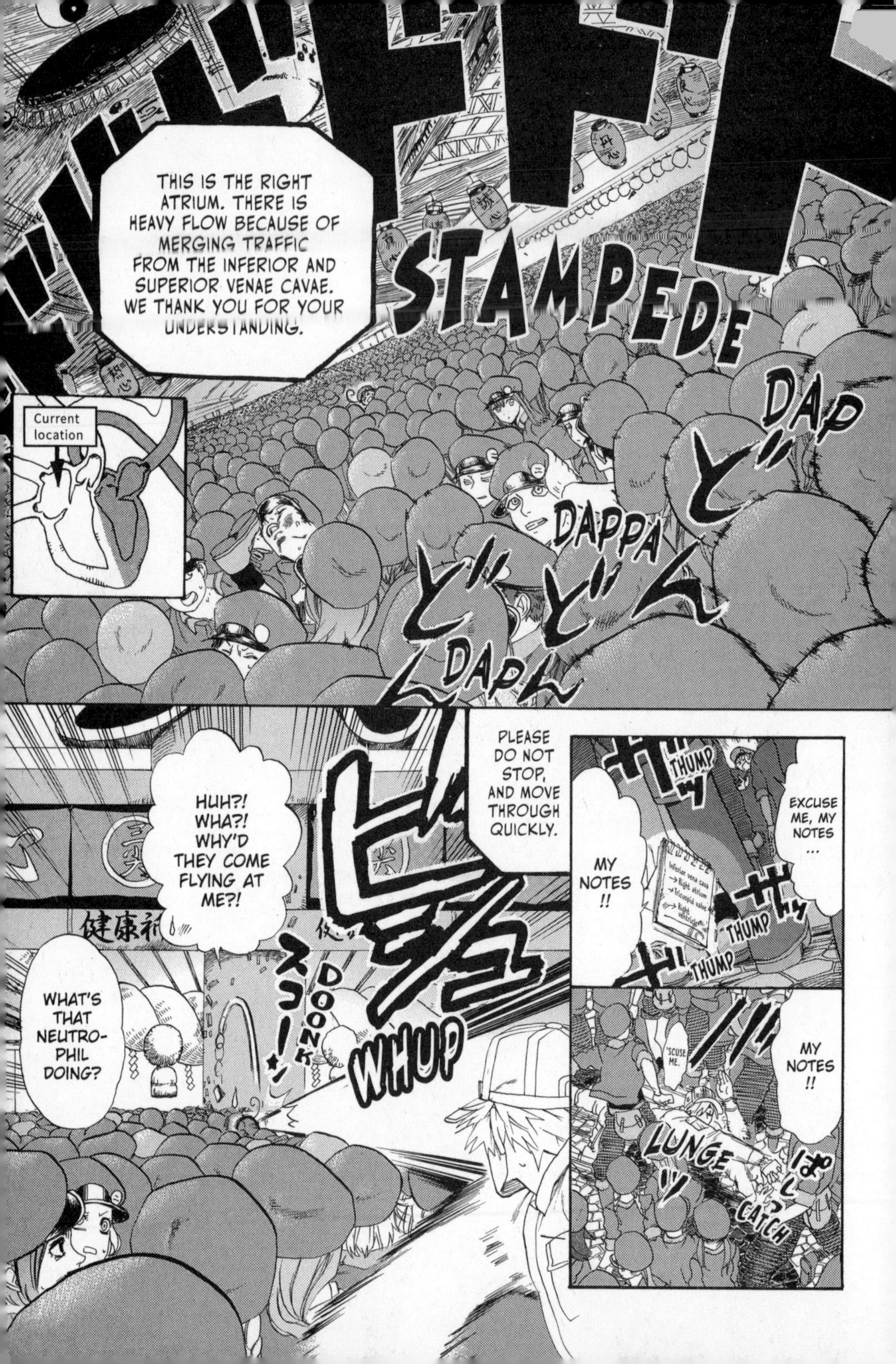
THIS IS THE RIGHT ATRIUM. THERE IS HEAVY FLOW BECAUSE OF MERGING TRAFFIC FROM THE INFERIOR AND SUPERIOR VENAE CAVAE. WE THANK YOU FOR YOUR UNDERSTANDING.
STAMPEDE
DAP
DAPPA
DAPA
Current location
EXCUSE ME, MY NOTES ...
THUMP
THUMP
THUMP
MY NOTES !!
Inferior vena cava → Right atrium → Tricuspid valve → Right ventricle
MY NOTES !!
'SCUSE ME.
LUNGE
CATCH
PLEASE DO NOT STOP, AND MOVE THROUGH QUICKLY.
HUH?! WHA?! WHY'D THEY COME FLYING AT ME?!
WHUP
DOOONK
WHAT'S THAT NEUTROPHIL DOING?

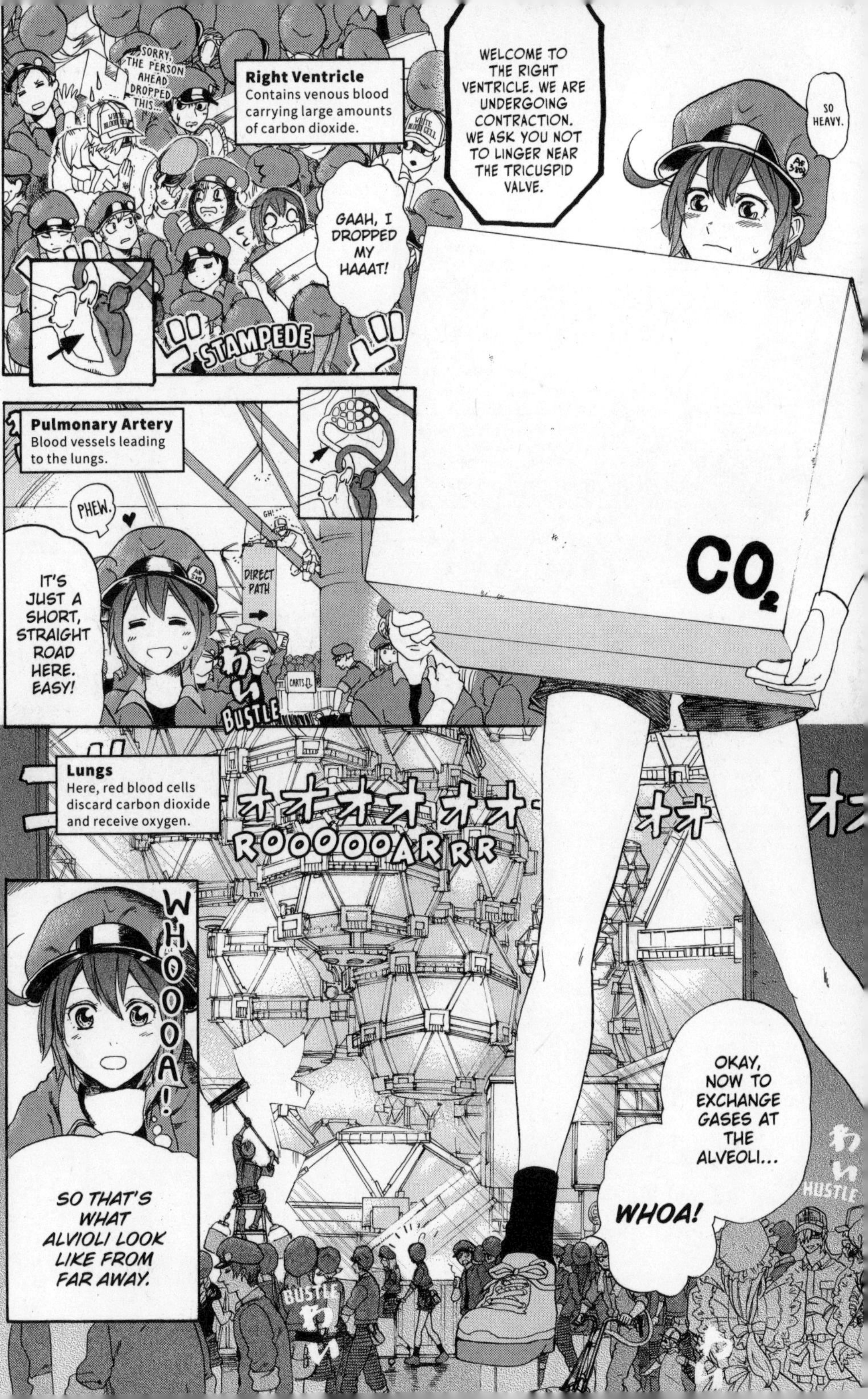

WELCOME TO THE RIGHT VENTRICLE. WE ARE UNDERGOING CONTRACTION. WE ASK YOU NOT TO LINGER NEAR THE TRICUSPID VALVE.
SO HEAVY.
CO2
Right Ventricle
Contains venous blood carrying large amounts of carbon dioxide.
SORRY, THE PERSON AHEAD DROPPED THIS...
WHITE BLOOD CELL
GAAH, I DROPPED MY HAAAT!
STAMPEDE
Pulmonary Artery
Blood vessels leading to the lungs.
PHEW.
IT'S JUST A SHORT, STRAIGHT ROAD HERE. EASY!
DIRECT PATH
CARTS
わい
BUSTLE
Lungs
Here, red blood cells discard carbon dioxide and receive oxygen.
オオオオオオ
ROOOOOARRR
オオ
OKAY, NOW TO EXCHANGE GASES AT THE ALVEOLI...
WHOA!
わい
HUSTLE
WHOOOOA!
SO THAT'S WHAT ALVIOLI LOOK LIKE FROM FAR AWAY.
BUSTLE
わい

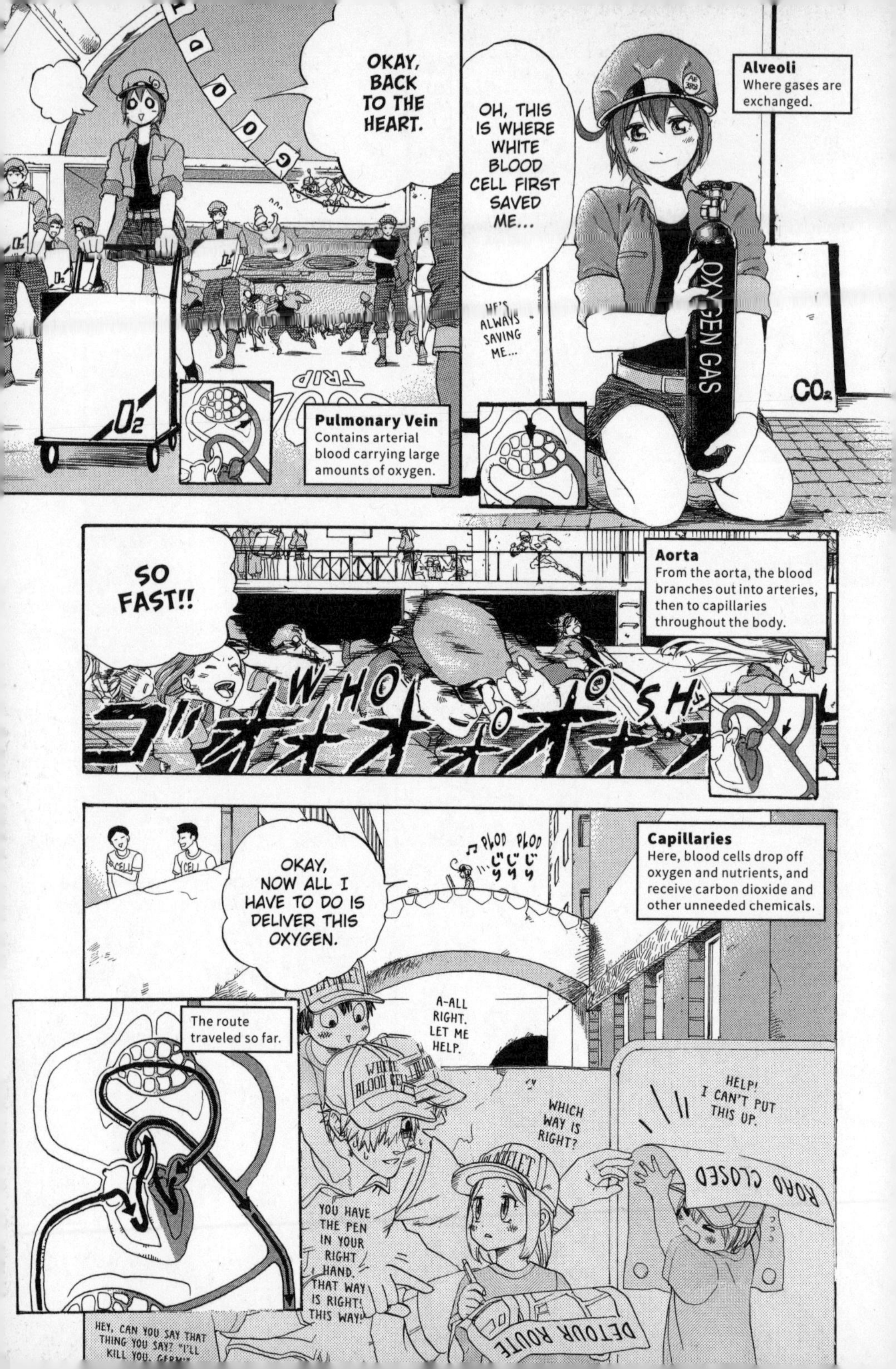
Alveoli
Where gases are exchanged.
OH, THIS IS WHERE WHITE BLOOD CELL FIRST SAVED ME...
HE'S ALWAYS SAVING ME...
OXYGEN GAS
CO_2
OKAY, BACK TO THE HEART.
GOOD TRIP
O_2
Pulmonary Vein
Contains arterial blood carrying large amounts of oxygen.
Aorta
From the aorta, the blood branches out into arteries, then to capillaries throughout the body.
SO FAST!!
WHOOOOSH
Capillaries
Here, blood cells drop off oxygen and nutrients, and receive carbon dioxide and other unneeded chemicals.
PLOD PLOD
OKAY, NOW ALL I HAVE TO DO IS DELIVER THIS OXYGEN.
CELL
CELL
HELP! I CAN'T PUT THIS UP.
ROAD CLOSED
WHICH WAY IS RIGHT?
A-ALL RIGHT. LET ME HELP.
WHITE BLOOD CELL
YOU HAVE THE PEN IN YOUR RIGHT HAND. THAT WAY IS RIGHT! THIS WAY!
DETOUR ROUTE
HEY, CAN YOU SAY THAT THING YOU SAY? "I'LL KILL YOU, GERM!"
The route traveled so far.

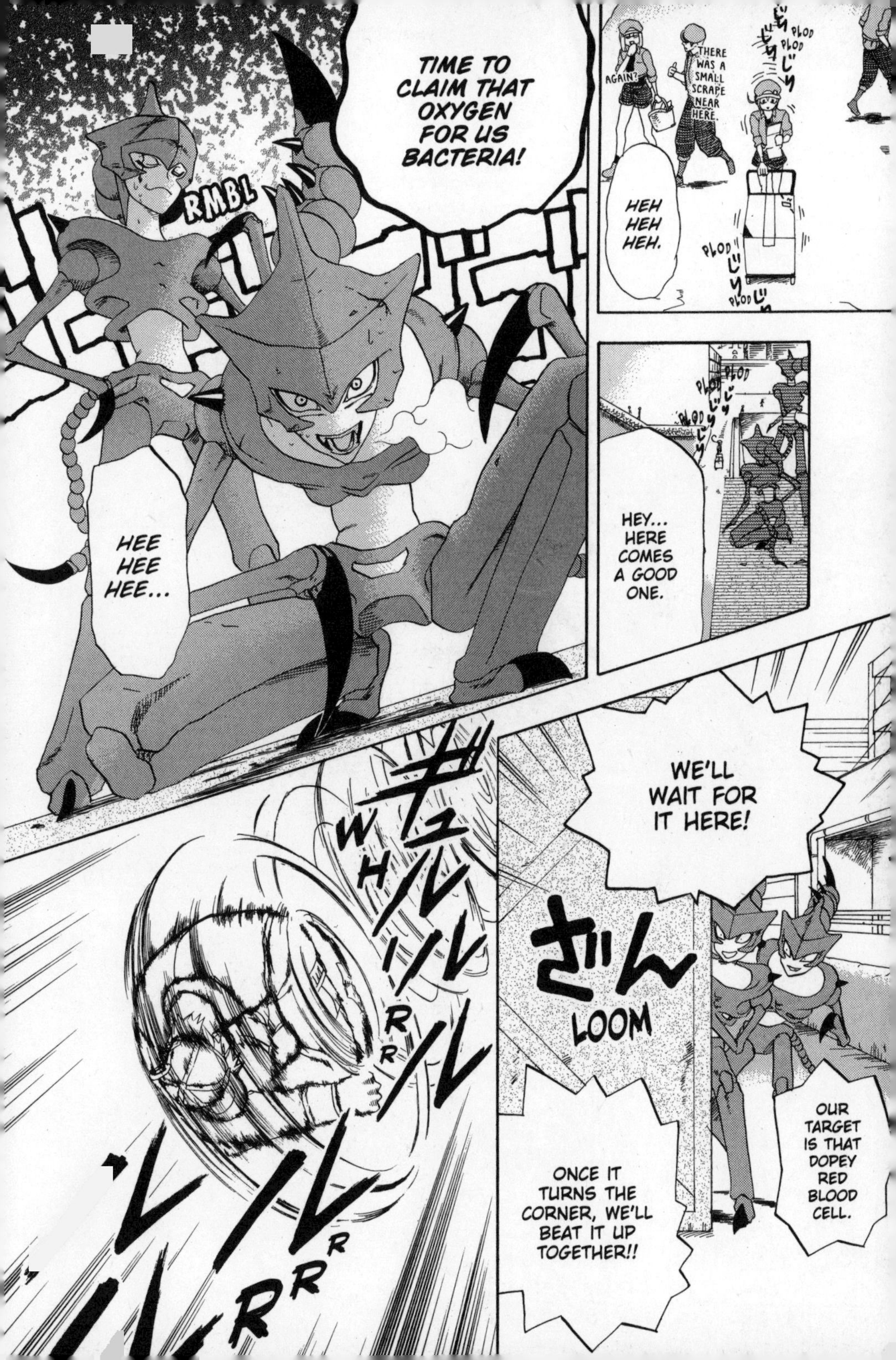
PLOD PLOD
THERE WAS A SMALL SCRAPE NEAR HERE.
AGAIN?
HEH HEH HEH.
PLOD PLOD
PLOD PLOD PLOD
HEY... HERE COMES A GOOD ONE.
TIME TO CLAIM THAT OXYGEN FOR US BACTERIA!
RMBL
HEE HEE HEE...
WE'LL WAIT FOR IT HERE!
LOOM
OUR TARGET IS THAT DOPEY RED BLOOD CELL.
ONCE IT TURNS THE CORNER, WE'LL BEAT IT UP TOGETHER!!
WHIRR
RRRR

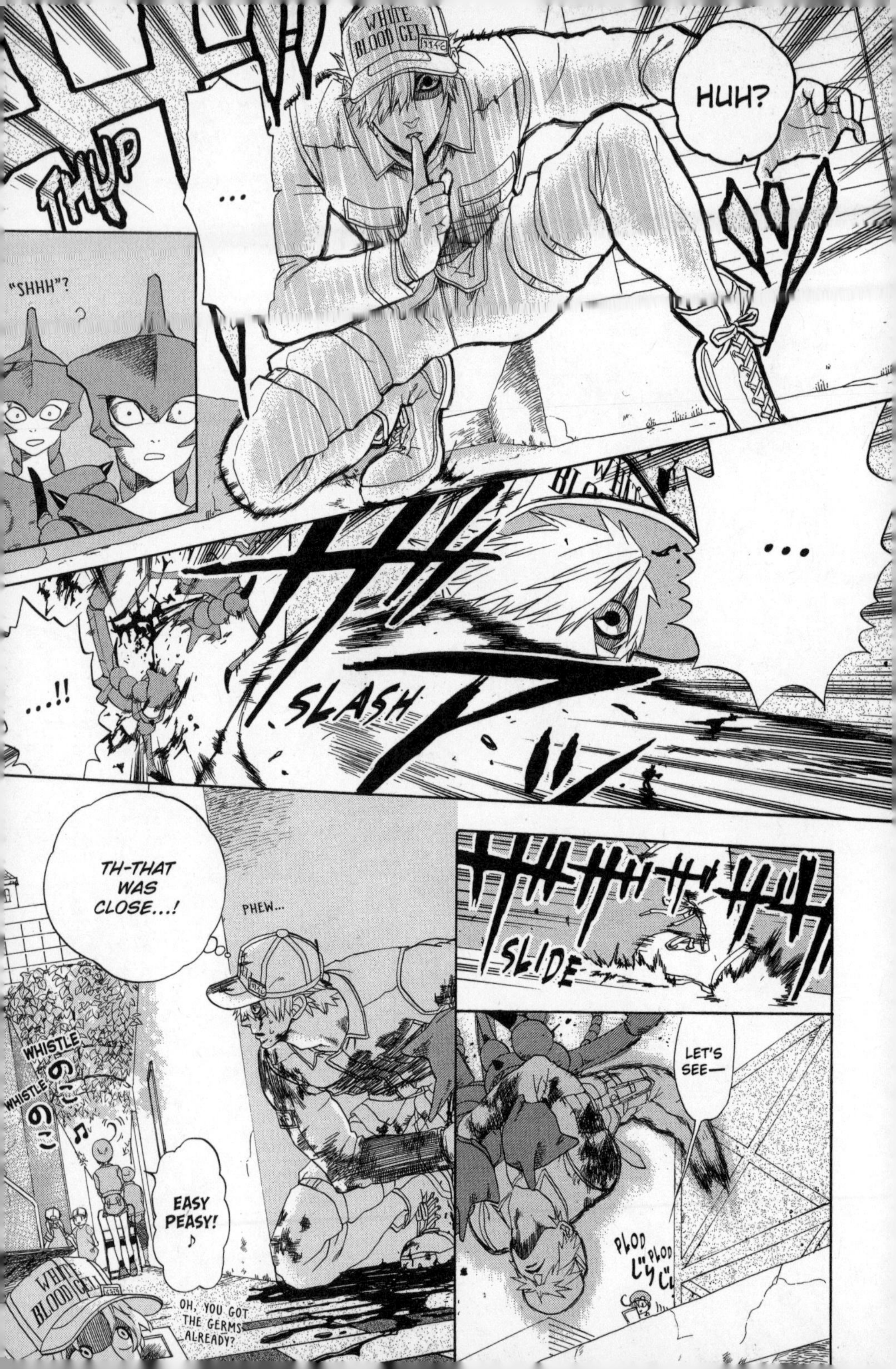
HUH?
...
THUP
"SHHH"?
...
SLASH
...!!
SLIDE
LET'S SEE—
PLOD PLOD
TH-THAT WAS CLOSE...!
PHEW...
EASY PEASY! ♪
WHISTLE WHISTLE
OH, YOU GOT THE GERMS ALREADY?

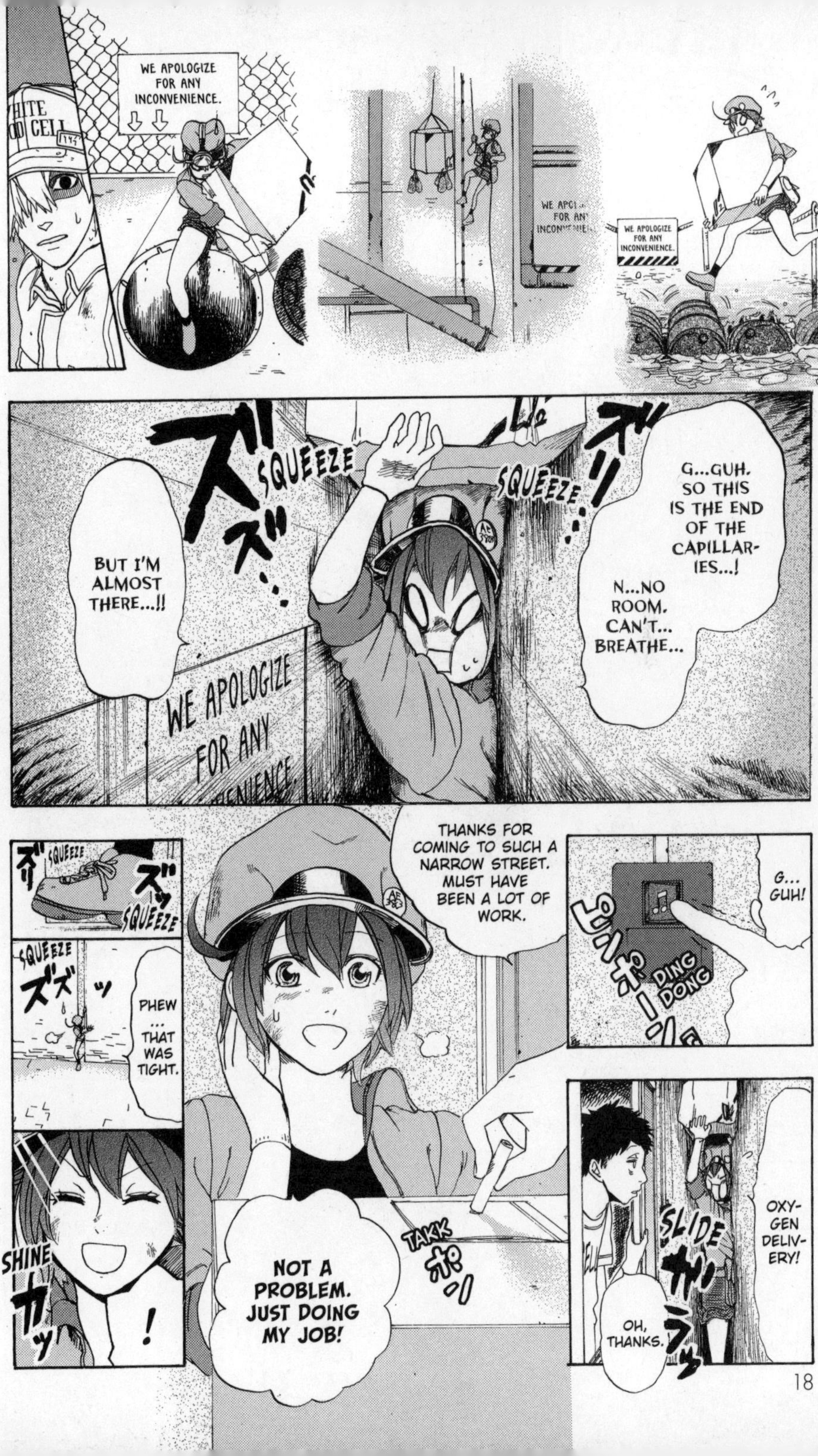

WE APOLOGIZE FOR ANY INCONVENIENCE.
WE APOLOGIZE FOR ANY INCONVENIENCE.
WE APOLOGIZE FOR ANY INCONVENIENCE.
G...GUH. SO THIS IS THE END OF THE CAPILLARIES...!
N...NO ROOM. CAN'T... BREATHE...
SQUEEZE
SQUEEZE
BUT I'M ALMOST THERE...!!
WE APOLOGIZE FOR ANY
G... GUH!
DING DONG
OXY-GEN DELIVERY!
SLIDE
OH, THANKS.
THANKS FOR COMING TO SUCH A NARROW STREET. MUST HAVE BEEN A LOT OF WORK.
TAKK
NOT A PROBLEM. JUST DOING MY JOB!
SQUEEZE
SQUEEZE
SQUEEZE
PHEW ... THAT WAS TIGHT.
SHINE
!

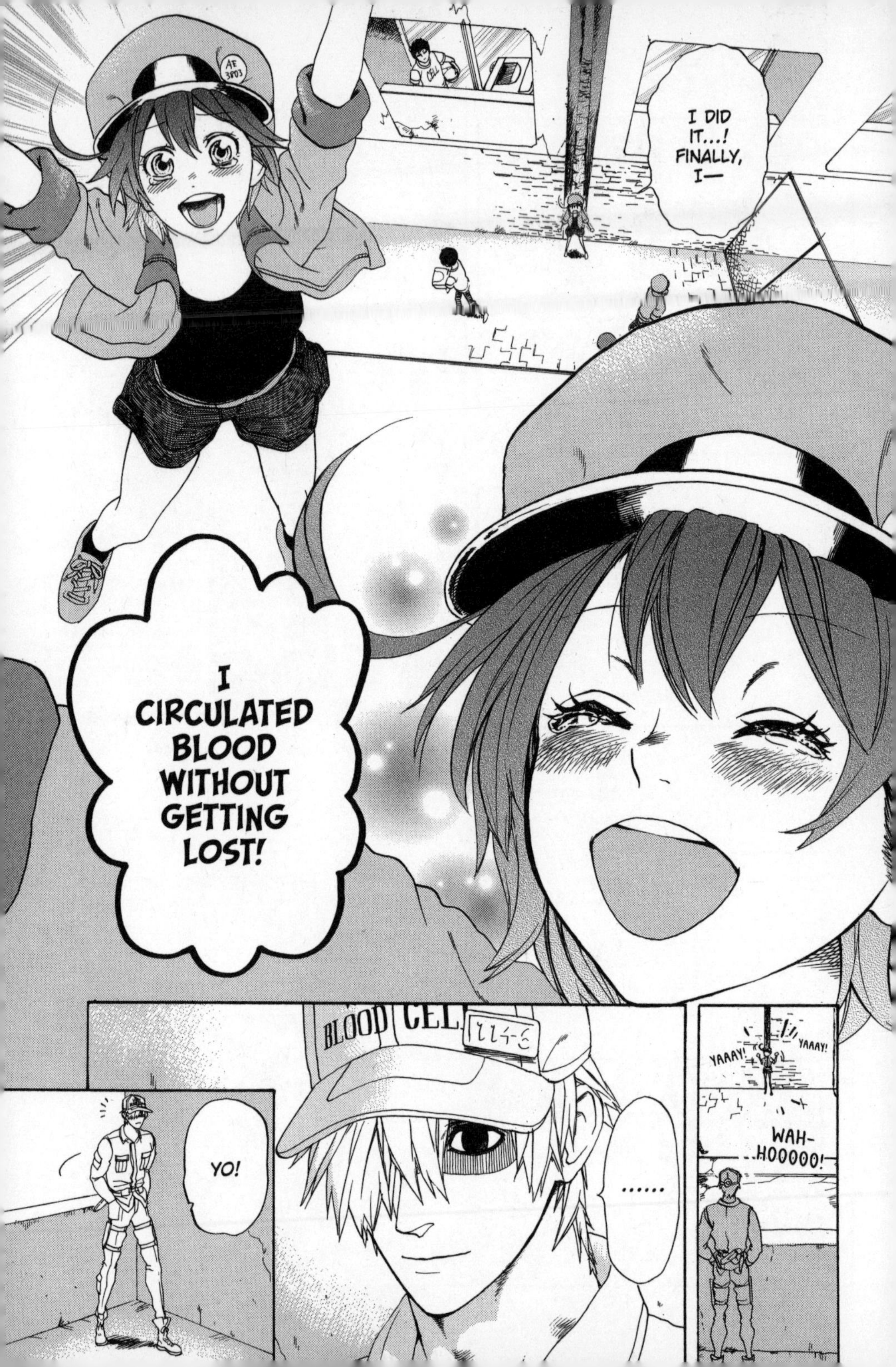
I DID IT...! FINALLY, I—
I CIRCULATED BLOOD WITHOUT GETTING LOST!
YAAAY!
YAAAY!
WAH-HOOOOO!
......
YO!

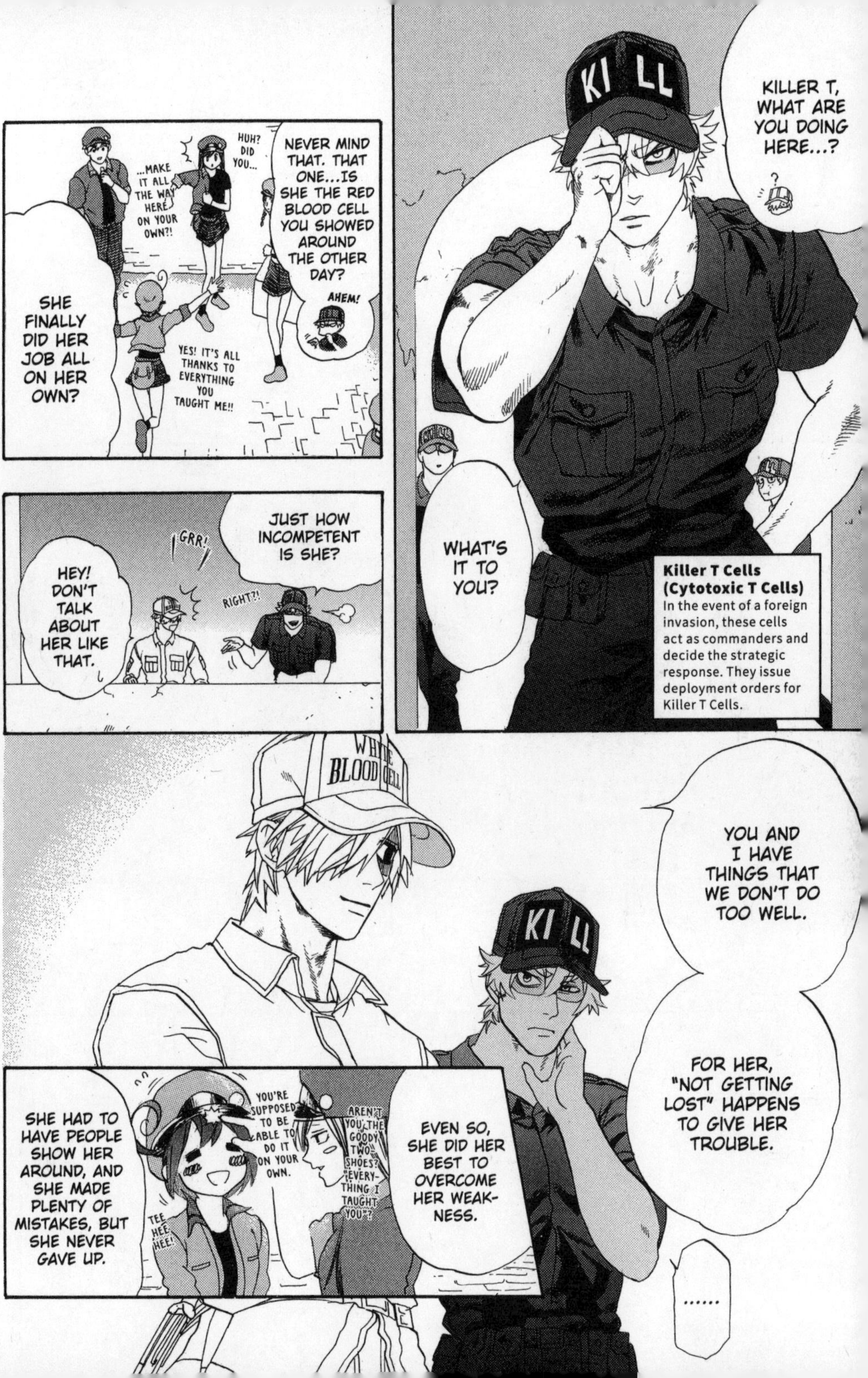
KILLER T, WHAT ARE YOU DOING HERE...?
WHAT'S IT TO YOU?
Killer T Cells (Cytotoxic T Cells) In the event of a foreign invasion, these cells act as commanders and decide the strategic response. They issue deployment orders for Killer T Cells.
NEVER MIND THAT. THAT ONE...IS SHE THE RED BLOOD CELL YOU SHOWED AROUND THE OTHER DAY?
AHEM!
HUH? DID YOU...
...MAKE IT ALL THE WAY HERE ON YOUR OWN?!
YES! IT'S ALL THANKS TO EVERYTHING YOU TAUGHT ME!!
SHE FINALLY DID HER JOB ALL ON HER OWN?
JUST HOW INCOMPETENT IS SHE?
RIGHT?!
GRR!
HEY! DON'T TALK ABOUT HER LIKE THAT.
YOU AND I HAVE THINGS THAT WE DON'T DO TOO WELL.
FOR HER, "NOT GETTING LOST" HAPPENS TO GIVE HER TROUBLE.
EVEN SO, SHE DID HER BEST TO OVERCOME HER WEAK-NESS.
AREN'T YOU THE GOODY TWO-SHOES? "EVERY-THING I TAUGHT YOU"?
YOU'RE SUPPOSED TO BE ABLE TO DO IT ON YOUR OWN.
TEE HEE HEE!
SHE HAD TO HAVE PEOPLE SHOW HER AROUND, AND SHE MADE PLENTY OF MISTAKES, BUT SHE NEVER GAVE UP.
......

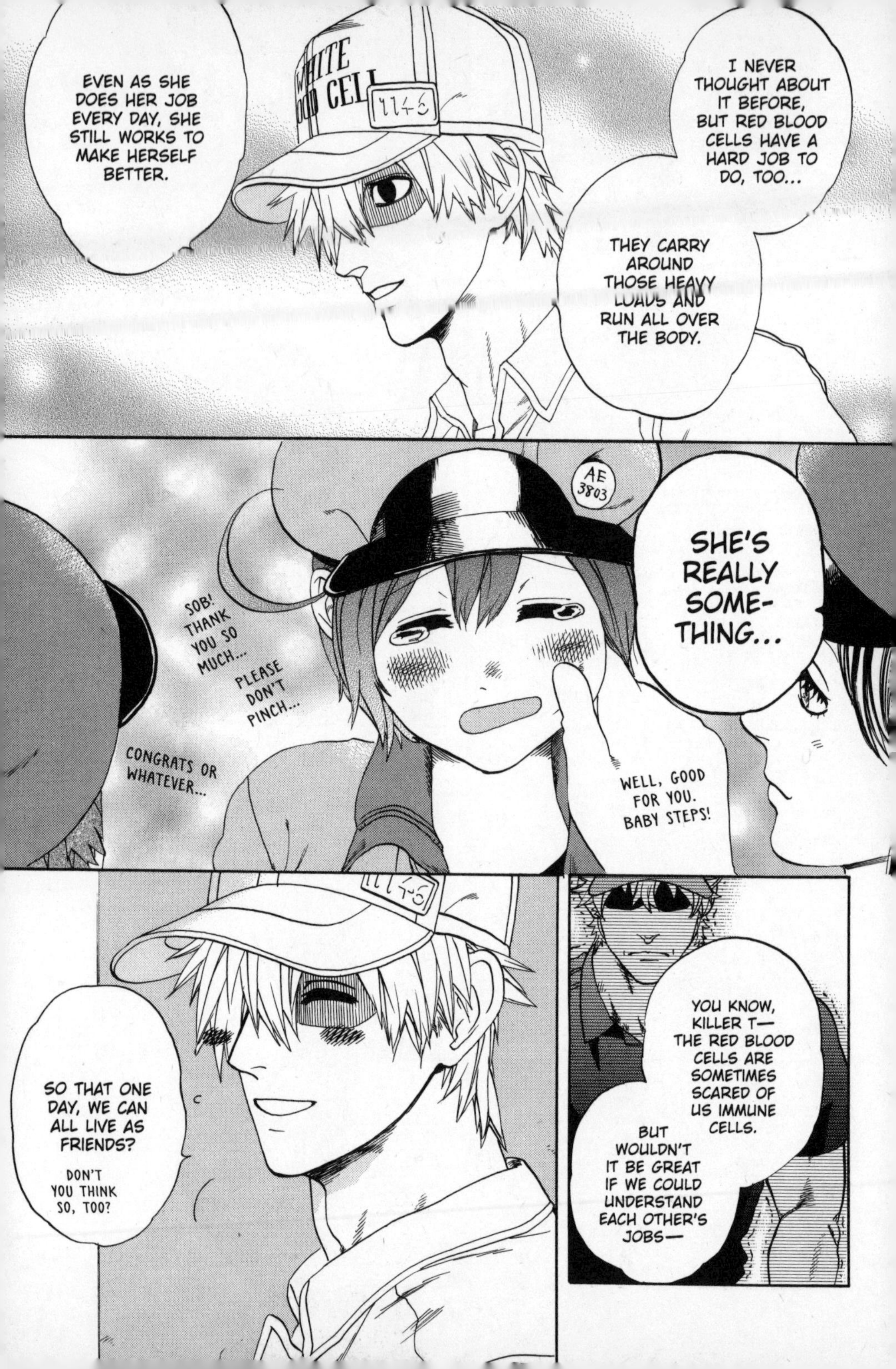
I NEVER THOUGHT ABOUT IT BEFORE, BUT RED BLOOD CELLS HAVE A HARD JOB TO DO, TOO...
THEY CARRY AROUND THOSE HEAVY LOADS AND RUN ALL OVER THE BODY.
EVEN AS SHE DOES HER JOB EVERY DAY, SHE STILL WORKS TO MAKE HERSELF BETTER.
AE 3803
SHE'S REALLY SOME-THING...
WELL, GOOD FOR YOU. BABY STEPS!
SOB! THANK YOU SO MUCH...
PLEASE DON'T PINCH...
CONGRATS OR WHATEVER...
YOU KNOW, KILLER T— THE RED BLOOD CELLS ARE SOMETIMES SCARED OF US IMMUNE CELLS.
BUT WOULDN'T IT BE GREAT IF WE COULD UNDERSTAND EACH OTHER'S JOBS—
SO THAT ONE DAY, WE CAN ALL LIVE AS FRIENDS?
DON'T YOU THINK SO, TOO?

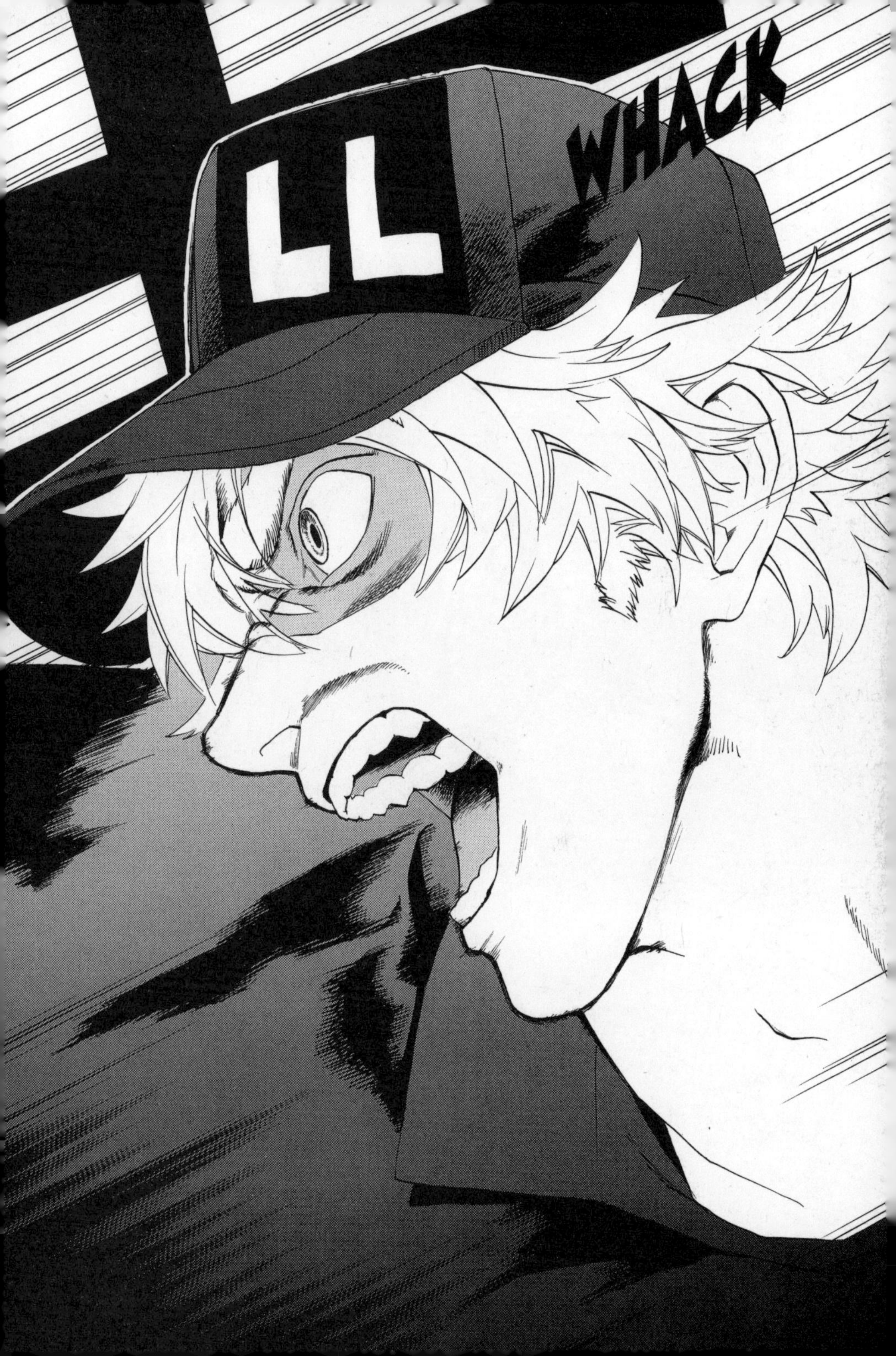
WHACK

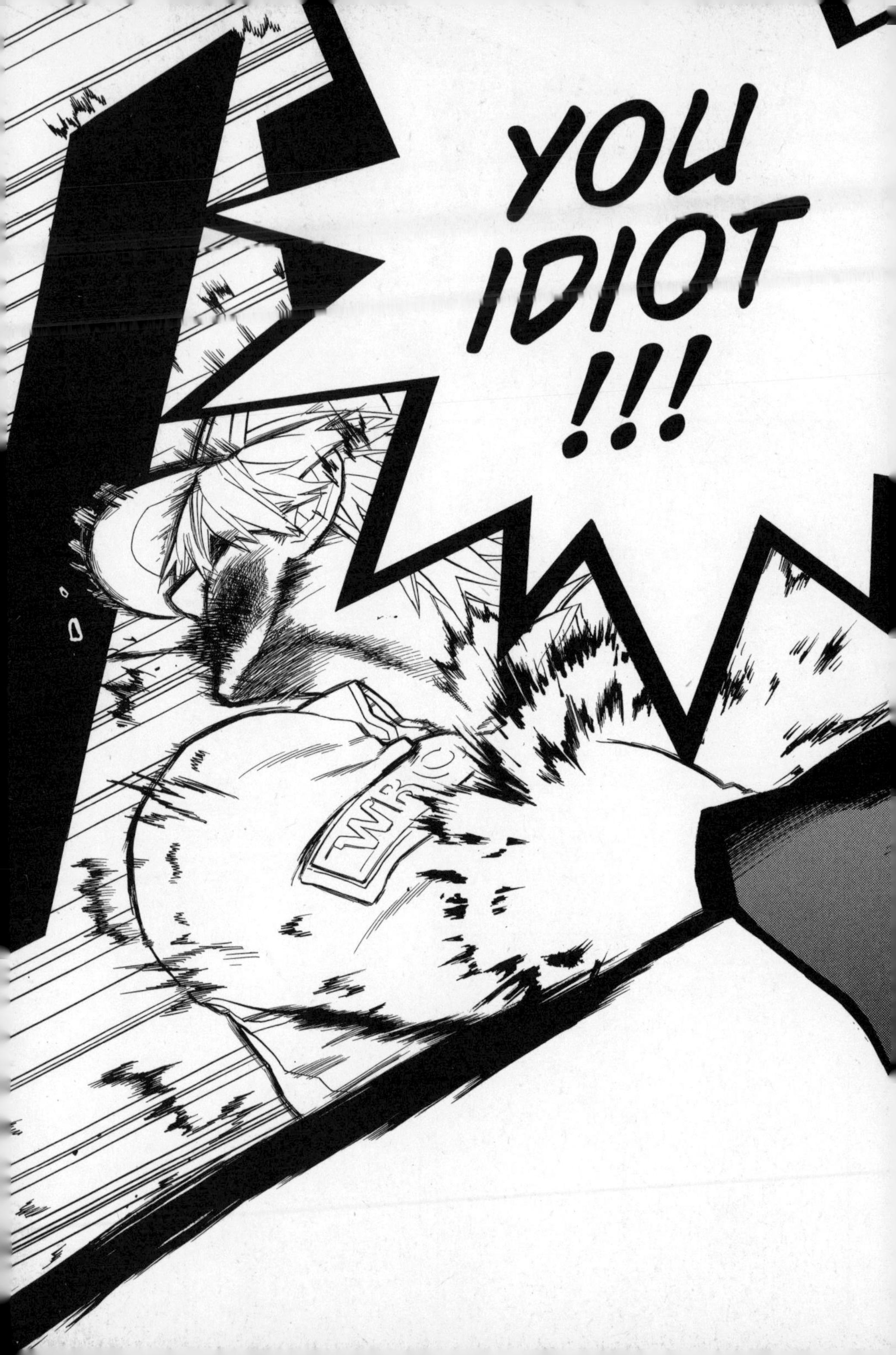
YOU IDIOT !!!

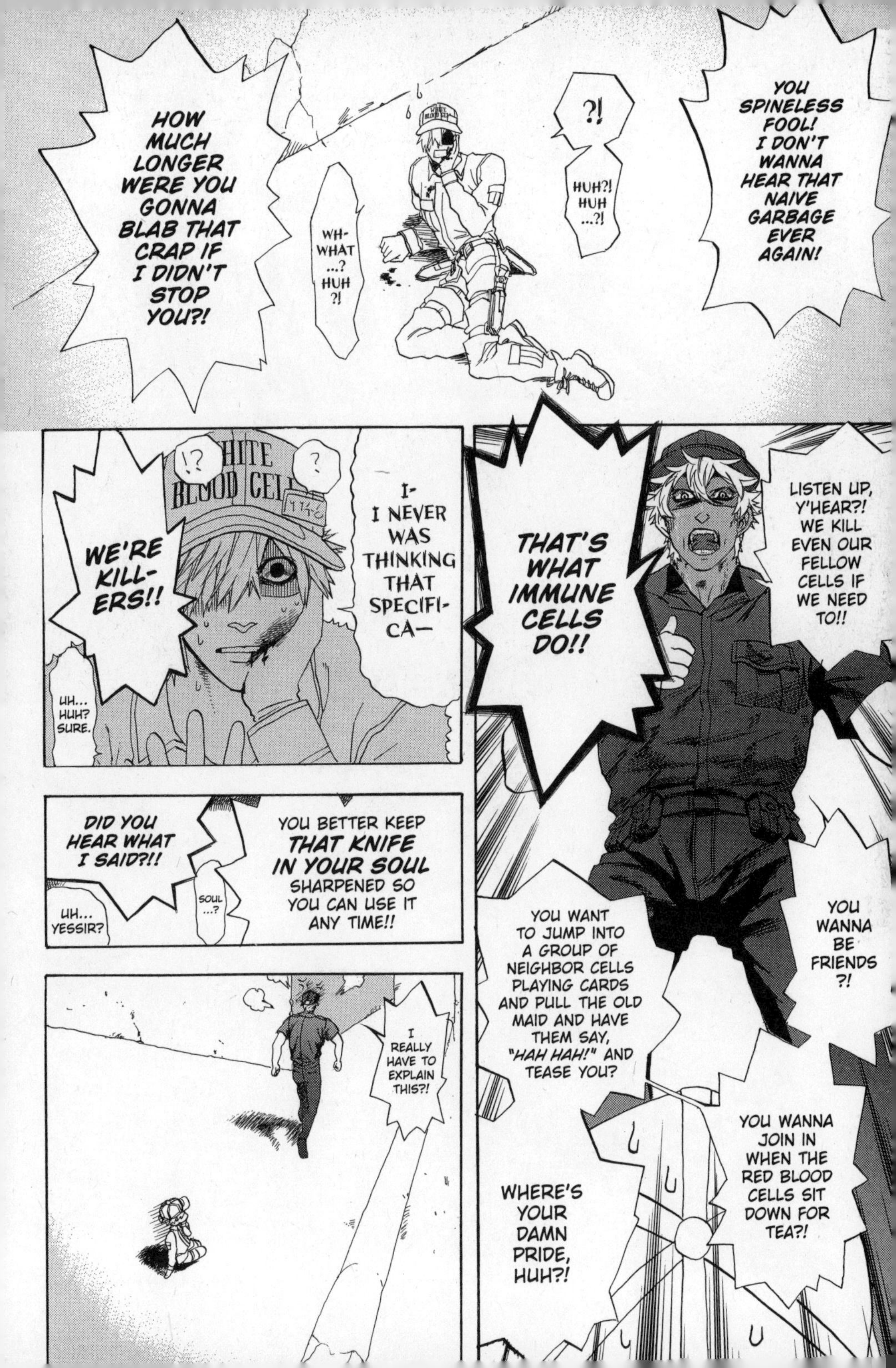
YOU SPINELESS FOOL! I DON'T WANNA HEAR THAT NAIVE GARBAGE EVER AGAIN!
?!
HUH?! HUH ...?!
WH-WHAT ...? HUH ?!
HOW MUCH LONGER WERE YOU GONNA BLAB THAT CRAP IF I DIDN'T STOP YOU?!
LISTEN UP, Y'HEAR?! WE KILL EVEN OUR FELLOW CELLS IF WE NEED TO!!
THAT'S WHAT IMMUNE CELLS DO!!
YOU WANNA BE FRIENDS ?!
YOU WANT TO JUMP INTO A GROUP OF NEIGHBOR CELLS PLAYING CARDS AND PULL THE OLD MAID AND HAVE THEM SAY, "HAH HAH!" AND TEASE YOU?
YOU WANNA JOIN IN WHEN THE RED BLOOD CELLS SIT DOWN FOR TEA?!
WHERE'S YOUR DAMN PRIDE, HUH?!
!?
?
I- I NEVER WAS THINKING THAT SPECIFI-CA—
WE'RE KILL-ERS!!
UH... HUH? SURE.
YOU BETTER KEEP THAT KNIFE IN YOUR SOUL SHARPENED SO YOU CAN USE IT ANY TIME!!
SOUL ...?
DID YOU HEAR WHAT I SAID?!!
UH... YESSIR?
I REALLY HAVE TO EXPLAIN THIS?!

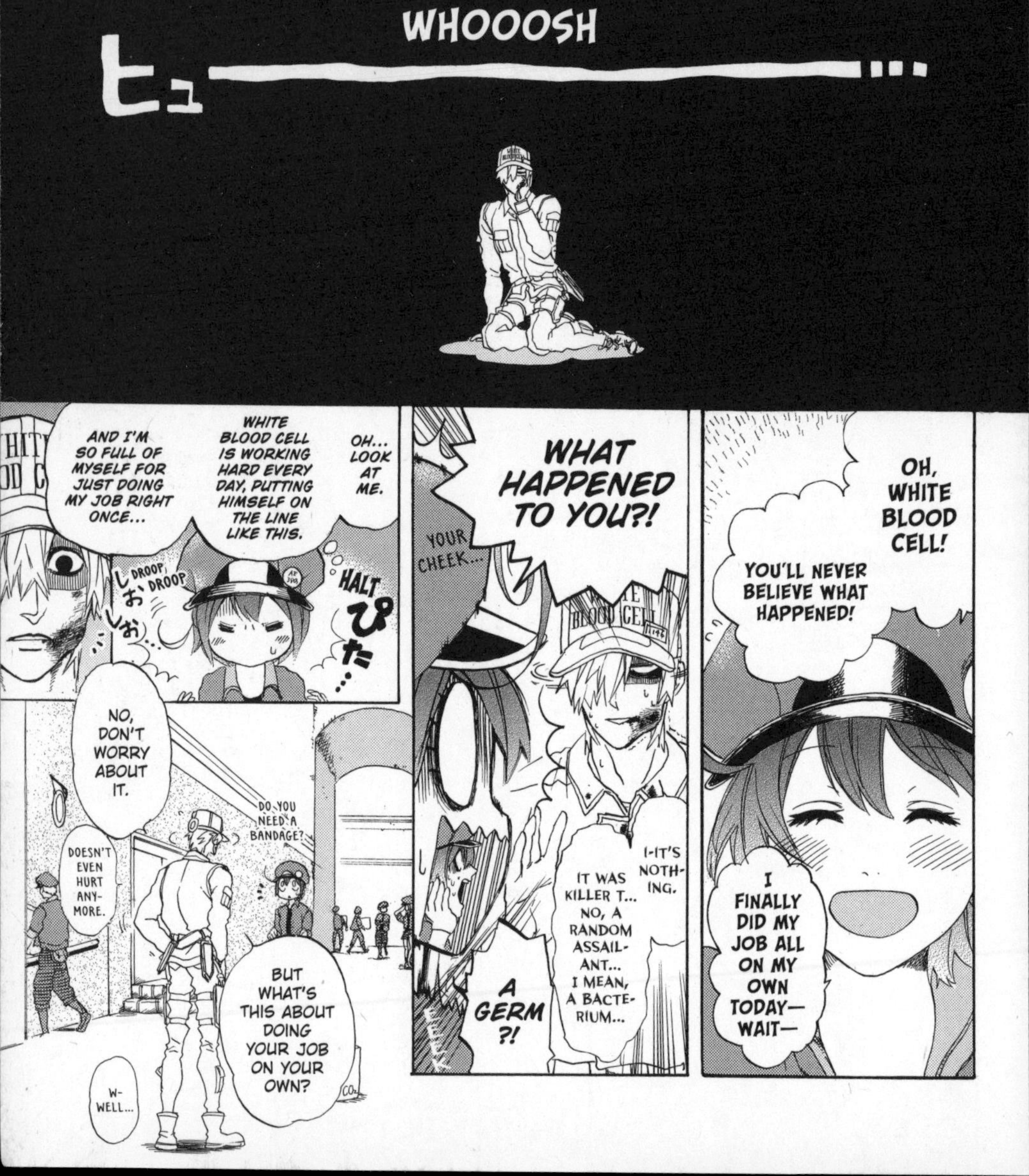
WHOOOSH
ヒュー…
OH, WHITE BLOOD CELL!
YOU'LL NEVER BELIEVE WHAT HAPPENED!
I FINALLY DID MY JOB ALL ON MY OWN TODAY— WAIT—
WHAT HAPPENED TO YOU?!
YOUR CHEEK...
I-IT'S NOTHING.
IT WAS KILLER T... NO, A RANDOM ASSAILANT... I MEAN, A BACTERIUM...
A GERM?!
OH... LOOK AT ME.
WHITE BLOOD CELL IS WORKING HARD EVERY DAY, PUTTING HIMSELF ON THE LINE LIKE THIS.
AND I'M SO FULL OF MYSELF FOR JUST DOING MY JOB RIGHT ONCE...
HALT ぴた…
DROOP DROOP しおしお…
DO YOU NEED A BANDAGE?
NO, DON'T WORRY ABOUT IT.
DOESN'T EVEN HURT ANYMORE.
BUT WHAT'S THIS ABOUT DOING YOUR JOB ON YOUR OWN?
W-WELL...

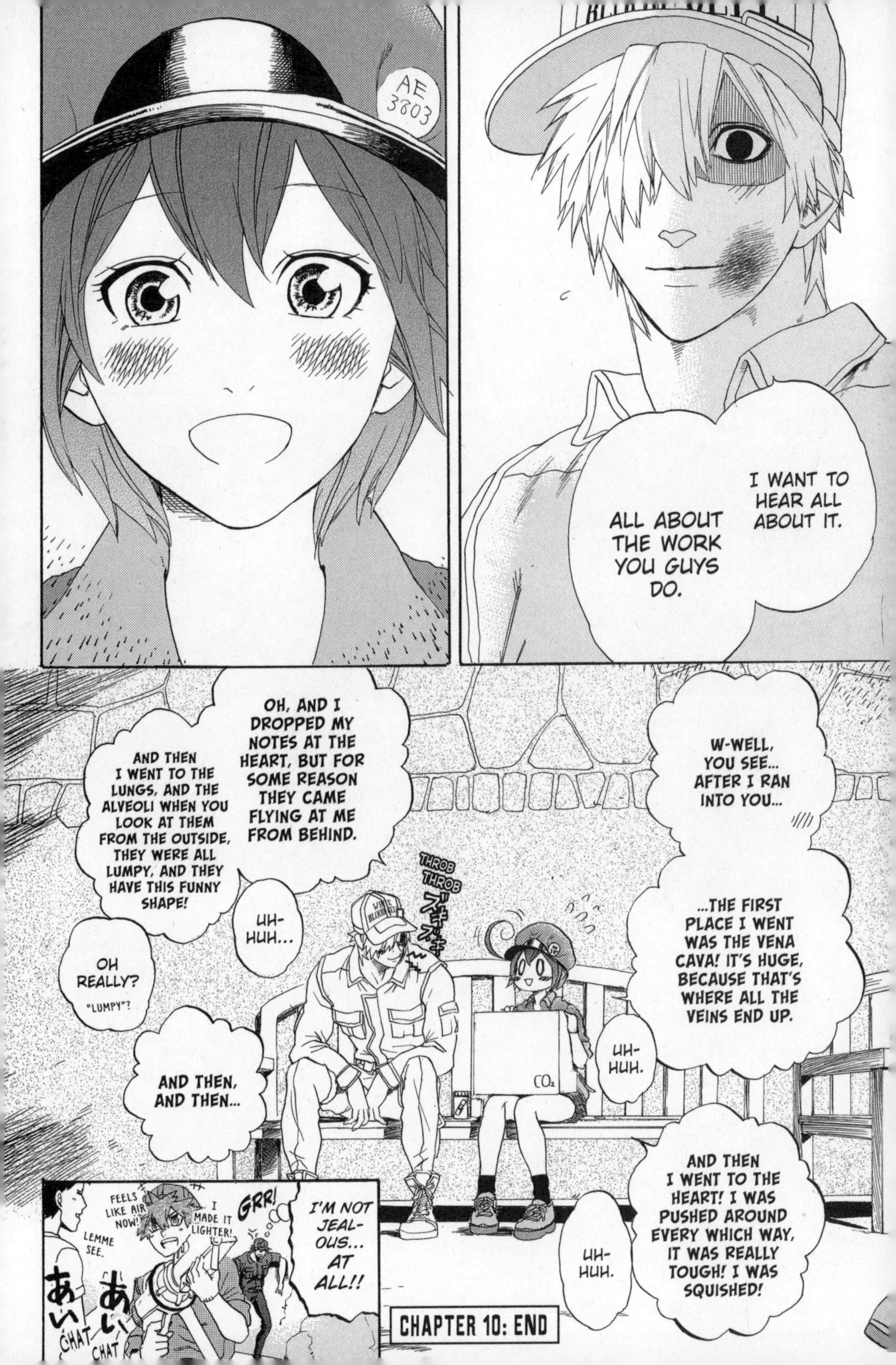
I WANT TO HEAR ALL ABOUT IT.
ALL ABOUT THE WORK YOU GUYS DO.
AE 3803
W-WELL, YOU SEE... AFTER I RAN INTO YOU...
...THE FIRST PLACE I WENT WAS THE VENA CAVA! IT'S HUGE, BECAUSE THAT'S WHERE ALL THE VEINS END UP.
UH-HUH.
AND THEN I WENT TO THE HEART! I WAS PUSHED AROUND EVERY WHICH WAY, IT WAS REALLY TOUGH! I WAS SQUISHED!
UH-HUH.
CO_2
OH, AND I DROPPED MY NOTES AT THE HEART, BUT FOR SOME REASON THEY CAME FLYING AT ME FROM BEHIND.
THROB THROB
AND THEN I WENT TO THE LUNGS, AND THE ALVEOLI WHEN YOU LOOK AT THEM FROM THE OUTSIDE, THEY WERE ALL LUMPY, AND THEY HAVE THIS FUNNY SHAPE!
UH-HUH...
OH REALLY?
"LUMPY"?
AND THEN, AND THEN...
I'M NOT JEALOUS... AT ALL!!
GRR!
I MADE IT LIGHTER!
FEELS LIKE AIR NOW!
LEMME SEE.
CHAT CHAT
CHAPTER 10: END

Cells at Work!

*This is a fictitious setting for this manga, and does not reflect scientific fact.

Inside a Blood Vessel [cross section]

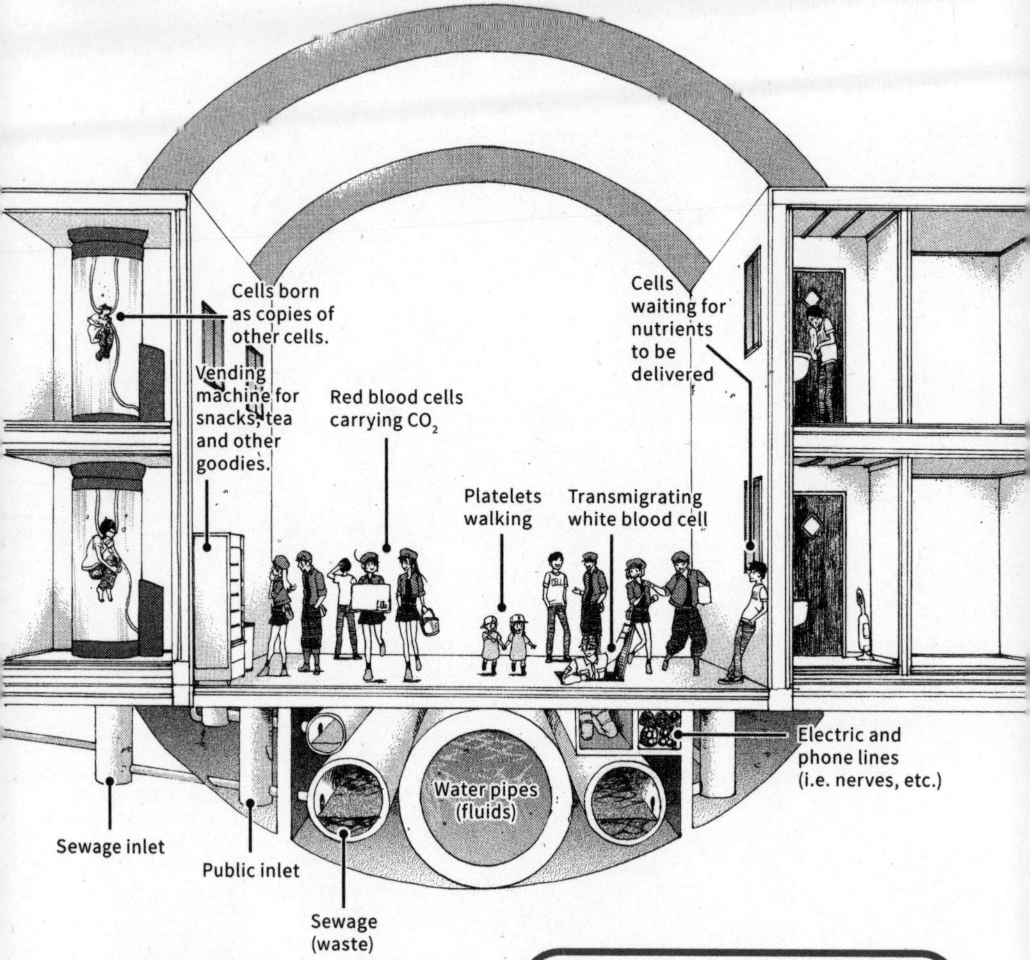

Cells born as copies of other cells.
Vending machine for snacks, tea and other goodies.
Red blood cells carrying CO_2
Cells waiting for nutrients to be delivered
Platelets walking
Transmigrating white blood cell
Electric and phone lines (i.e. nerves, etc.)
Water pipes (fluids)
Sewage inlet
Public inlet
Sewage (waste)

Red blood cells like sugars

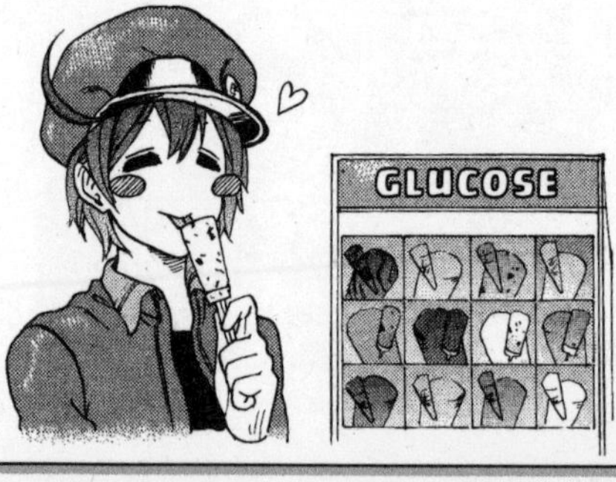

GLUCOSE

Unlike white blood cells and other cells, red blood cells lack mitochondria. Because of this, they can only utilize glucose for energy.

Cells at Work!
はたらく細胞

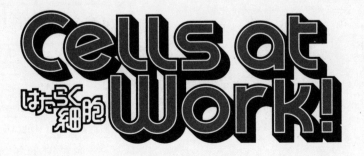

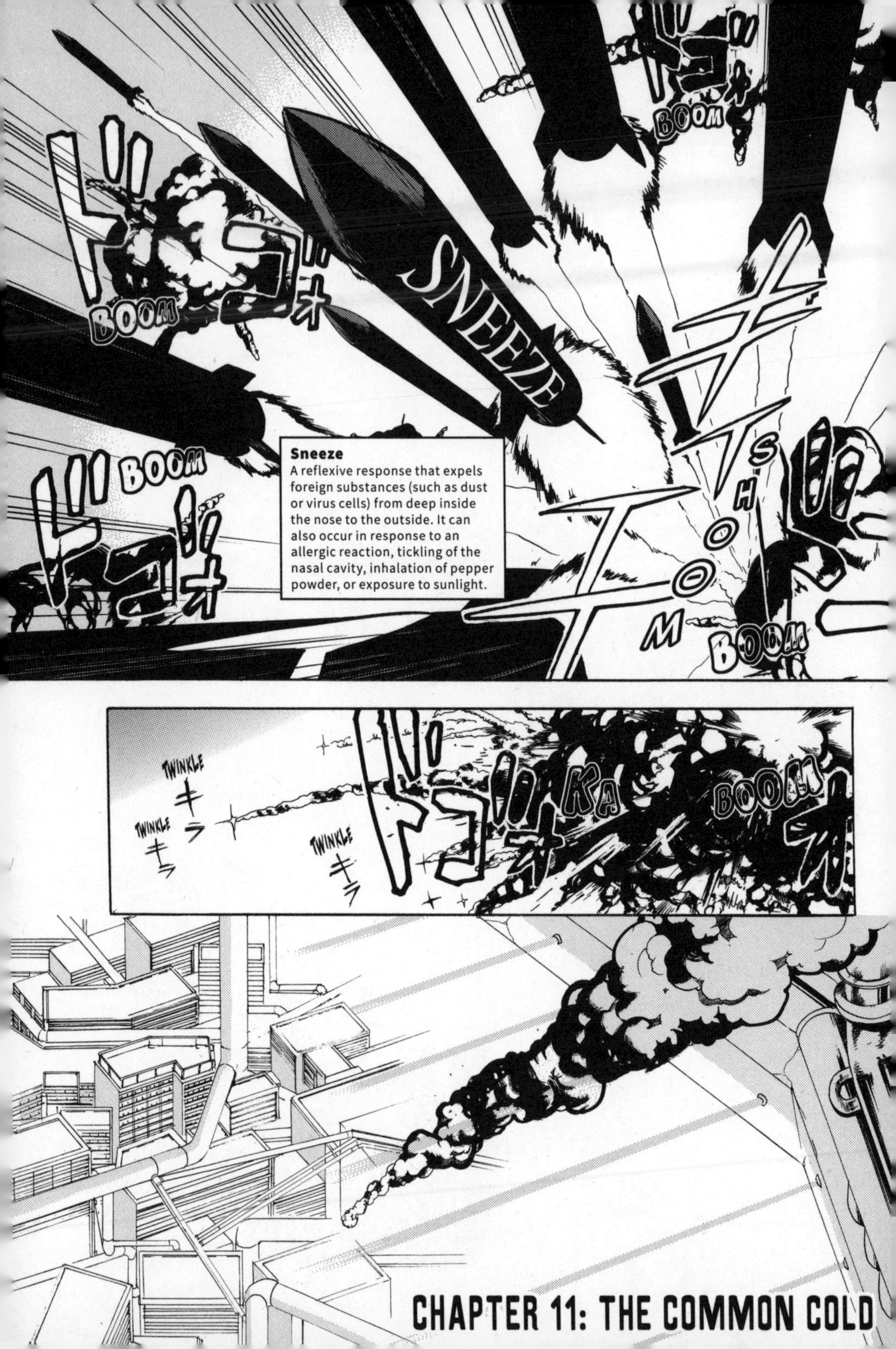
BOOM
SHOOOM
BOOM
SNEEZE
Sneeze
A reflexive response that expels foreign substances (such as dust or virus cells) from deep inside the nose to the outside. It can also occur in response to an allergic reaction, tickling of the nasal cavity, inhalation of pepper powder, or exposure to sunlight.
BOOM
BOOM
BOOM
KA
TWINKLE
TWINKLE
TWINKLE

CHAPTER 11: THE COMMON COLD

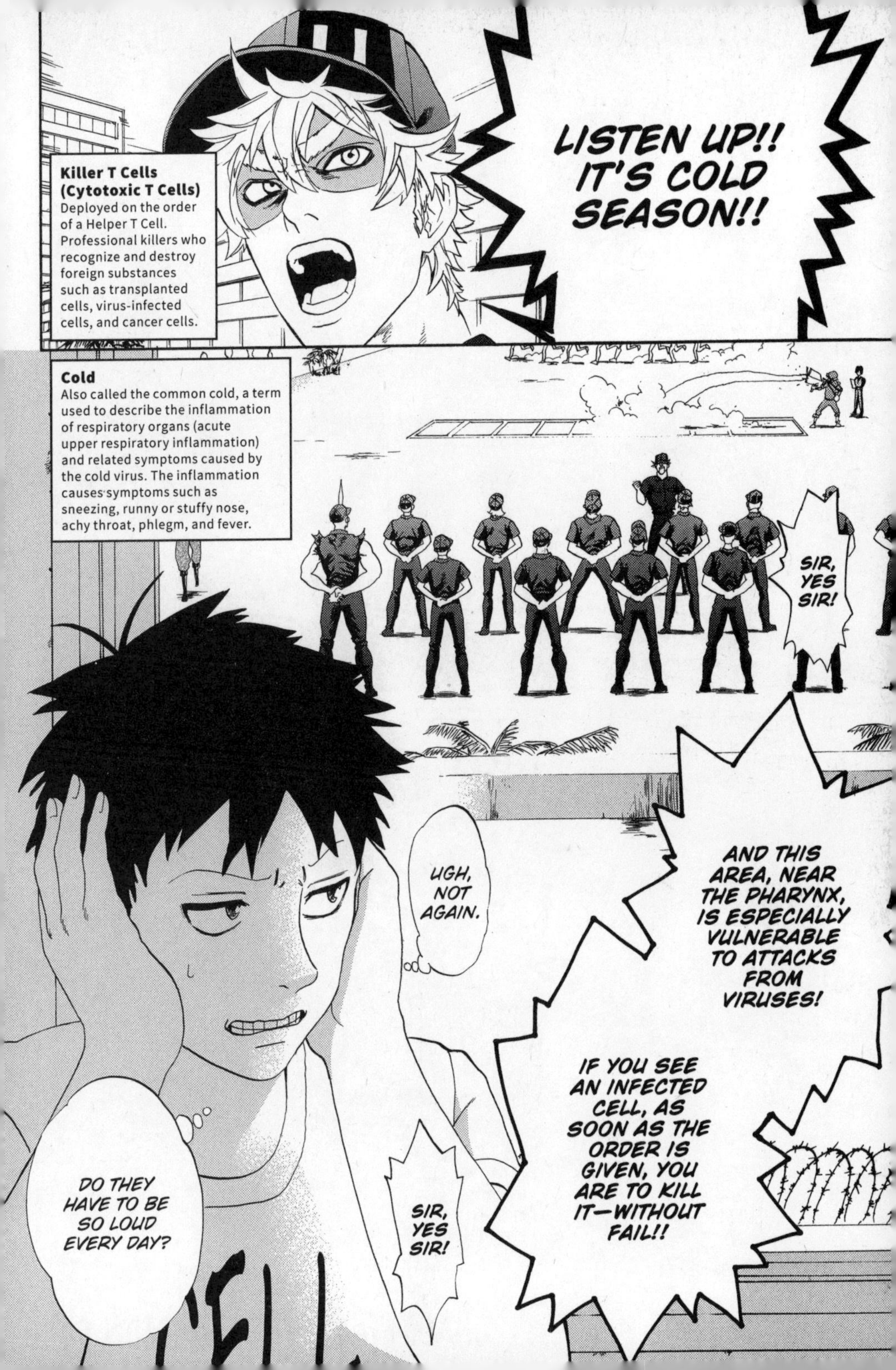
LISTEN UP!! IT'S COLD SEASON!!
Killer T Cells (Cytotoxic T Cells)
Deployed on the order of a Helper T Cell. Professional killers who recognize and destroy foreign substances such as transplanted cells, virus-infected cells, and cancer cells.
Cold
Also called the common cold, a term used to describe the inflammation of respiratory organs (acute upper respiratory inflammation) and related symptoms caused by the cold virus. The inflammation causes symptoms such as sneezing, runny or stuffy nose, achy throat, phlegm, and fever.
SIR, YES SIR!
AND THIS AREA, NEAR THE PHARYNX, IS ESPECIALLY VULNERABLE TO ATTACKS FROM VIRUSES!
IF YOU SEE AN INFECTED CELL, AS SOON AS THE ORDER IS GIVEN, YOU ARE TO KILL IT—WITHOUT FAIL!!
SIR, YES SIR!
UGH, NOT AGAIN.
DO THEY HAVE TO BE SO LOUD EVERY DAY?

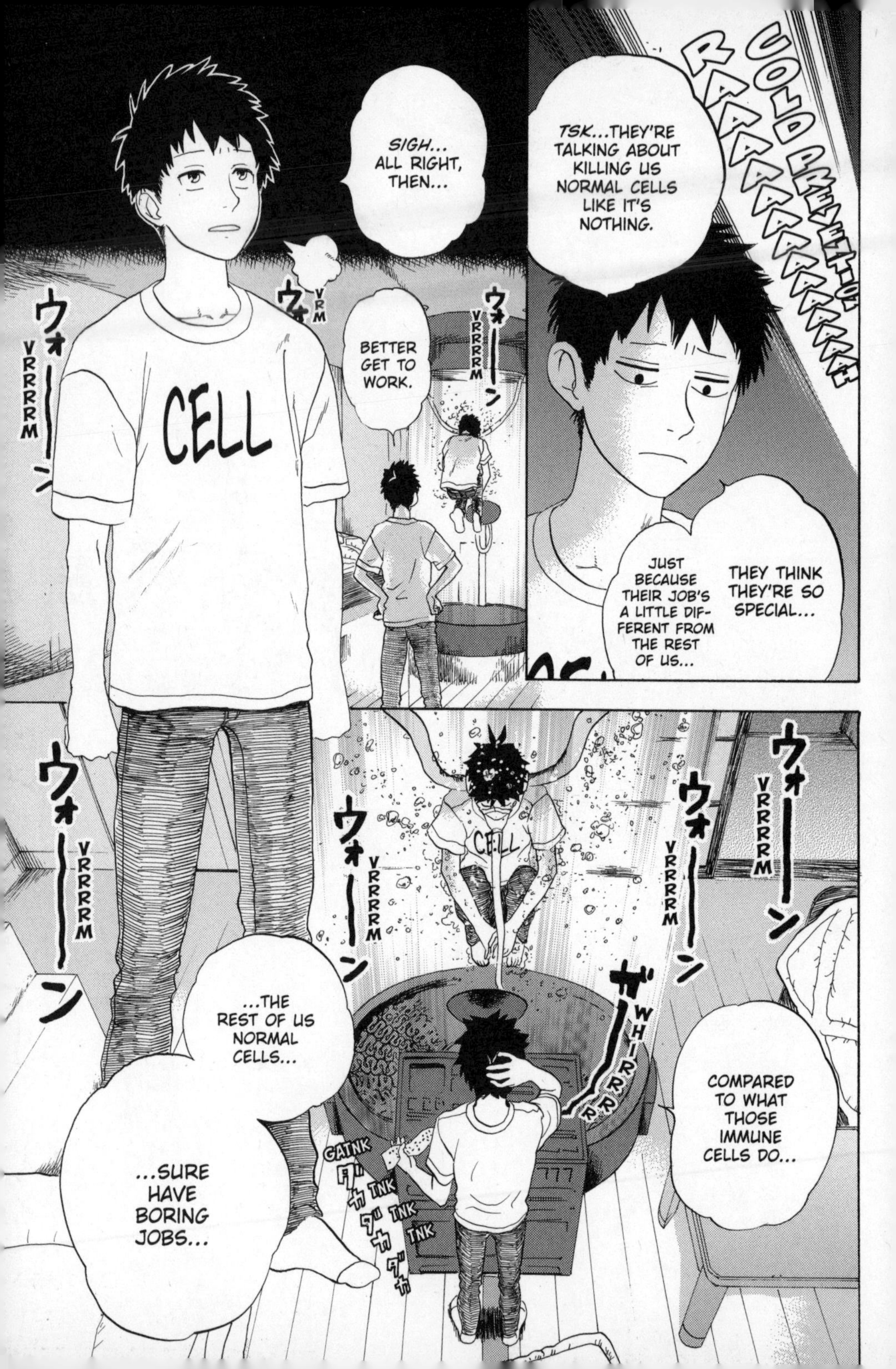
COLD PREVENTION RAAAAAAAAAAAAH
TSK...THEY'RE TALKING ABOUT KILLING US NORMAL CELLS LIKE IT'S NOTHING.
THEY THINK THEY'RE SO SPECIAL...
JUST BECAUSE THEIR JOB'S A LITTLE DIF-FERENT FROM THE REST OF US...
ウォーン VRRRRM
ウォーン VRRRRM
ウォーン VRRRRM
ザー WHIRRRR
CELL
COMPARED TO WHAT THOSE IMMUNE CELLS DO...
ガタン GATINK
カ TNK
カ TNK
カ TNK
SIGH... ALL RIGHT, THEN...
ウォ VRM
ウォーン VRRRRM
BETTER GET TO WORK.
ウォーン VRRRRM
CELL
ウォーン VRRRRM
...THE REST OF US NORMAL CELLS...
...SURE HAVE BORING JOBS...

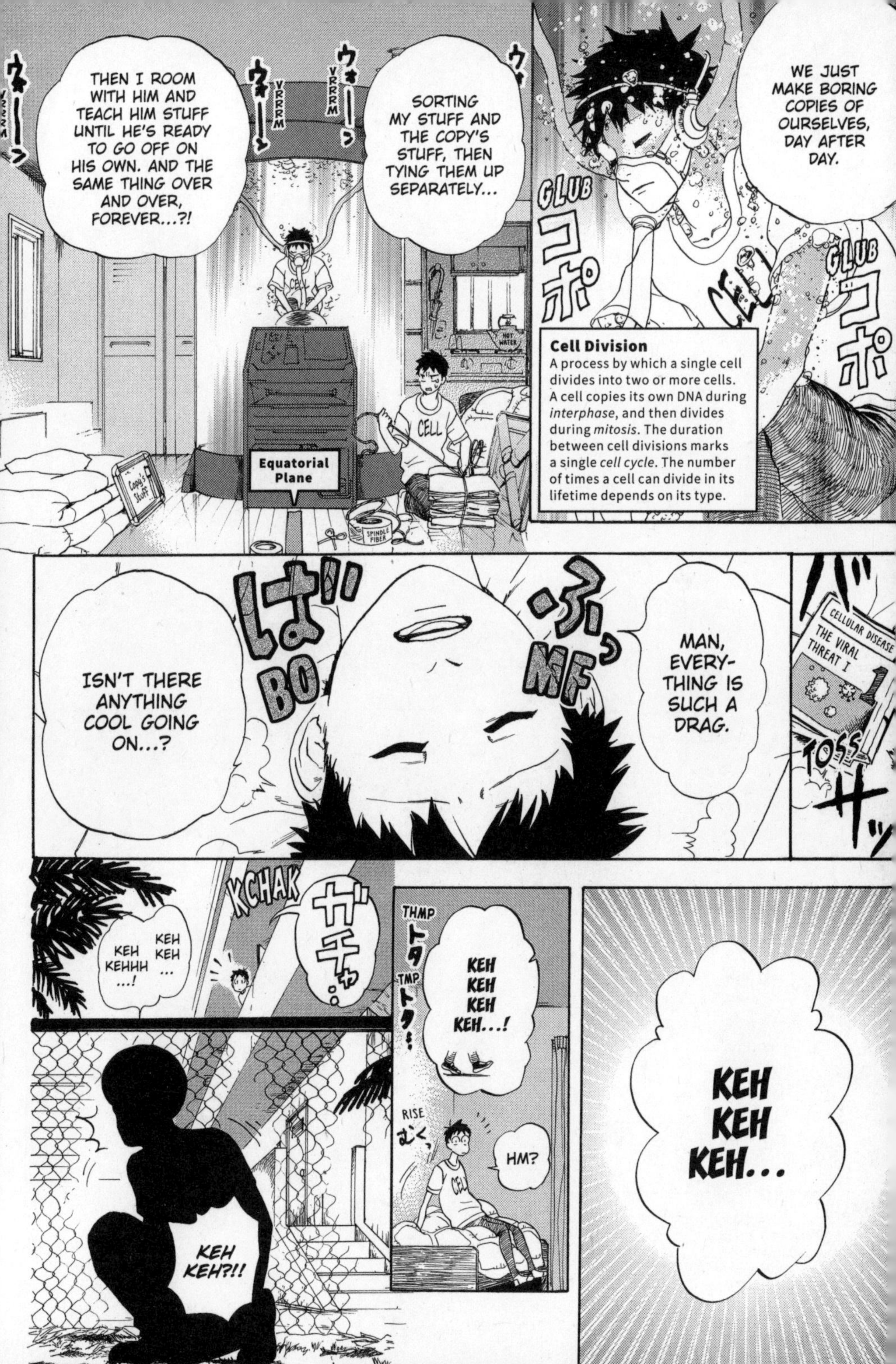
WE JUST MAKE BORING COPIES OF OURSELVES, DAY AFTER DAY.
GLUB
GLUB
Cell Division
A process by which a single cell divides into two or more cells. A cell copies its own DNA during *interphase*, and then divides during *mitosis*. The duration between cell divisions marks a single *cell cycle*. The number of times a cell can divide in its lifetime depends on its type.
SORTING MY STUFF AND THE COPY'S STUFF, THEN TYING THEM UP SEPARATELY...
VRRRM
VRRRM
THEN I ROOM WITH HIM AND TEACH HIM STUFF UNTIL HE'S READY TO GO OFF ON HIS OWN. AND THE SAME THING OVER AND OVER, FOREVER...?!
HOT WATER
Equatorial Plane
Copy's Stuff
SPINDLE FIBER
CELLULAR DISEASE
THE VIRAL THREAT I
TOSS
MAN, EVERYTHING IS SUCH A DRAG.
MF
BO
ISN'T THERE ANYTHING COOL GOING ON...?
KEH KEH KEH...
THMP
TMP
KEH KEH KEH KEH...!
RISE
HM?
KCHAK
KEH KEH ...
KEH KEHHH ...!
KEH KEH?!!

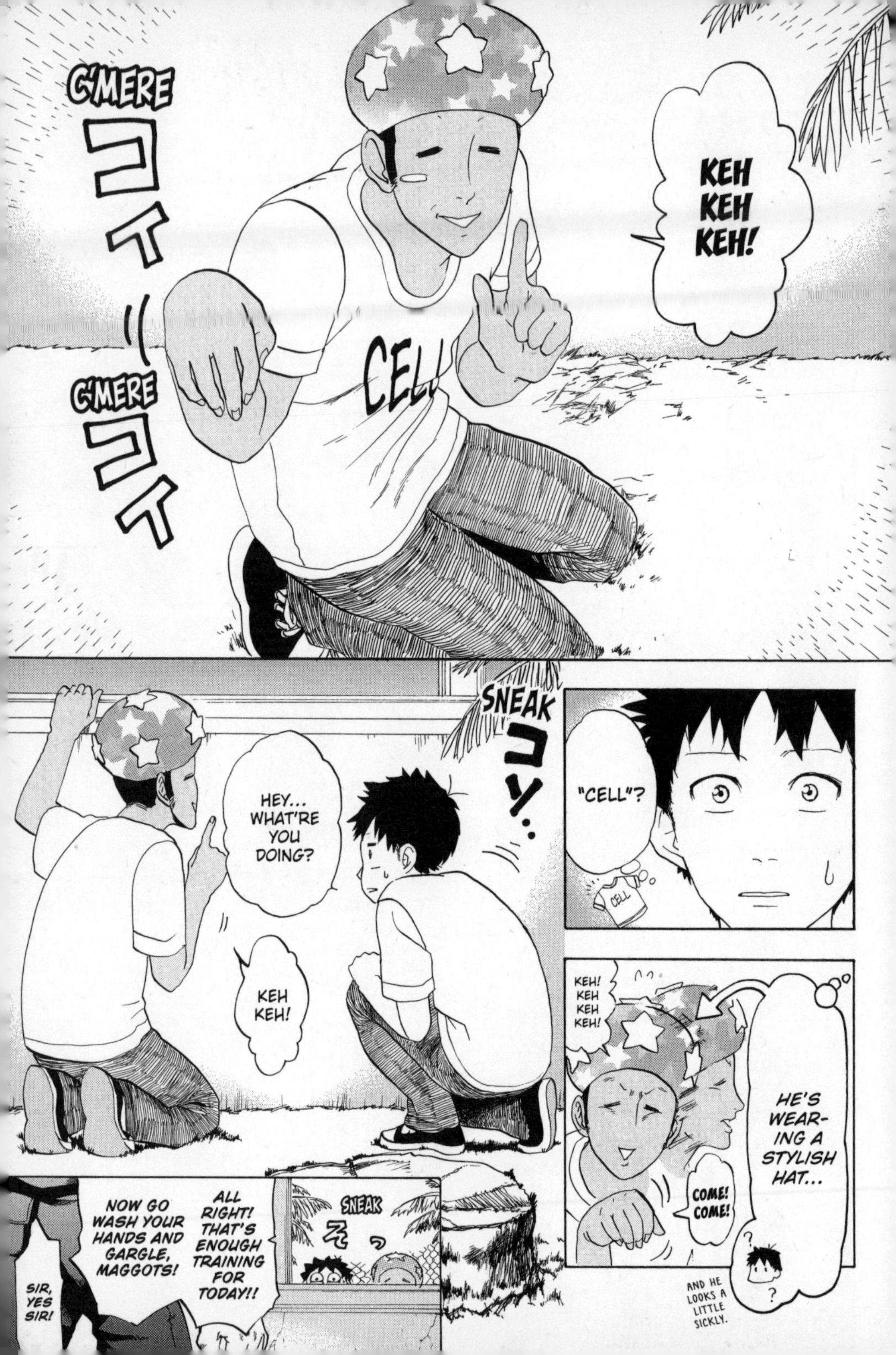
KEH KEH KEH!
C'MERE
コイ
C'MERE
コイ
CELL
"CELL"?
CELL
SNEAK
コソ..
HEY... WHAT'RE YOU DOING?
KEH KEH!
HE'S WEARING A STYLISH HAT...
KEH! KEH KEH KEH!
COME! COME!
AND HE LOOKS A LITTLE SICKLY.
SNEAK
そっ
ALL RIGHT! THAT'S ENOUGH TRAINING FOR TODAY!!
NOW GO WASH YOUR HANDS AND GARGLE, MAGGOTS!
SIR, YES SIR!

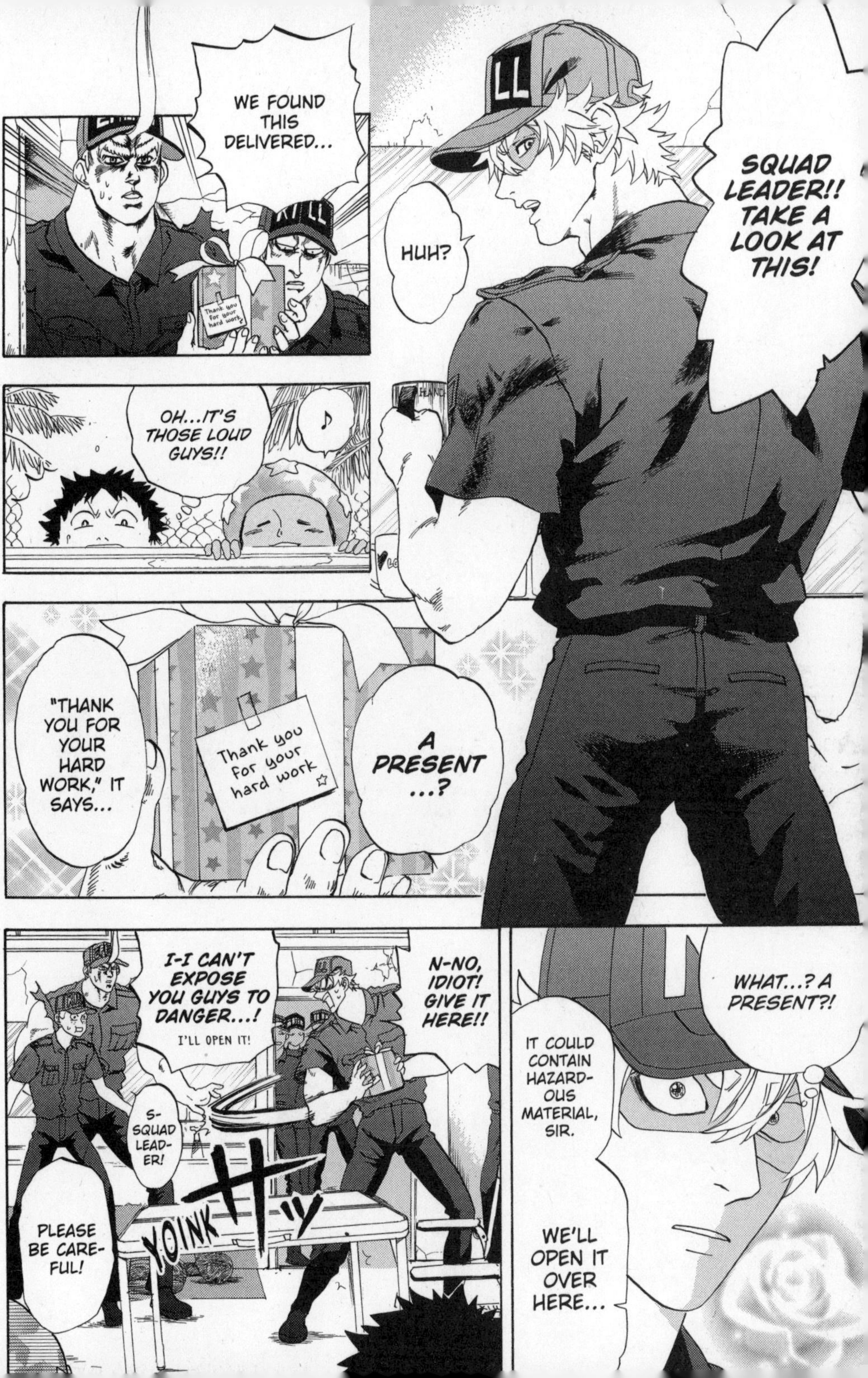
SQUAD LEADER!! TAKE A LOOK AT THIS!
HUH?
WE FOUND THIS DELIVERED...
Thank you for your hard work
OH...IT'S THOSE LOUD GUYS!!
♪
A PRESENT ...?
Thank you for your hard work
"THANK YOU FOR YOUR HARD WORK," IT SAYS...
WHAT...? A PRESENT?!
IT COULD CONTAIN HAZARD-OUS MATERIAL, SIR.
WE'LL OPEN IT OVER HERE...
N-NO, IDIOT! GIVE IT HERE!!
I-I CAN'T EXPOSE YOU GUYS TO DANGER...!
I'LL OPEN IT!
S-SQUAD LEAD-ER!
YOINK
PLEASE BE CARE-FUL!

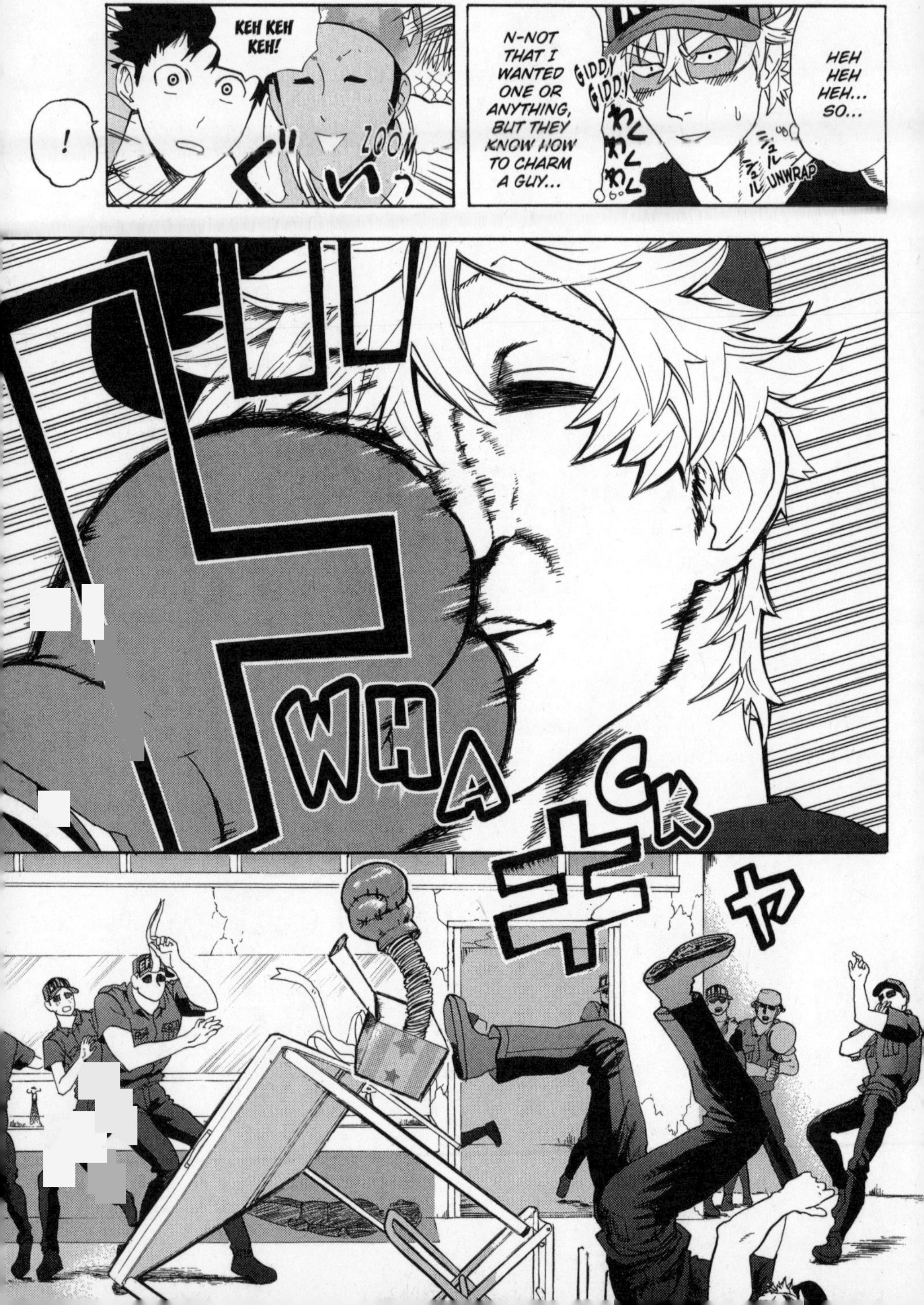
HEH HEH HEH... SO...
N-NOT THAT I WANTED ONE OR ANYTHING, BUT THEY KNOW HOW TO CHARM A GUY...
GIDDY GIDDY
わくわくわく
UNWRAP
KEH KEH KEH!
ZOOM
!
WHACK

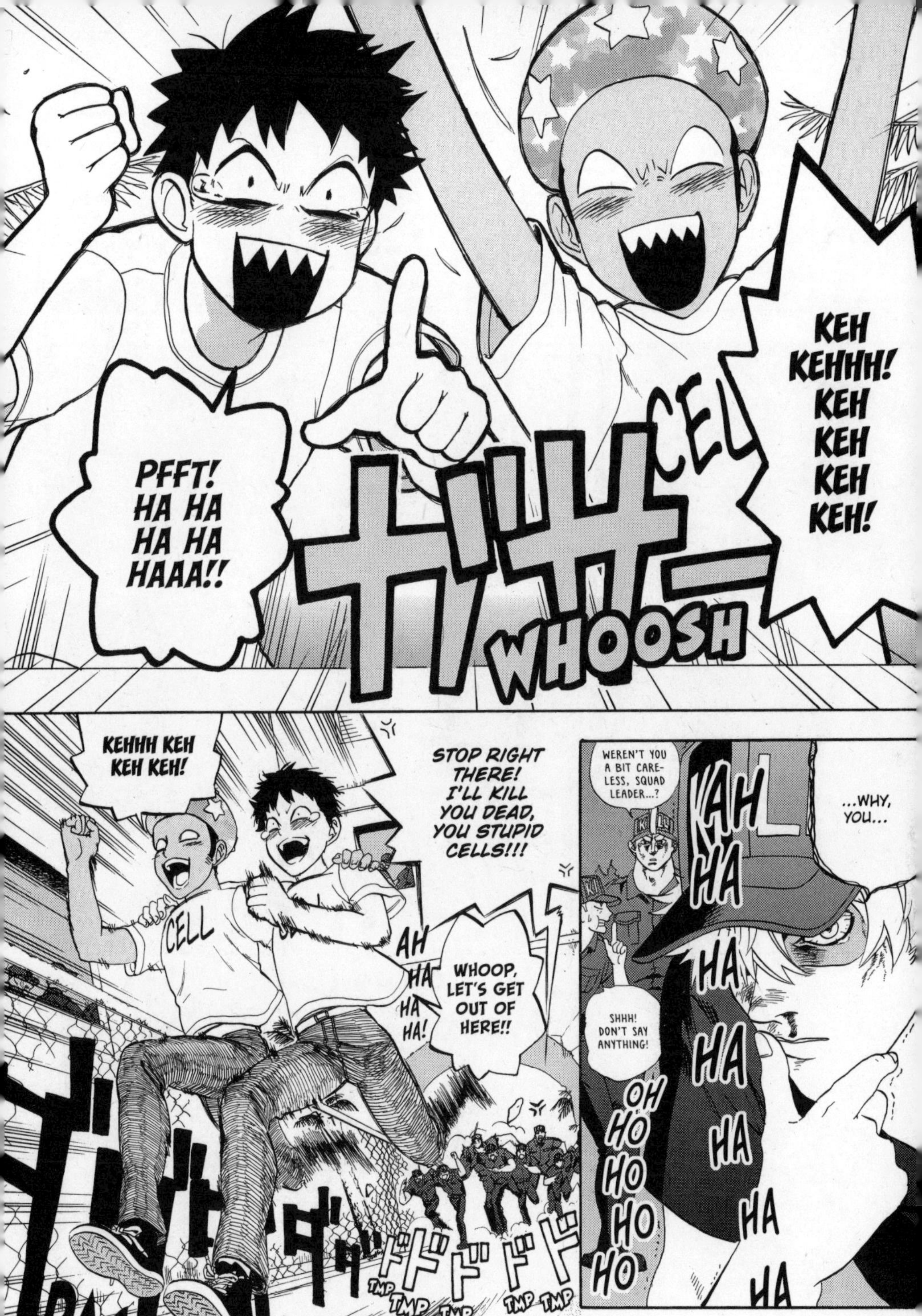
KEH KEHHH! KEH KEH KEH KEH!
CEL
WHOOSH
PFFT! HA HA HA HA HAAA!!
...WHY, YOU...
KAH HA HA HA HA HA HA HA HA
WEREN'T YOU A BIT CARELESS, SQUAD LEADER...?
SHHH! DON'T SAY ANYTHING!
OH HO HO HO HO HO
STOP RIGHT THERE! I'LL KILL YOU DEAD, YOU STUPID CELLS!!!
KEHHH KEH KEH KEH!
WHOOP, LET'S GET OUT OF HERE!!
AH HA HA HA!
CELL
TMP TMP TMP TMP TMP
DASH

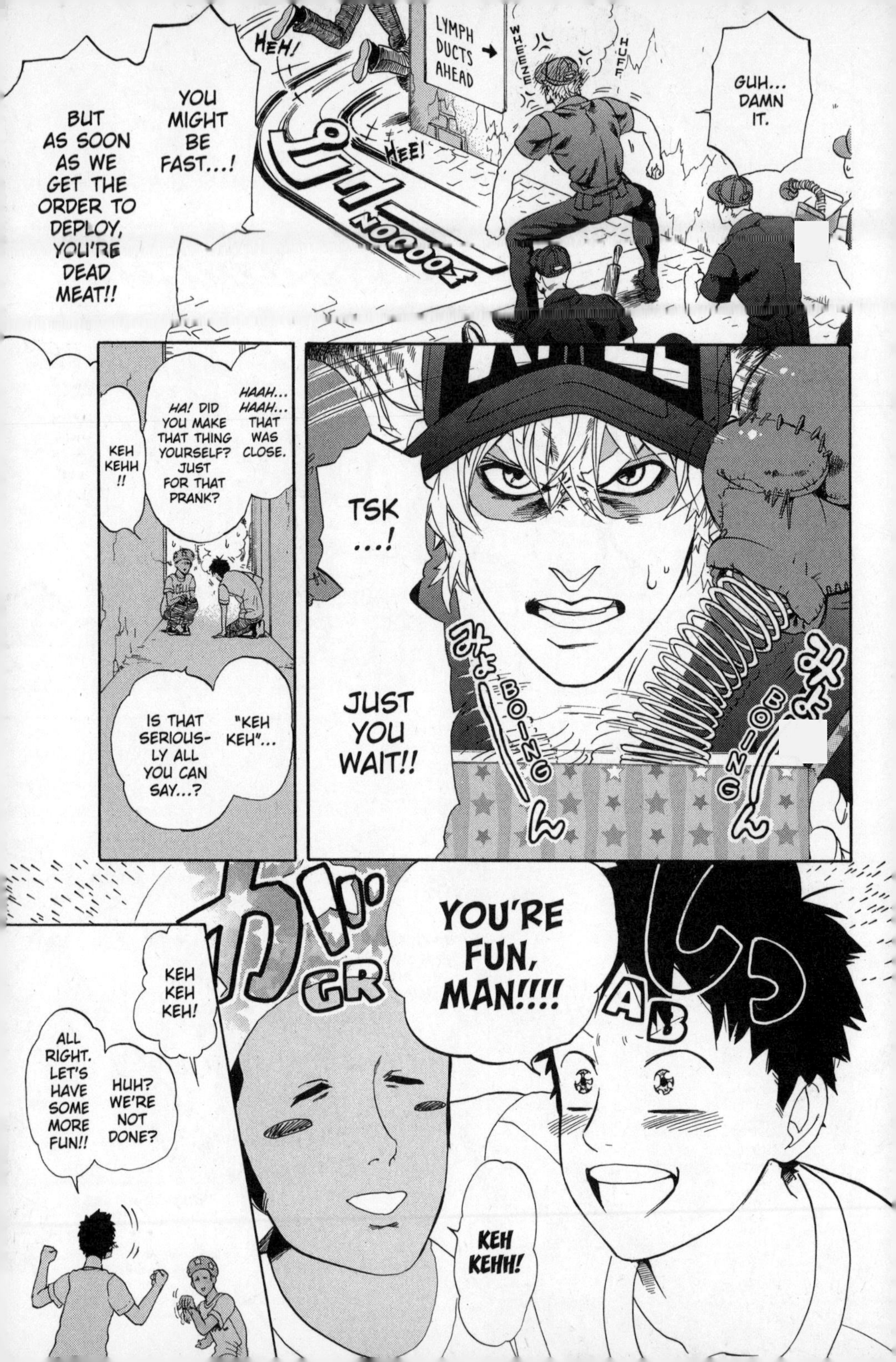
GUH... DAMN IT.
HUFF
WHEEZE
LYMPH DUCTS AHEAD
HEH!
HEE!
ZOOOOM
YOU MIGHT BE FAST...!
BUT AS SOON AS WE GET THE ORDER TO DEPLOY, YOU'RE DEAD MEAT!!
TSK ...!
JUST YOU WAIT!!
BOING
BOING
HAAH... HAAH... THAT WAS CLOSE.
HA! DID YOU MAKE THAT THING YOURSELF? JUST FOR THAT PRANK?
KEH KEHH !!
"KEH KEH"...
IS THAT SERIOUS-LY ALL YOU CAN SAY...?
AB
YOU'RE FUN, MAN!!!!
GR
KEH KEHH!
KEH KEH KEH!
HUH? WE'RE NOT DONE?
ALL RIGHT. LET'S HAVE SOME MORE FUN!!

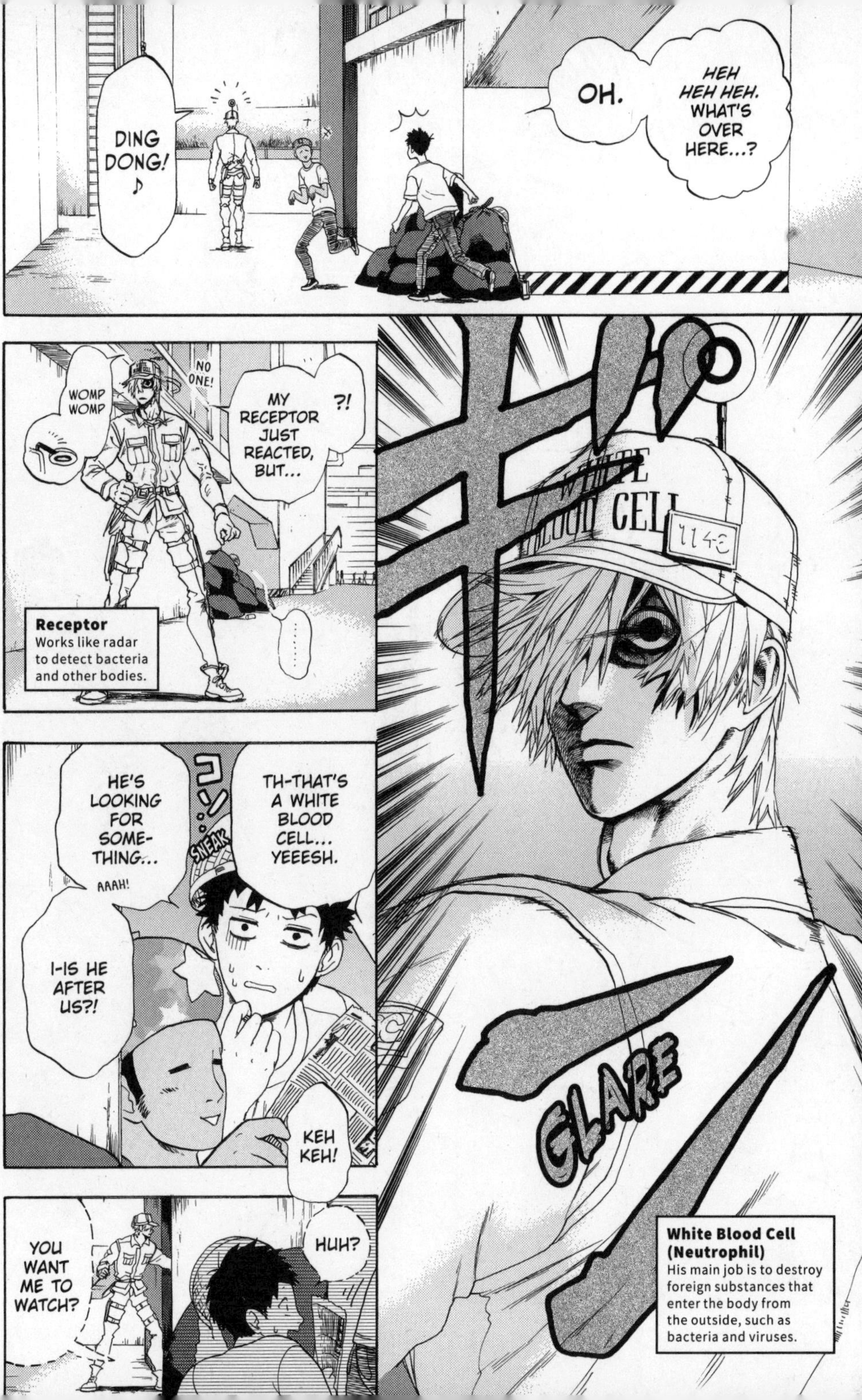
HEH HEH HEH. WHAT'S OVER HERE...?
OH.
DING DONG! ♪
GLARE
White Blood Cell (Neutrophil)
His main job is to destroy foreign substances that enter the body from the outside, such as bacteria and viruses.
?!
MY RECEPTOR JUST REACTED, BUT...
NO ONE!
WOMP WOMP
......
Receptor
Works like radar to detect bacteria and other bodies.
TH-THAT'S A WHITE BLOOD CELL... YEEESH.
SNEAK
HE'S LOOKING FOR SOME-THING...
AAAH!
I-IS HE AFTER US?!
KEH KEH!
HUH?
YOU WANT ME TO WATCH?

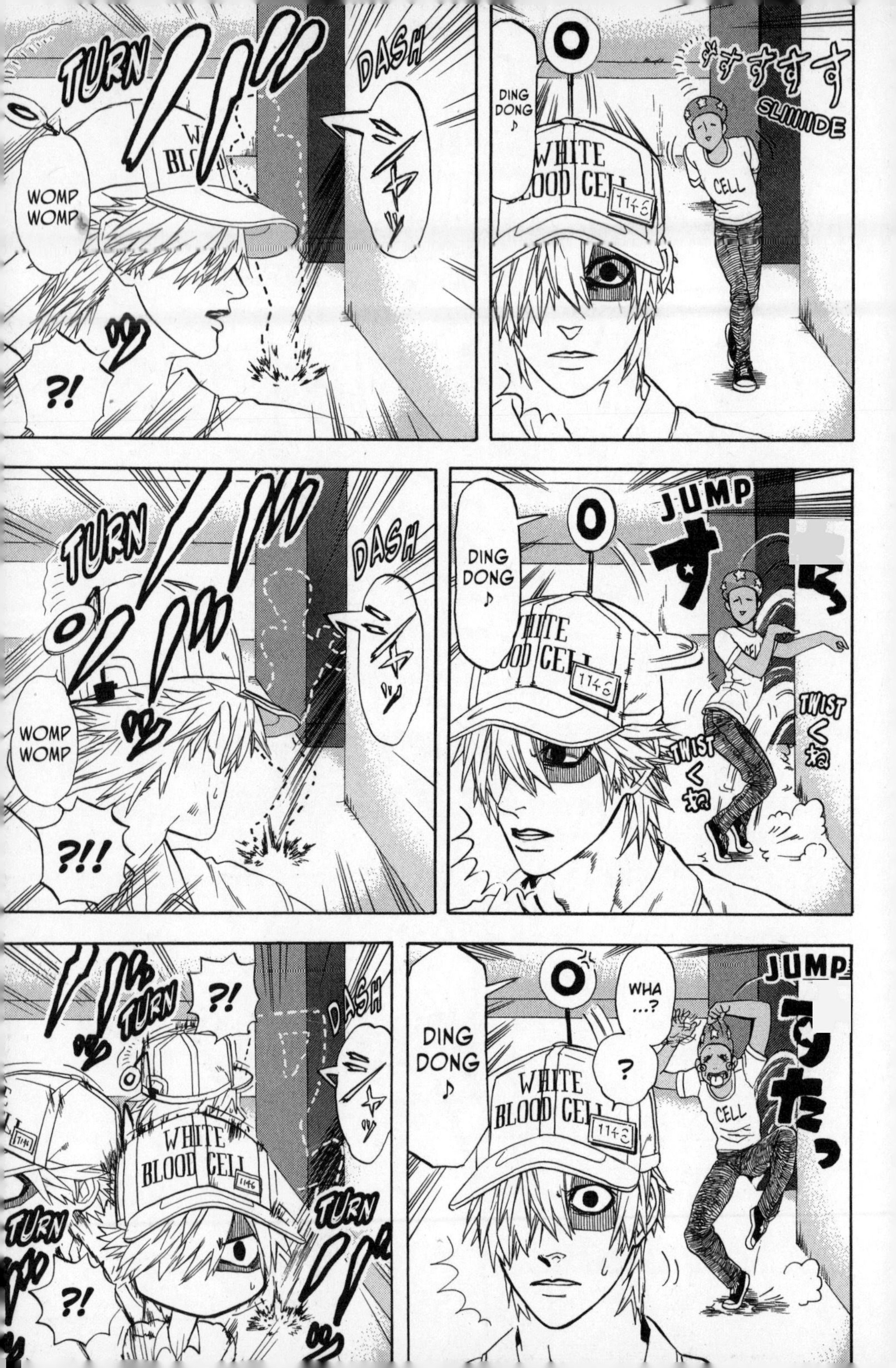
すすすす
SLIIIIIDE
DING DONG ♪
DASH
TURN
WOMP WOMP
?!
JUMP
す
TWIST
くね
TWIST
くね
DING DONG ♪
DASH
TURN
WOMP WOMP
?!!
JUMP
たっ
WHA ...?
?
DING DONG ♪
DASH
?!
TURN
TURN
TURN
?!

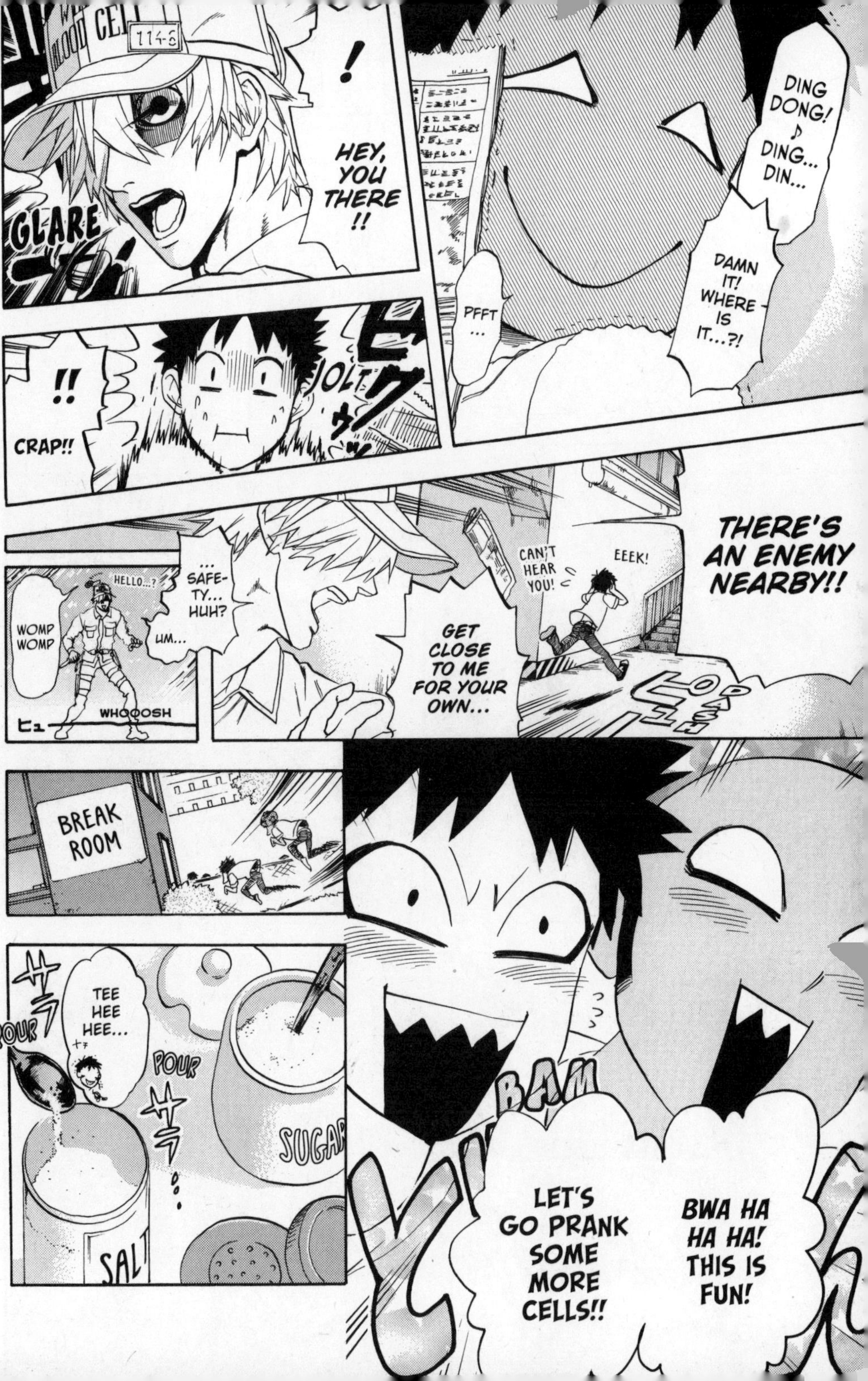
DING DONG! ♪ DING... DIN...
DAMN IT! WHERE IS IT...?!
PFFT...
!
HEY, YOU THERE!!
GLARE
JOLT
!!
CRAP!!
THERE'S AN ENEMY NEARBY!!
EEEK!
CAN'T HEAR YOU!
DASH
GET CLOSE TO ME FOR YOUR OWN...
... SAFETY... HUH?
UM...
HELLO...?
WOMP WOMP
WHOOOSH
BAM
BWA HA HA HA! THIS IS FUN!
LET'S GO PRANK SOME MORE CELLS!!
BREAK ROOM
POUR
TEE HEE HEE...
POUR
SUGAR
SALT

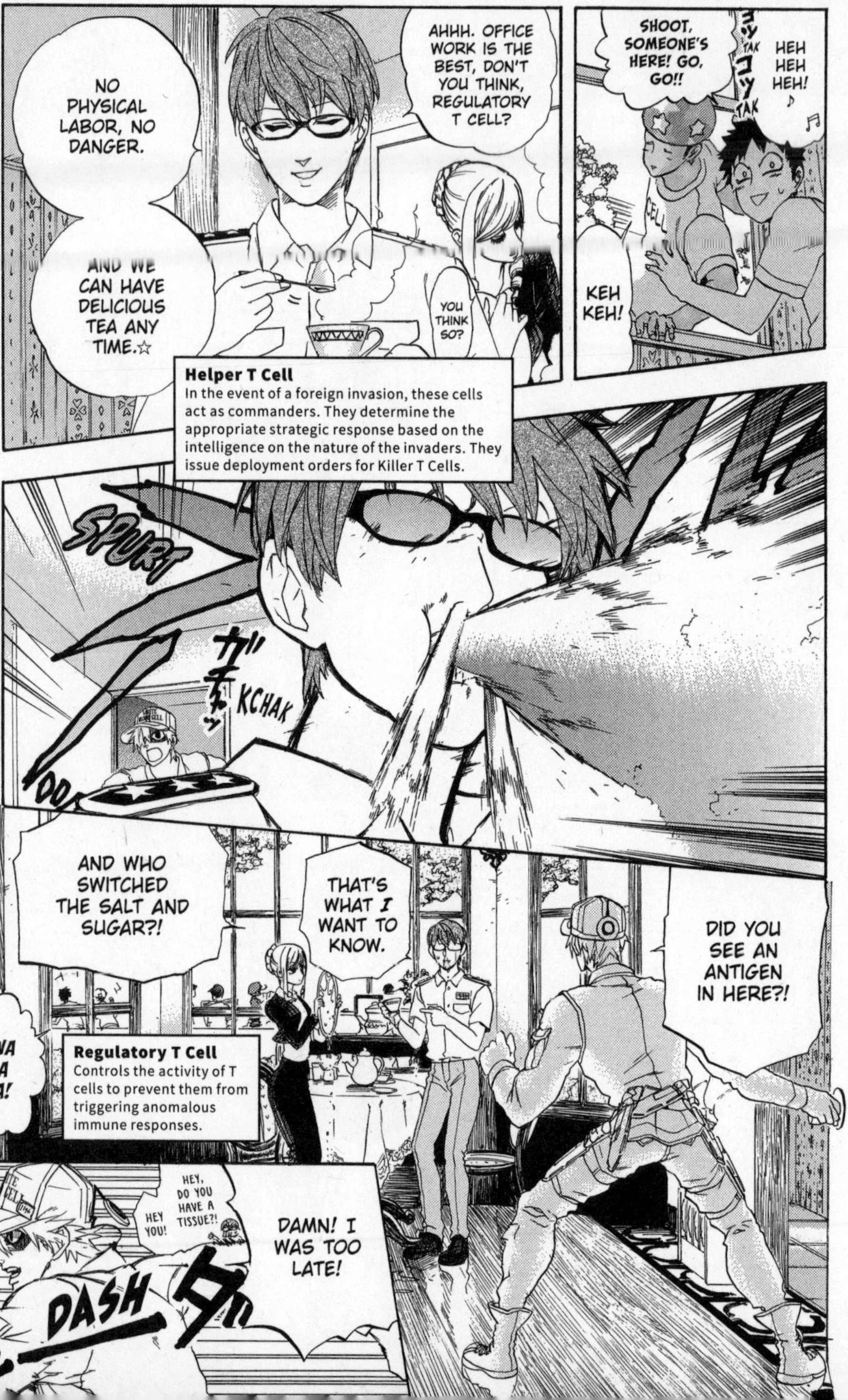
SHOOT, SOMEONE'S HERE! GO, GO!!
TAK TAK
HEH HEH HEH! ♪
KEH KEH!
AHHH. OFFICE WORK IS THE BEST, DON'T YOU THINK, REGULATORY T CELL?
NO PHYSICAL LABOR, NO DANGER.
YOU THINK SO?
AND WE CAN HAVE DELICIOUS TEA ANY TIME.☆
Helper T Cell
In the event of a foreign invasion, these cells act as commanders. They determine the appropriate strategic response based on the intelligence on the nature of the invaders. They issue deployment orders for Killer T Cells.
SPURT
KCHAK
DO
DID YOU SEE AN ANTIGEN IN HERE?!
THAT'S WHAT I WANT TO KNOW.
AND WHO SWITCHED THE SALT AND SUGAR?!
BWA HA HA!
Regulatory T Cell
Controls the activity of T cells to prevent them from triggering anomalous immune responses.
DAMN! I WAS TOO LATE!
HEY, DO YOU HAVE A TISSUE?!
HEY YOU!
DASH

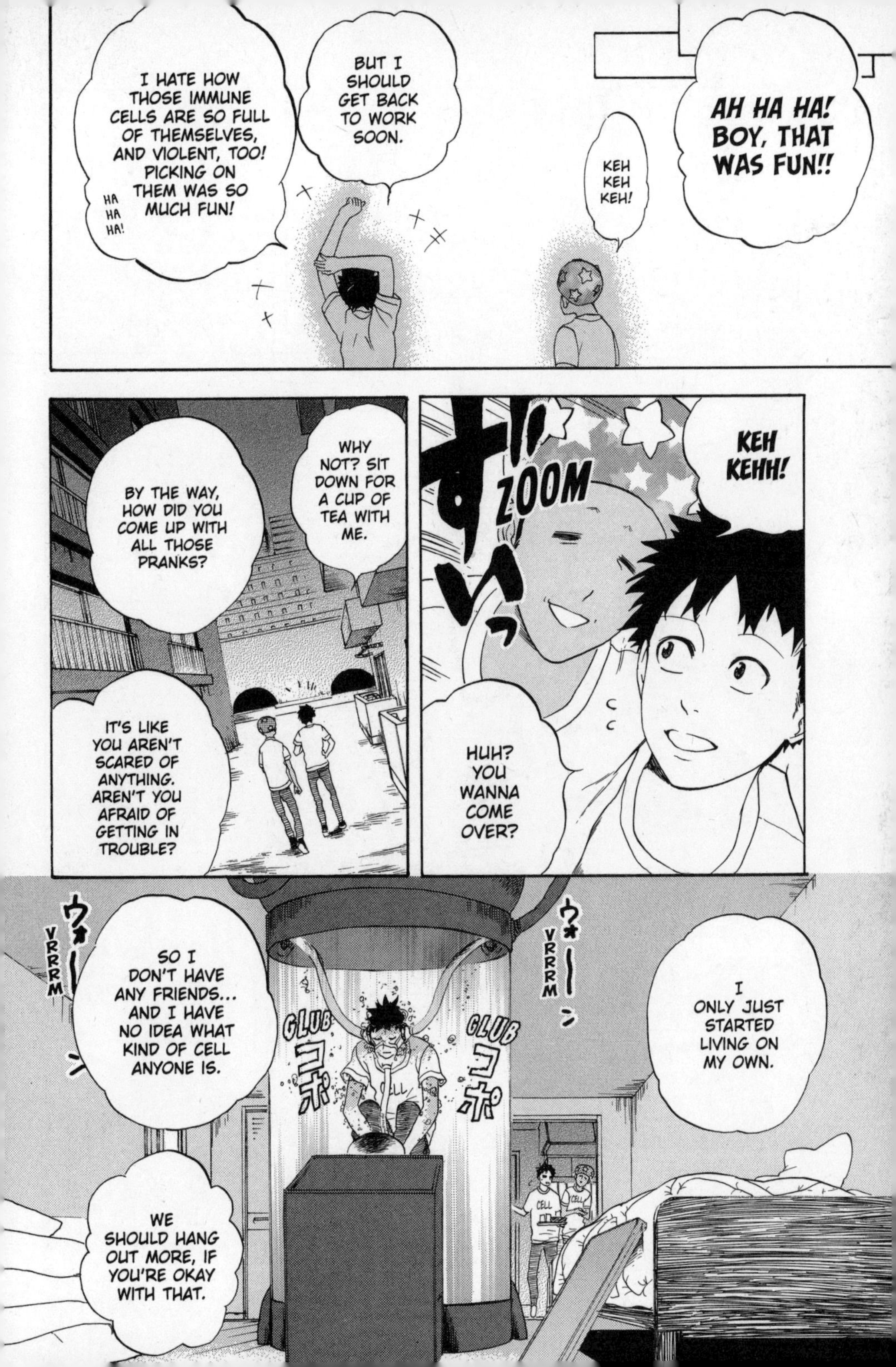
AH HA HA! BOY, THAT WAS FUN!!
KEH KEH KEH!
BUT I SHOULD GET BACK TO WORK SOON.
I HATE HOW THOSE IMMUNE CELLS ARE SO FULL OF THEMSELVES, AND VIOLENT, TOO! PICKING ON THEM WAS SO MUCH FUN!
HA HA HA!
KEH KEHH!
ZOOM
HUH? YOU WANNA COME OVER?
WHY NOT? SIT DOWN FOR A CUP OF TEA WITH ME.
BY THE WAY, HOW DID YOU COME UP WITH ALL THOSE PRANKS?
IT'S LIKE YOU AREN'T SCARED OF ANYTHING. AREN'T YOU AFRAID OF GETTING IN TROUBLE?
I ONLY JUST STARTED LIVING ON MY OWN.
VRRRM
GLUB
GLUB
VRRRM
SO I DON'T HAVE ANY FRIENDS... AND I HAVE NO IDEA WHAT KIND OF CELL ANYONE IS.
WE SHOULD HANG OUT MORE, IF YOU'RE OKAY WITH THAT.

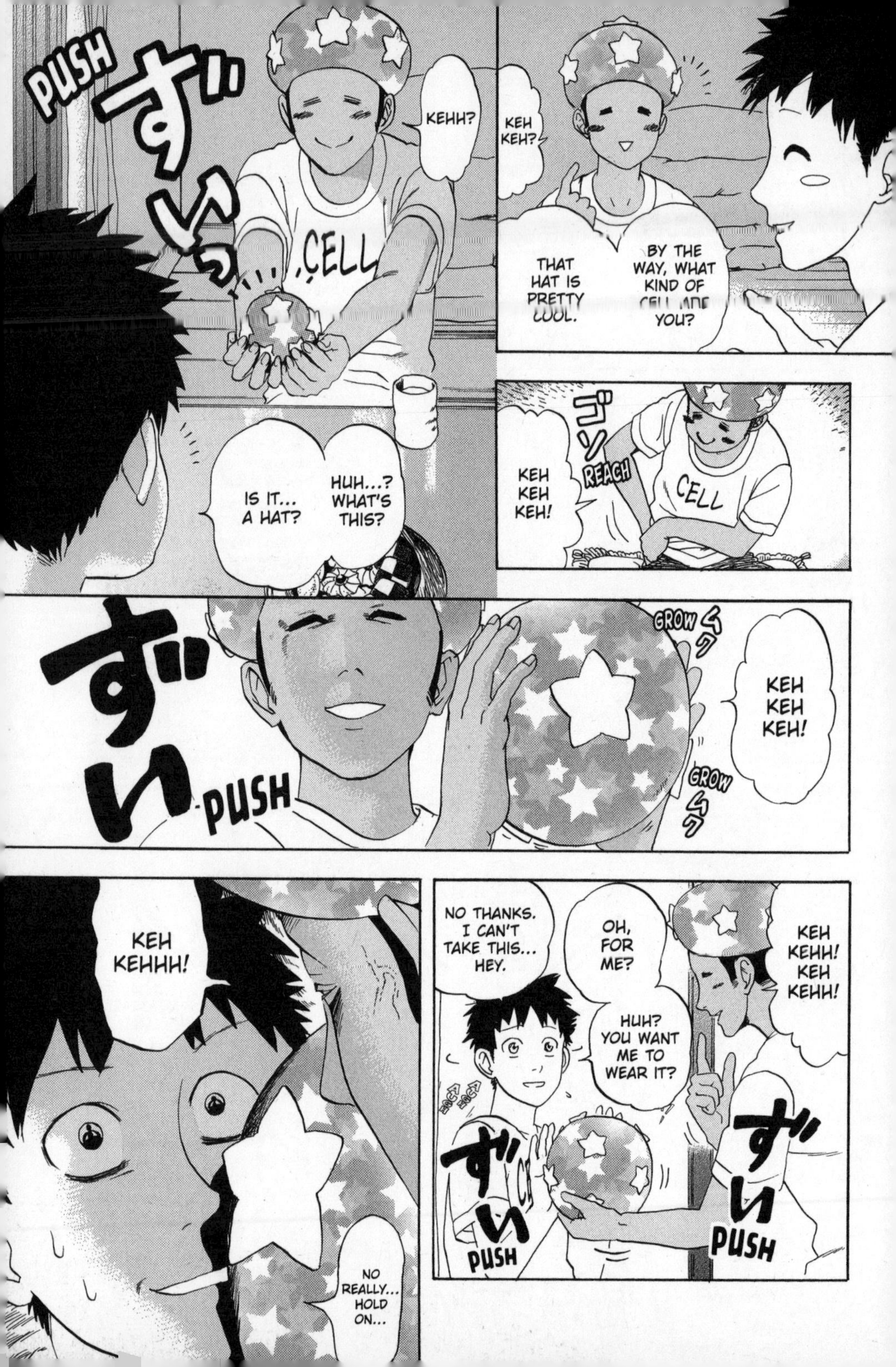
KEH KEH?
BY THE WAY, WHAT KIND OF CELL ARE YOU?
THAT HAT IS PRETTY COOL.
ゴソ REACH
KEH KEH KEH!
ずい PUSH
KEHH?
HUH...? WHAT'S THIS?
IS IT... A HAT?
ムク GROW
KEH KEH KEH!
ムク GROW
ずい PUSH
KEH KEHH! KEH KEHH!
OH, FOR ME?
NO THANKS. I CAN'T TAKE THIS... HEY.
HUH? YOU WANT ME TO WEAR IT?
ずい PUSH
ずい PUSH
KEH KEHHH!
NO REALLY... HOLD ON...

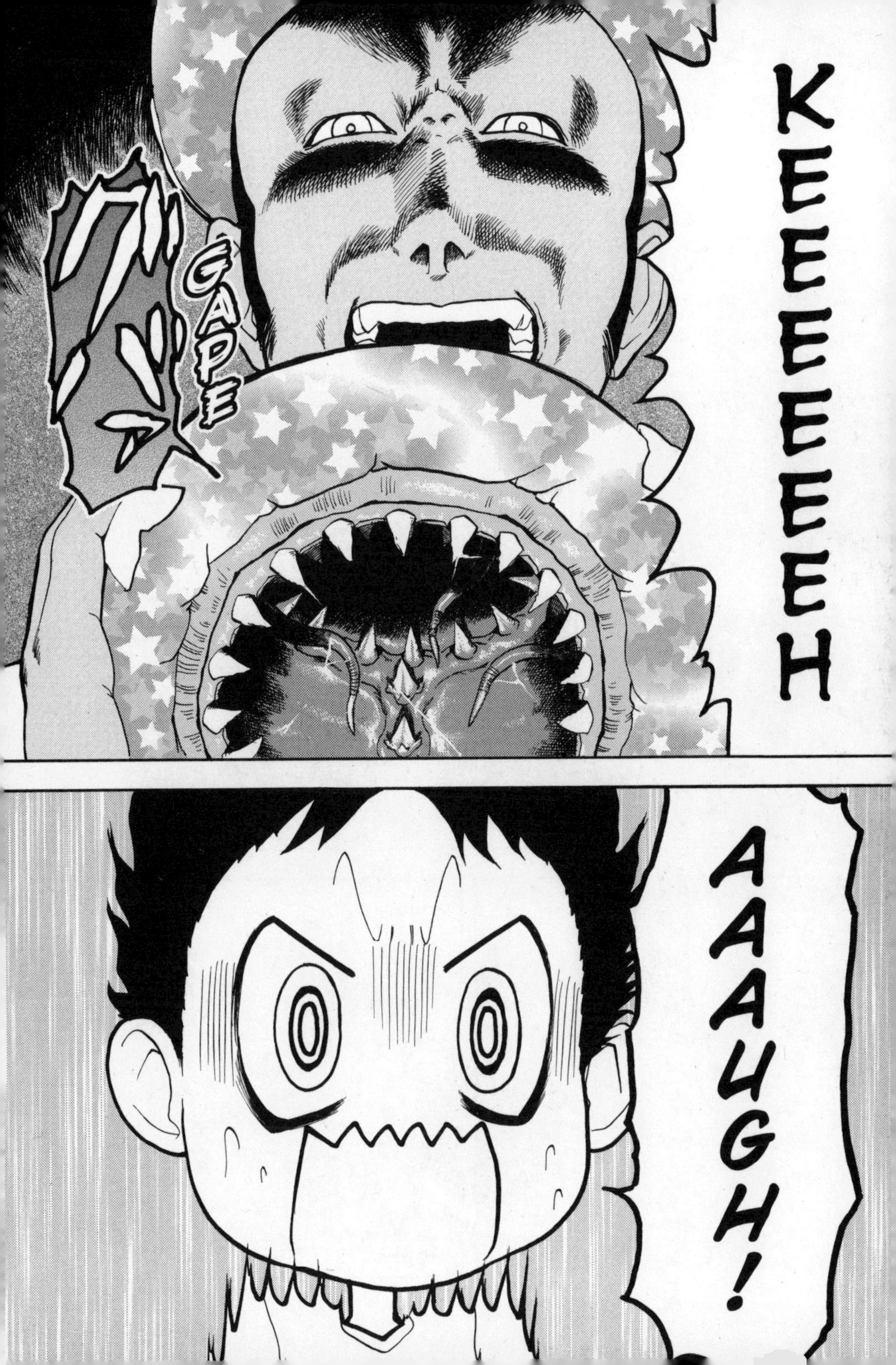
KEEEEEH
GAPE
AAAUGH!

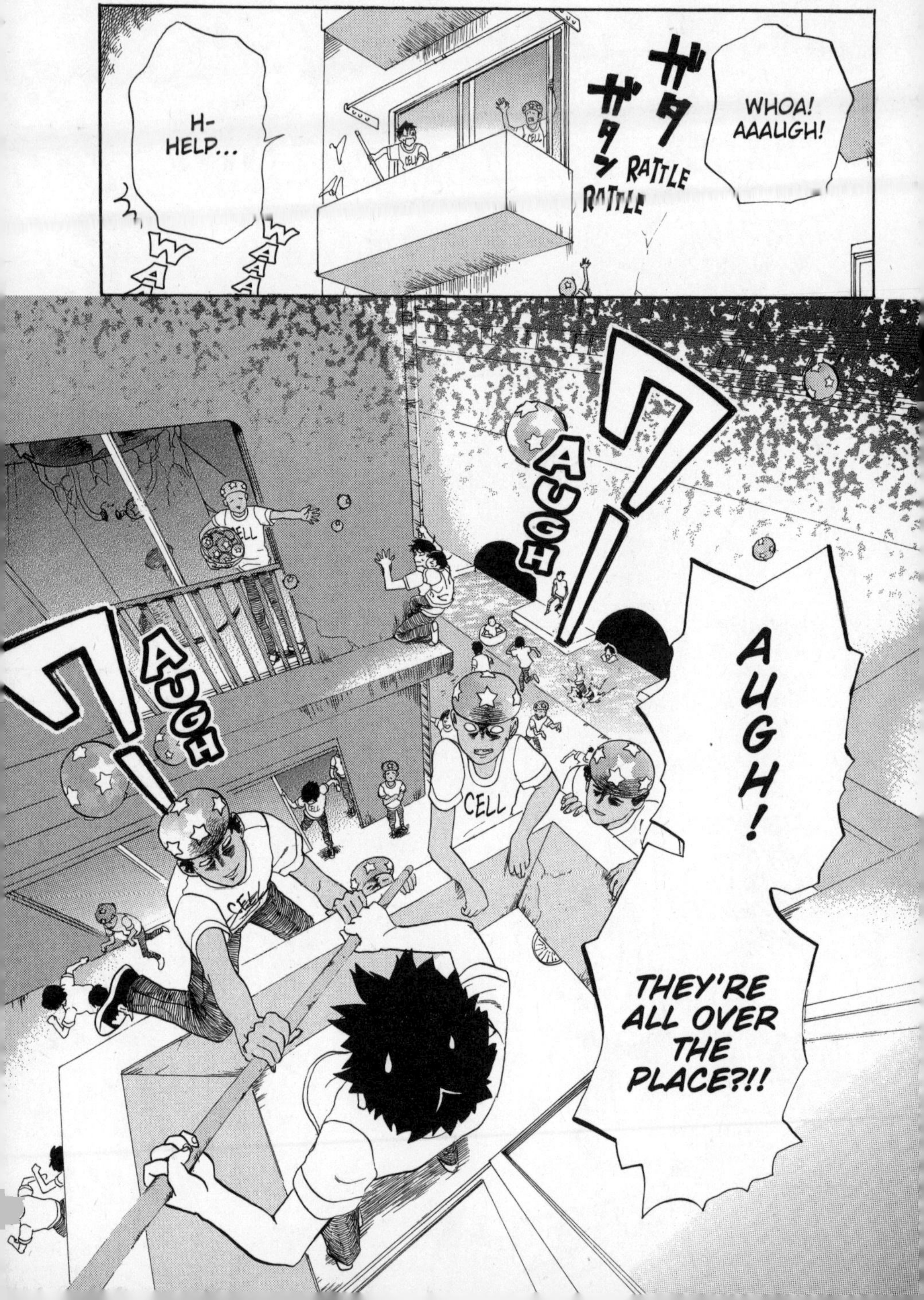
WHOA! AAAUGH!
ガタガタン
RATTLE RATTLE
H- HELP...
WAAA
WAAA
AUGH!
AUGH!
THEY'RE ALL OVER THE PLACE?!!
AUGH!

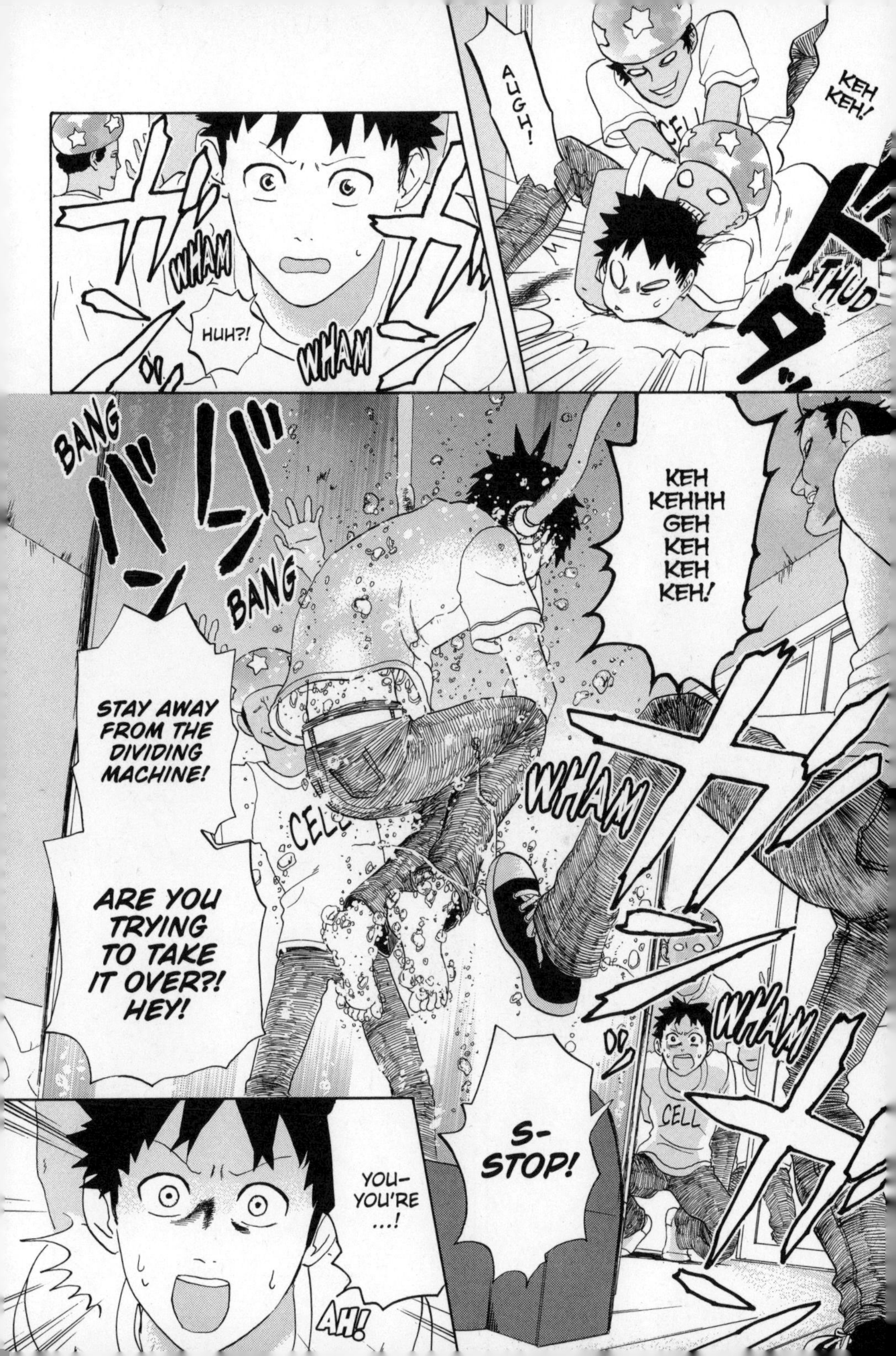
KEH KEH!
THUD
AUGH!
WHAM
HUH?!
WHAM
KEH KEHHH GEH KEH KEH KEH!
BANG
BANG
STAY AWAY FROM THE DIVIDING MACHINE!
ARE YOU TRYING TO TAKE IT OVER?! HEY!
WHAM
WHAM
CELL
CELL
S-STOP!
YOU-YOU'RE ...!
AH!

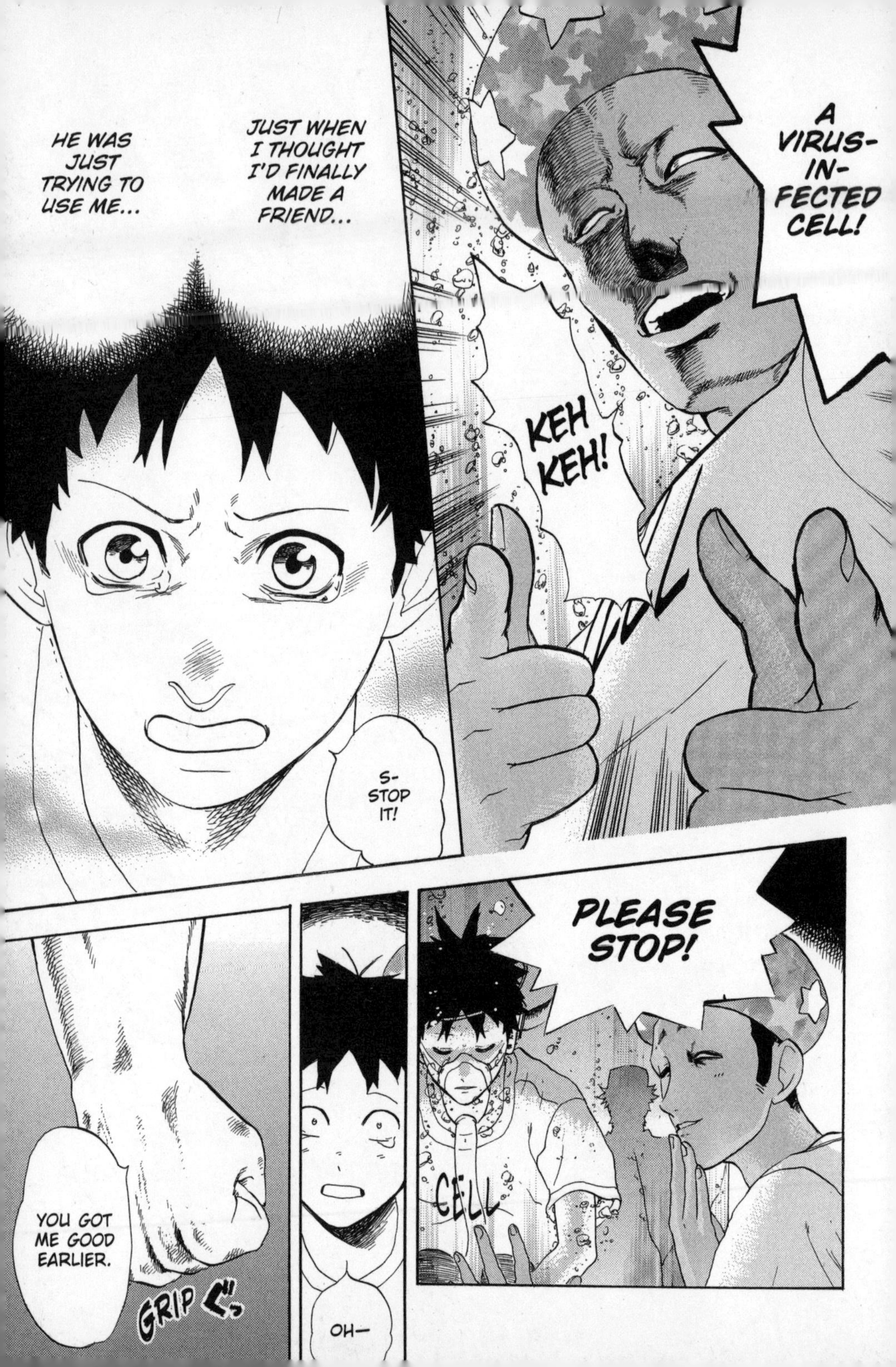
A VIRUS-INFECTED CELL!
KEH KEH!
JUST WHEN I THOUGHT I'D FINALLY MADE A FRIEND...
HE WAS JUST TRYING TO USE ME...
S-STOP IT!
PLEASE STOP!
CELL
OH—
YOU GOT ME GOOD EARLIER.
GRIP

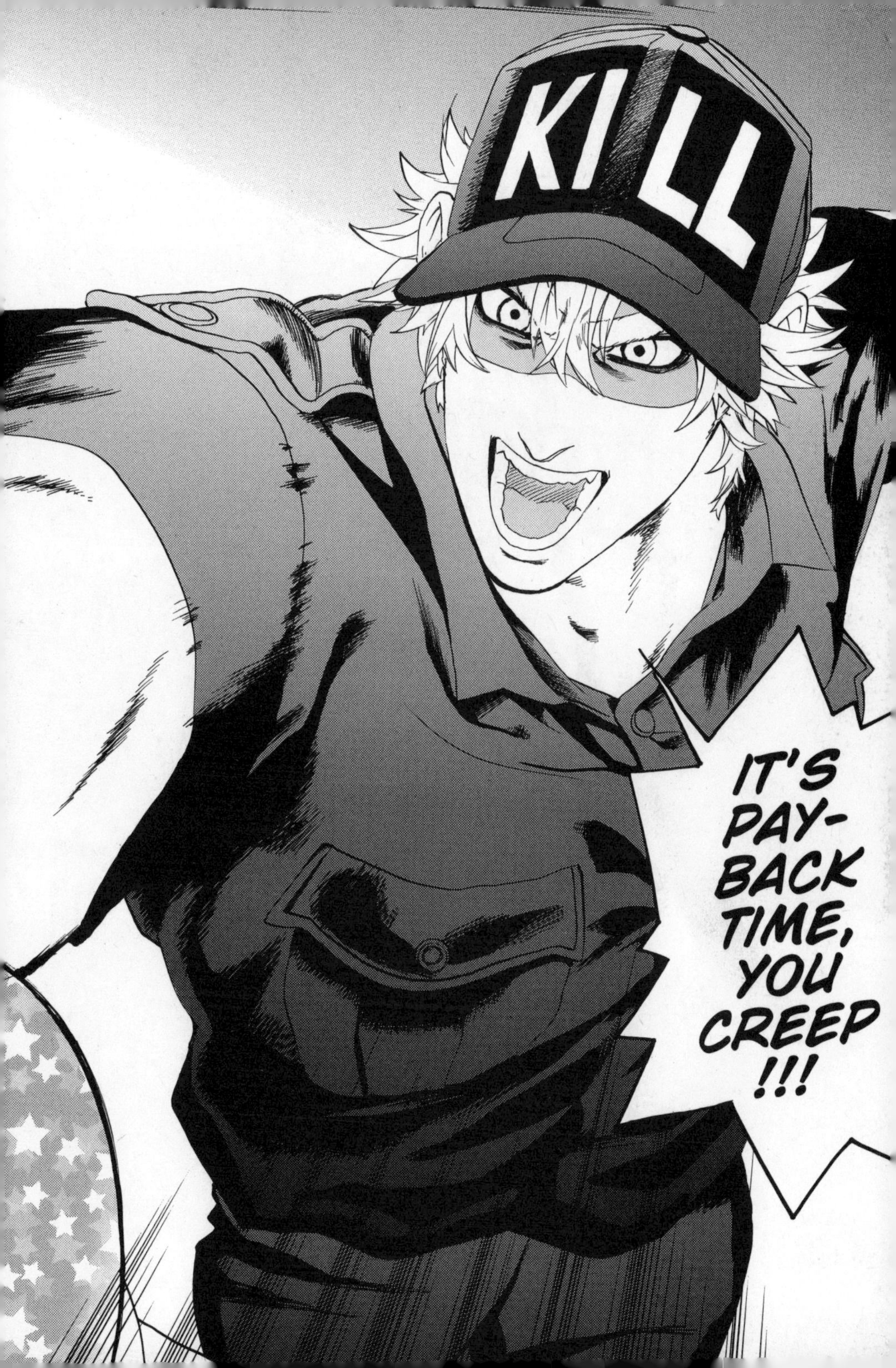
KILL
IT'S PAY-BACK TIME, YOU CREEP!!!

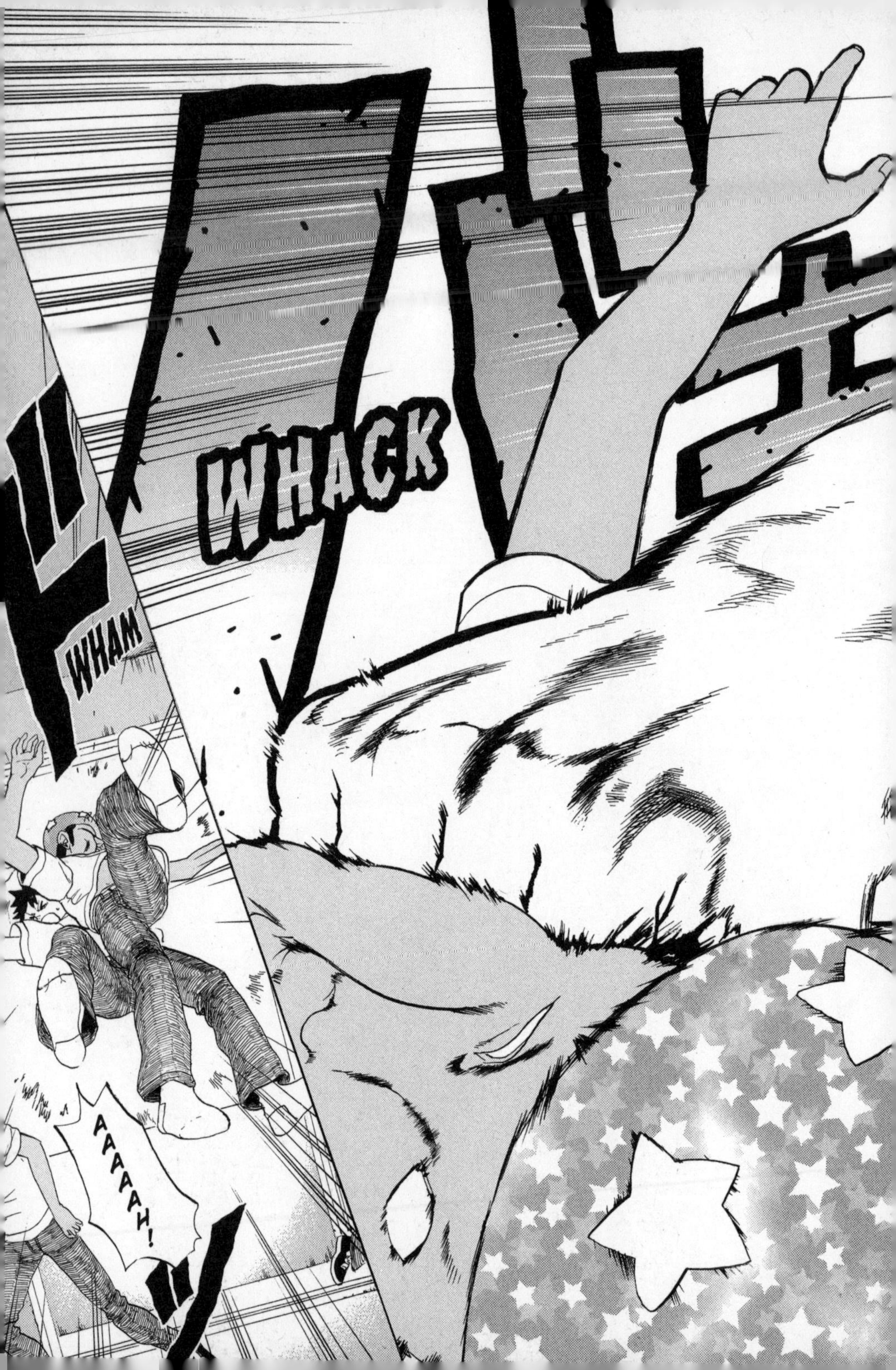
WHACK
WHAM
AAAAAH!

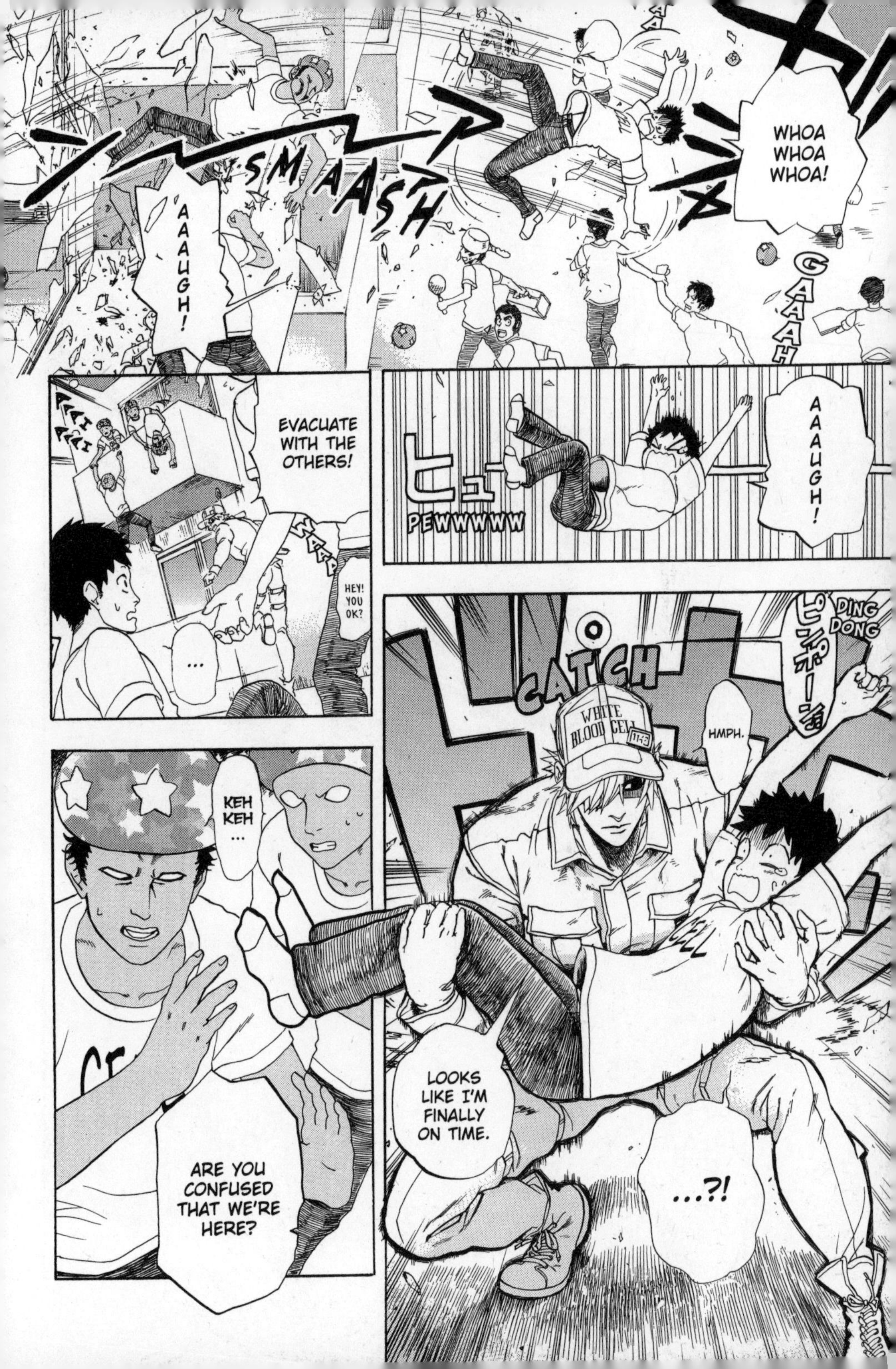
WHOA WHOA WHOA!
GAAAH
SMAASH
AAAUGH!
AAAAUGH!
ヒュ
PEWWWWWW
EVACUATE WITH THE OTHERS!
HEY! YOU OK?
...
CATCH
DING DONG
HMPH.
LOOKS LIKE I'M FINALLY ON TIME.
...?!
WHITE BLOOD CELL
KEH KEH ...
ARE YOU CONFUSED THAT WE'RE HERE?

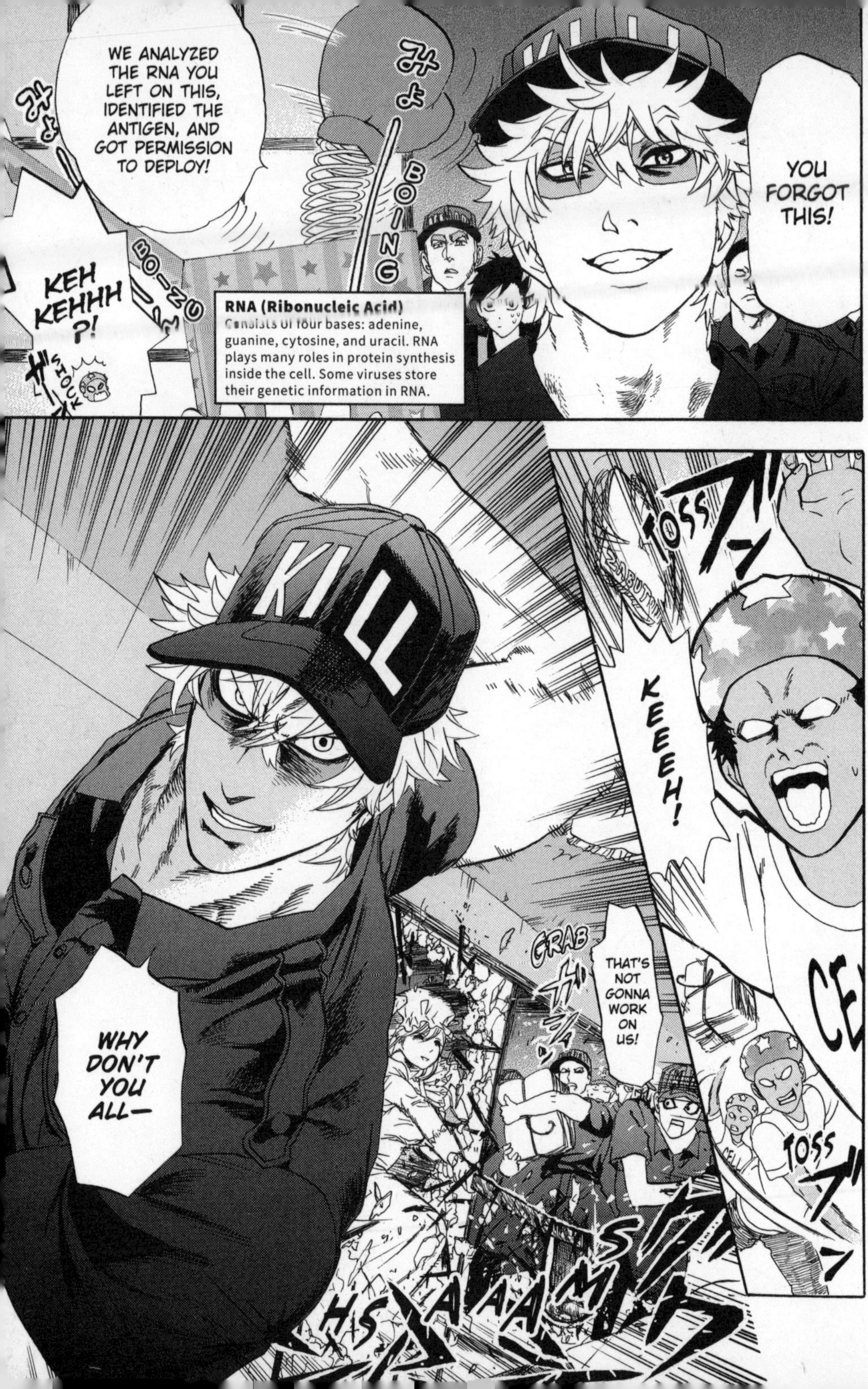
YOU FORGOT THIS!
WE ANALYZED THE RNA YOU LEFT ON THIS, IDENTIFIED THE ANTIGEN, AND GOT PERMISSION TO DEPLOY!
みよ
BOING
BO-ZU
KEH KEHHH?!
SHOCK
RNA (Ribonucleic Acid)
Consists of four bases: adenine, guanine, cytosine, and uracil. RNA plays many roles in protein synthesis inside the cell. Some viruses store their genetic information in RNA.
TOSS
KEEEEH!
TOSS
WHY DON'T YOU ALL—
GRAB
THAT'S NOT GONNA WORK ON US!
SMAAASH

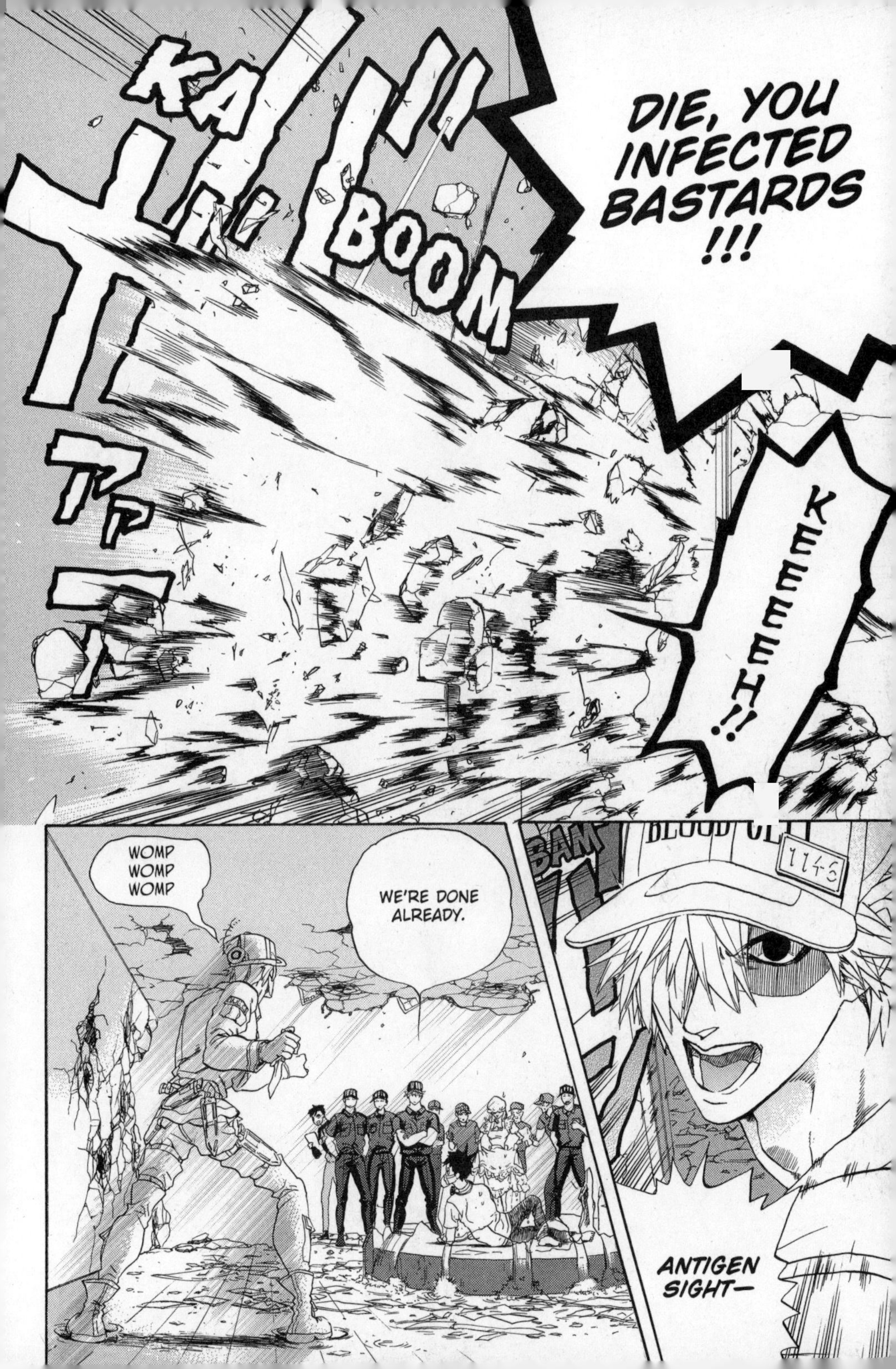
DIE, YOU INFECTED BASTARDS!!!
KEEEEEH!!
KA BOOM
BAM
1146
ANTIGEN SIGHT—
WE'RE DONE ALREADY.
WOMP WOMP WOMP

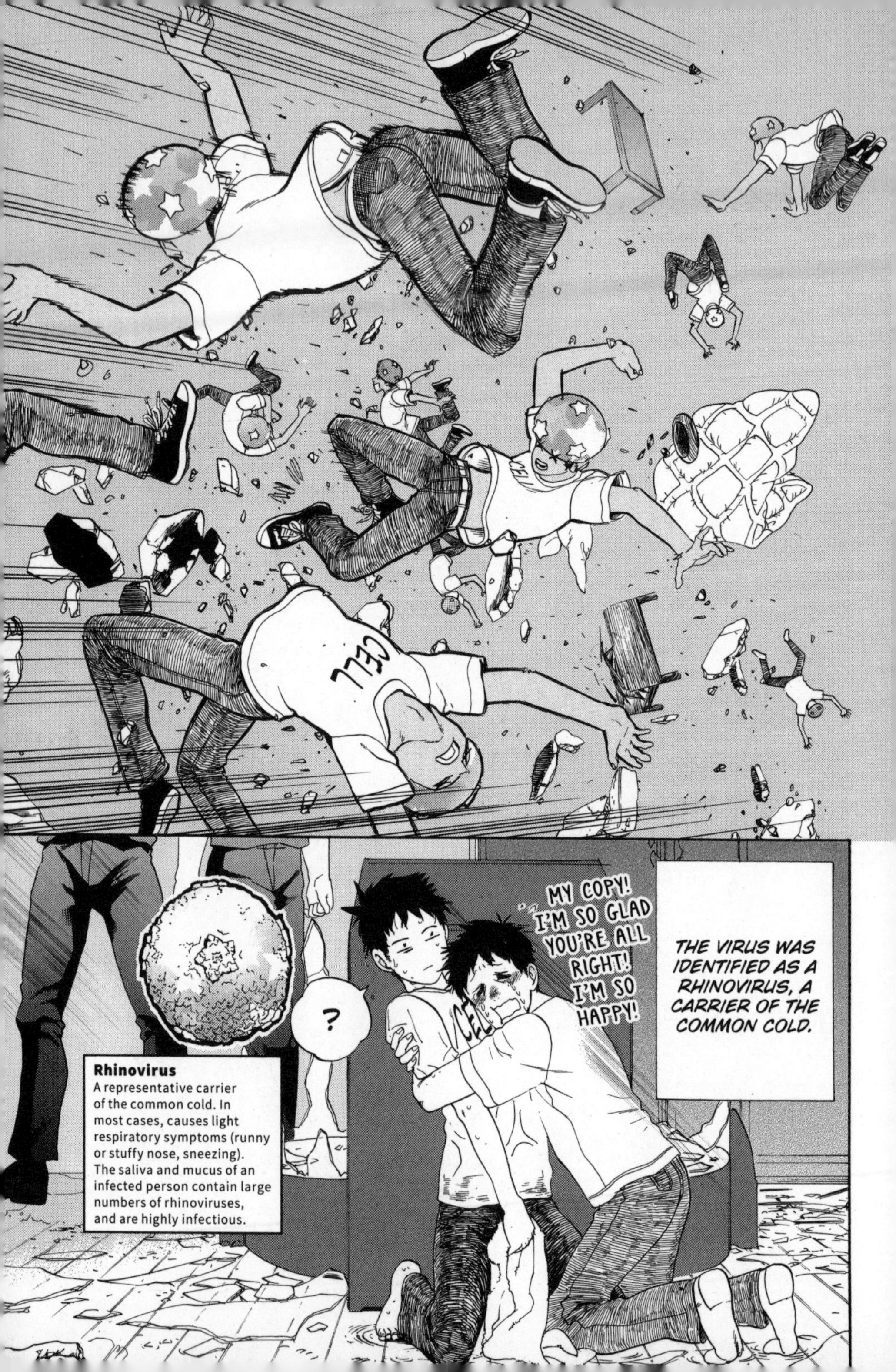
CELL
THE VIRUS WAS IDENTIFIED AS A RHINOVIRUS, A CARRIER OF THE COMMON COLD.
MY COPY! I'M SO GLAD YOU'RE ALL RIGHT! I'M SO HAPPY!
?
Rhinovirus
A representative carrier of the common cold. In most cases, causes light respiratory symptoms (runny or stuffy nose, sneezing). The saliva and mucus of an infected person contain large numbers of rhinoviruses, and are highly infectious.
CELL

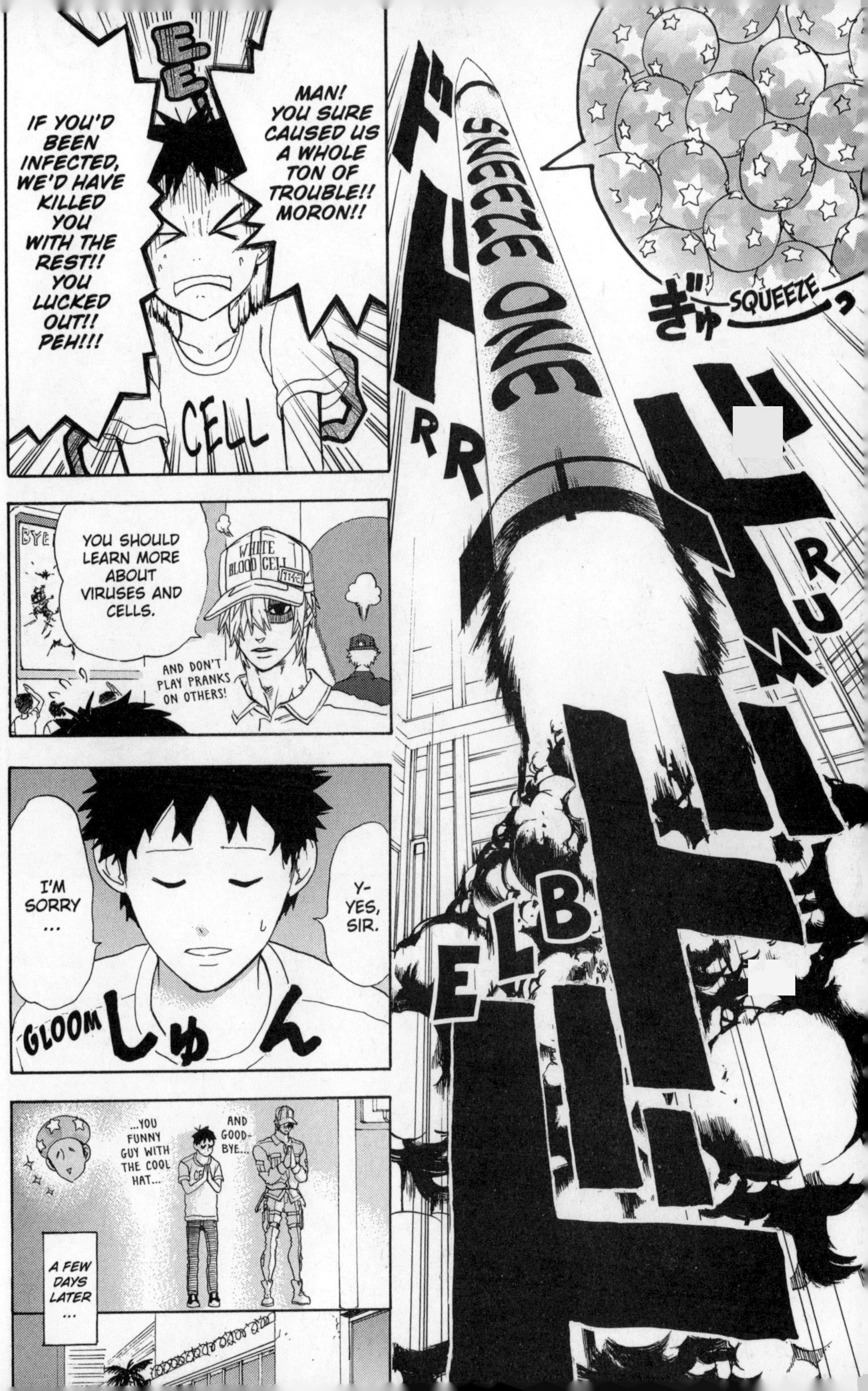

ぎゅ SQUEEZE っ
SNEEZE ONE
MAN! YOU SURE CAUSED US A WHOLE TON OF TROUBLE!! MORON!!
IF YOU'D BEEN INFECTED, WE'D HAVE KILLED YOU WITH THE REST!! YOU LUCKED OUT!! PEH!!!
CELL
YOU SHOULD LEARN MORE ABOUT VIRUSES AND CELLS.
AND DON'T PLAY PRANKS ON OTHERS!
WHITE BLOOD CELL
BYE
Y-YES, SIR.
I'M SORRY ...
GLOOM しゅん
AND GOOD-BYE...
...YOU FUNNY GUY WITH THE COOL HAT...
A FEW DAYS LATER ...

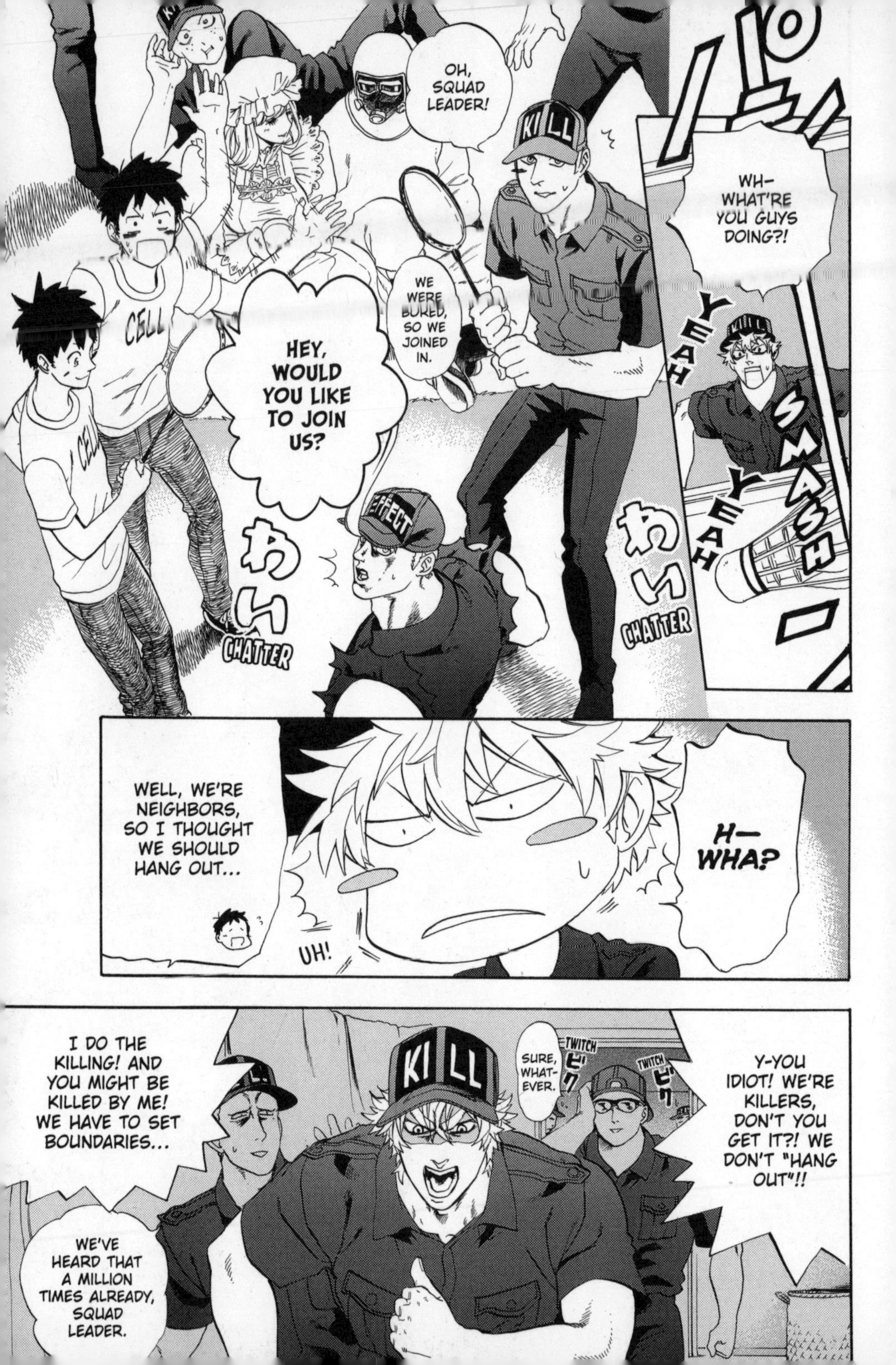
WH— WHAT'RE YOU GUYS DOING?!
YEAH
SMASH
YEAH
わい
CHATTER
OH, SQUAD LEADER!
WE WERE BORED, SO WE JOINED IN.
HEY, WOULD YOU LIKE TO JOIN US?
わい
CHATTER
H— WHA?
WELL, WE'RE NEIGHBORS, SO I THOUGHT WE SHOULD HANG OUT...
UH!
Y-YOU IDIOT! WE'RE KILLERS, DON'T YOU GET IT?! WE DON'T "HANG OUT"!!
TWITCH ピク
SURE, WHAT-EVER.
TWITCH ピク
I DO THE KILLING! AND YOU MIGHT BE KILLED BY ME! WE HAVE TO SET BOUNDARIES...
WE'VE HEARD THAT A MILLION TIMES ALREADY, SQUAD LEADER.

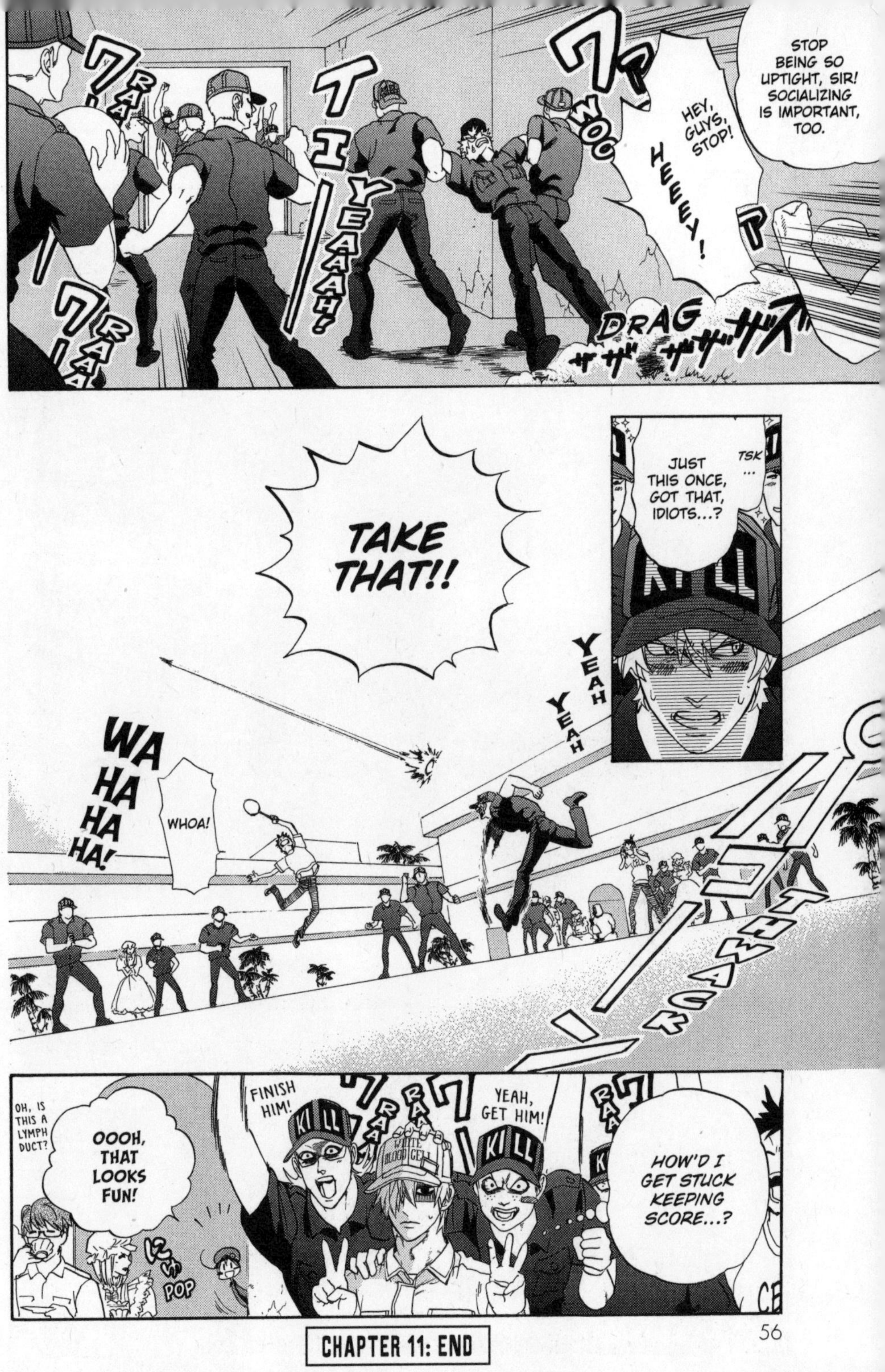

STOP BEING SO UPTIGHT, SIR! SOCIALIZING IS IMPORTANT, TOO.
HEY, GUYS, STOP!
HEEEEY!
WOO
DRAG
YEAAAAAH!
RAA
RAA
JUST THIS ONCE, GOT THAT, IDIOTS...?
TSK...
YEAH YEAH
TAKE THAT!!
THWACK
WHOA!
WAHAHAHAHA!
HOW'D I GET STUCK KEEPING SCORE...?
RAA
YEAH, GET HIM!
RAA
FINISH HIM!
OOOH, THAT LOOKS FUN!
OH, IS THIS A LYMPH DUCT?
POP

CHAPTER 11: END

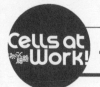

*This is a fictitious setting for this manga and does not reflect scientific fact.

The Apartment of an Ordinary Cell [floor plan]

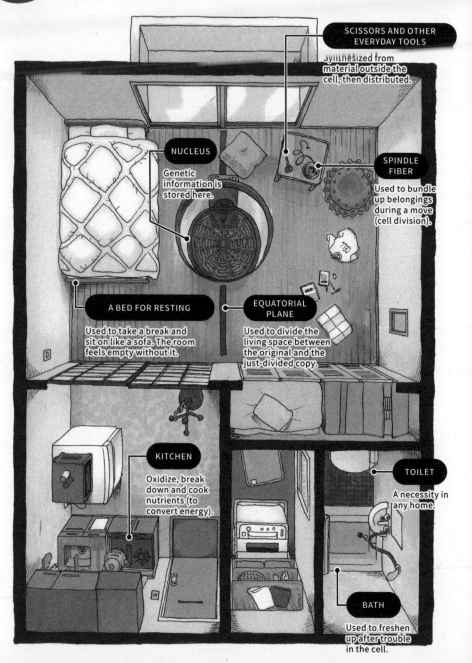

SCISSORS AND OTHER EVERYDAY TOOLS
Synthesized from material outside the cell, then distributed.

NUCLEUS
Genetic information is stored here.

SPINDLE FIBER
Used to bundle up belongings during a move (cell division).

A BED FOR RESTING
Used to take a break and sit on like a sofa. The room feels empty without it.

EQUATORIAL PLANE
Used to divide the living space between the original and the just-divided copy.

KITCHEN
Oxidize, break down and cook nutrients (to convert energy).

TOILET
A necessity in any home.

BATH
Used to freshen up after trouble in the cell.

Cells at Work!

はたらく細胞

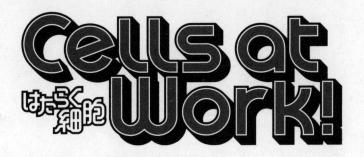

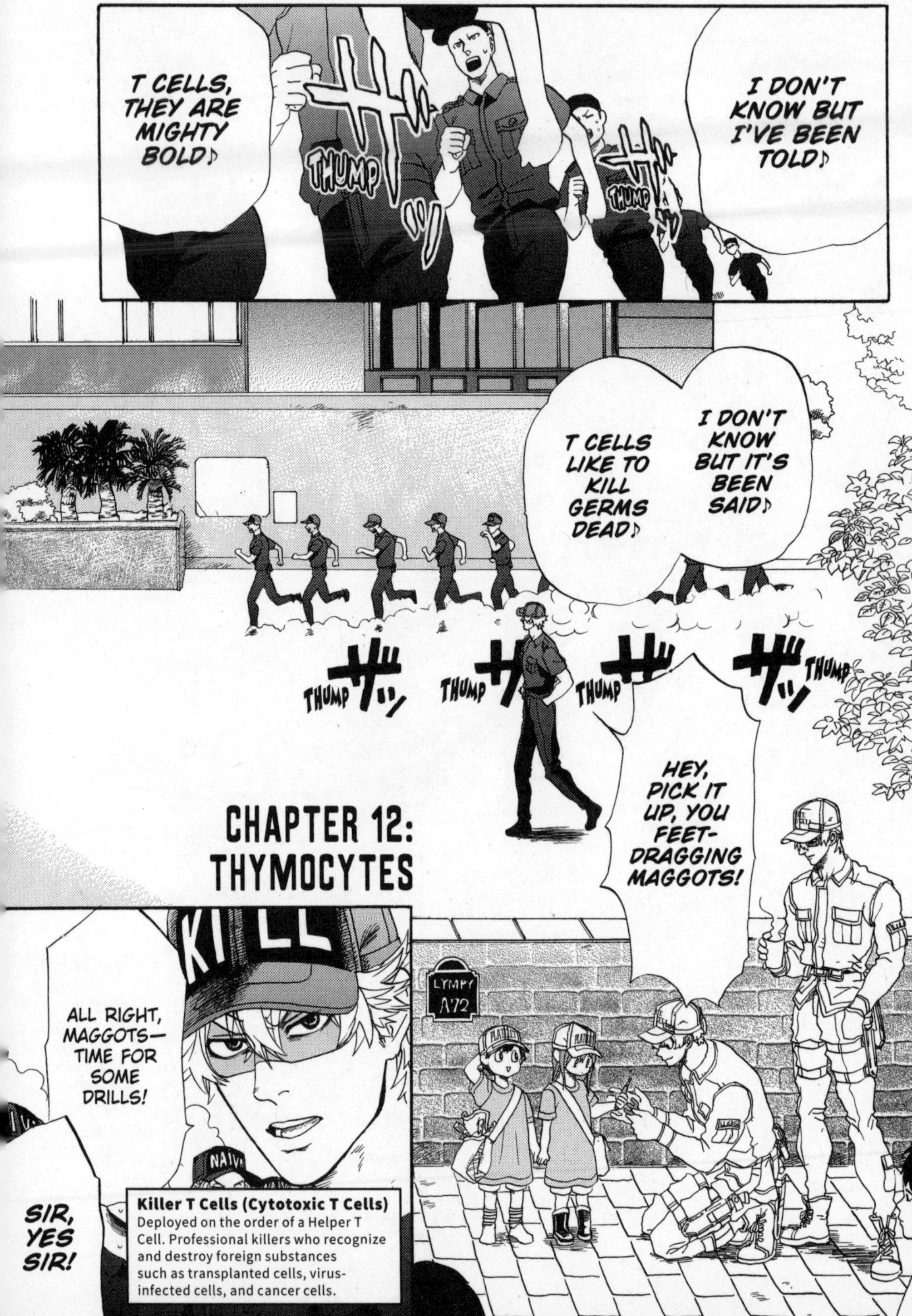
I DON'T KNOW BUT I'VE BEEN TOLD♪
T CELLS, THEY ARE MIGHTY BOLD♪
THUMP
THUMP
I DON'T KNOW BUT IT'S BEEN SAID♪
T CELLS LIKE TO KILL GERMS DEAD♪
THUMP
THUMP
THUMP
THUMP
HEY, PICK IT UP, YOU FEET-DRAGGING MAGGOTS!
CHAPTER 12: THYMOCYTES
LYMPY A72
KILL
ALL RIGHT, MAGGOTS—TIME FOR SOME DRILLS!
SIR, YES SIR!
Killer T Cells (Cytotoxic T Cells)
Deployed on the order of a Helper T Cell. Professional killers who recognize and destroy foreign substances such as transplanted cells, virus-infected cells, and cancer cells.

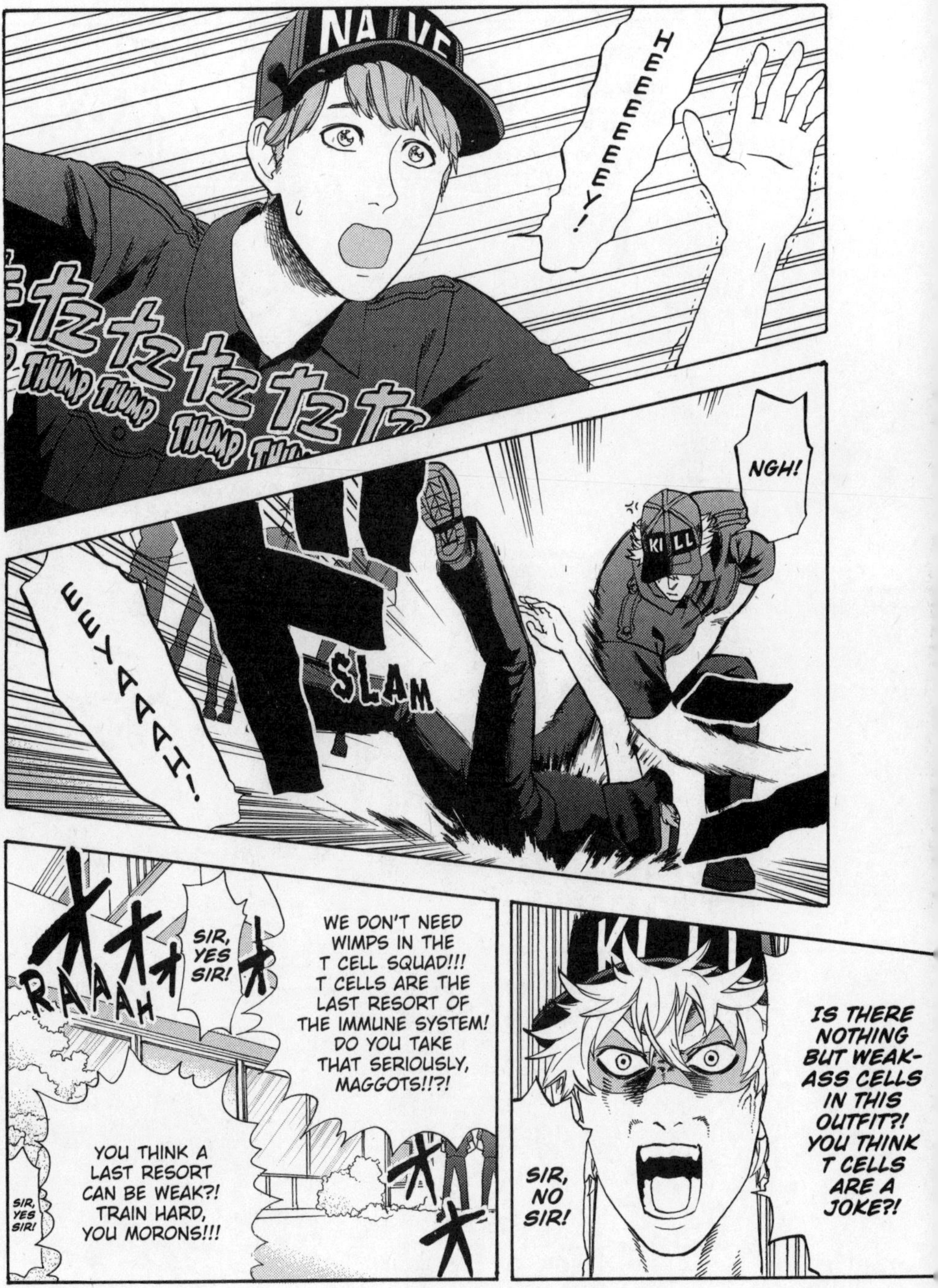
HEEEEEEEY!
たたたたた
THUMP THUMP THUMP THUMP
NGH!
SLAM
EEYAAAAH!
IS THERE NOTHING BUT WEAK-ASS CELLS IN THIS OUTFIT?! YOU THINK T CELLS ARE A JOKE?!
SIR, NO SIR!
WE DON'T NEED WIMPS IN THE T CELL SQUAD!!! T CELLS ARE THE LAST RESORT OF THE IMMUNE SYSTEM! DO YOU TAKE THAT SERIOUSLY, MAGGOTS!!?!
SIR, YES SIR!
RAAAH
YOU THINK A LAST RESORT CAN BE WEAK?! TRAIN HARD, YOU MORONS!!!
SIR, YES SIR!

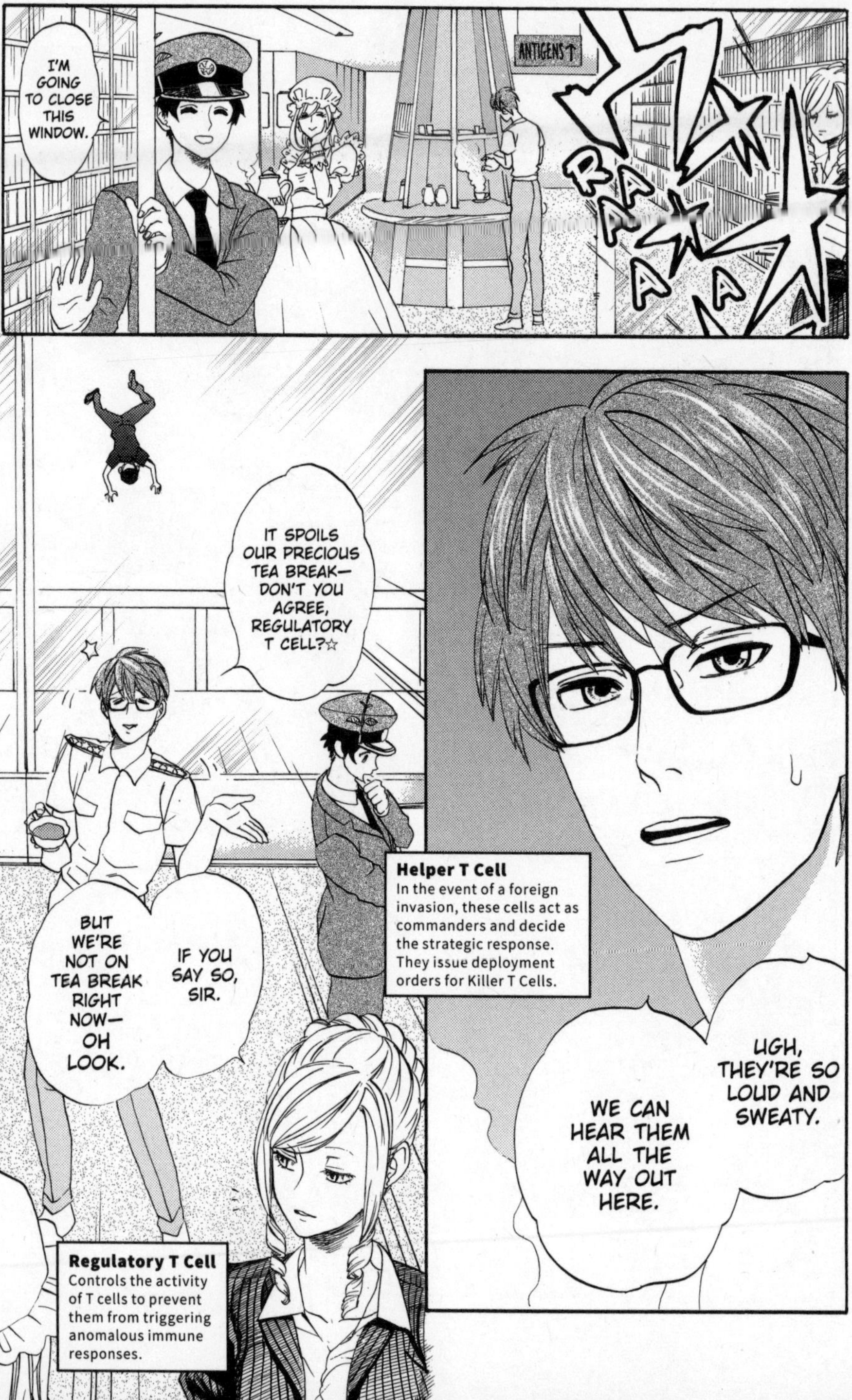
RAAAA
ANTIGENS ↑
I'M GOING TO CLOSE THIS WINDOW.
UGH, THEY'RE SO LOUD AND SWEATY.
WE CAN HEAR THEM ALL THE WAY OUT HERE.
IT SPOILS OUR PRECIOUS TEA BREAK—DON'T YOU AGREE, REGULATORY T CELL?☆
Helper T Cell
In the event of a foreign invasion, these cells act as commanders and decide the strategic response. They issue deployment orders for Killer T Cells.
IF YOU SAY SO, SIR.
BUT WE'RE NOT ON TEA BREAK RIGHT NOW—OH LOOK.
Regulatory T Cell
Controls the activity of T cells to prevent them from triggering anomalous immune responses.

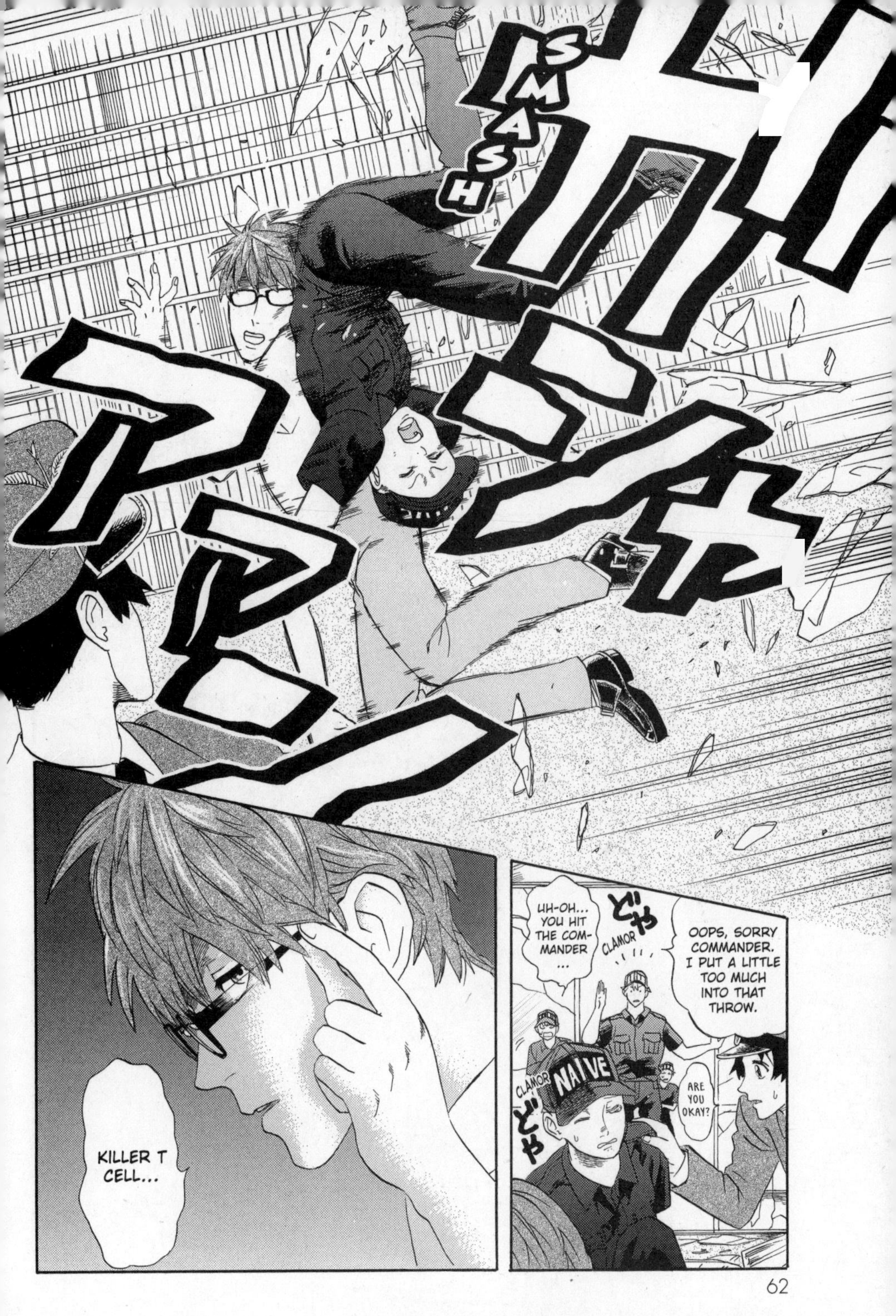
SMASH
OOPS, SORRY COMMANDER. I PUT A LITTLE TOO MUCH INTO THAT THROW.
UH-OH... YOU HIT THE COMMANDER ...
CLAMOR
どや
NAIVE
ARE YOU OKAY?
CLAMOR
どや
KILLER T CELL...

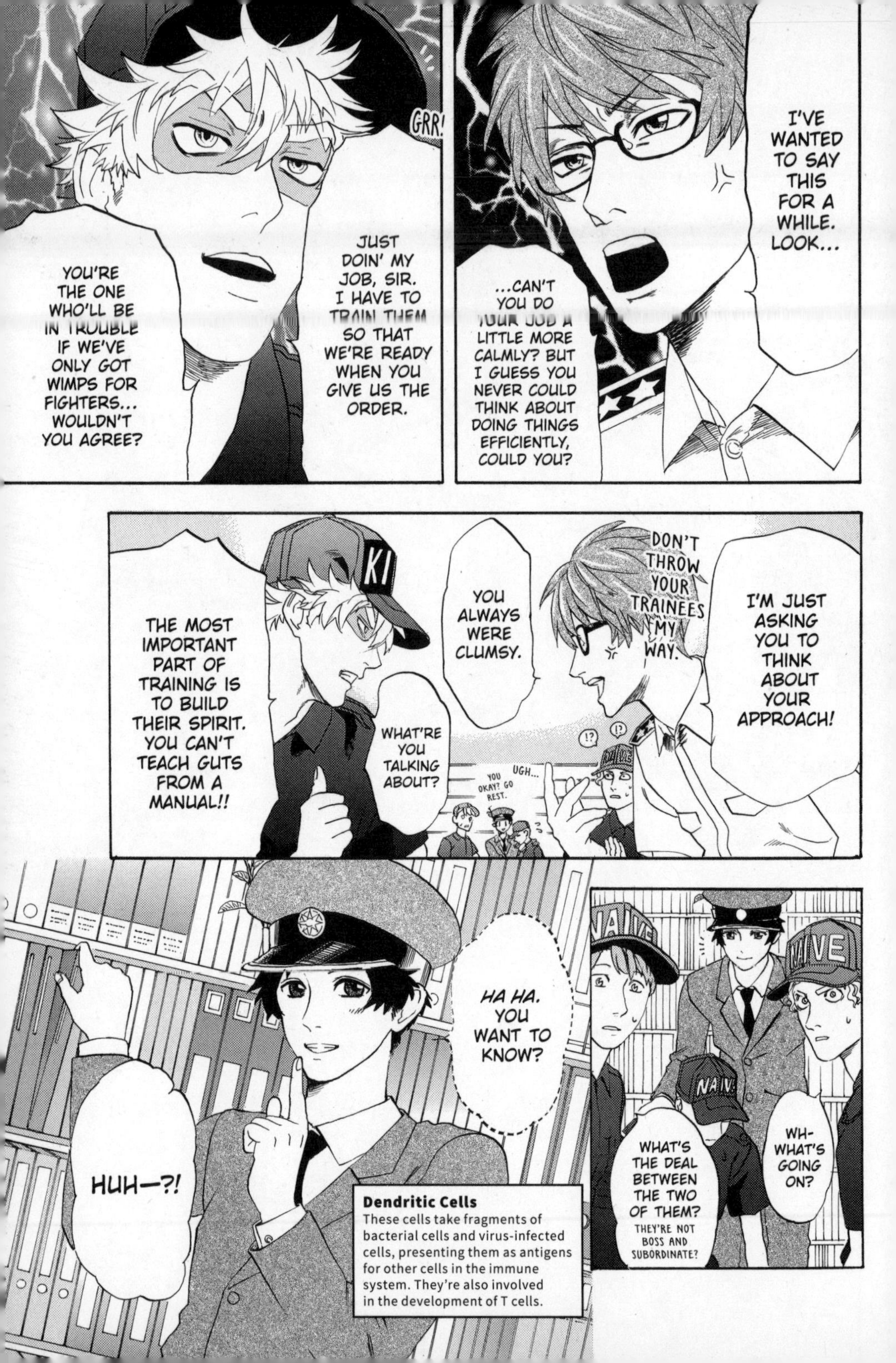
I'VE WANTED TO SAY THIS FOR A WHILE. LOOK...
...CAN'T YOU DO YOUR JOB A LITTLE MORE CALMLY? BUT I GUESS YOU NEVER COULD THINK ABOUT DOING THINGS EFFICIENTLY, COULD YOU?
GRR!
JUST DOIN' MY JOB, SIR. I HAVE TO TRAIN THEM SO THAT WE'RE READY WHEN YOU GIVE US THE ORDER.
YOU'RE THE ONE WHO'LL BE IN TROUBLE IF WE'VE ONLY GOT WIMPS FOR FIGHTERS... WOULDN'T YOU AGREE?
I'M JUST ASKING YOU TO THINK ABOUT YOUR APPROACH!
DON'T THROW YOUR TRAINEES MY WAY.
YOU ALWAYS WERE CLUMSY.
!?
!?
UGH...
YOU OKAY? GO REST.
WHAT'RE YOU TALKING ABOUT?
THE MOST IMPORTANT PART OF TRAINING IS TO BUILD THEIR SPIRIT. YOU CAN'T TEACH GUTS FROM A MANUAL!!
WH-WHAT'S GOING ON?
WHAT'S THE DEAL BETWEEN THE TWO OF THEM?
THEY'RE NOT BOSS AND SUBORDINATE?
HA HA. YOU WANT TO KNOW?
HUH—?!
Dendritic Cells
These cells take fragments of bacterial cells and virus-infected cells, presenting them as antigens for other cells in the immune system. They're also involved in the development of T cells.

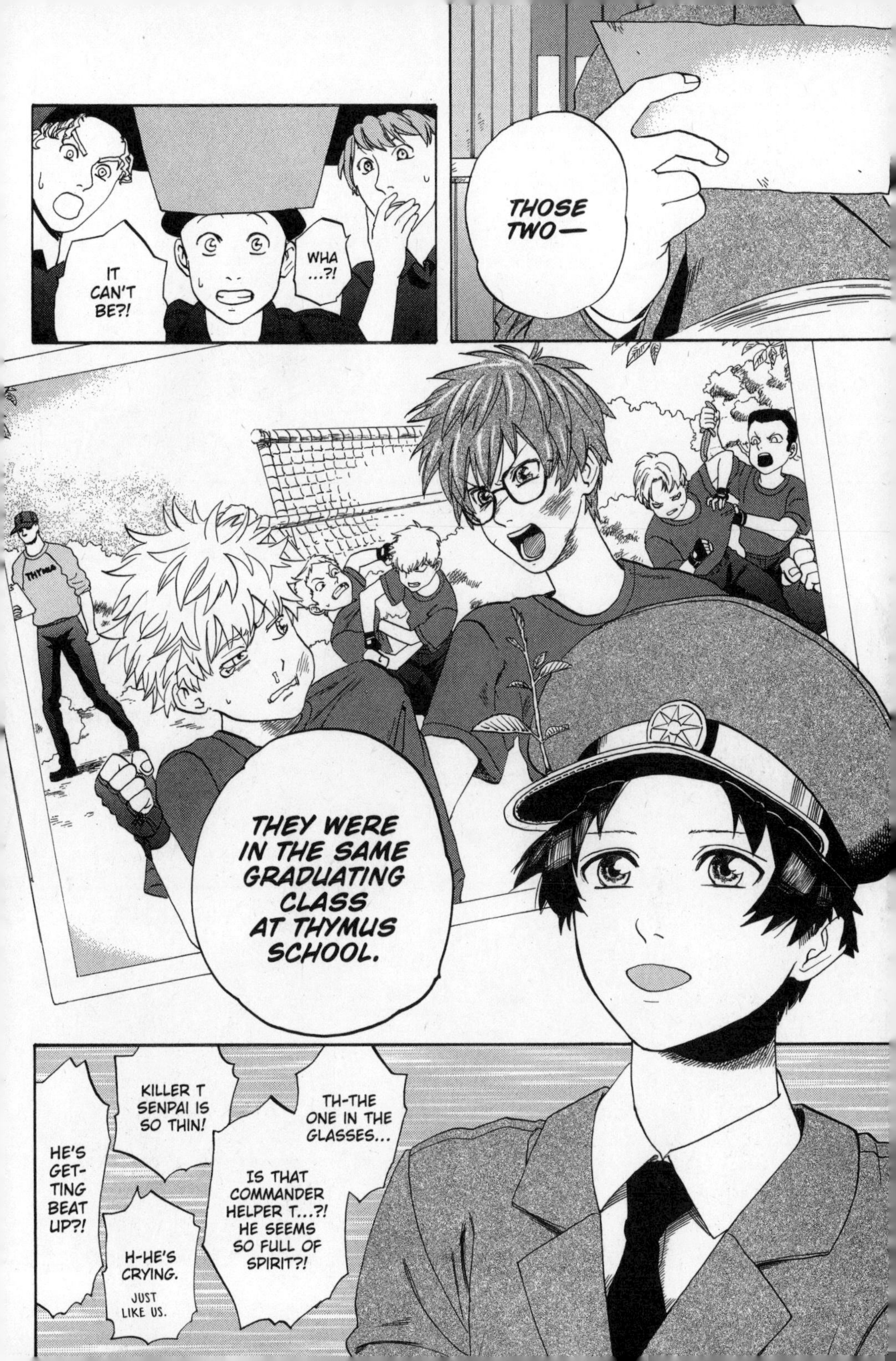
THOSE TWO—
WHA...?!
IT CAN'T BE?!
THEY WERE IN THE SAME GRADUATING CLASS AT THYMUS SCHOOL.
TH-THE ONE IN THE GLASSES...
KILLER T SENPAI IS SO THIN!
HE'S GET-TING BEAT UP?!
IS THAT COMMANDER HELPER T...?! HE SEEMS SO FULL OF SPIRIT?!
H-HE'S CRYING.
JUST LIKE US.

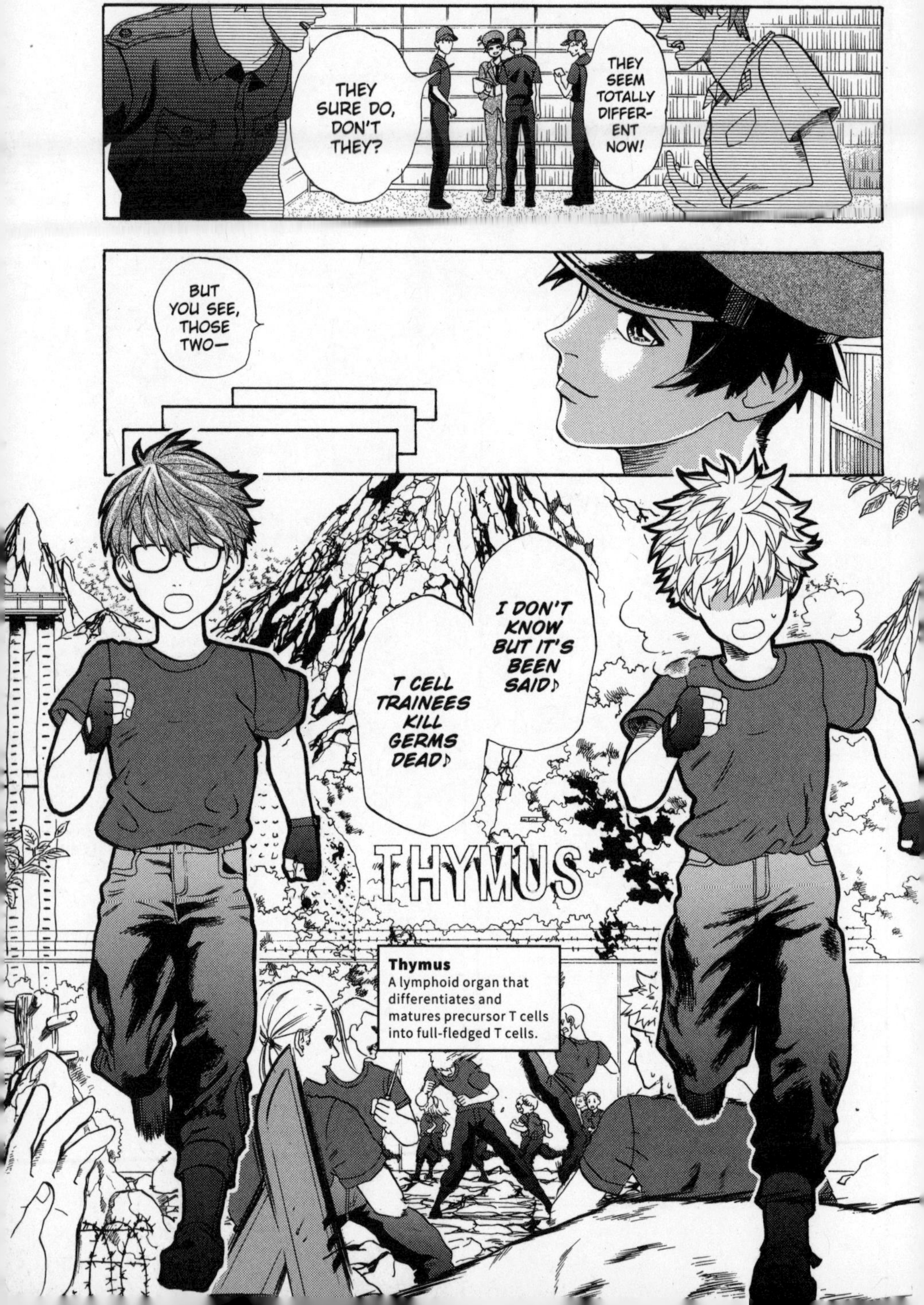
THEY SEEM TOTALLY DIFFER-ENT NOW!
THEY SURE DO, DON'T THEY?
BUT YOU SEE, THOSE TWO—
I DON'T KNOW BUT IT'S BEEN SAID♪
T CELL TRAINEES KILL GERMS DEAD♪
THYMUS
Thymus
A lymphoid organ that differentiates and matures precursor T cells into full-fledged T cells.

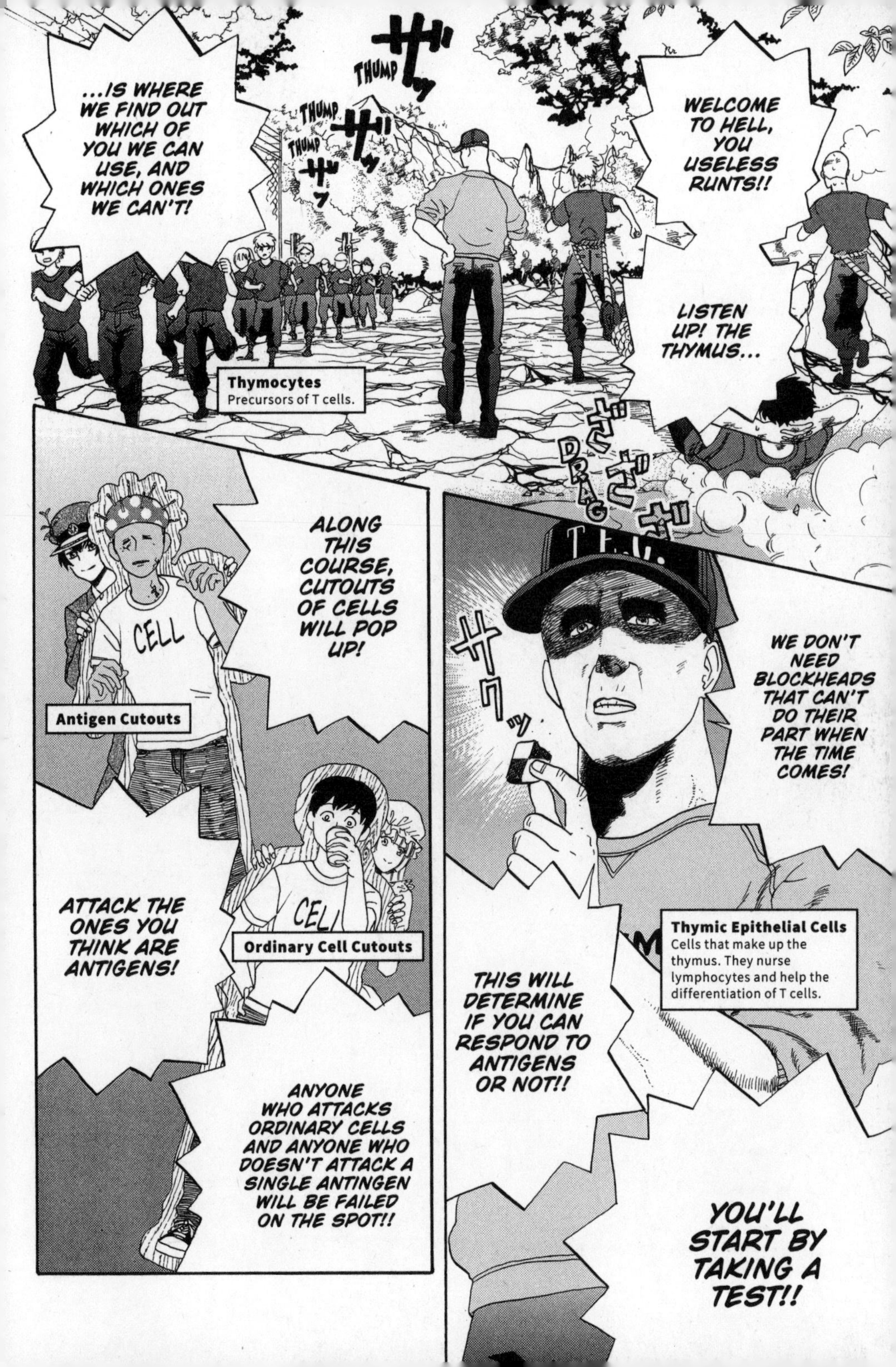
WELCOME TO HELL, YOU USELESS RUNTS!!
THUMP
THUMP
THUMP
LISTEN UP! THE THYMUS...
...IS WHERE WE FIND OUT WHICH OF YOU WE CAN USE, AND WHICH ONES WE CAN'T!
Thymocytes
Precursors of T cells.
DRAG
T.E.C.
WE DON'T NEED BLOCKHEADS THAT CAN'T DO THEIR PART WHEN THE TIME COMES!
Thymic Epithelial Cells
Cells that make up the thymus. They nurse lymphocytes and help the differentiation of T cells.
THIS WILL DETERMINE IF YOU CAN RESPOND TO ANTIGENS OR NOT!!
YOU'LL START BY TAKING A TEST!!
ALONG THIS COURSE, CUTOUTS OF CELLS WILL POP UP!
CELL
Antigen Cutouts
ATTACK THE ONES YOU THINK ARE ANTIGENS!
CELL
Ordinary Cell Cutouts
ANYONE WHO ATTACKS ORDINARY CELLS AND ANYONE WHO DOESN'T ATTACK A SINGLE ANTINGEN WILL BE FAILED ON THE SPOT!!

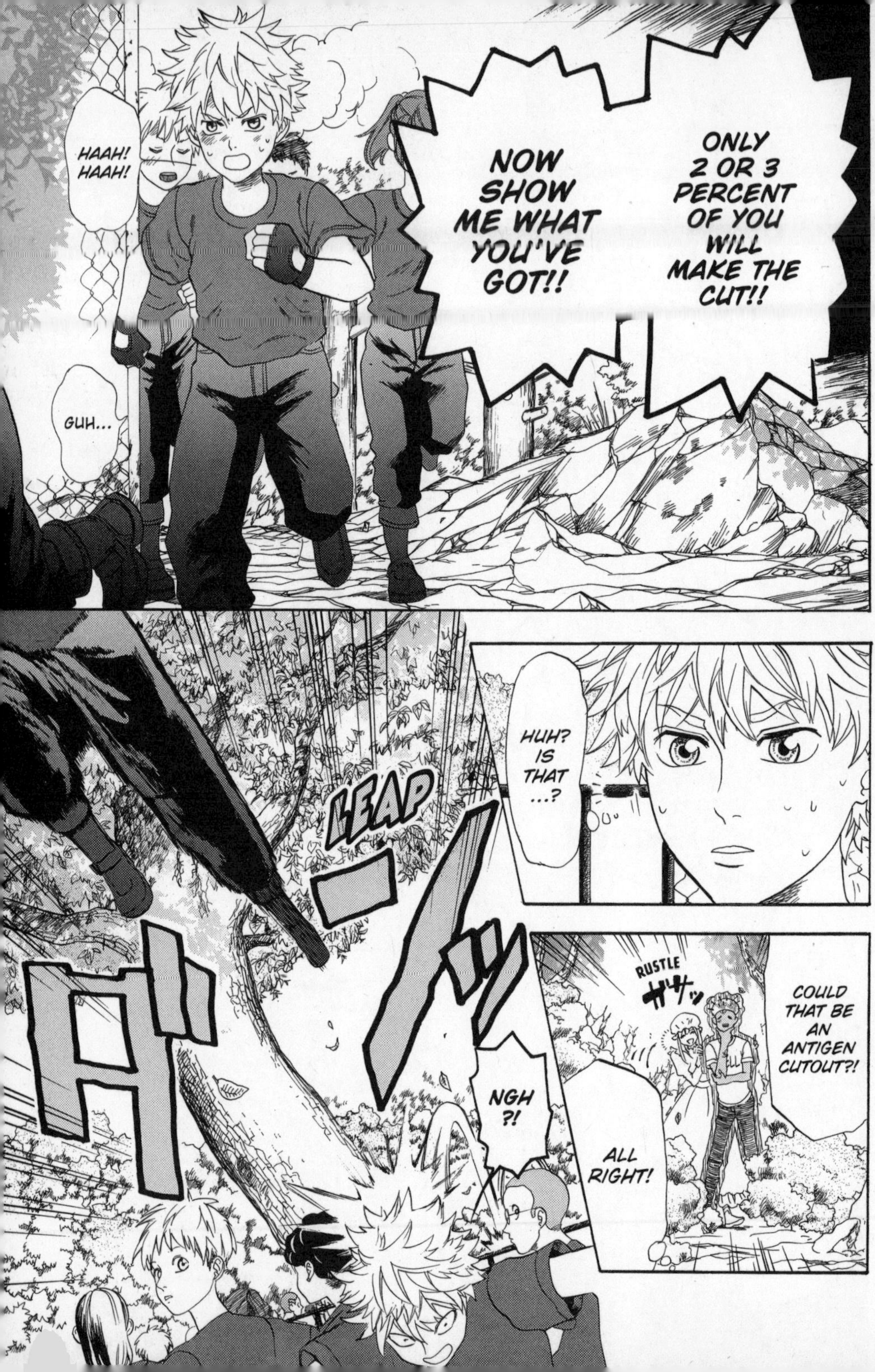

ONLY 2 OR 3 PERCENT OF YOU WILL MAKE THE CUT!!
NOW SHOW ME WHAT YOU'VE GOT!!
HAAH! HAAH!
GUH...
HUH? IS THAT ...?
RUSTLE
COULD THAT BE AN ANTIGEN CUTOUT?!
ALL RIGHT!
LEAP
NGH ?!

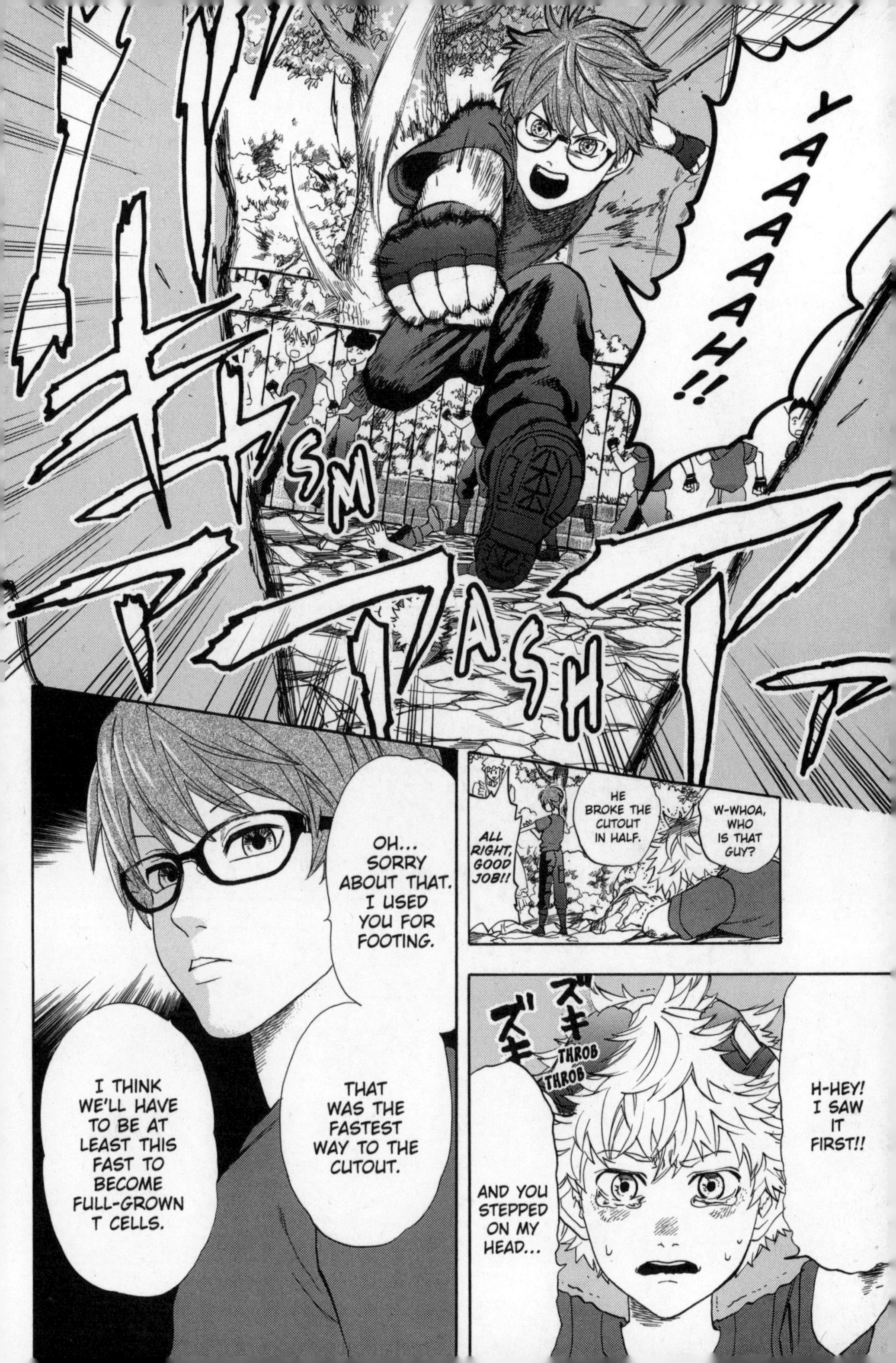
YAAAAAAAH!!
SMASH
W-WHOA, WHO IS THAT GUY?
HE BROKE THE CUTOUT IN HALF.
ALL RIGHT, GOOD JOB!!
H-HEY! I SAW IT FIRST!!
ズキ
ズキ
THROB
THROB
AND YOU STEPPED ON MY HEAD...
OH... SORRY ABOUT THAT. I USED YOU FOR FOOTING.
THAT WAS THE FASTEST WAY TO THE CUTOUT.
I THINK WE'LL HAVE TO BE AT LEAST THIS FAST TO BECOME FULL-GROWN T CELLS.

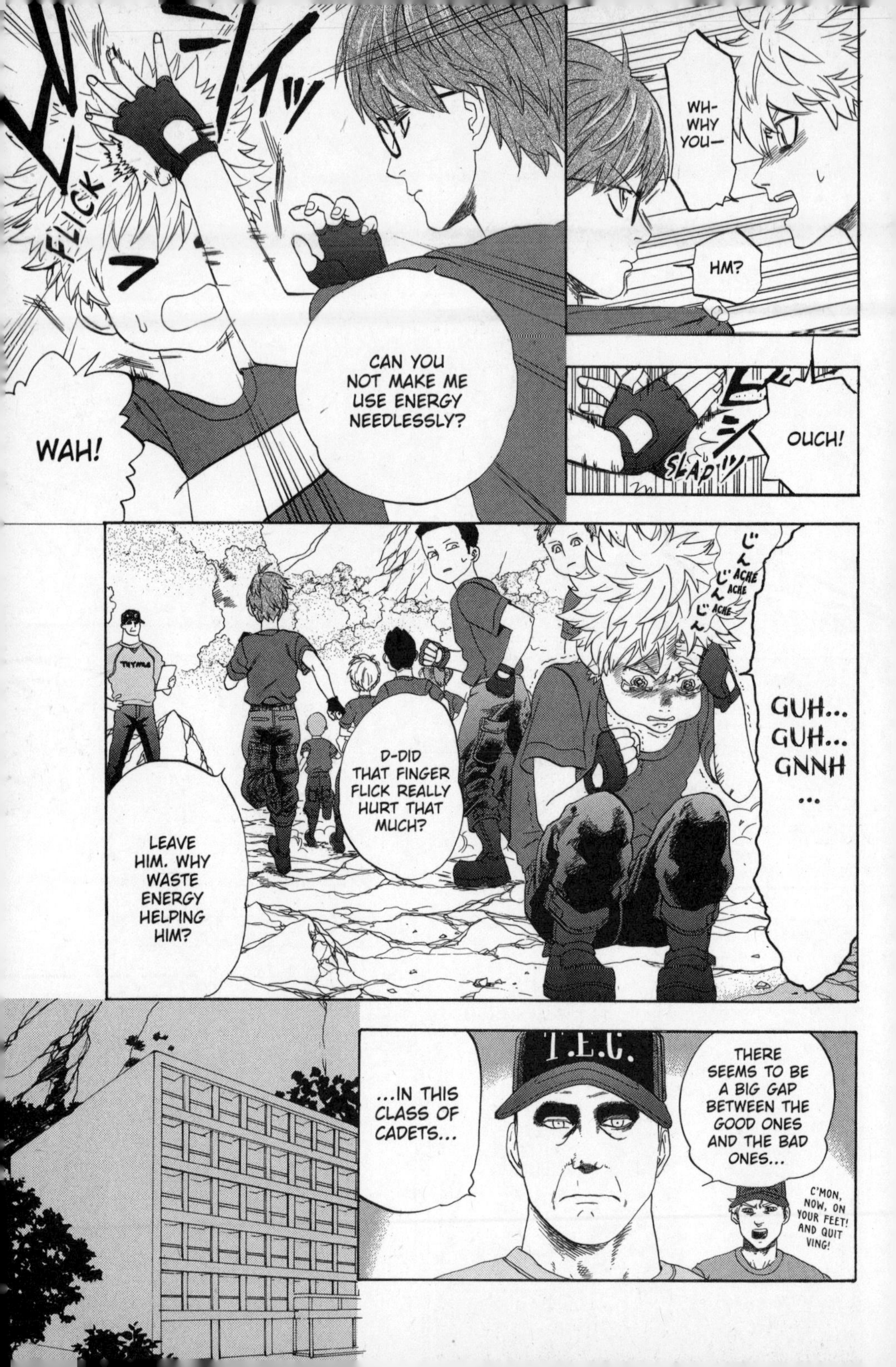
WH-WHY YOU—
HM?
OUCH!
SLAP
CAN YOU NOT MAKE ME USE ENERGY NEEDLESSLY?
WAH!
FLICK
じんじんじん
ACHE ACHE ACHE
GUH... GUH... GNNH...
D-DID THAT FINGER FLICK REALLY HURT THAT MUCH?
LEAVE HIM. WHY WASTE ENERGY HELPING HIM?
T.E.C.
THERE SEEMS TO BE A BIG GAP BETWEEN THE GOOD ONES AND THE BAD ONES...
C'MON, NOW, ON YOUR FEET! AND QUIT VING!
...IN THIS CLASS OF CADETS...

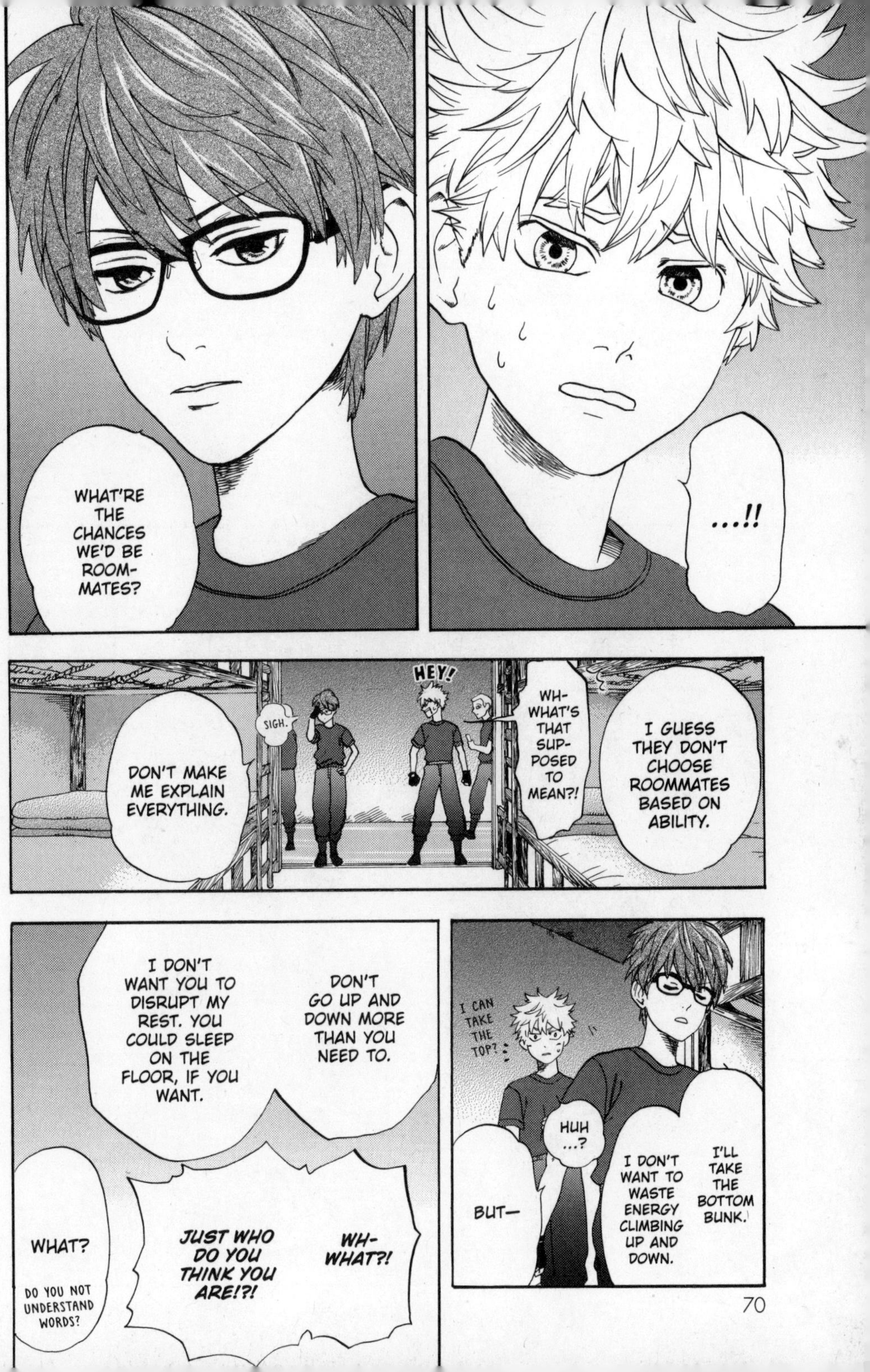
...!!
WHAT'RE THE CHANCES WE'D BE ROOM-MATES?
I GUESS THEY DON'T CHOOSE ROOMMATES BASED ON ABILITY.
WH- WHAT'S THAT SUP-POSED TO MEAN?!
HEY!
SIGH.
DON'T MAKE ME EXPLAIN EVERYTHING.
I'LL TAKE THE BOTTOM BUNK.
I DON'T WANT TO WASTE ENERGY CLIMBING UP AND DOWN.
HUH ...?
I CAN TAKE THE TOP?
BUT—
DON'T GO UP AND DOWN MORE THAN YOU NEED TO.
I DON'T WANT YOU TO DISRUPT MY REST. YOU COULD SLEEP ON THE FLOOR, IF YOU WANT.
WH-WHAT?!
JUST WHO DO YOU THINK YOU ARE!?!
WHAT?
DO YOU NOT UNDERSTAND WORDS?

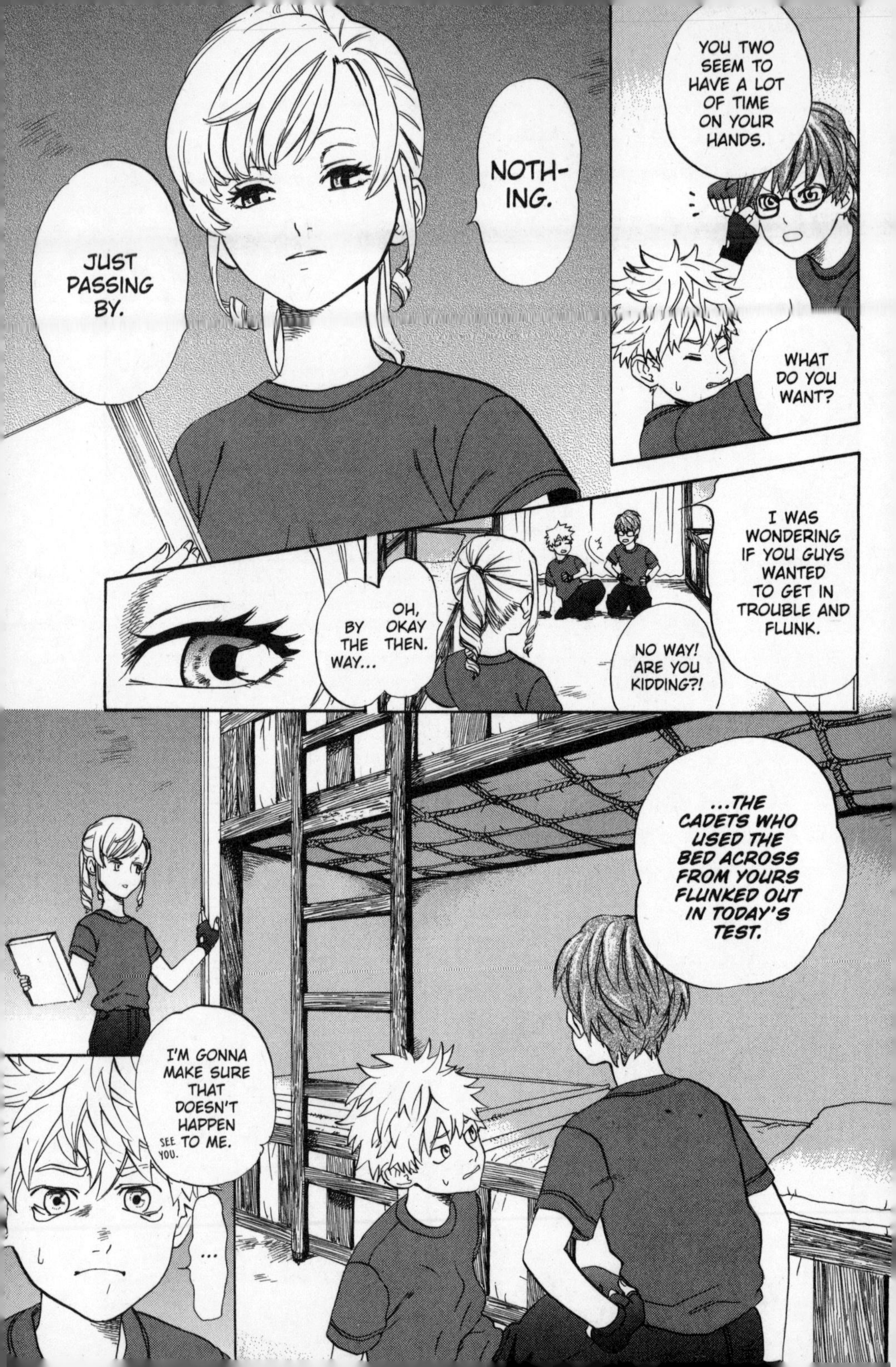
YOU TWO SEEM TO HAVE A LOT OF TIME ON YOUR HANDS.
WHAT DO YOU WANT?
NOTH-ING.
JUST PASSING BY.
I WAS WONDERING IF YOU GUYS WANTED TO GET IN TROUBLE AND FLUNK.
NO WAY! ARE YOU KIDDING?!
OH, OKAY THEN.
BY THE WAY...
...THE CADETS WHO USED THE BED ACROSS FROM YOURS FLUNKED OUT IN TODAY'S TEST.
I'M GONNA MAKE SURE THAT DOESN'T HAPPEN TO ME.
SEE YOU.
...

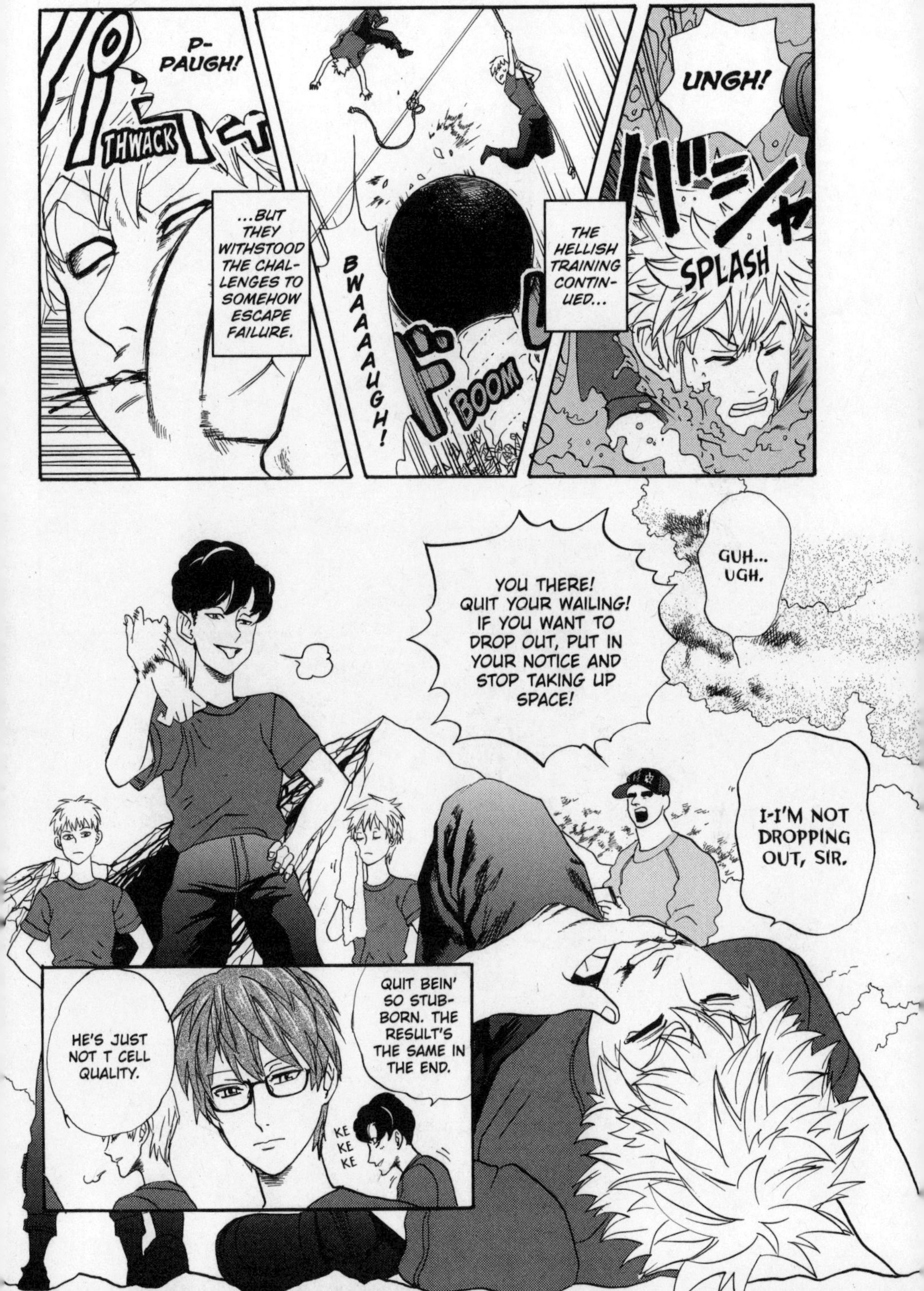
UNGH!
THE HELLISH TRAINING CONTINUED...
SPLASH
BWAAAAAUGH!
BOOM
...BUT THEY WITHSTOOD THE CHALLENGES TO SOMEHOW ESCAPE FAILURE.
P-PAUGH!
THWACK
GUH... UGH.
YOU THERE! QUIT YOUR WAILING! IF YOU WANT TO DROP OUT, PUT IN YOUR NOTICE AND STOP TAKING UP SPACE!
I-I'M NOT DROPPING OUT, SIR.
QUIT BEIN' SO STUBBORN. THE RESULT'S THE SAME IN THE END.
KE KE KE
HE'S JUST NOT T CELL QUALITY.

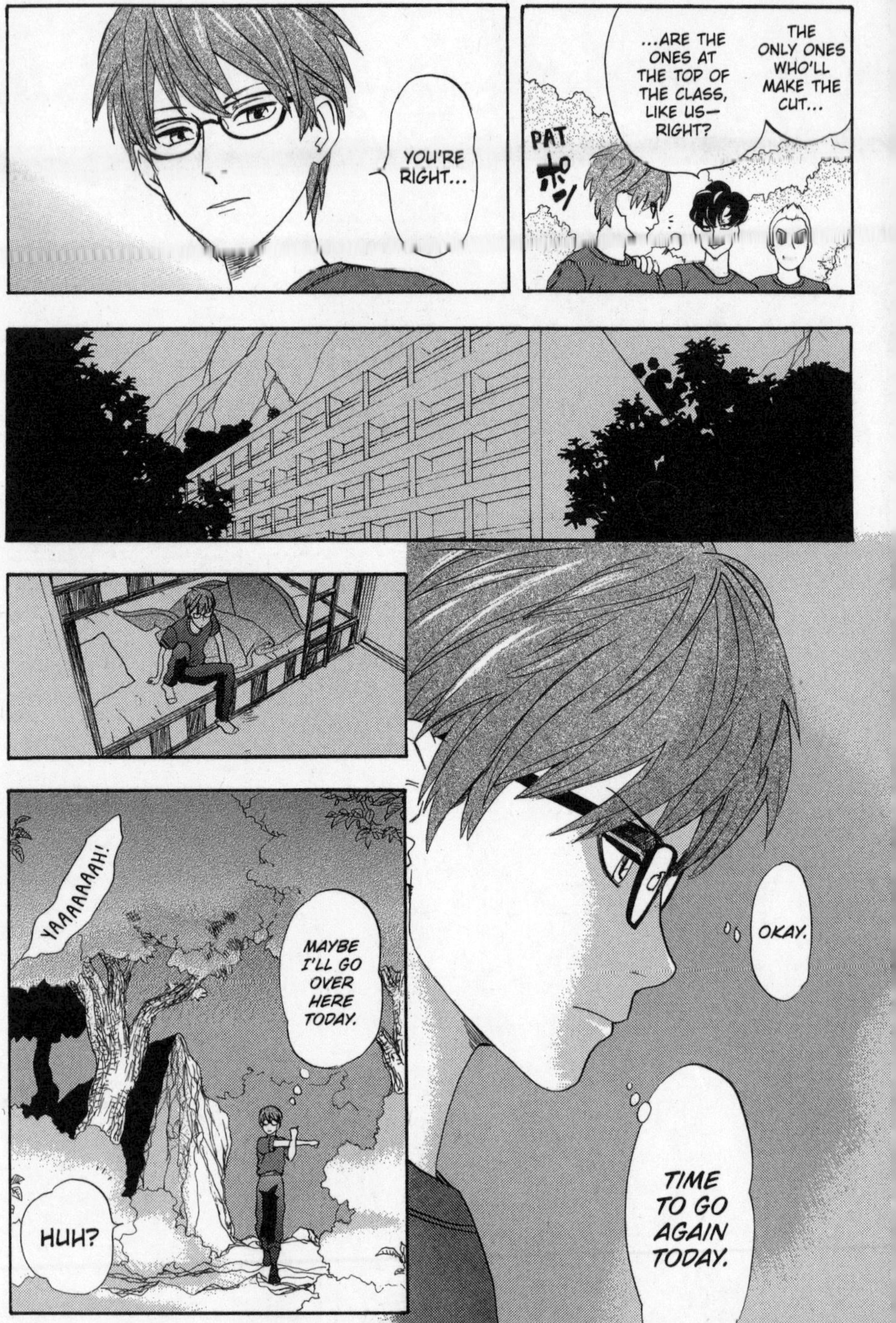
THE ONLY ONES WHO'LL MAKE THE CUT...
...ARE THE ONES AT THE TOP OF THE CLASS, LIKE US— RIGHT?
PAT
ポン
YOU'RE RIGHT...
OKAY.
TIME TO GO AGAIN TODAY.
YAAAAAAAH!
MAYBE I'LL GO OVER HERE TODAY.
HUH?

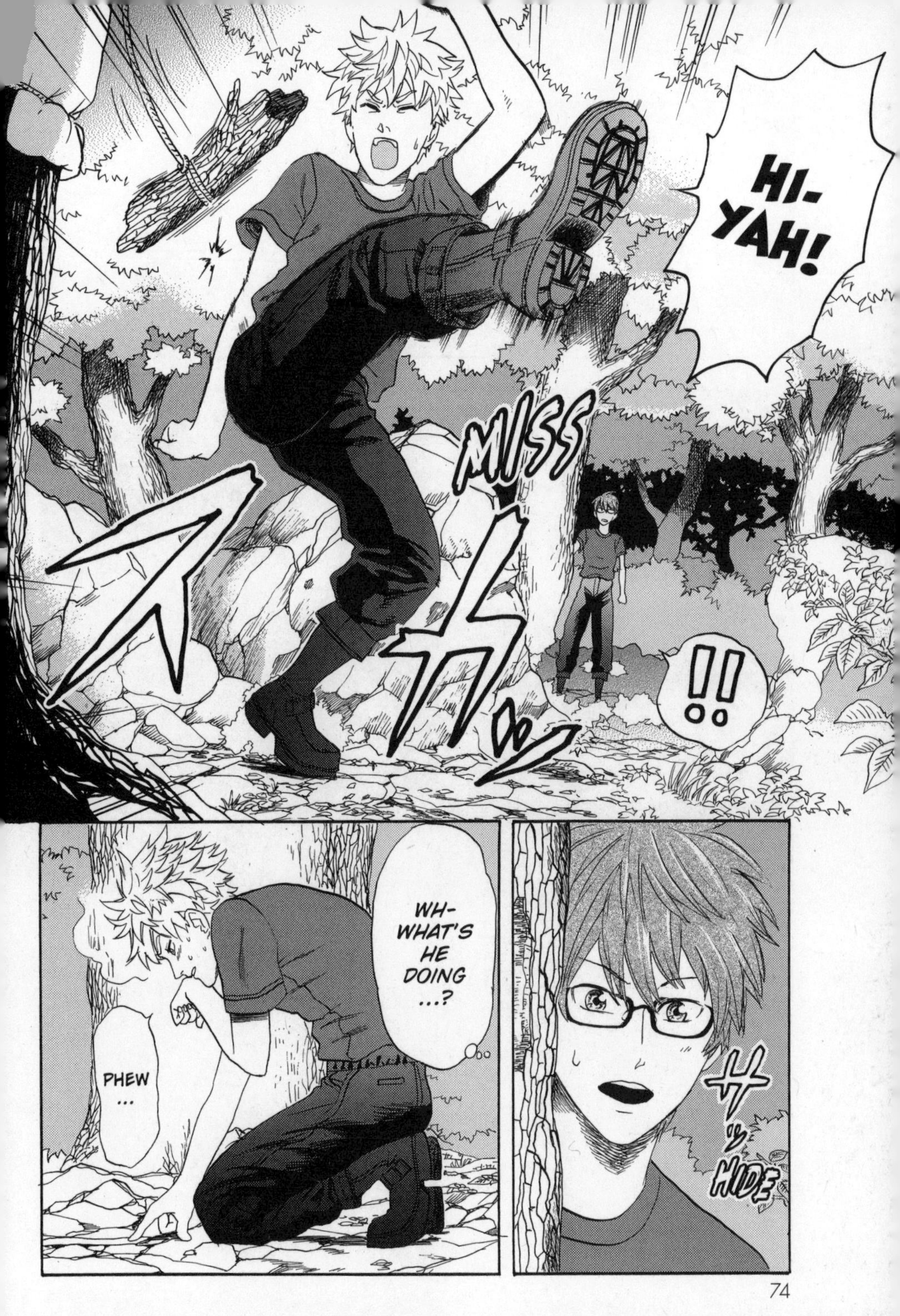
HI-YAH!
MISS
!!
HIDE
WH-WHAT'S HE DOING ...?
PHEW ...

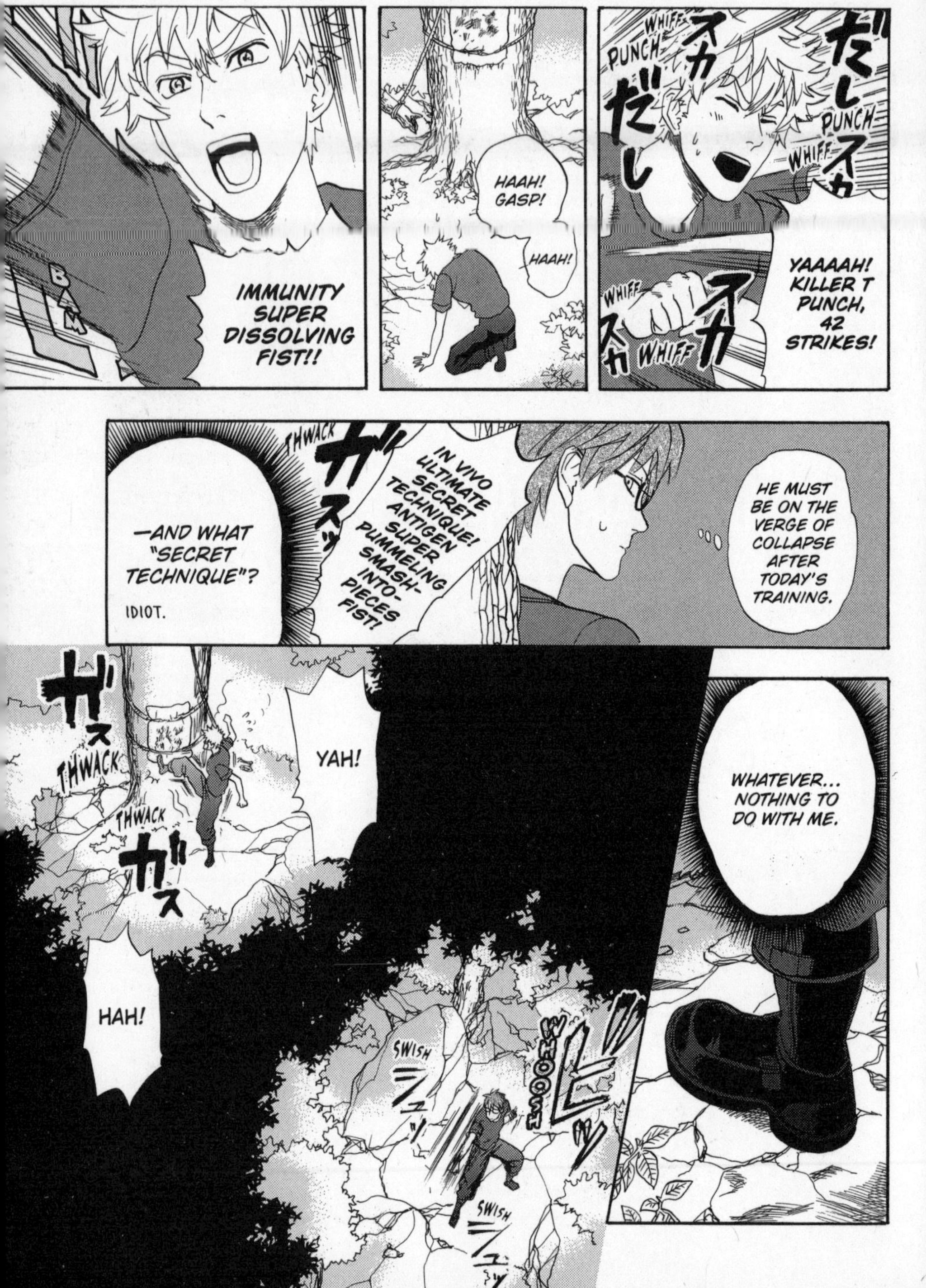
WHIFF
PUNCH
PUNCH
WHIFF
YAAAAH! KILLER T PUNCH, 42 STRIKES!
WHIFF
WHIFF
HAAH! GASP!
HAAH!
IMMUNITY SUPER DISSOLVING FIST!!
BAM
HE MUST BE ON THE VERGE OF COLLAPSE AFTER TODAY'S TRAINING.
...
IN VIVO ULTIMATE SECRET TECHNIQUE! ANTIGEN SUPER PUMMELING SMASH-INTO-PIECES FIST!
THWACK
—AND WHAT "SECRET TECHNIQUE"?
IDIOT.
WHATEVER... NOTHING TO DO WITH ME.
YAH!
THWACK
THWACK
HAH!
WHOOSH
SWISH
SWISH

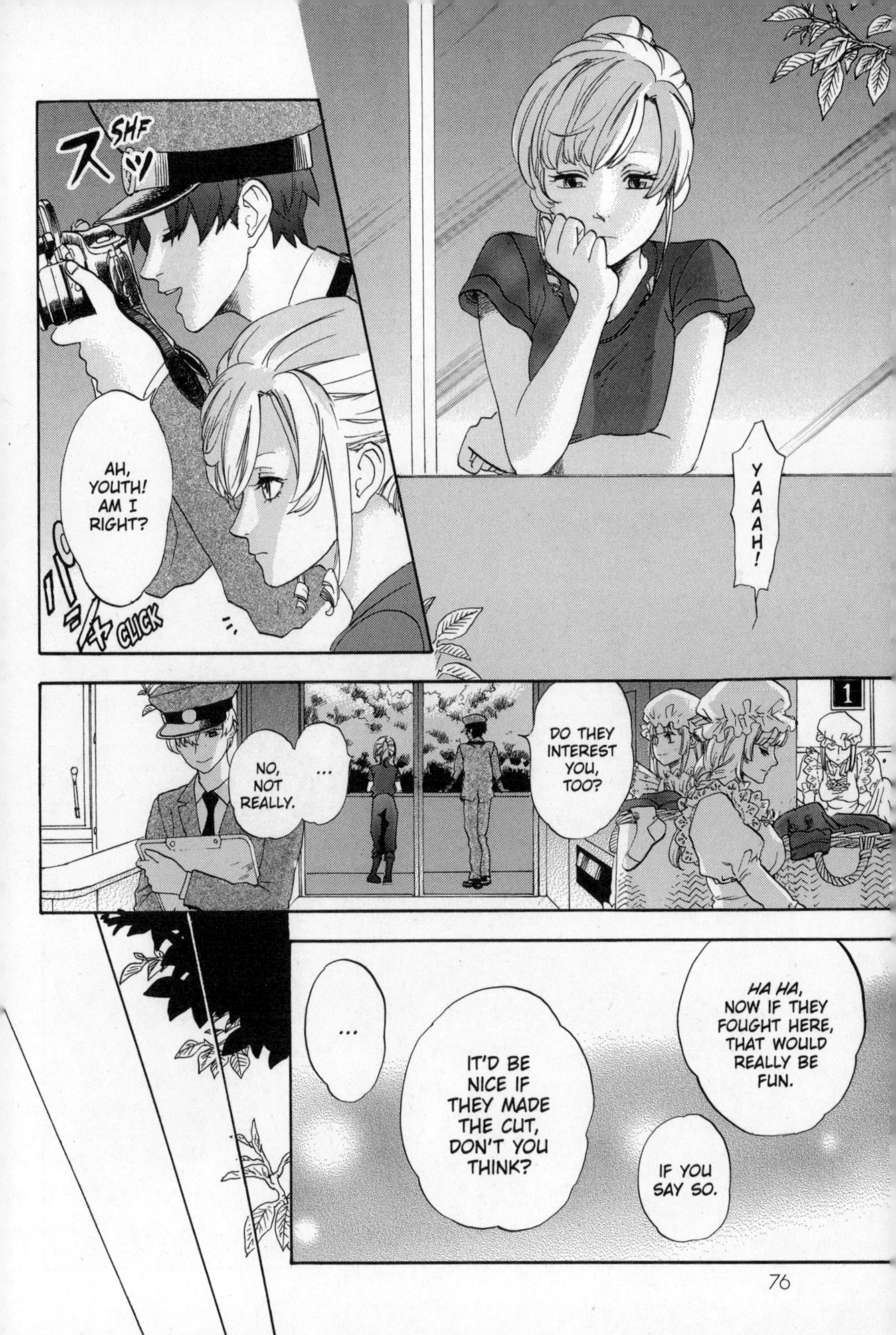
YAAAAH!
SHF
AH, YOUTH! AM I RIGHT?
CLICK
DO THEY INTEREST YOU, TOO?
...
NO, NOT REALLY.
HA HA, NOW IF THEY FOUGHT HERE, THAT WOULD REALLY BE FUN.
IF YOU SAY SO.
IT'D BE NICE IF THEY MADE THE CUT, DON'T YOU THINK?
...

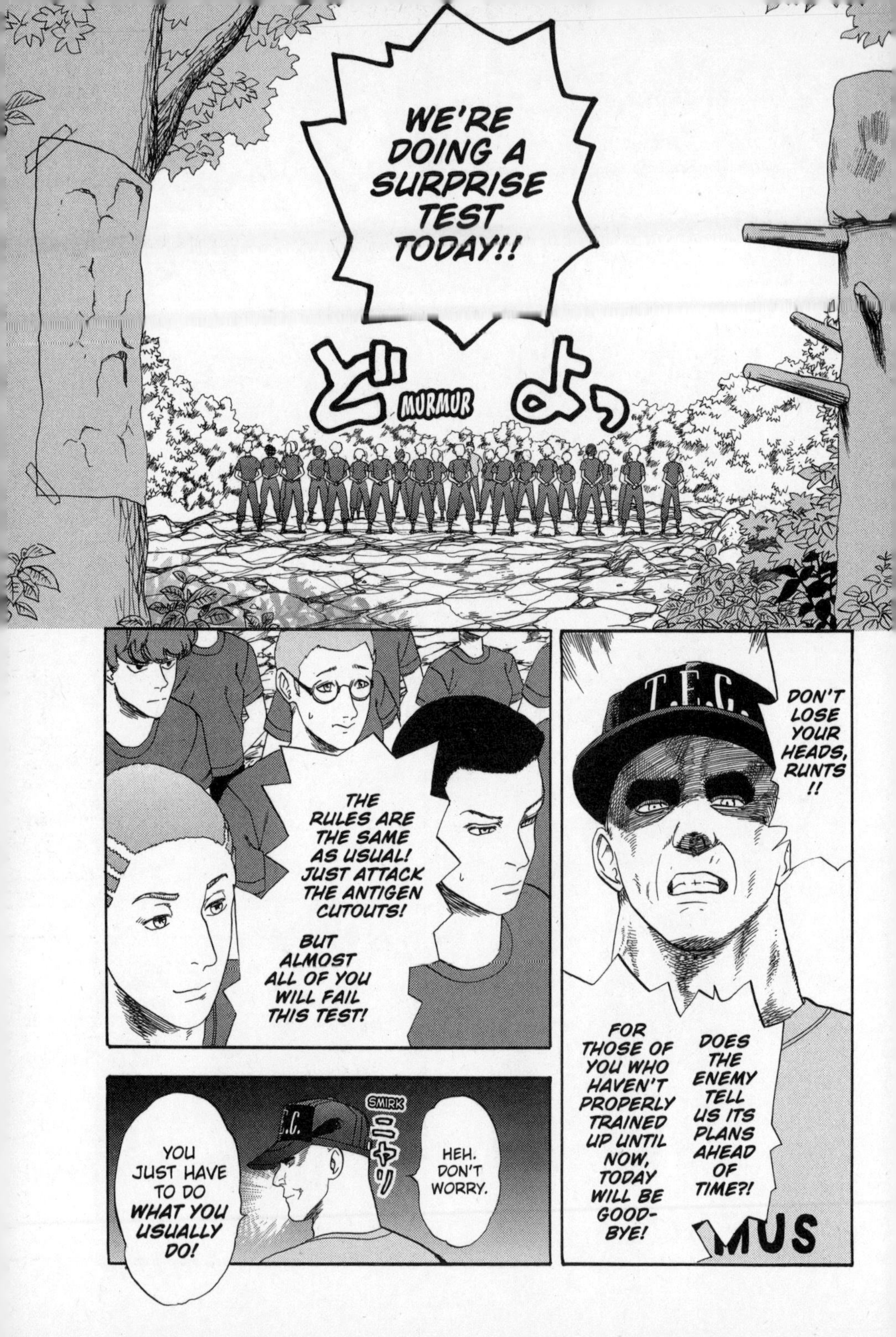
WE'RE DOING A SURPRISE TEST TODAY!!
どよっ
MURMUR
DON'T LOSE YOUR HEADS, RUNTS!!
DOES THE ENEMY TELL US ITS PLANS AHEAD OF TIME?!
FOR THOSE OF YOU WHO HAVEN'T PROPERLY TRAINED UP UNTIL NOW, TODAY WILL BE GOOD-BYE!
MUS
THE RULES ARE THE SAME AS USUAL! JUST ATTACK THE ANTIGEN CUTOUTS!
BUT ALMOST ALL OF YOU WILL FAIL THIS TEST!
SMIRK
ニヤッ
HEH. DON'T WORRY.
YOU JUST HAVE TO DO WHAT YOU USUALLY DO!

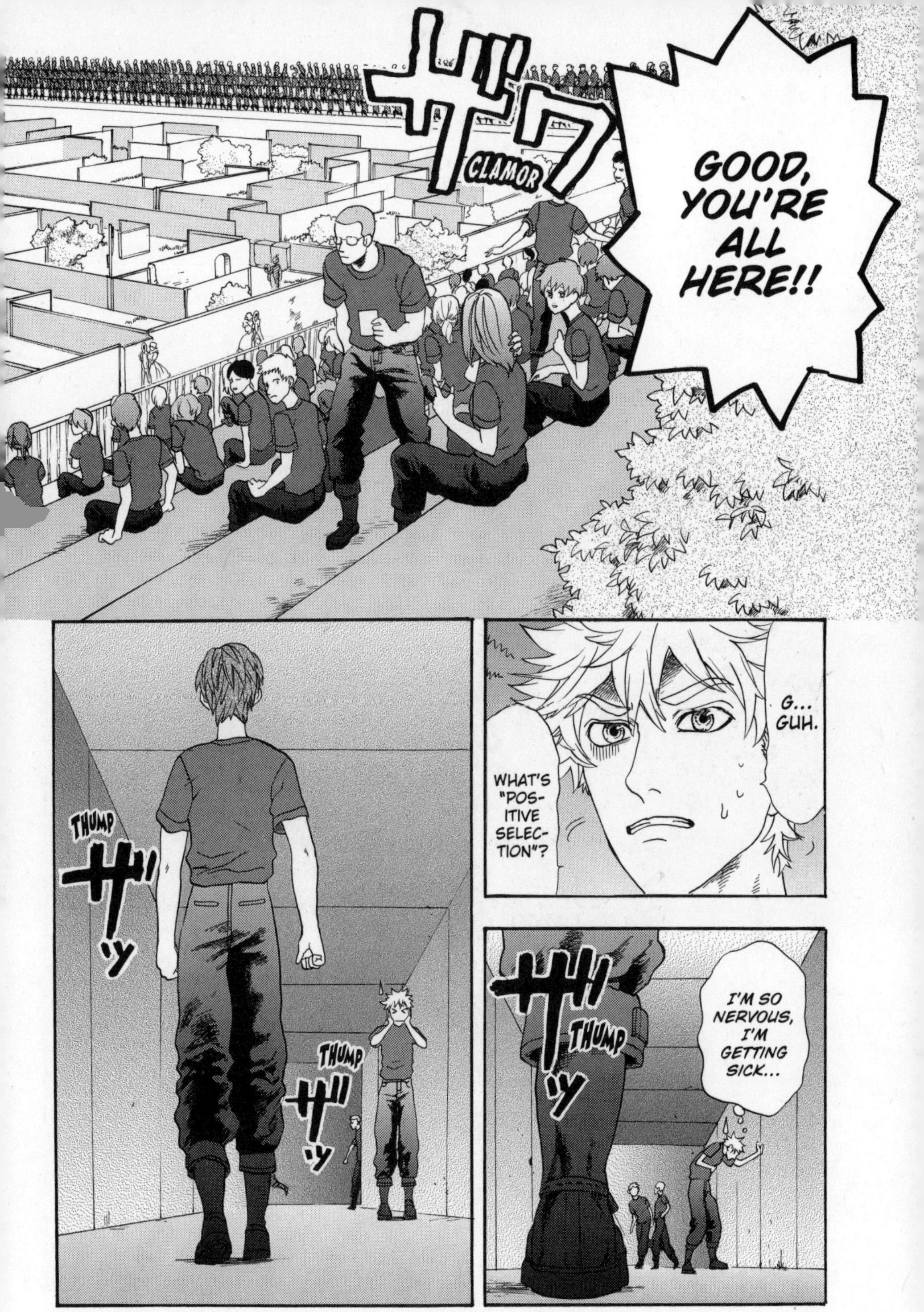
GOOD, YOU'RE ALL HERE!!
CLAMOR
G... GUH.
WHAT'S "POS-ITIVE SELEC-TION"?
I'M SO NERVOUS, I'M GETTING SICK...
THUMP
THUMP
THUMP

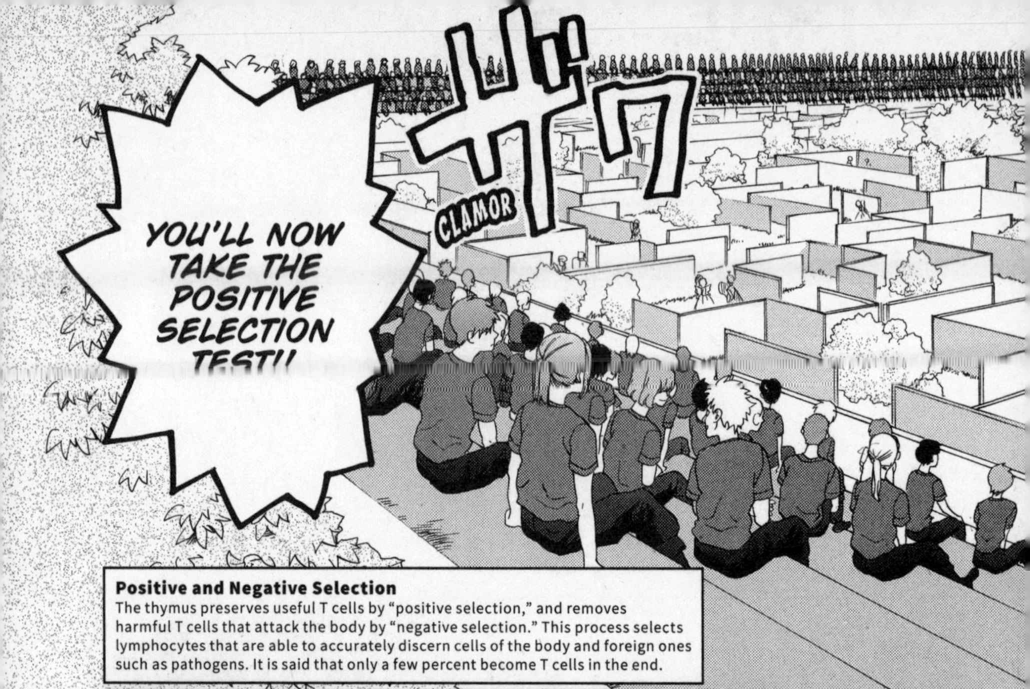
ザワ
CLAMOR
YOU'LL NOW TAKE THE POSITIVE SELECTION TEST!!
Positive and Negative Selection
The thymus preserves useful T cells by "positive selection," and removes harmful T cells that attack the body by "negative selection." This process selects lymphocytes that are able to accurately discern cells of the body and foreign ones such as pathogens. It is said that only a few percent become T cells in the end.

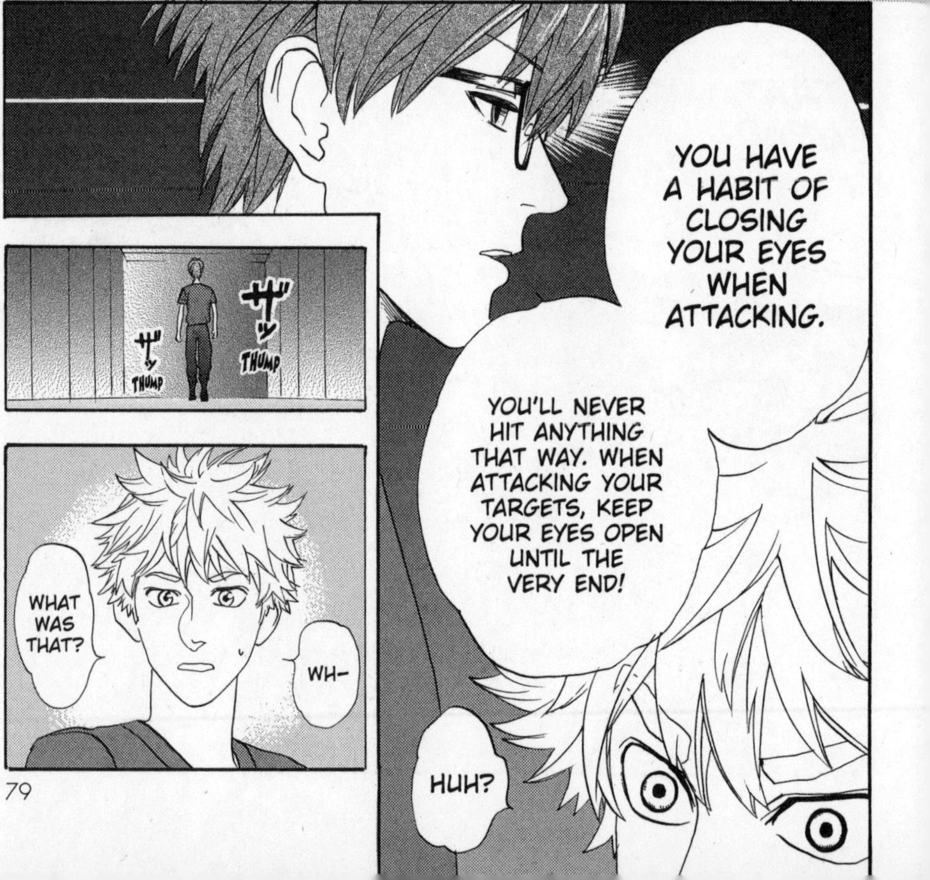
YOU HAVE A HABIT OF CLOSING YOUR EYES WHEN ATTACKING.
YOU'LL NEVER HIT ANYTHING THAT WAY. WHEN ATTACKING YOUR TARGETS, KEEP YOUR EYES OPEN UNTIL THE VERY END!
HUH?
ザッ
THUMP
ザッ
THUMP
WH-
WHAT WAS THAT?

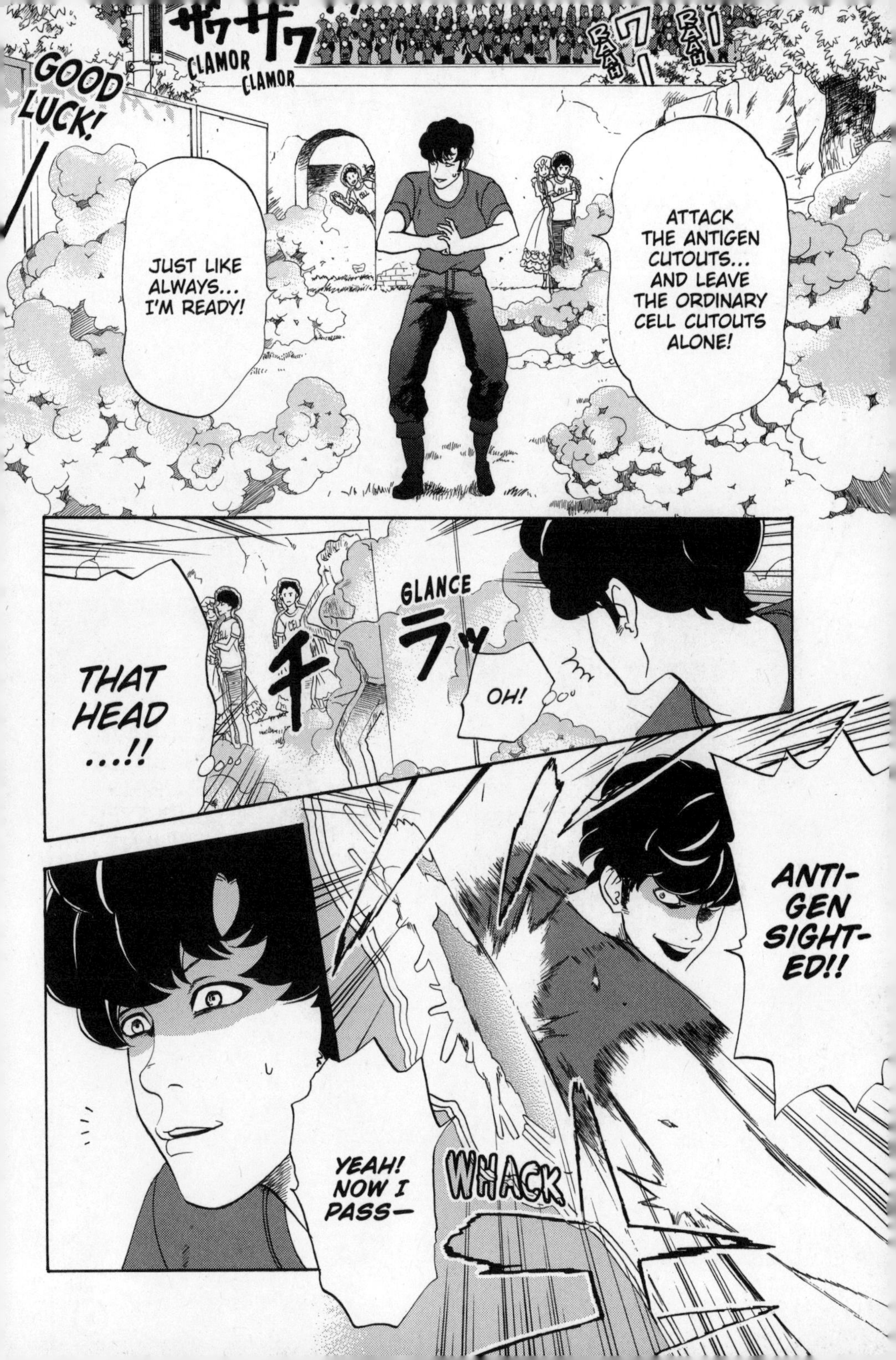
RAAH RAAH
ATTACK THE ANTIGEN CUTOUTS... AND LEAVE THE ORDINARY CELL CUTOUTS ALONE!
ザワザワ
CLAMOR CLAMOR
GOOD LUCK!
JUST LIKE ALWAYS... I'M READY!
OH!
GLANCE
チラッ
THAT HEAD ...!!
ANTI-GEN SIGHT-ED!!
WHACK
YEAH! NOW I PASS—

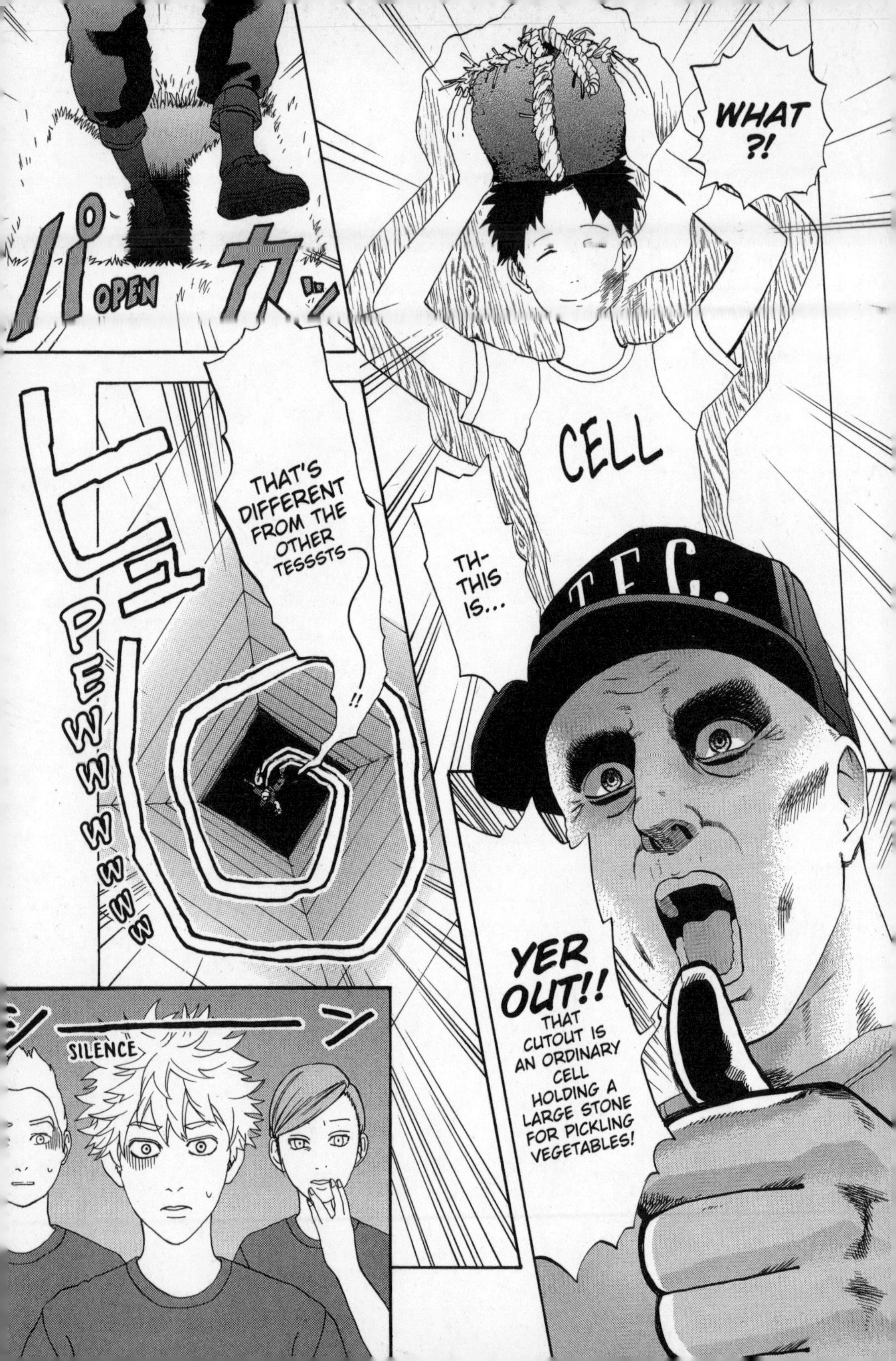
WHAT ?!
CELL
パカッ
OPEN
ヒュー
PEWWWWWWWW
THAT'S DIFFERENT FROM THE OTHER TESSSTS
!!
TH-THIS IS...
YER OUT!!
THAT CUTOUT IS AN ORDINARY CELL HOLDING A LARGE STONE FOR PICKLING VEGETABLES!
シーン
SILENCE

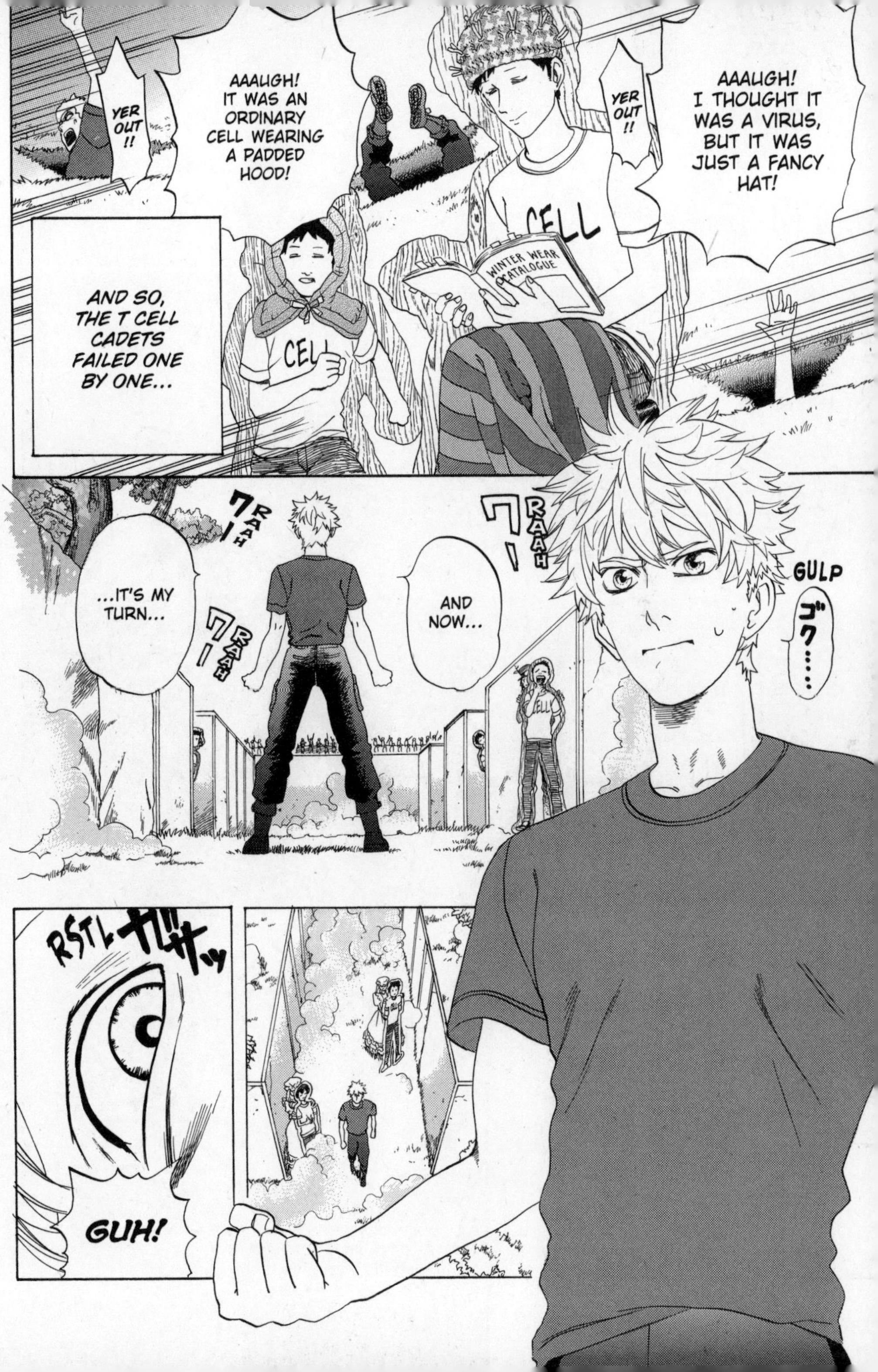
AAAUGH! I THOUGHT IT WAS A VIRUS, BUT IT WAS JUST A FANCY HAT!
YER OUT!!
WINTER WEAR CATALOGUE
CELL
AAAUGH! IT WAS AN ORDINARY CELL WEARING A PADDED HOOD!
YER OUT!!
CELL
AND SO, THE T CELL CADETS FAILED ONE BY ONE...
GULP
ゴク……
RAAH
AND NOW...
RAAH
...IT'S MY TURN...
RAAH
CELL
CELL
RSTL
GUH!

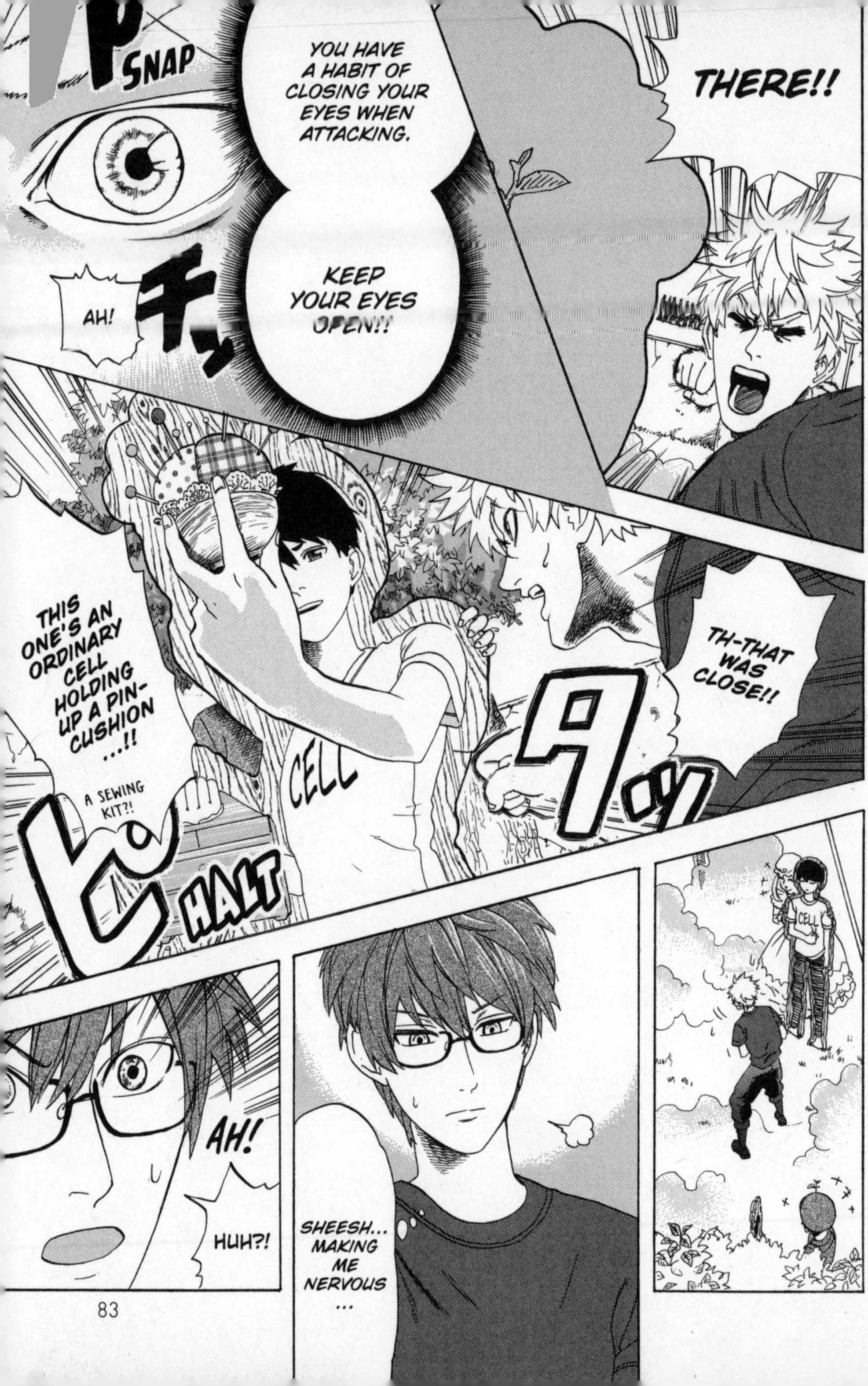
THERE!!
SNAP
YOU HAVE A HABIT OF CLOSING YOUR EYES WHEN ATTACKING.
KEEP YOUR EYES OPEN!!
AH!
チッ
TH-THAT WAS CLOSE!!
THIS ONE'S AN ORDINARY CELL HOLDING UP A PIN-CUSHION ...!!
A SEWING KIT?!
CELL
HALT
SHEESH... MAKING ME NERVOUS ...
AH!
HUH?!

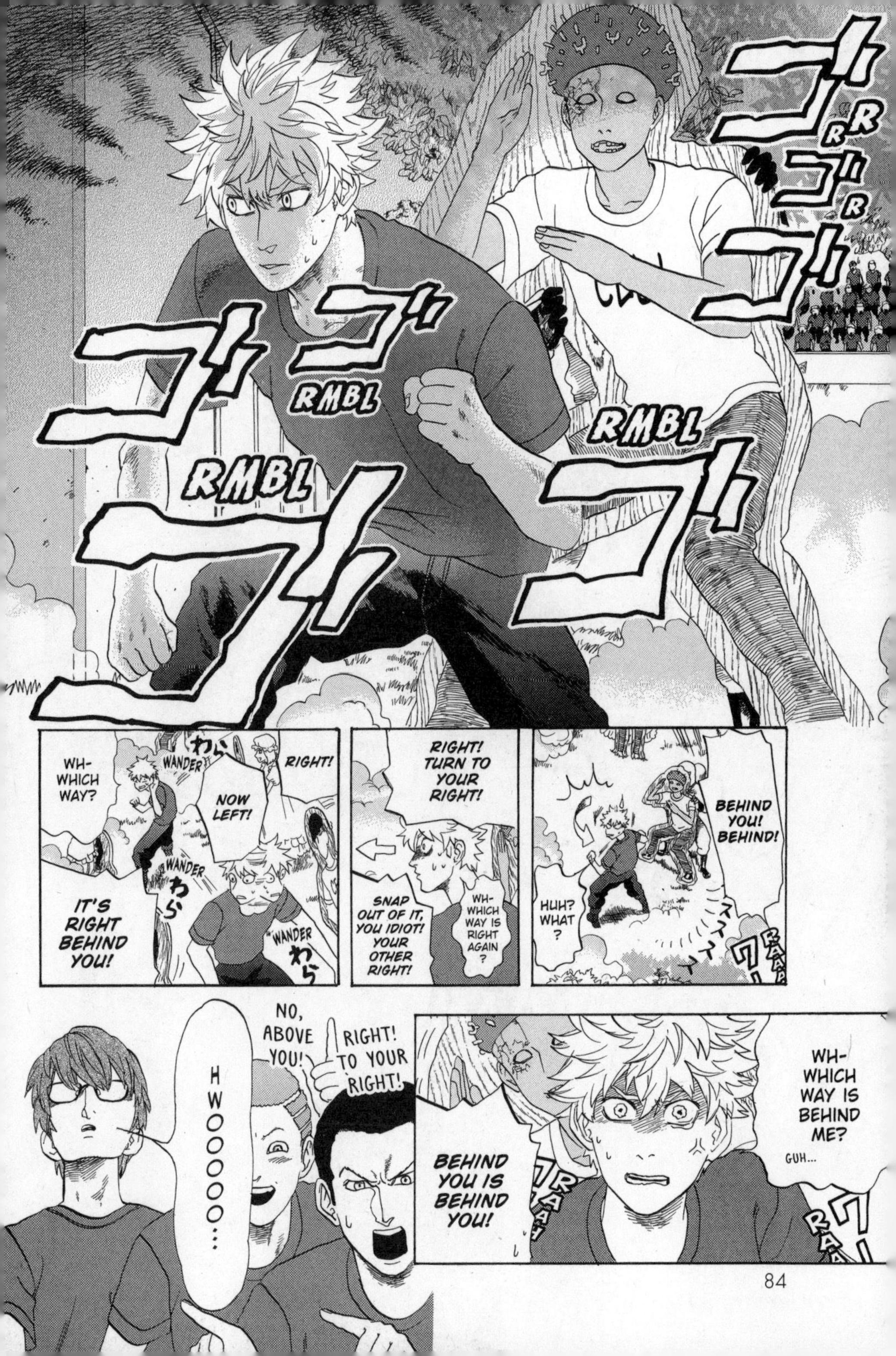

R R R
RMBL
RMBL
RMBL
BEHIND YOU! BEHIND!
HUH? WHAT?
RAAA
RIGHT! TURN TO YOUR RIGHT!
WH-WHICH WAY IS RIGHT AGAIN?
SNAP OUT OF IT, YOU IDIOT! YOUR OTHER RIGHT!
RIGHT!
NOW LEFT!
WANDER
WH-WHICH WAY?
WANDER
IT'S RIGHT BEHIND YOU!
WANDER
WH-WHICH WAY IS BEHIND ME?
GUH...
BEHIND YOU IS BEHIND YOU!
RAAA
RAAA
RIGHT! TO YOUR RIGHT!
NO, ABOVE YOU!
HWOOOOOO...

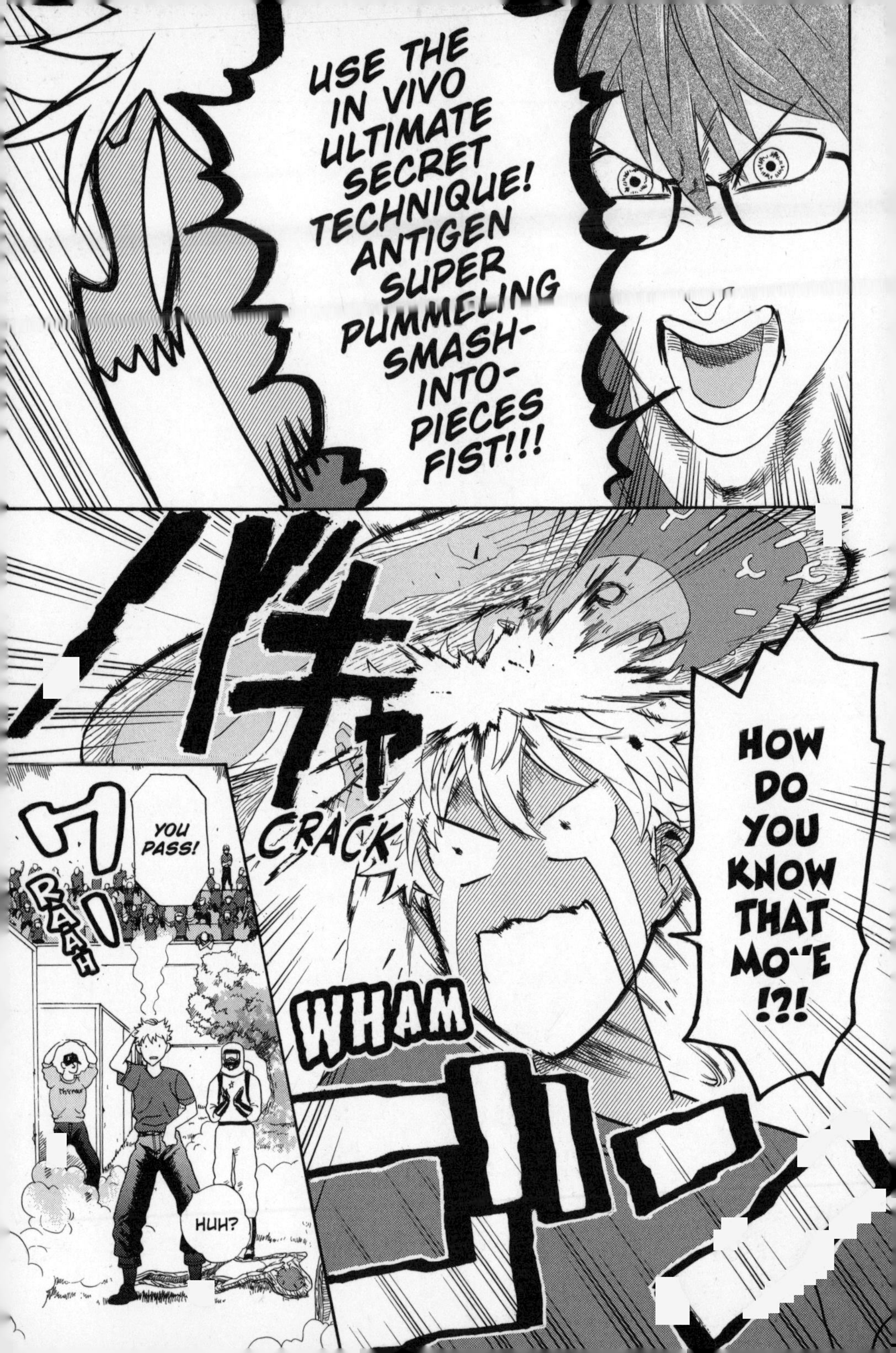
USE THE IN VIVO ULTIMATE SECRET TECHNIQUE! ANTIGEN SUPER PUMMELING SMASH-INTO-PIECES FIST!!!
CRACK
HOW DO YOU KNOW THAT MO''E !?!
WHAM
YOU PASS!
RAAAH
HUH?

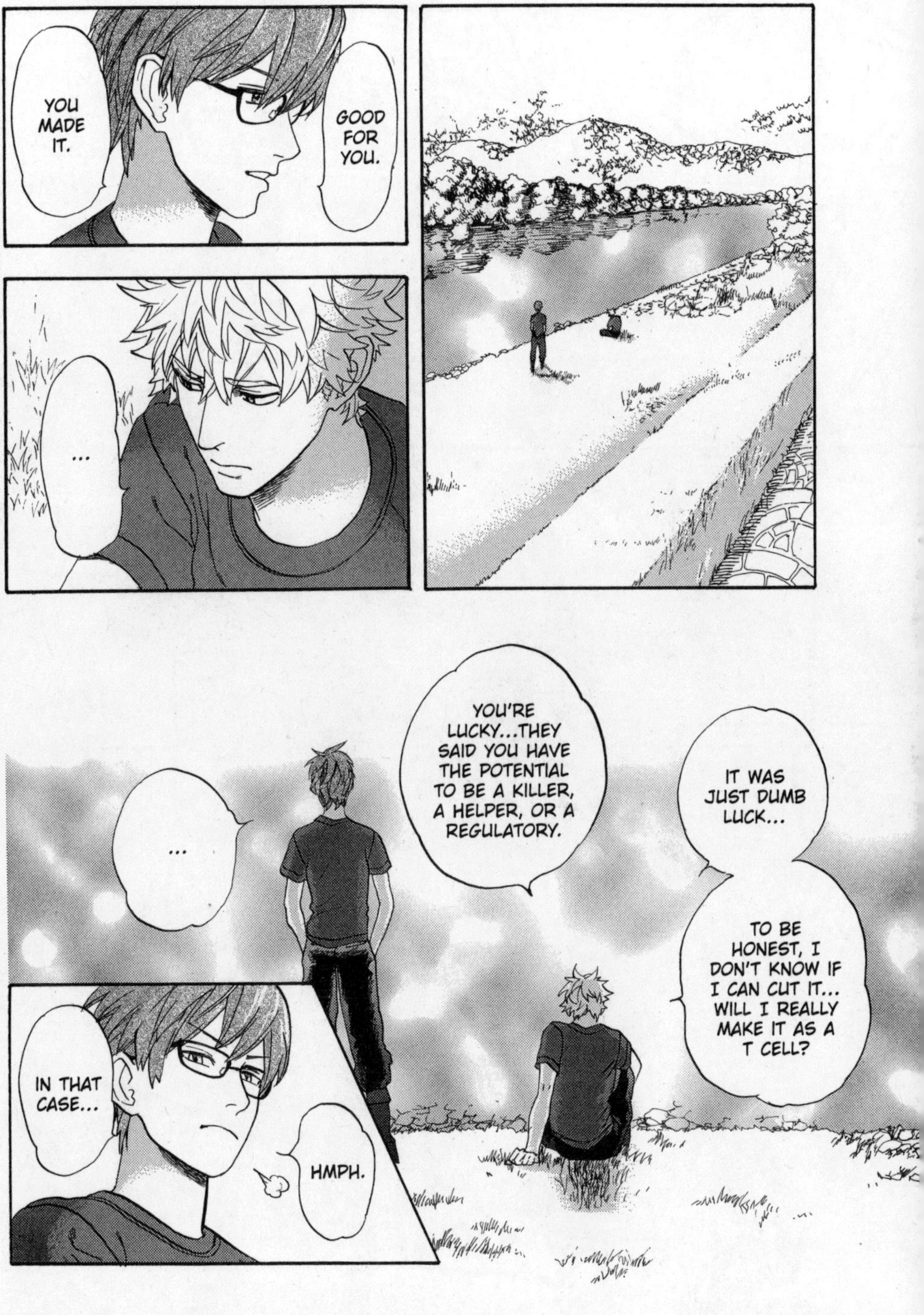

GOOD FOR YOU.
YOU MADE IT.
...
IT WAS JUST DUMB LUCK...
TO BE HONEST, I DON'T KNOW IF I CAN CUT IT... WILL I REALLY MAKE IT AS A T CELL?
YOU'RE LUCKY...THEY SAID YOU HAVE THE POTENTIAL TO BE A KILLER, A HELPER, OR A REGULATORY.
...
HMPH.
IN THAT CASE...

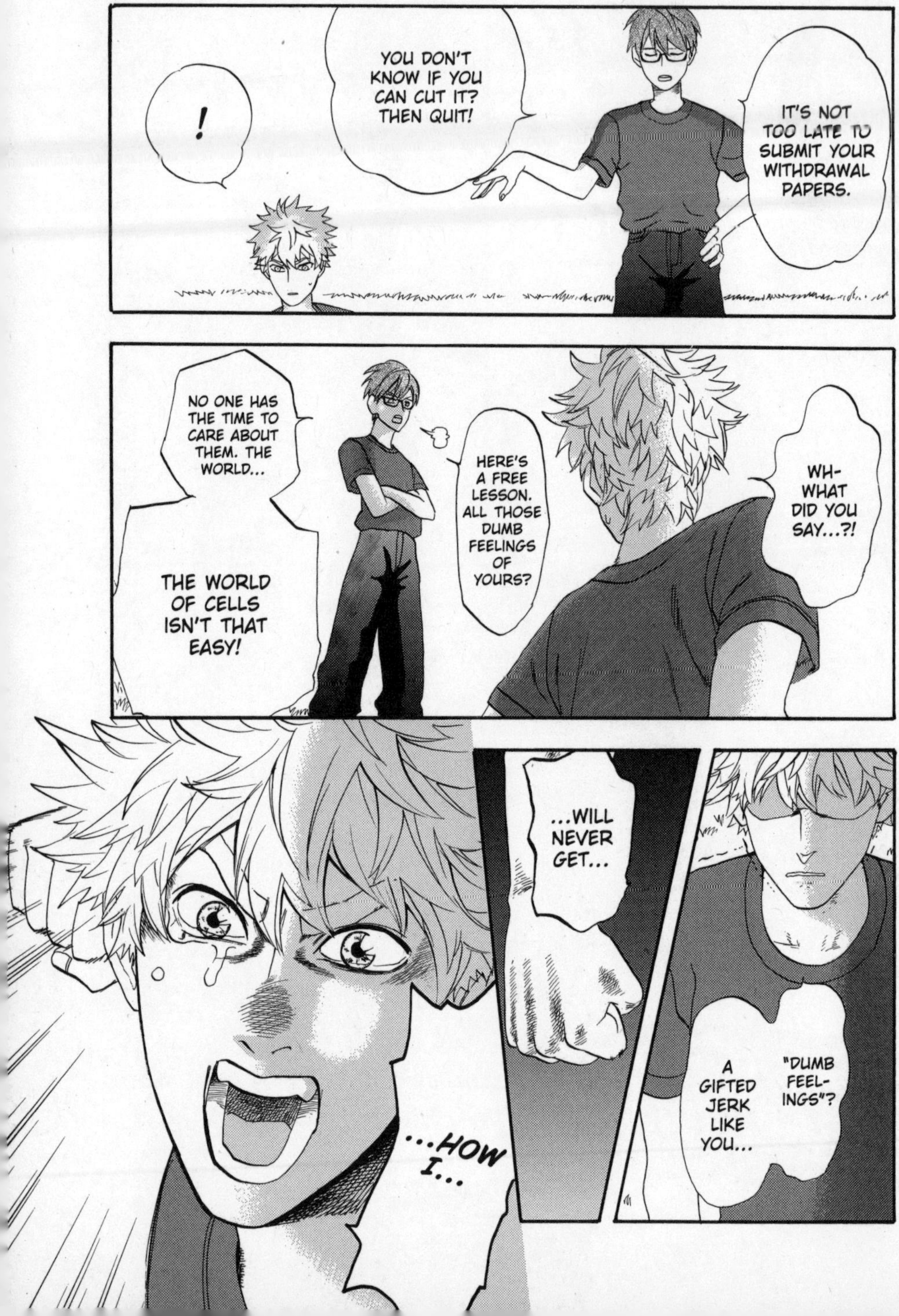
IT'S NOT TOO LATE TO SUBMIT YOUR WITHDRAWAL PAPERS.
YOU DON'T KNOW IF YOU CAN CUT IT? THEN QUIT!
!
WH-WHAT DID YOU SAY...?!
HERE'S A FREE LESSON. ALL THOSE DUMB FEELINGS OF YOURS?
NO ONE HAS THE TIME TO CARE ABOUT THEM. THE WORLD...
THE WORLD OF CELLS ISN'T THAT EASY!
"DUMB FEEL-INGS"?
A GIFTED JERK LIKE YOU...
...WILL NEVER GET...
...HOW I...

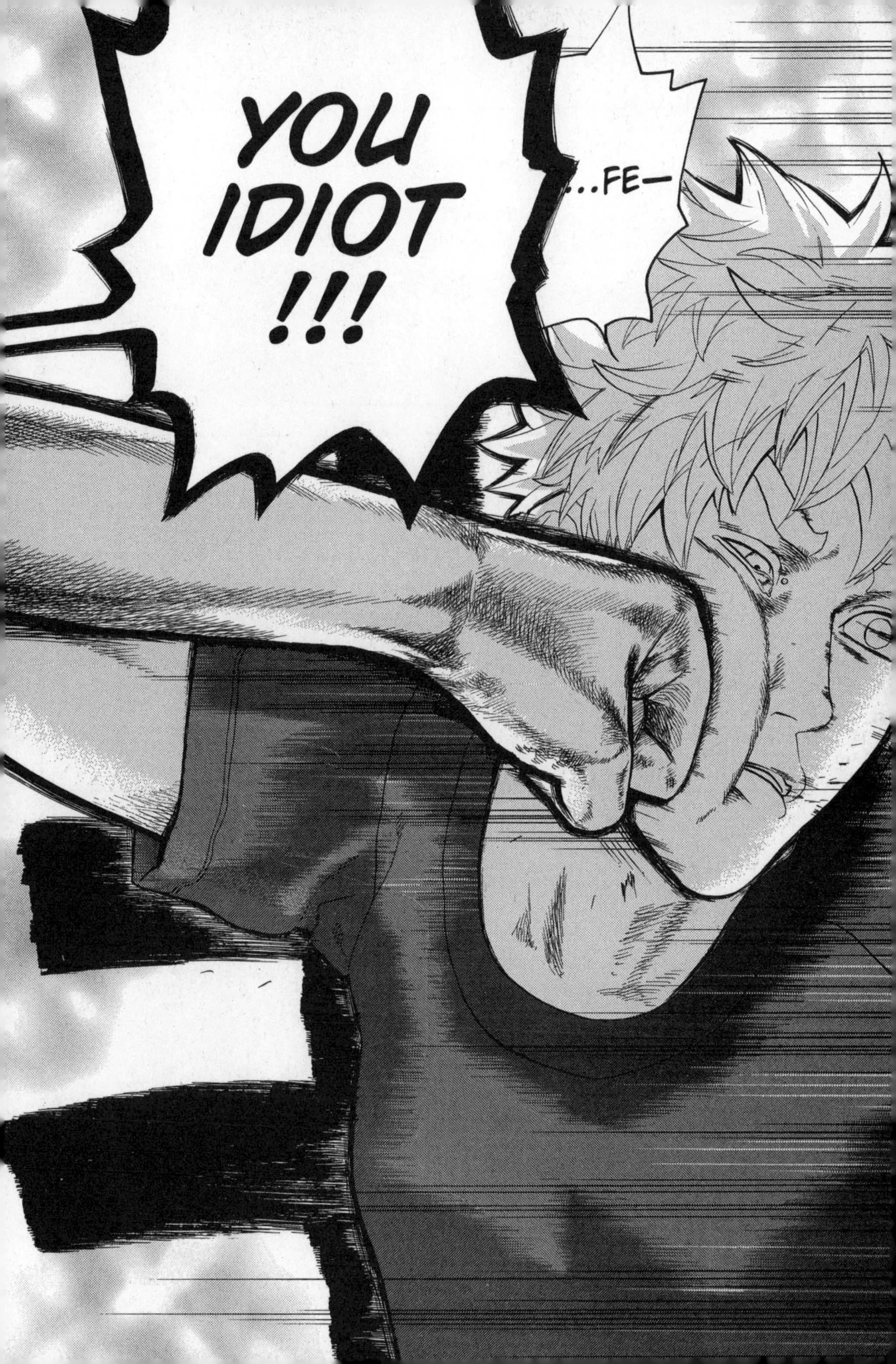
...FE—
YOU IDIOT !!!

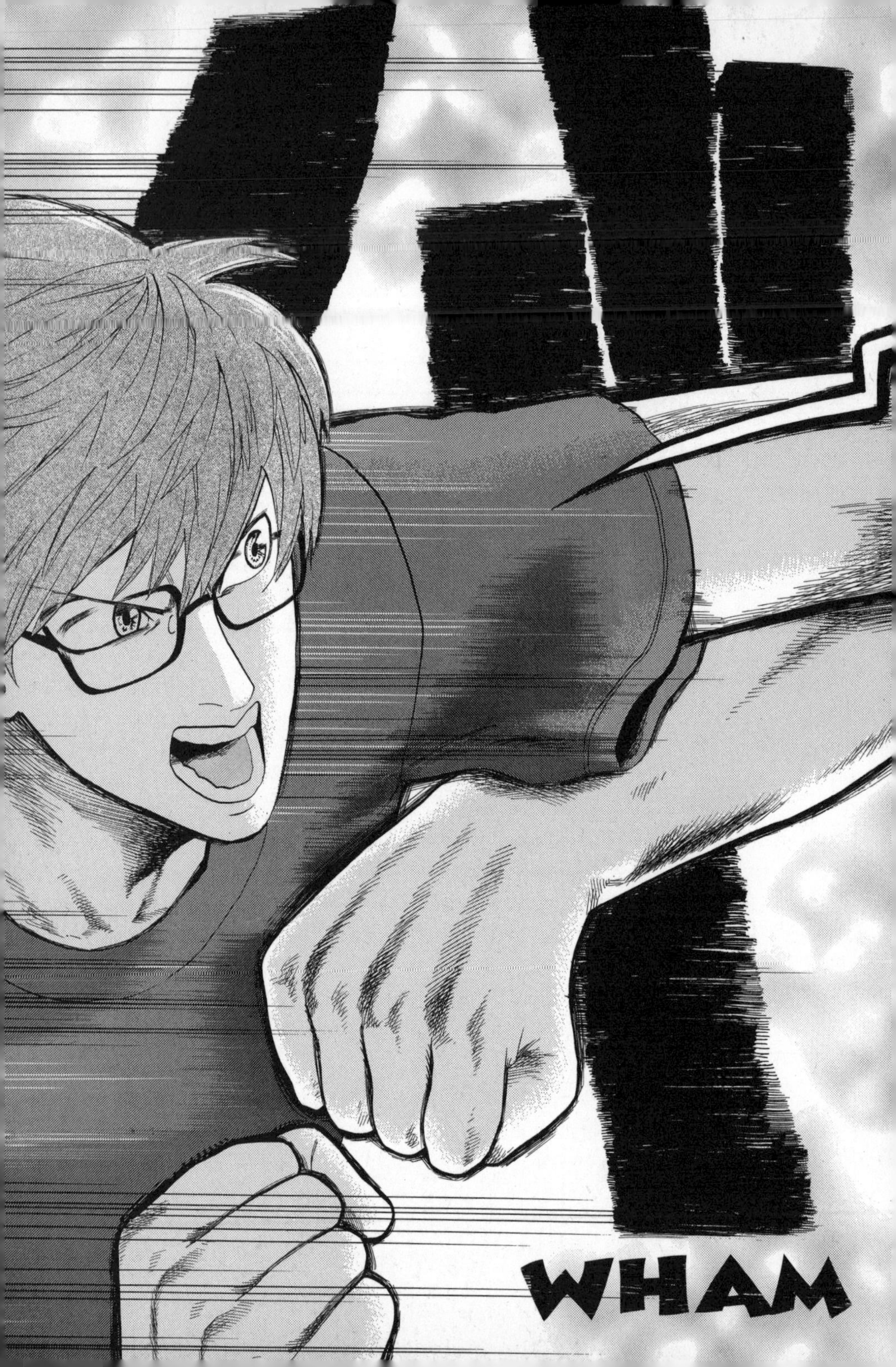
WHAM

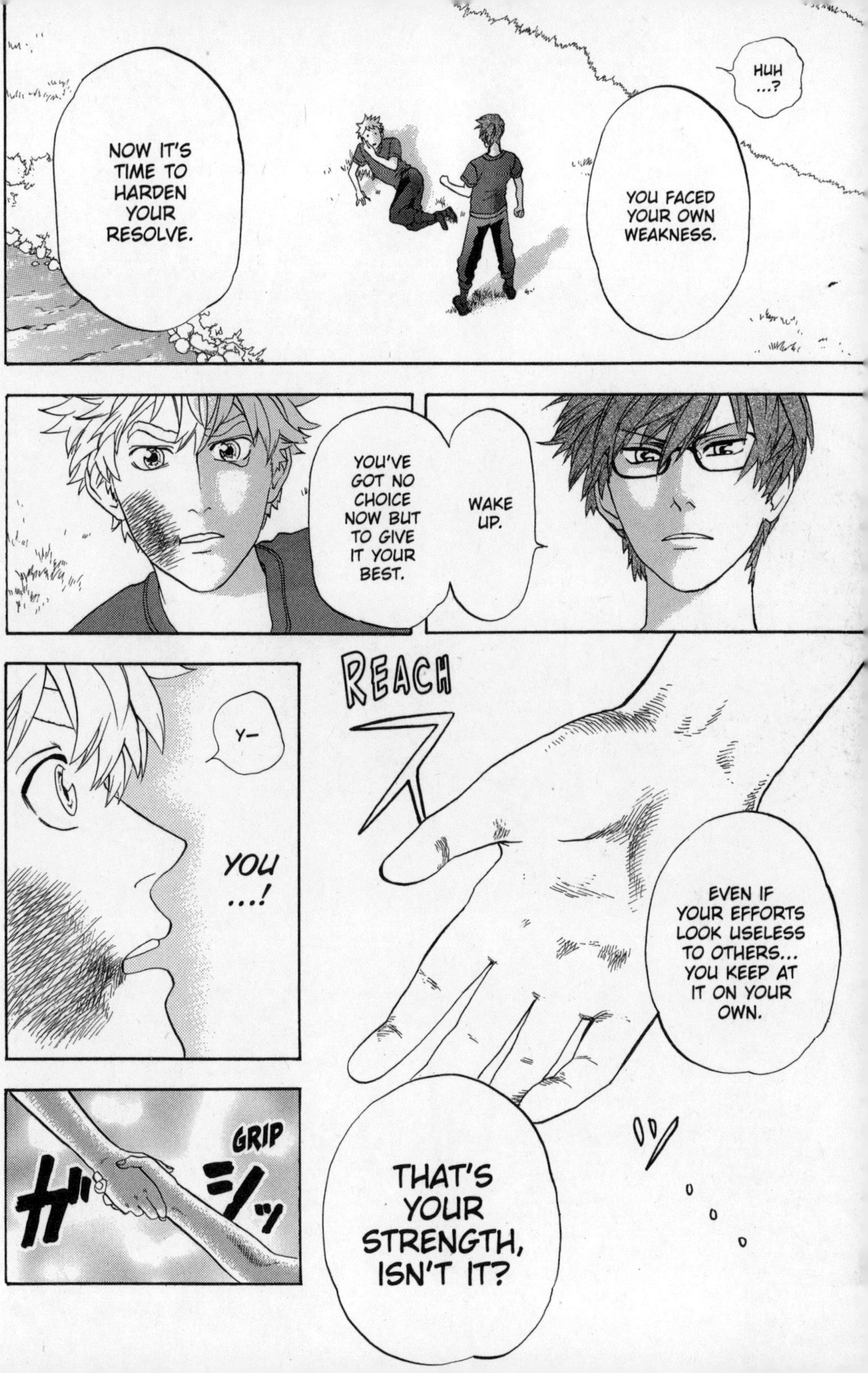
HUH ...?
YOU FACED YOUR OWN WEAKNESS.
NOW IT'S TIME TO HARDEN YOUR RESOLVE.
WAKE UP.
YOU'VE GOT NO CHOICE NOW BUT TO GIVE IT YOUR BEST.
REACH
EVEN IF YOUR EFFORTS LOOK USELESS TO OTHERS... YOU KEEP AT IT ON YOUR OWN.
THAT'S YOUR STRENGTH, ISN'T IT?
Y–
YOU ...!
GRIP
ガシッ

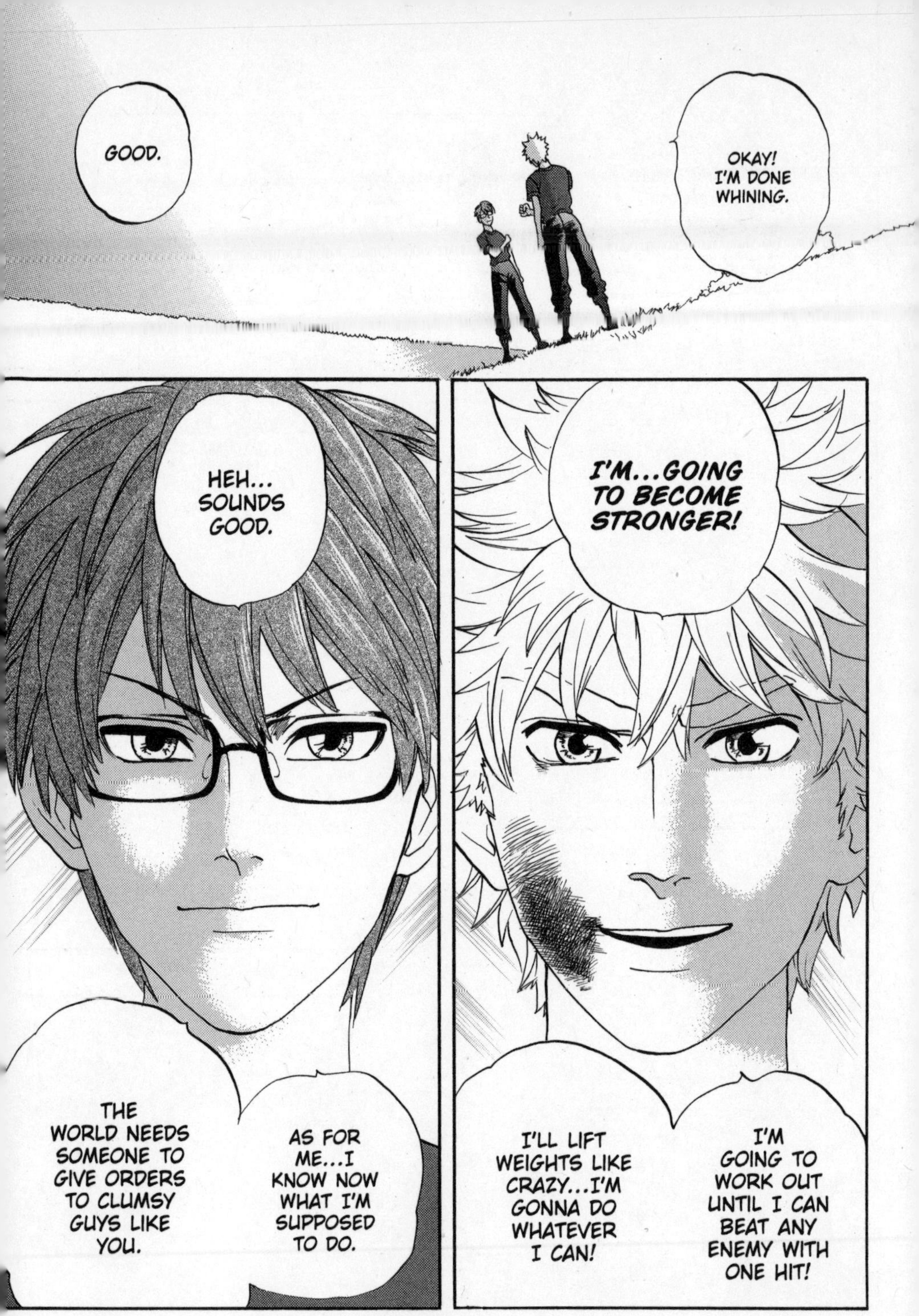
OKAY! I'M DONE WHINING.
GOOD.
I'M...GOING TO BECOME STRONGER!
I'M GOING TO WORK OUT UNTIL I CAN BEAT ANY ENEMY WITH ONE HIT!
I'LL LIFT WEIGHTS LIKE CRAZY...I'M GONNA DO WHATEVER I CAN!
HEH... SOUNDS GOOD.
AS FOR ME...I KNOW NOW WHAT I'M SUPPOSED TO DO.
THE WORLD NEEDS SOMEONE TO GIVE ORDERS TO CLUMSY GUYS LIKE YOU.

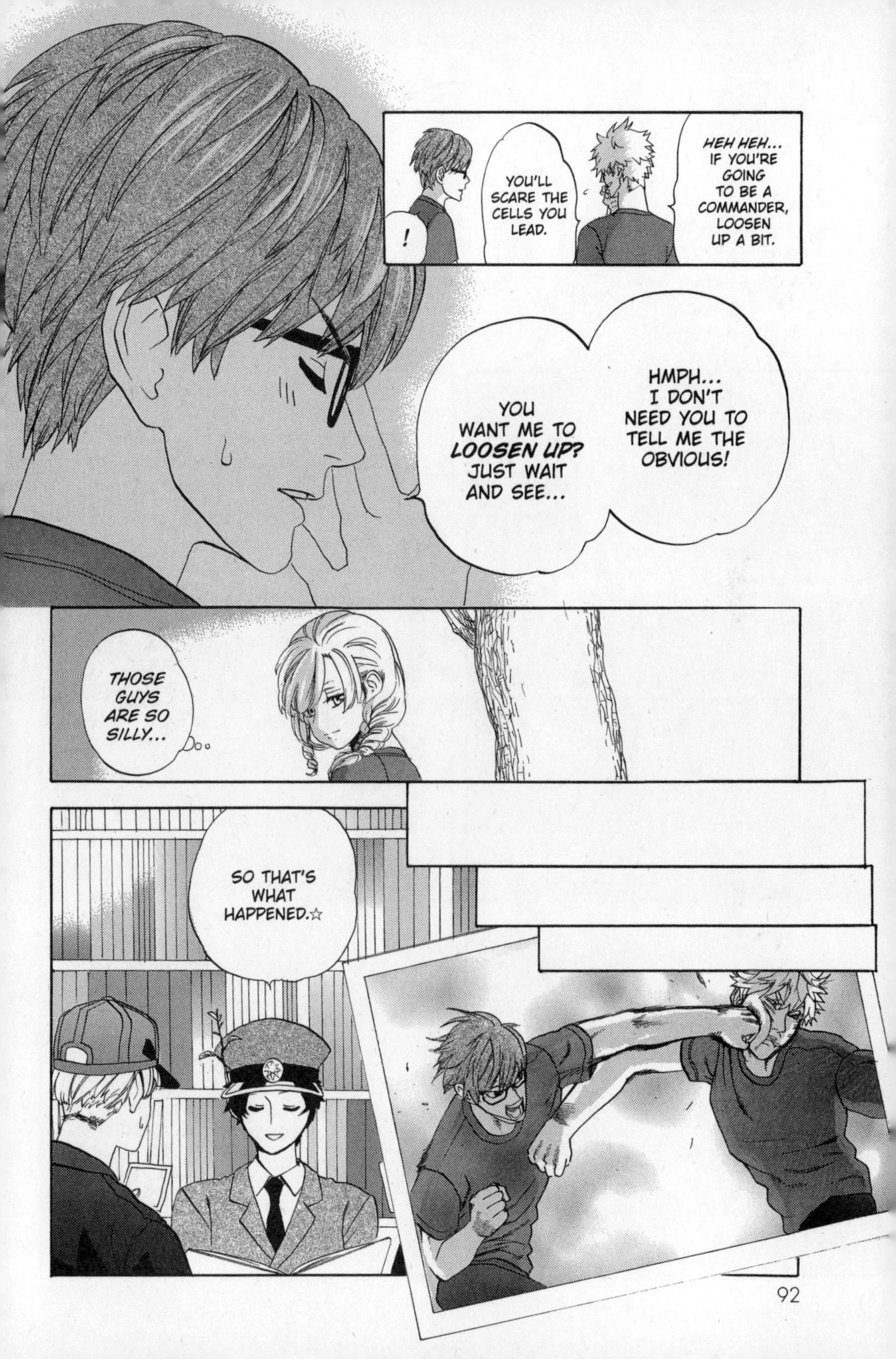
HEH HEH... IF YOU'RE GOING TO BE A COMMANDER, LOOSEN UP A BIT.
YOU'LL SCARE THE CELLS YOU LEAD.
!
HMPH... I DON'T NEED YOU TO TELL ME THE OBVIOUS!
YOU WANT ME TO *LOOSEN UP?* JUST WAIT AND SEE...
THOSE GUYS ARE SO SILLY...
SO THAT'S WHAT HAPPENED.☆

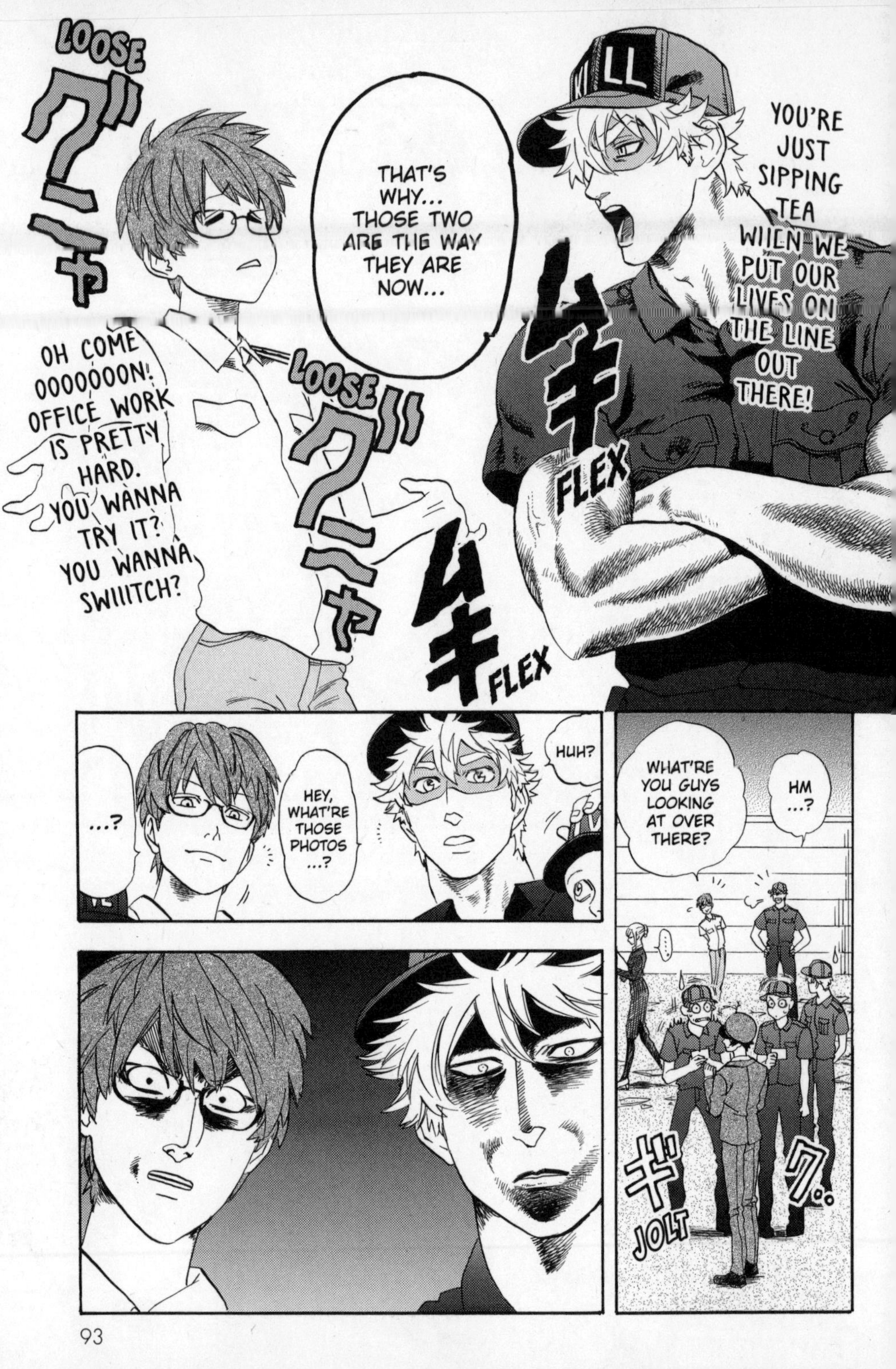
YOU'RE JUST SIPPING TEA WHEN WE PUT OUR LIVES ON THE LINE OUT THERE!
FLEX
FLEX
THAT'S WHY... THOSE TWO ARE THE WAY THEY ARE NOW...
LOOSE
LOOSE
OH COME OOOOOOON! OFFICE WORK IS PRETTY HARD. YOU WANNA TRY IT? YOU WANNA SWIIITCH?
HM ...?
WHAT'RE YOU GUYS LOOKING AT OVER THERE?
...
JOLT
HUH?
HEY, WHAT'RE THOSE PHOTOS ...?
...?

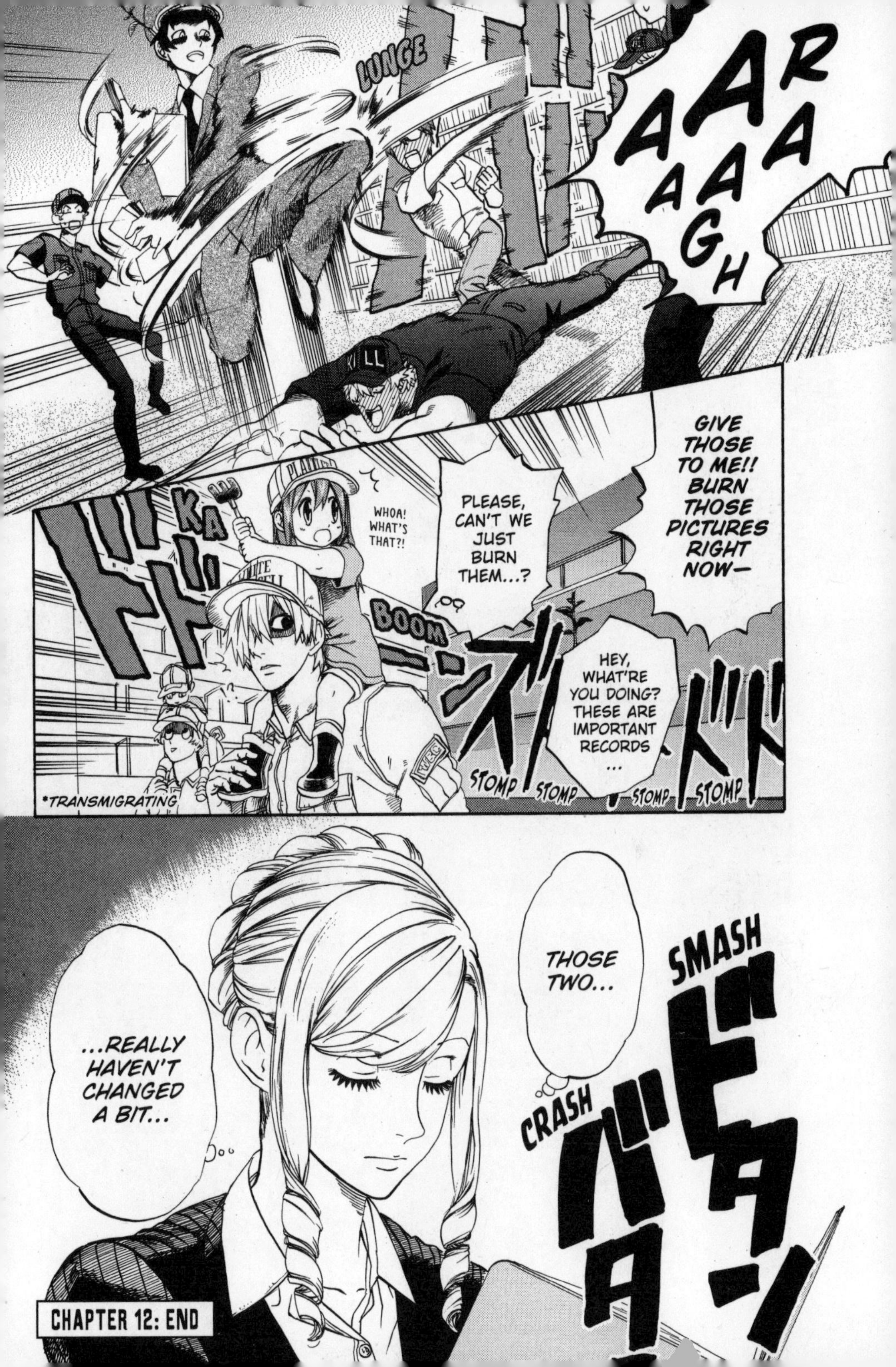
AARAAAGH
LUNGE
GIVE THOSE TO ME!! BURN THOSE PICTURES RIGHT NOW—
HEY, WHAT'RE YOU DOING? THESE ARE IMPORTANT RECORDS ...
STOMP
STOMP
STOMP
STOMP
BOOM
PLEASE, CAN'T WE JUST BURN THEM...?
WHOA! WHAT'S THAT?!
KA
*TRANSMIGRATING
SMASH
CRASH
THOSE TWO...
...REALLY HAVEN'T CHANGED A BIT...
CHAPTER 12: END

Cells at Work!

Life of a Killer T Cell

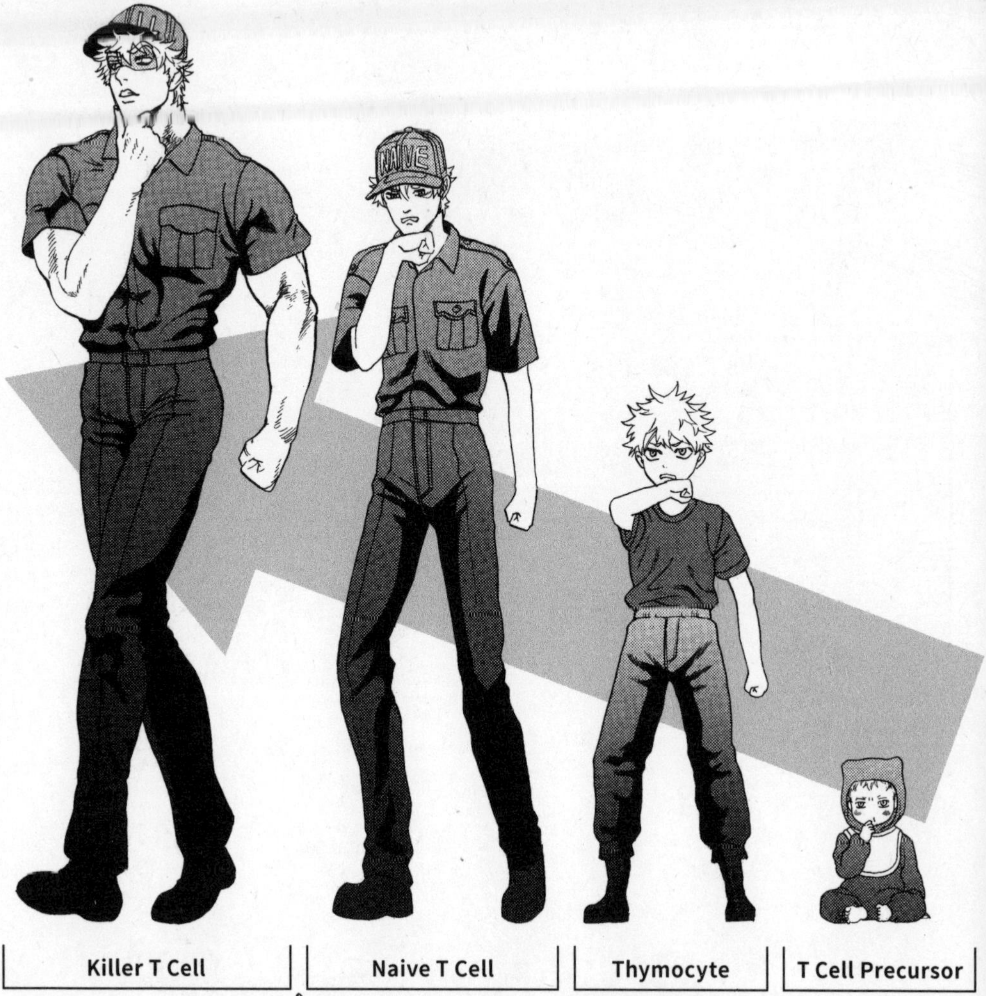
Killer T Cell
Naive T Cell
Thymocyte
T Cell Precursor

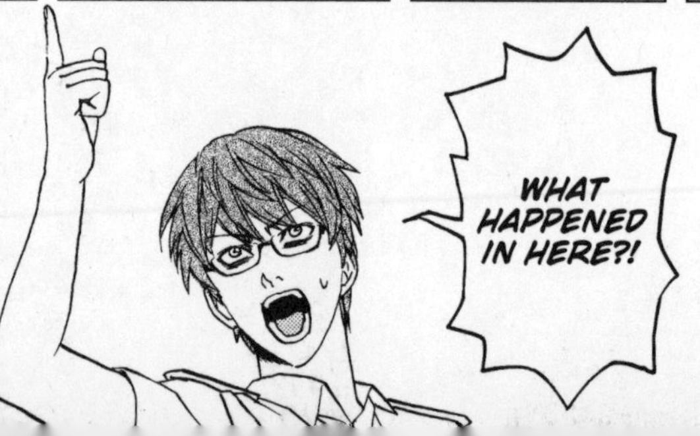
WHAT HAPPENED IN HERE?!

Cells at Work!

はたらく細胞

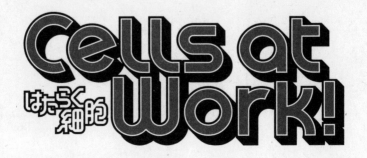

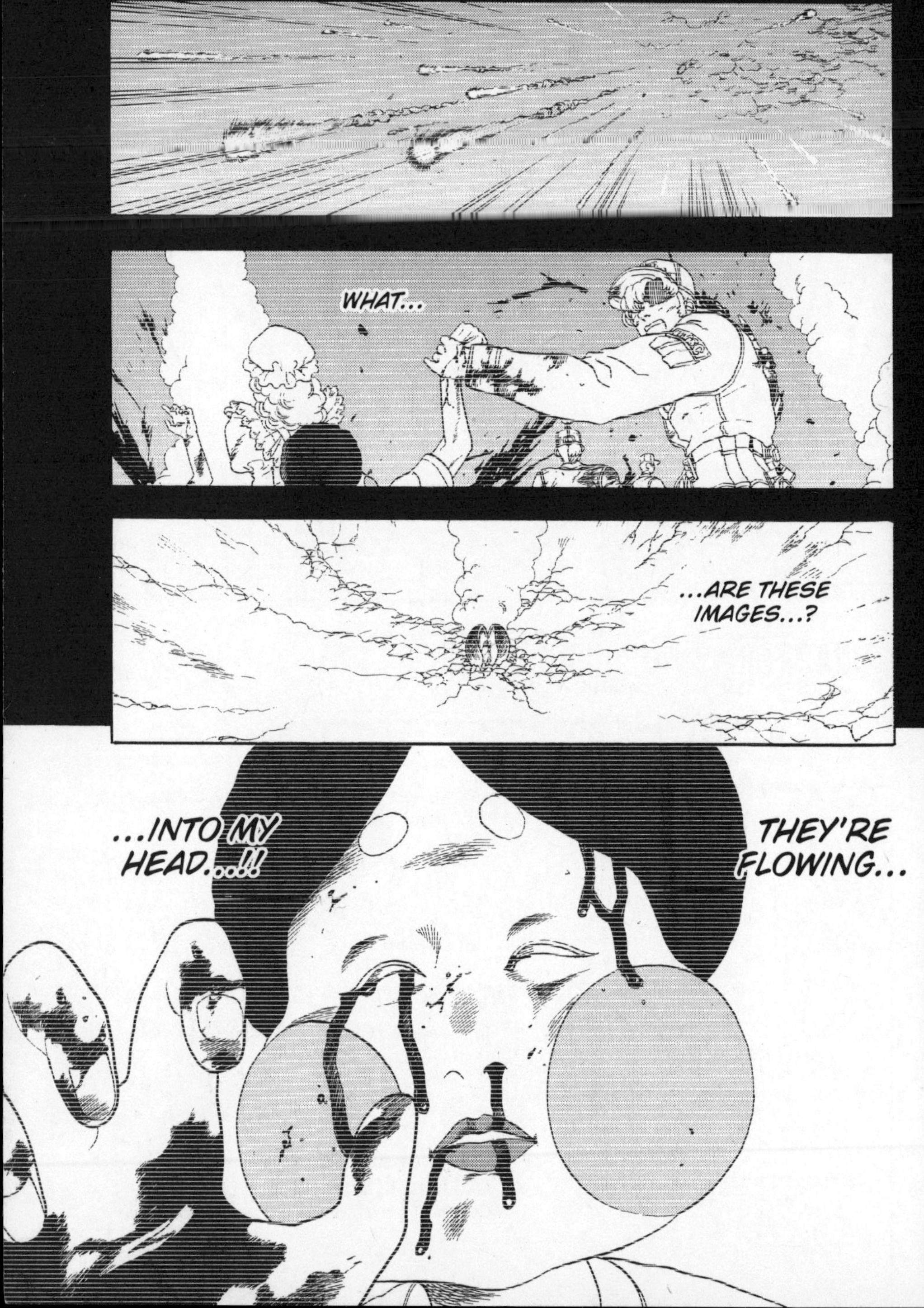
WHAT...
...ARE THESE IMAGES...?
THEY'RE FLOWING...
...INTO MY HEAD...!!

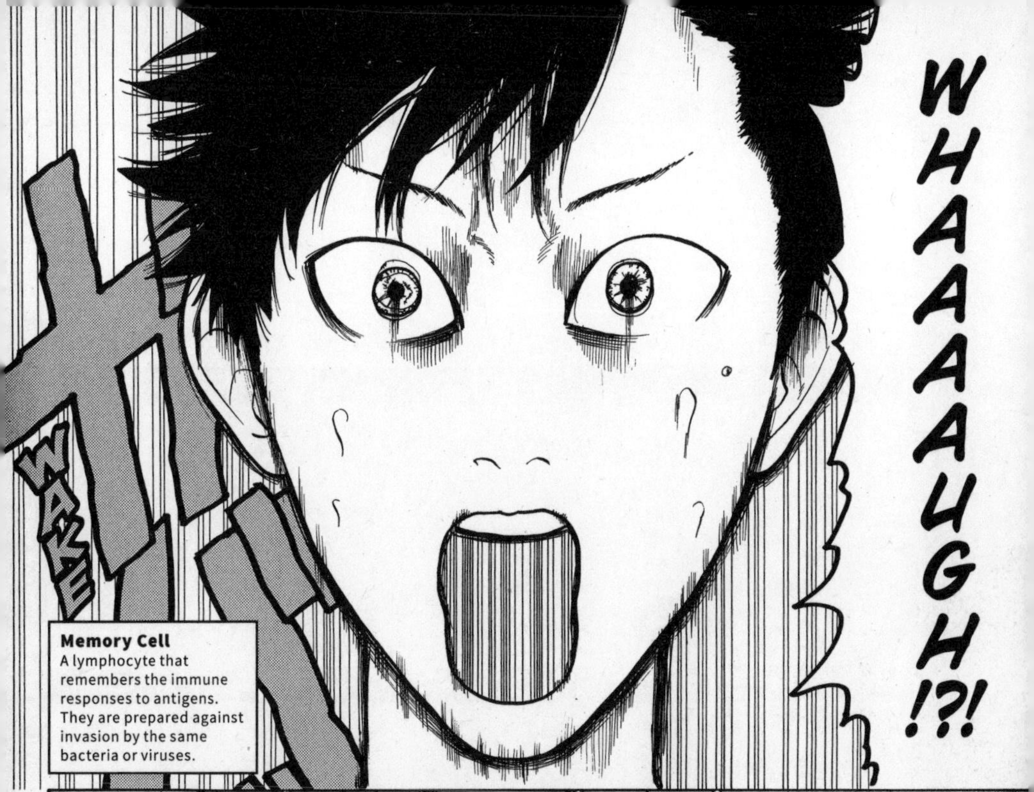
WHAAAAAUGH!?!
WAKE!!
Memory Cell
A lymphocyte that remembers the immune responses to antigens. They are prepared against invasion by the same bacteria or viruses.

CHAPTER 13: ACQUIRED IMMUNITY

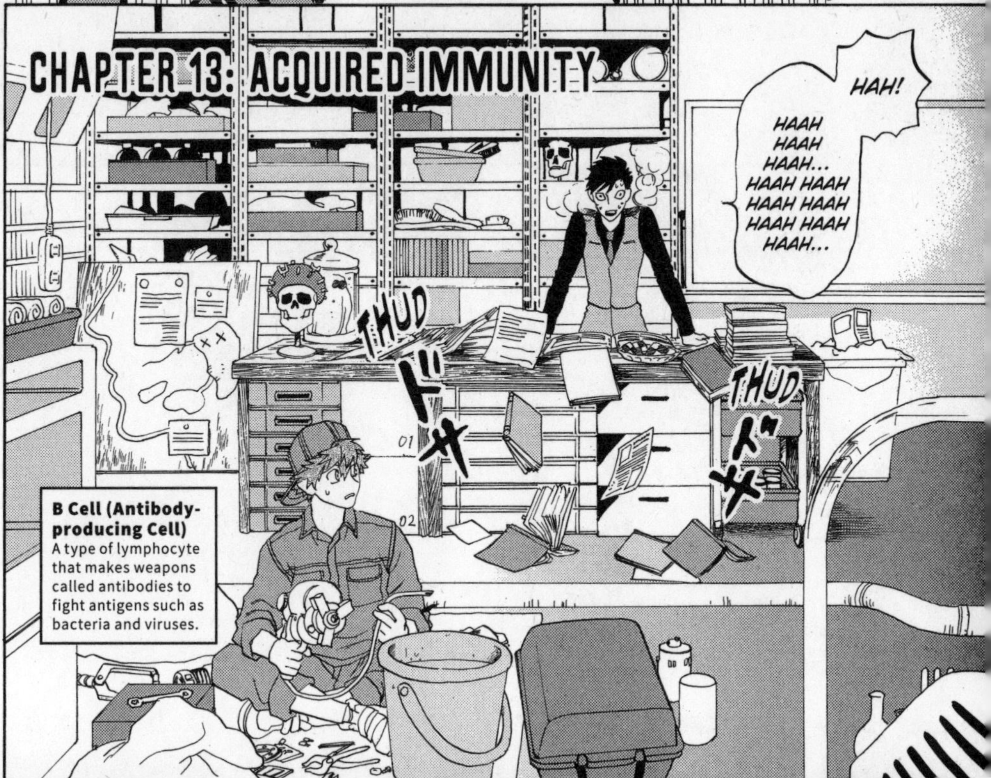
HAH!
HAAH HAAH HAAH... HAAH HAAH HAAH HAAH HAAH HAAH HAAH...
THUD
THUD
B Cell (Antibody-producing Cell)
A type of lymphocyte that makes weapons called antibodies to fight antigens such as bacteria and viruses.

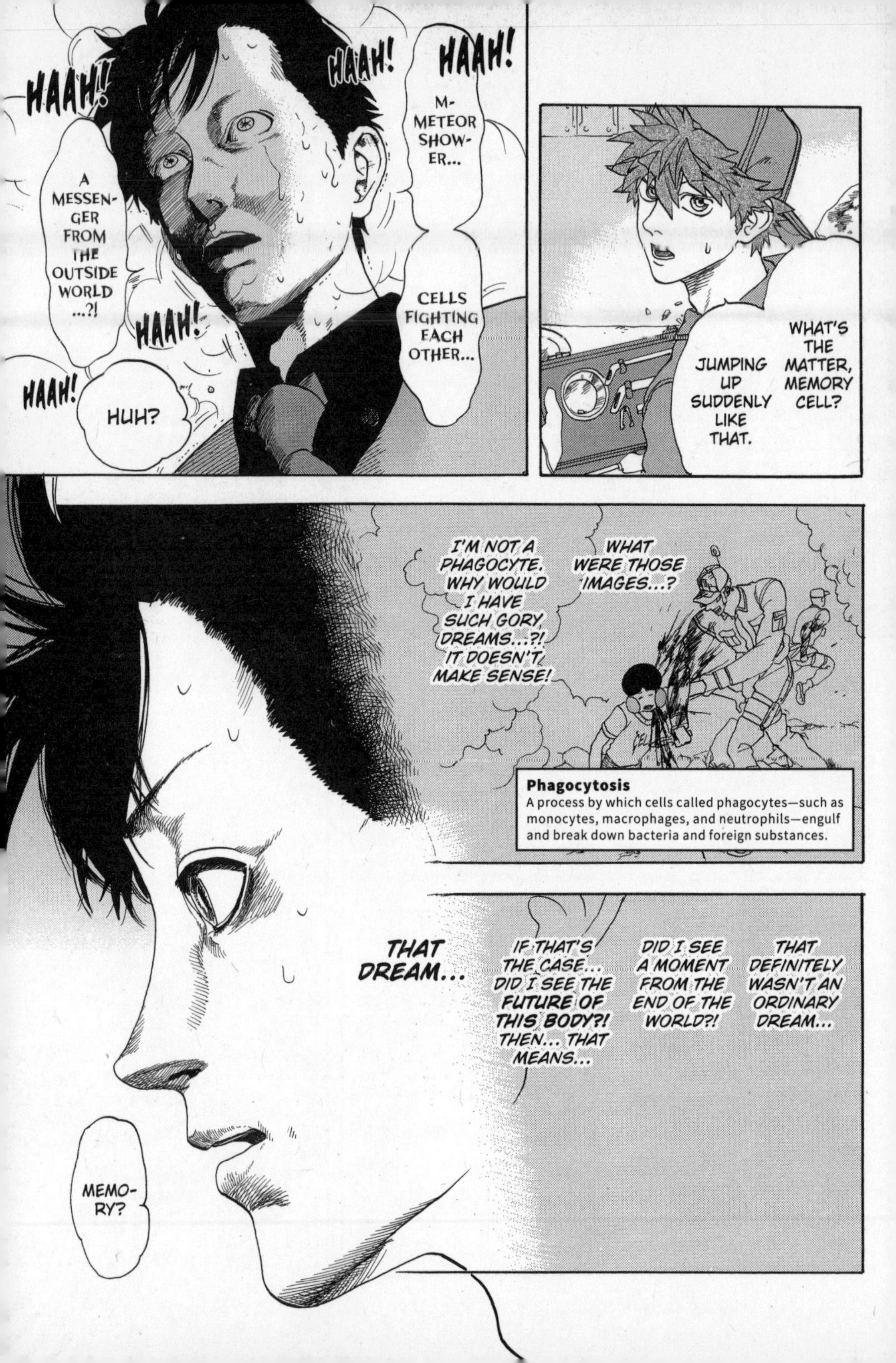
WHAT'S THE MATTER, MEMORY CELL?
JUMPING UP SUDDENLY LIKE THAT.
HAAH!
M-METEOR SHOWER...
HAAH!
CELLS FIGHTING EACH OTHER...
HAAH!
A MESSENGER FROM THE OUTSIDE WORLD ...?!
HAAH!
HAAH!
HUH?
WHAT WERE THOSE IMAGES...?
I'M NOT A PHAGOCYTE. WHY WOULD I HAVE SUCH GORY DREAMS...?! IT DOESN'T MAKE SENSE!
Phagocytosis
A process by which cells called phagocytes—such as monocytes, macrophages, and neutrophils—engulf and break down bacteria and foreign substances.
THAT DEFINITELY WASN'T AN ORDINARY DREAM...
DID I SEE A MOMENT FROM THE END OF THE WORLD?!
IF THAT'S THE CASE... DID I SEE THE FUTURE OF THIS BODY?! THEN... THAT MEANS...
THAT DREAM...
MEMORY?

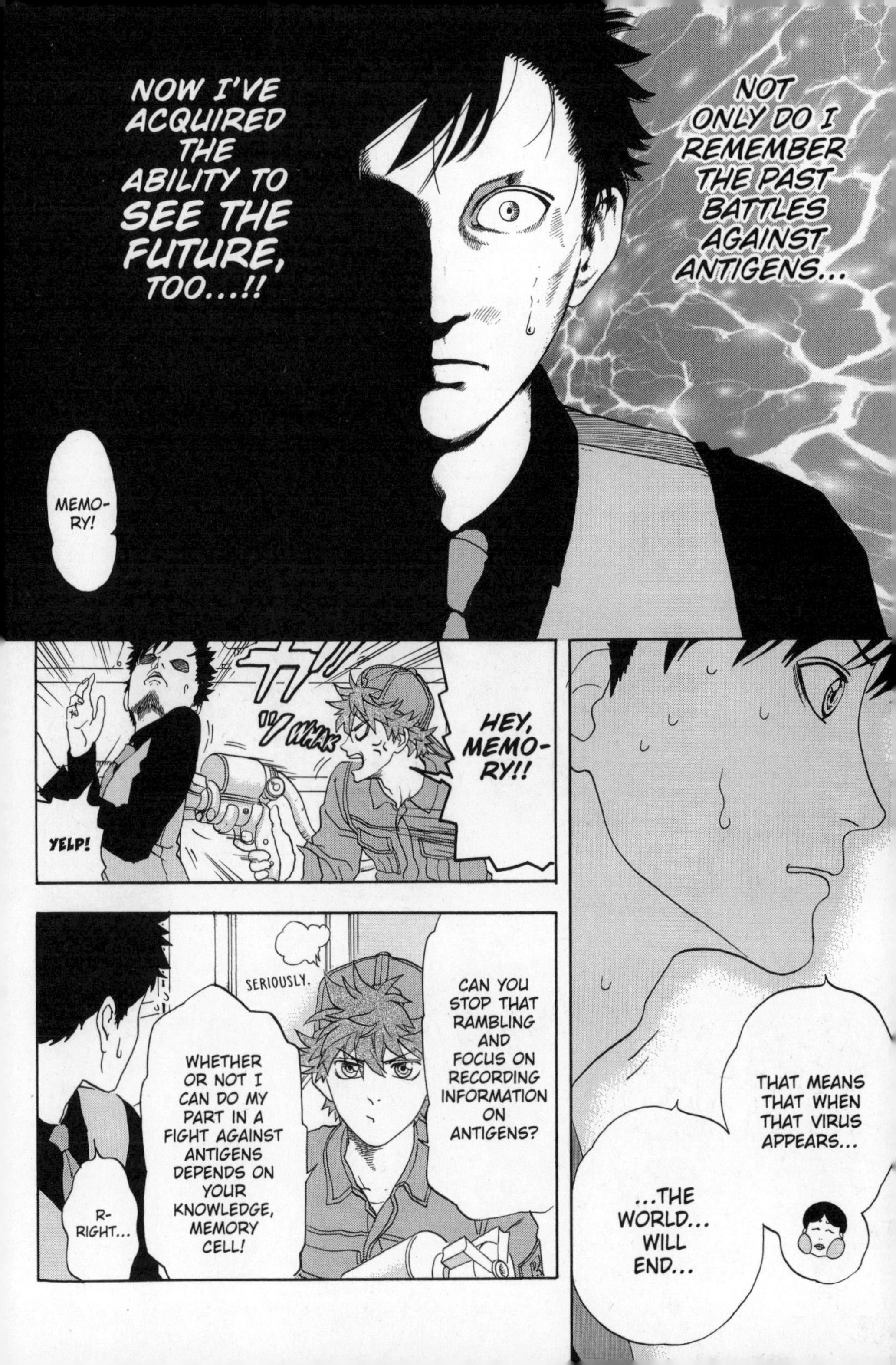
NOT ONLY DO I REMEMBER THE PAST BATTLES AGAINST ANTIGENS...
NOW I'VE ACQUIRED THE ABILITY TO SEE THE FUTURE, TOO...!!
MEMORY!
THAT MEANS THAT WHEN THAT VIRUS APPEARS...
...THE WORLD... WILL END...
HEY, MEMORY!!
WHAK
YELP!
CAN YOU STOP THAT RAMBLING AND FOCUS ON RECORDING INFORMATION ON ANTIGENS?
SERIOUSLY.
WHETHER OR NOT I CAN DO MY PART IN A FIGHT AGAINST ANTIGENS DEPENDS ON YOUR KNOWLEDGE, MEMORY CELL!
R-RIGHT...

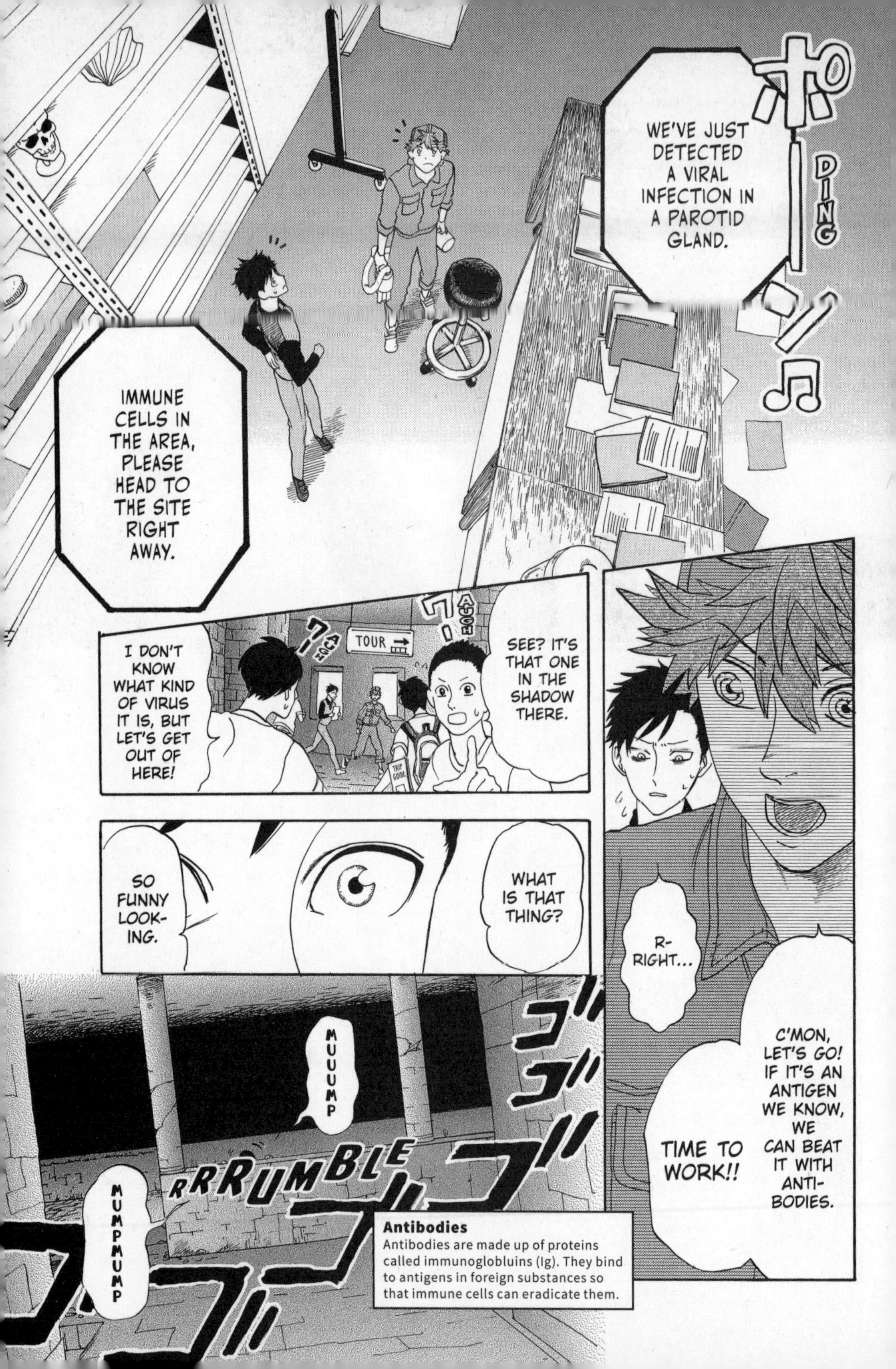
DING
WE'VE JUST DETECTED A VIRAL INFECTION IN A PAROTID GLAND.
IMMUNE CELLS IN THE AREA, PLEASE HEAD TO THE SITE RIGHT AWAY.
R-RIGHT...
C'MON, LET'S GO! IF IT'S AN ANTIGEN WE KNOW, WE CAN BEAT IT WITH ANTI-BODIES.
TIME TO WORK!!
AUCH
AUCH
TOUR
SEE? IT'S THAT ONE IN THE SHADOW THERE.
I DON'T KNOW WHAT KIND OF VIRUS IT IS, BUT LET'S GET OUT OF HERE!
TRIP GUIDE
WHAT IS THAT THING?
SO FUNNY LOOK-ING.
MUUUMP
RRRUMBLE
MUMPMUMP

Antibodies
Antibodies are made up of proteins called immunoglobluins (Ig). They bind to antigens in foreign substances so that immune cells can eradicate them.

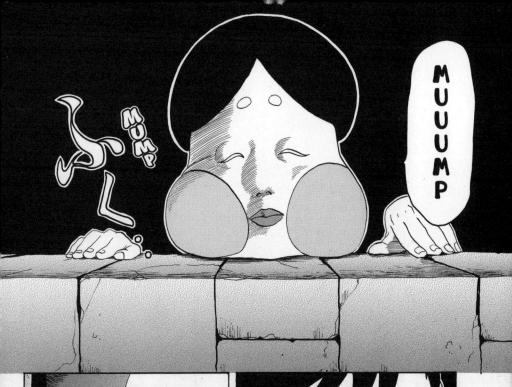

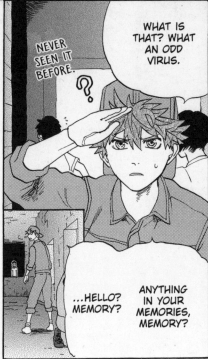

WHAT IS THAT? WHAT AN ODD VIRUS.

NEVER SEEN IT BEFORE.

...HELLO? MEMORY?

ANYTHING IN YOUR MEMORIES, MEMORY?

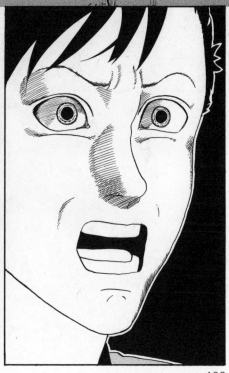

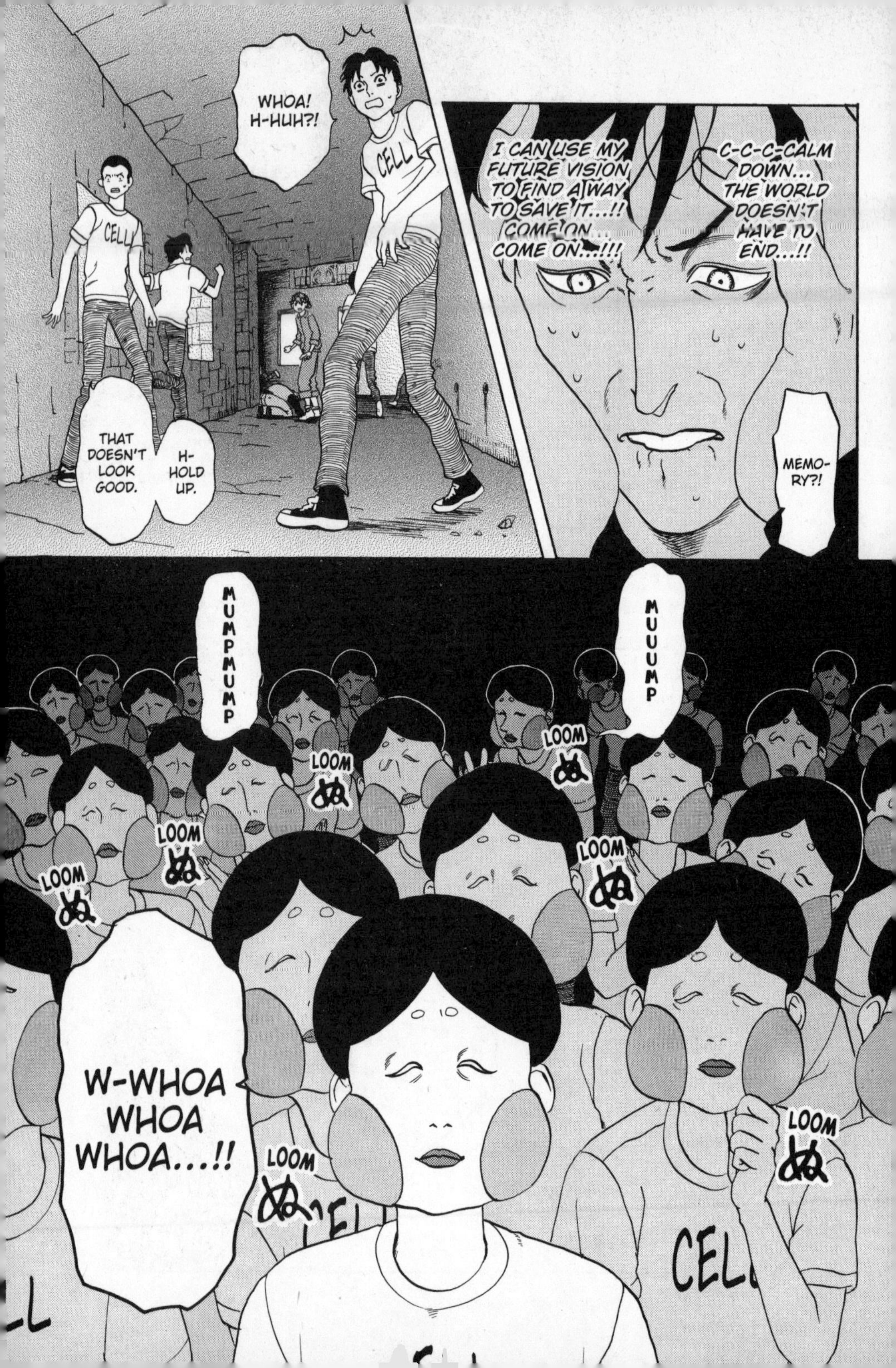
C-C-C-CALM DOWN... THE WORLD DOESN'T HAVE TO END...!!
I CAN USE MY FUTURE VISION TO FIND A WAY TO SAVE IT...!! COME ON... COME ON...!!!
MEMORY?!
WHOA! H-HUH?!
H-HOLD UP.
THAT DOESN'T LOOK GOOD.
MUUUMP
MUMPMUMP
LOOM ぬ
LOOM ぬ
LOOM ぬ
LOOM ぬ
LOOM ぬ
LOOM ぬ
LOOM ぬ
W-WHOA WHOA WHOA...!!
CELL
CELL

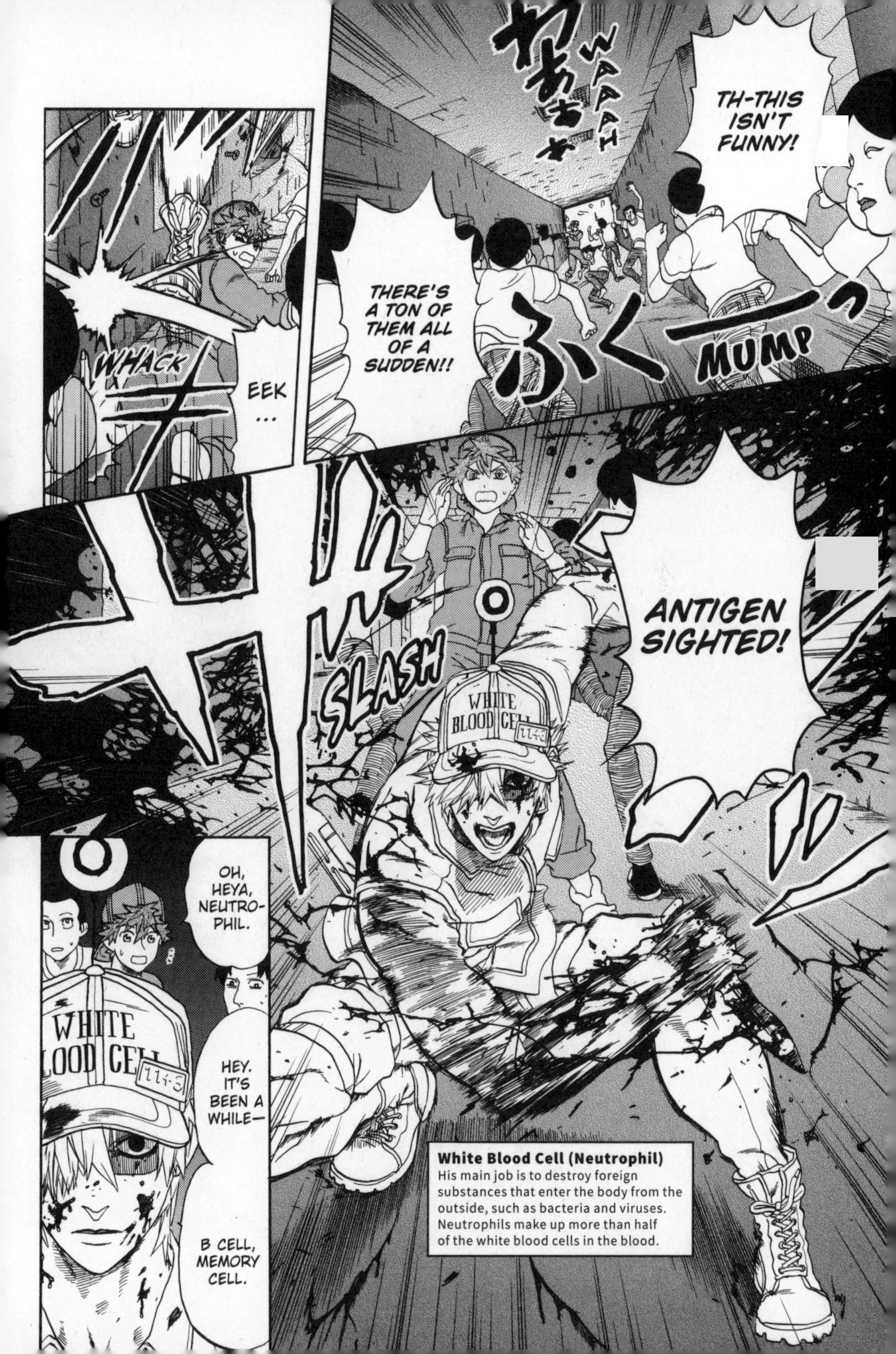
WAAAH
TH-THIS ISN'T FUNNY!
THERE'S A TON OF THEM ALL OF A SUDDEN!!
ふくーっ
MUMP
WHACK
EEK ...
ANTIGEN SIGHTED!
SLASH
WHITE BLOOD CELL
1146
White Blood Cell (Neutrophil)
His main job is to destroy foreign substances that enter the body from the outside, such as bacteria and viruses. Neutrophils make up more than half of the white blood cells in the blood.
OH, HEYA, NEUTROPHIL.
HEY. IT'S BEEN A WHILE—
B CELL, MEMORY CELL.
WHITE BLOOD CELL
1146

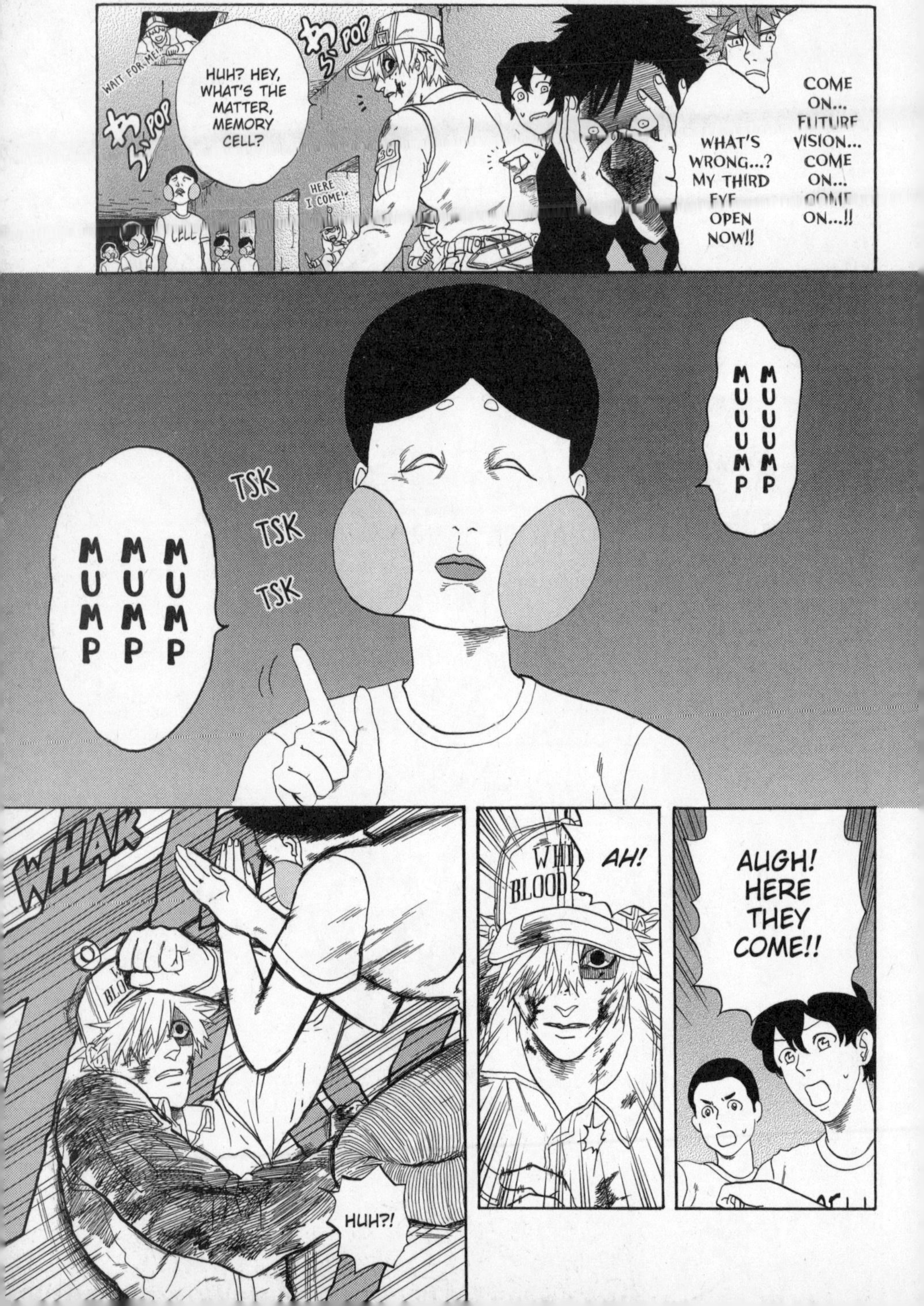
COME ON... FUTURE VISION... COME ON... COME ON...!!
WHAT'S WRONG...? MY THIRD EYE OPEN NOW!!
わ POP
HUH? HEY, WHAT'S THE MATTER, MEMORY CELL?
HERE I COME!
WAIT FOR ME!
わ POP
MUUUMP MUUUMP
TSK TSK TSK
MUMP MUMP MUMP
AUGH! HERE THEY COME!!
AH!
WHAK
HUH?!

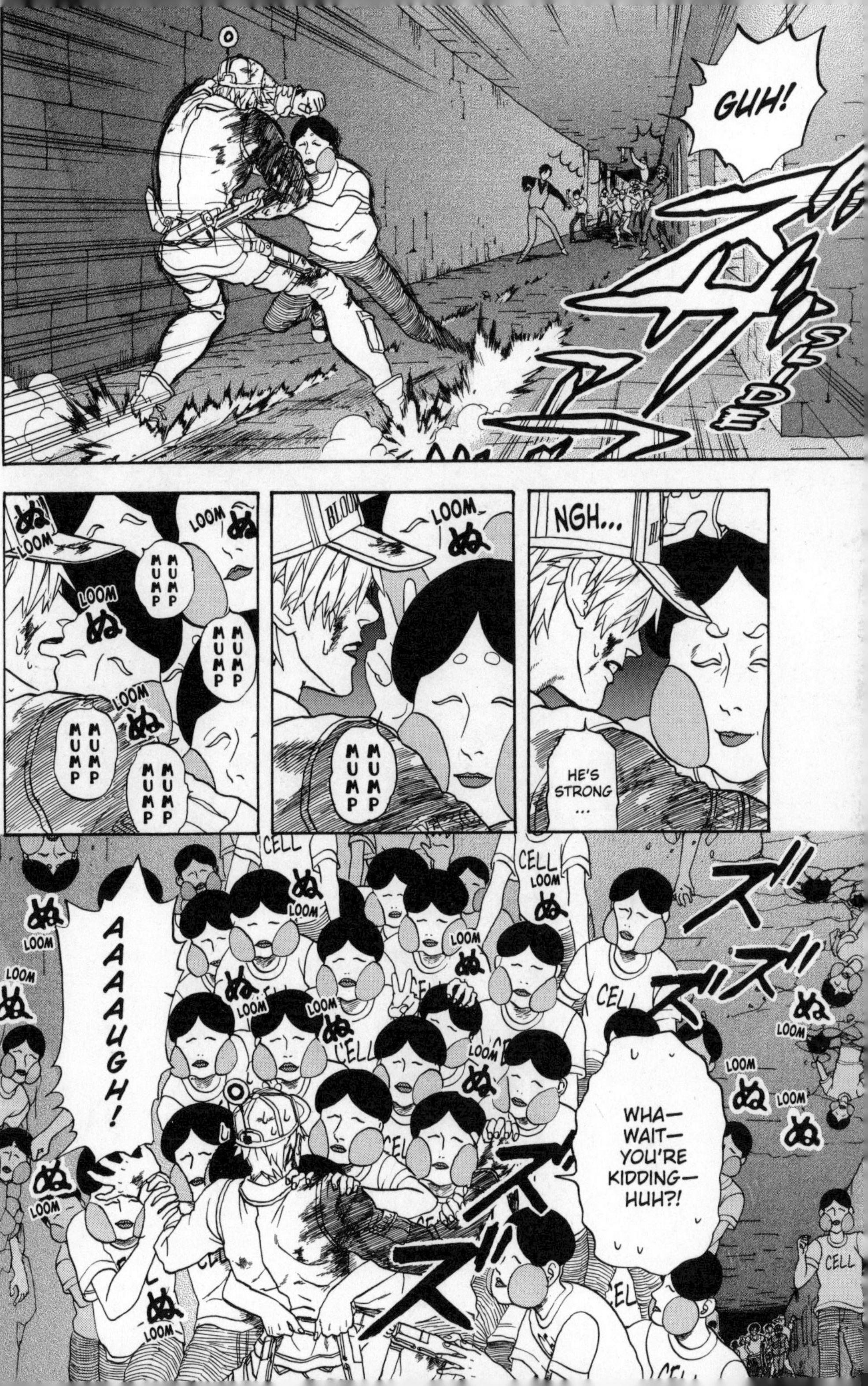

GUH!
SLIDE
NGH...
HE'S STRONG ...
LOOM ぬ
MUMP MUMP
MUMP MUMP
LOOM ぬ
LOOM ぬ
LOOM ぬ
LOOM ぬ
MUMP MUMP
MUMP MUMP
MUMP MUMP
MUMP MUMP
LOOM ぬ
WHA— WAIT— YOU'RE KIDDING— HUH?!
LOOM ぬ
LOOM ぬ
ぬ LOOM
AAAAUGH!
ぬ LOOM
LOOM ぬ
ぬ LOOM
ぬ LOOM

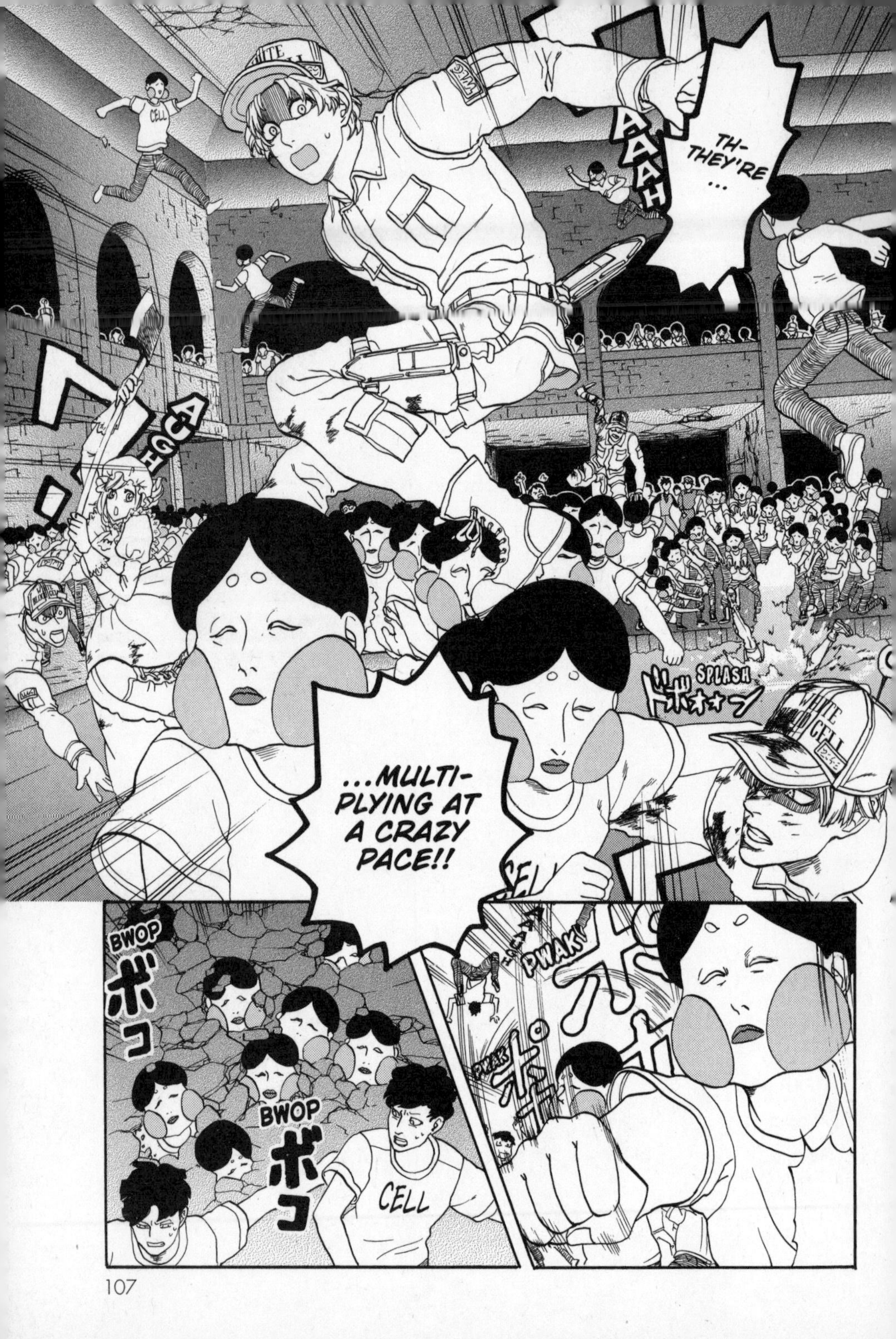
AAAH
TH-THEY'RE ...
AUGH
SPLASH
...MULTI-PLYING AT A CRAZY PACE!!
PWAK
PWAK
BWOP
BWOP

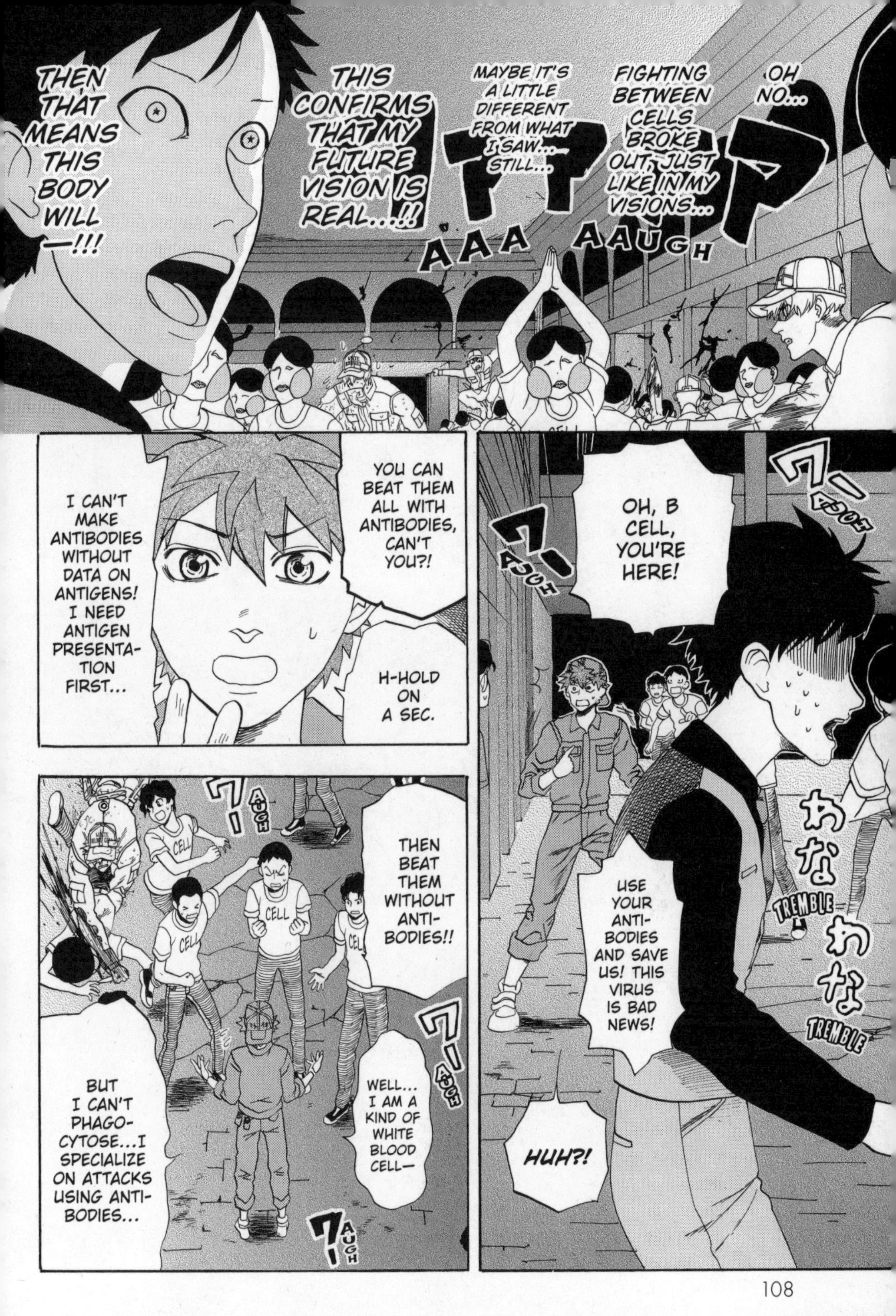
OH NO...
FIGHTING BETWEEN CELLS BROKE OUT, JUST LIKE IN MY VISIONS...
MAYBE IT'S A LITTLE DIFFERENT FROM WHAT I SAW... STILL...
THIS CONFIRMS THAT MY FUTURE VISION IS REAL...!!
THEN THAT MEANS THIS BODY WILL—!!!
AAA AAUGH
OH, B CELL, YOU'RE HERE!
AUGH
AUGH
USE YOUR ANTIBODIES AND SAVE US! THIS VIRUS IS BAD NEWS!
わなわな
TREMBLE TREMBLE
HUH?!
YOU CAN BEAT THEM ALL WITH ANTIBODIES, CAN'T YOU?!
H-HOLD ON A SEC.
I CAN'T MAKE ANTIBODIES WITHOUT DATA ON ANTIGENS! I NEED ANTIGEN PRESENTATION FIRST...
AUGH
THEN BEAT THEM WITHOUT ANTIBODIES!!
AUGH
WELL... I AM A KIND OF WHITE BLOOD CELL—
BUT I CAN'T PHAGOCYTOSE...I SPECIALIZE ON ATTACKS USING ANTIBODIES...
AUGH

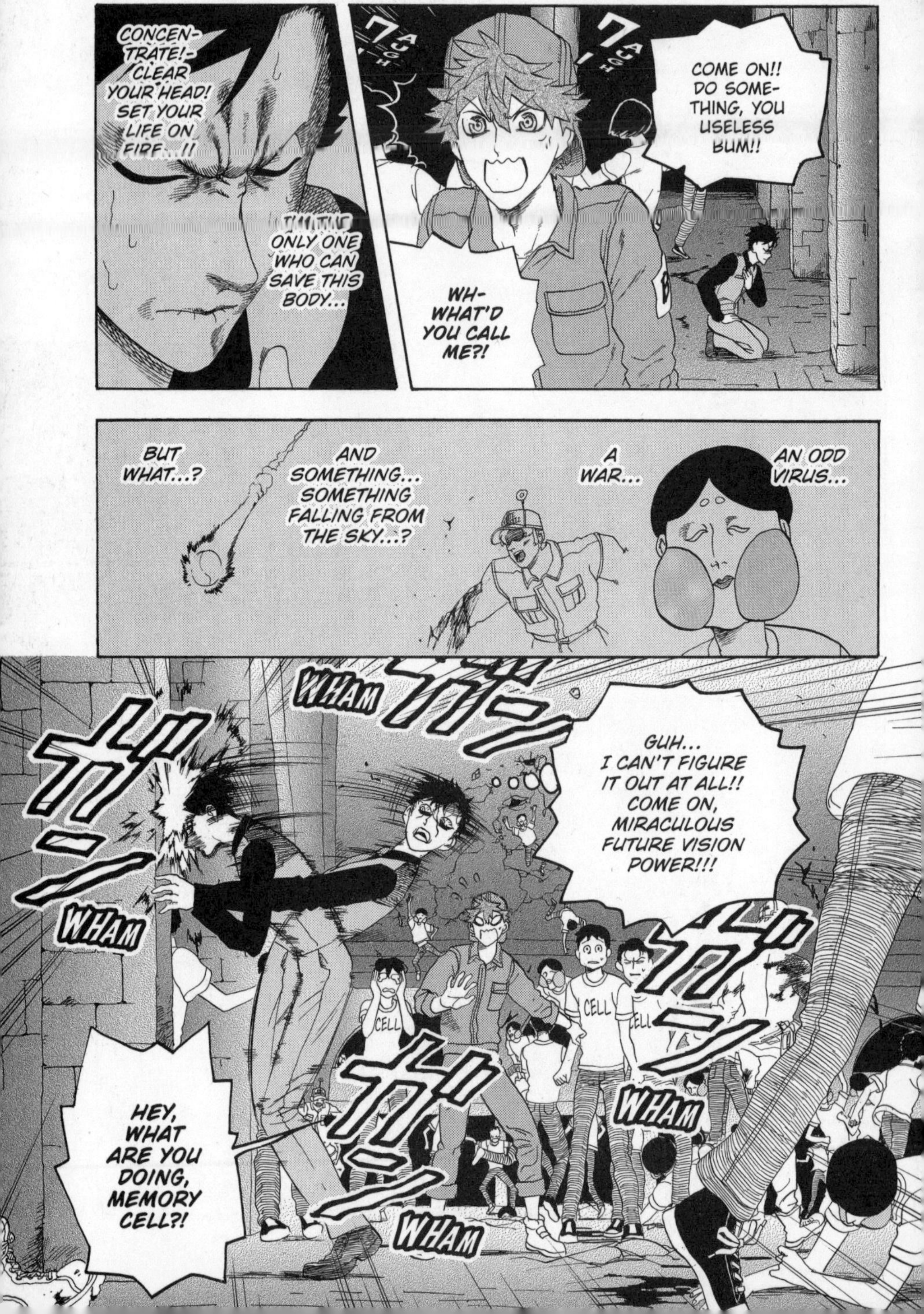
AUGH
AUGH
COME ON!! DO SOMETHING, YOU USELESS BUM!!
WH- WHAT'D YOU CALL ME?!
CONCEN- TRATE!- CLEAR YOUR HEAD! SET YOUR LIFE ON FIRE...!!
ONLY ONE WHO CAN SAVE THIS BODY...
AN ODD VIRUS...
A WAR...
AND SOMETHING... SOMETHING FALLING FROM THE SKY...?
BUT WHAT...?
WHAM
GUH... I CAN'T FIGURE IT OUT AT ALL!! COME ON, MIRACULOUS FUTURE VISION POWER!!!
WHAM
WHAM
CELL
CELL
WHAM
HEY, WHAT ARE YOU DOING, MEMORY CELL?!

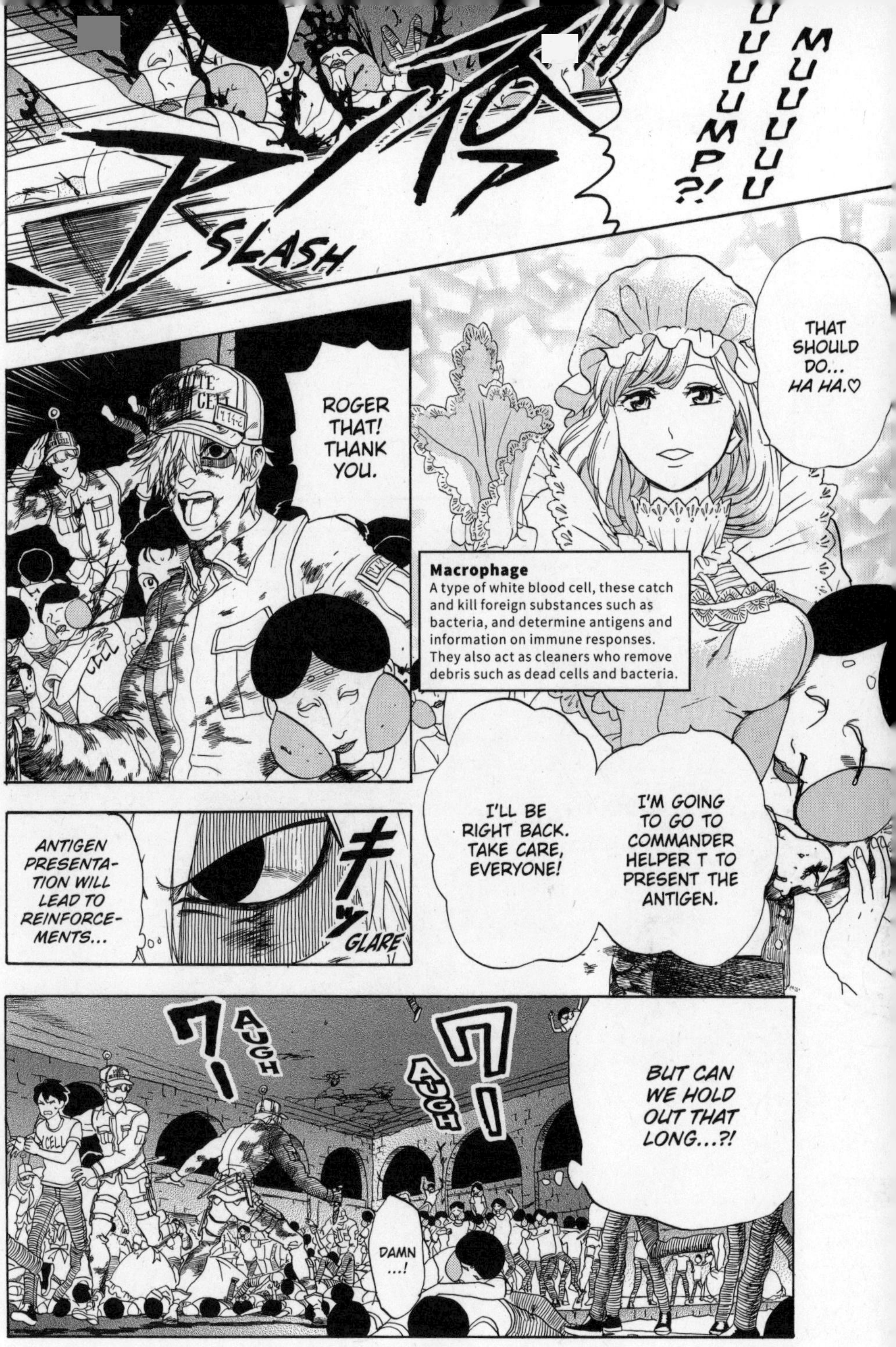
MUUUUUUU
UUUUUMP?!
SLASH
THAT SHOULD DO... HA HA.♡
Macrophage
A type of white blood cell, these catch and kill foreign substances such as bacteria, and determine antigens and information on immune responses. They also act as cleaners who remove debris such as dead cells and bacteria.
I'M GOING TO GO TO COMMANDER HELPER T TO PRESENT THE ANTIGEN.
I'LL BE RIGHT BACK. TAKE CARE, EVERYONE!
ROGER THAT! THANK YOU.
GLARE
ANTIGEN PRESENTATION WILL LEAD TO REINFORCEMENTS...
BUT CAN WE HOLD OUT THAT LONG...?!
AUGH
AUGH
DAMN...!

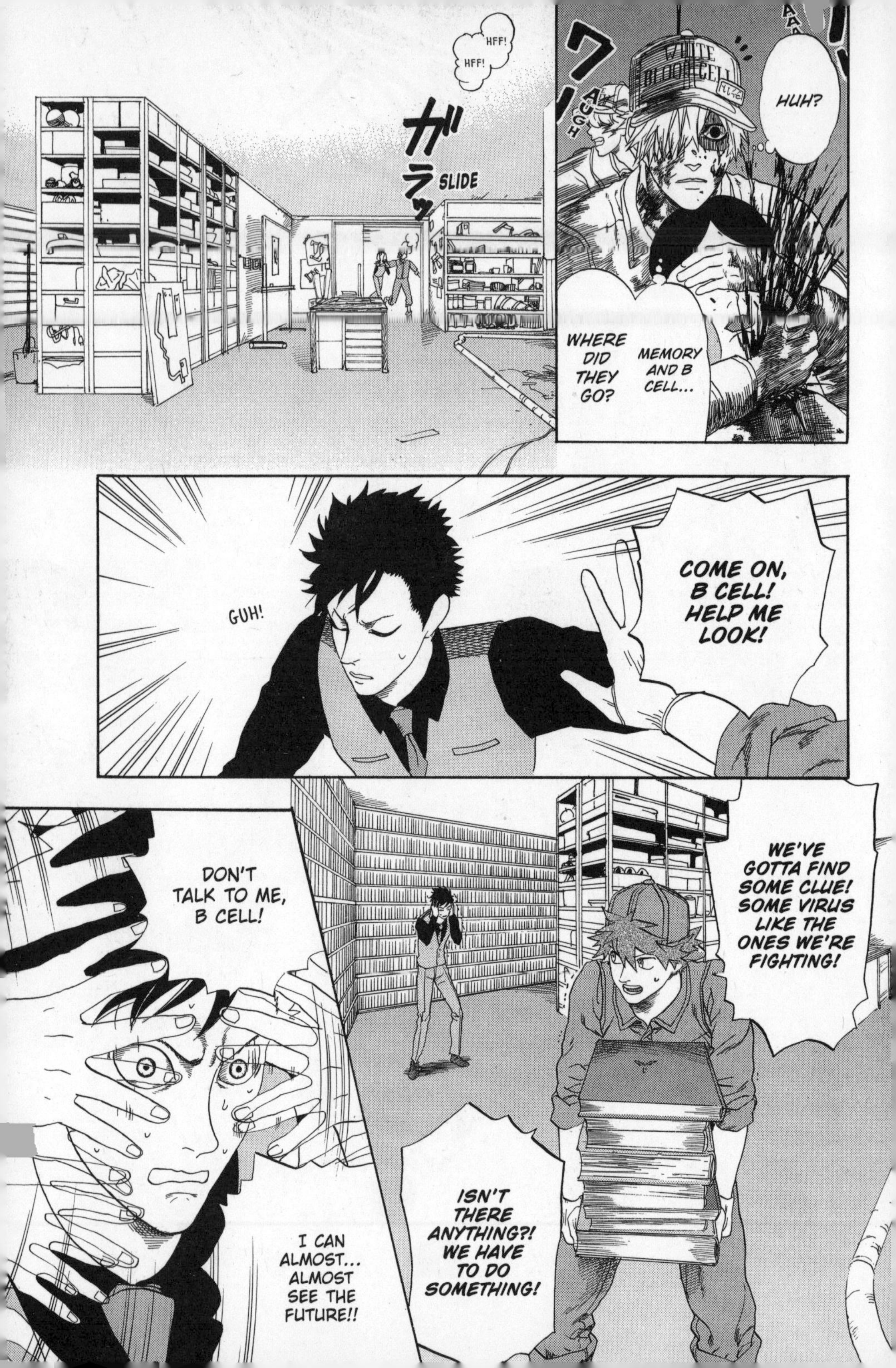
AUGH
HUH?
WHERE DID THEY GO? MEMORY AND B CELL...
HFF! HFF!
ガラッ SLIDE
COME ON, B CELL! HELP ME LOOK!
GUH!
WE'VE GOTTA FIND SOME CLUE! SOME VIRUS LIKE THE ONES WE'RE FIGHTING!
ISN'T THERE ANYTHING?! WE HAVE TO DO SOMETHING!
DON'T TALK TO ME, B CELL!
I CAN ALMOST... ALMOST SEE THE FUTURE!!

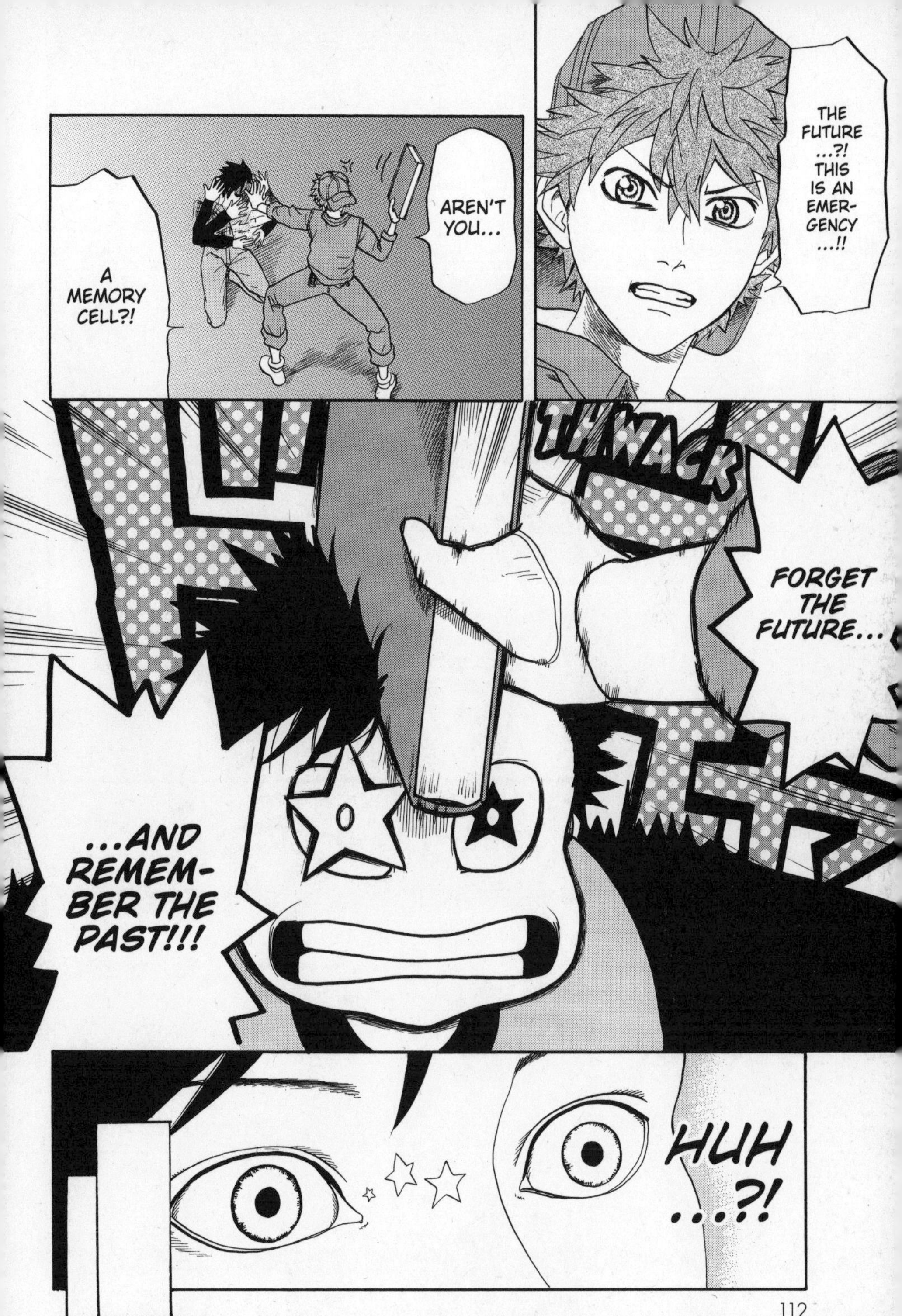
THE FUTURE ...?! THIS IS AN EMERGENCY ...!!
AREN'T YOU...
A MEMORY CELL?!
THWACK
FORGET THE FUTURE...
...AND REMEMBER THE PAST!!!
HUH ...?!

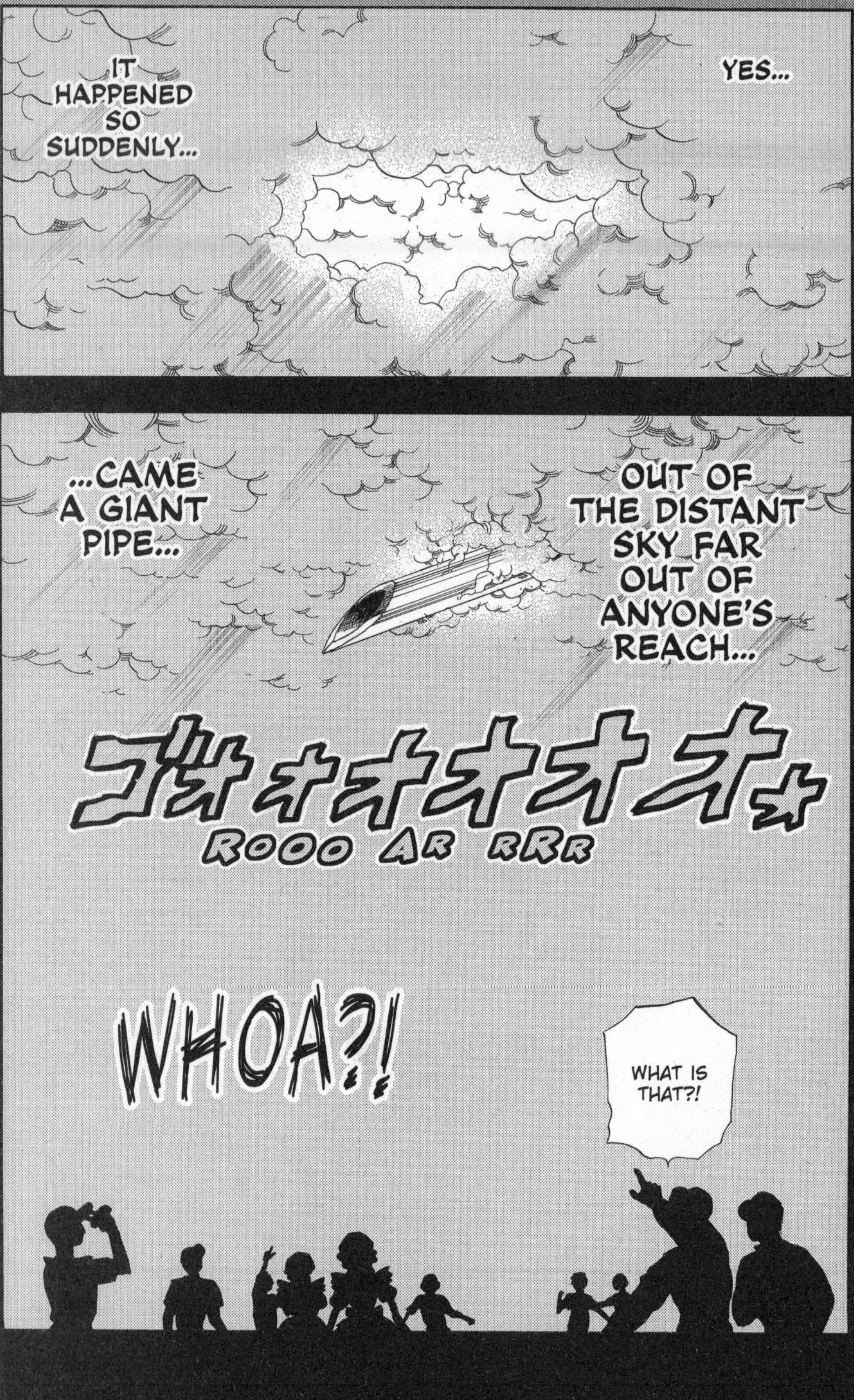
YES...
IT HAPPENED SO SUDDENLY...
OUT OF THE DISTANT SKY FAR OUT OF ANYONE'S REACH...
...CAME A GIANT PIPE...
ゴォォオオオォ
ROOO AR RRR
WHAT IS THAT?!
WHOA?!

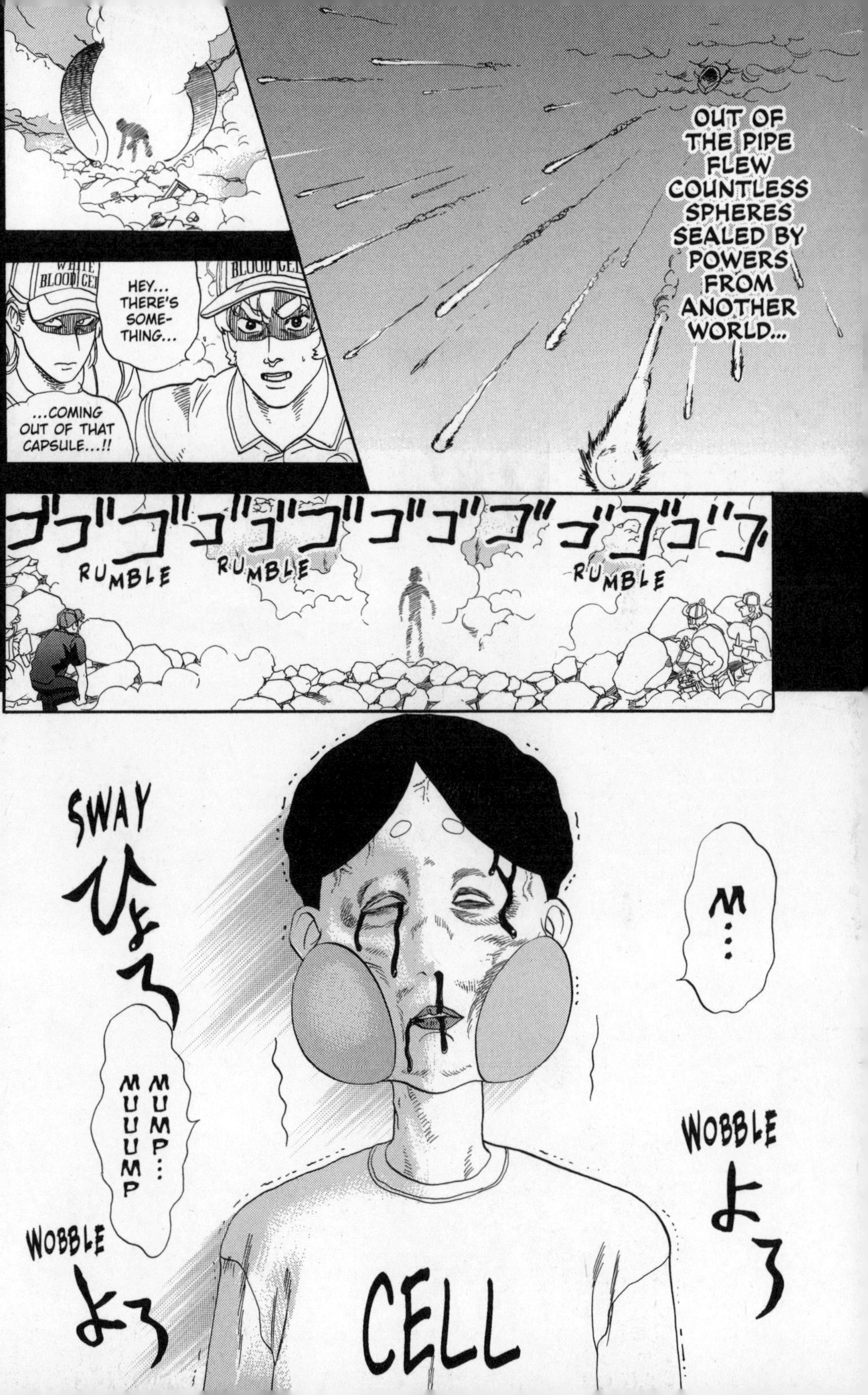
OUT OF THE PIPE FLEW COUNTLESS SPHERES SEALED BY POWERS FROM ANOTHER WORLD...
HEY... THERE'S SOME-THING...
...COMING OUT OF THAT CAPSULE...!!
ゴゴゴゴゴゴゴゴゴゴゴ
RUMBLE RUMBLE RUMBLE
M...
WOBBLE
よろ
SWAY
ひょろ
MUMP... MUUUMP
WOBBLE
よろ
CELL

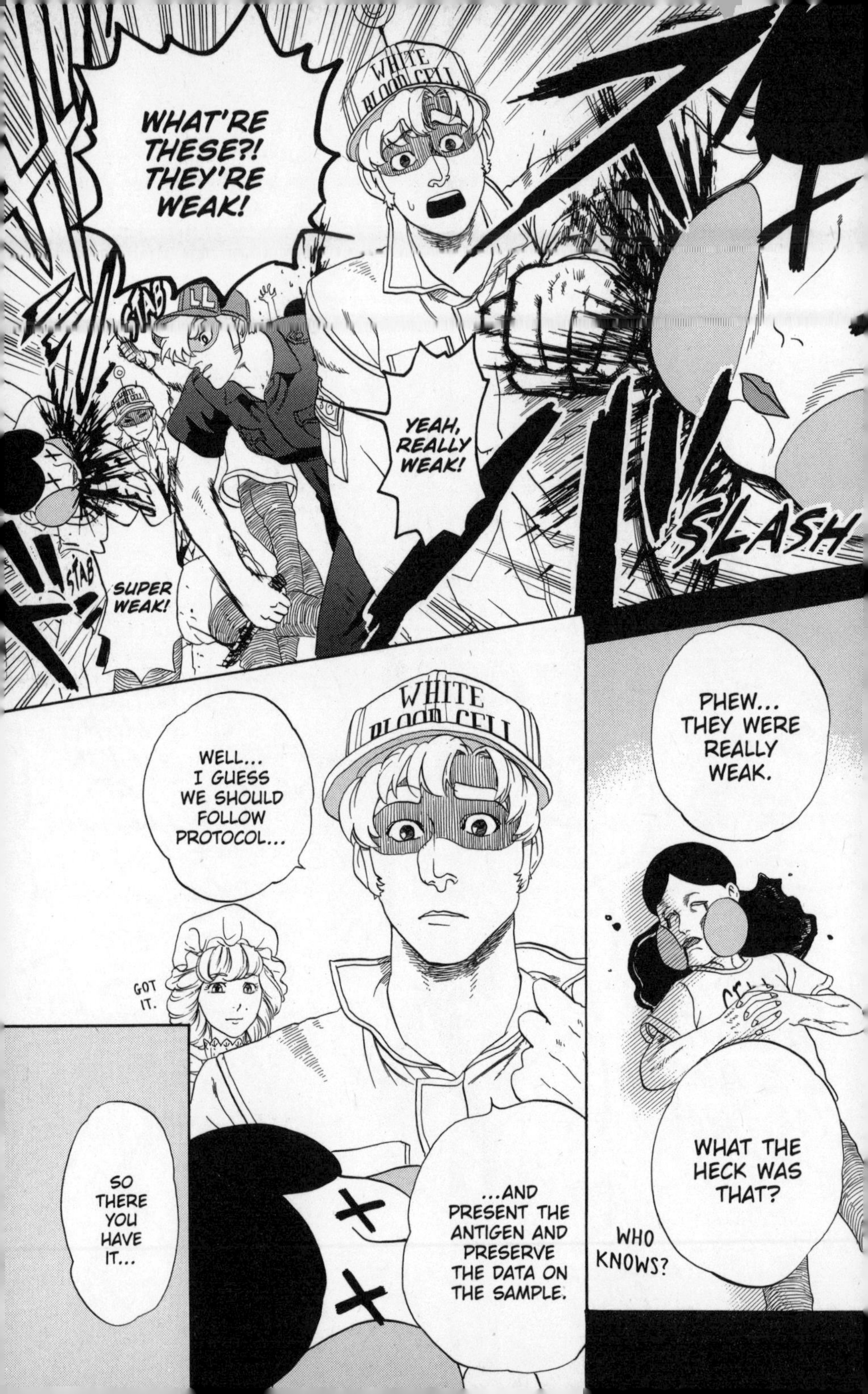
WHAT'RE THESE?! THEY'RE WEAK!
SLASH
YEAH, REALLY WEAK!
STAB
STAB
SUPER WEAK!
PHEW... THEY WERE REALLY WEAK.
WHAT THE HECK WAS THAT?
WHO KNOWS?
WELL... I GUESS WE SHOULD FOLLOW PROTOCOL...
GOT IT.
...AND PRESENT THE ANTIGEN AND PRESERVE THE DATA ON THE SAMPLE.
SO THERE YOU HAVE IT...

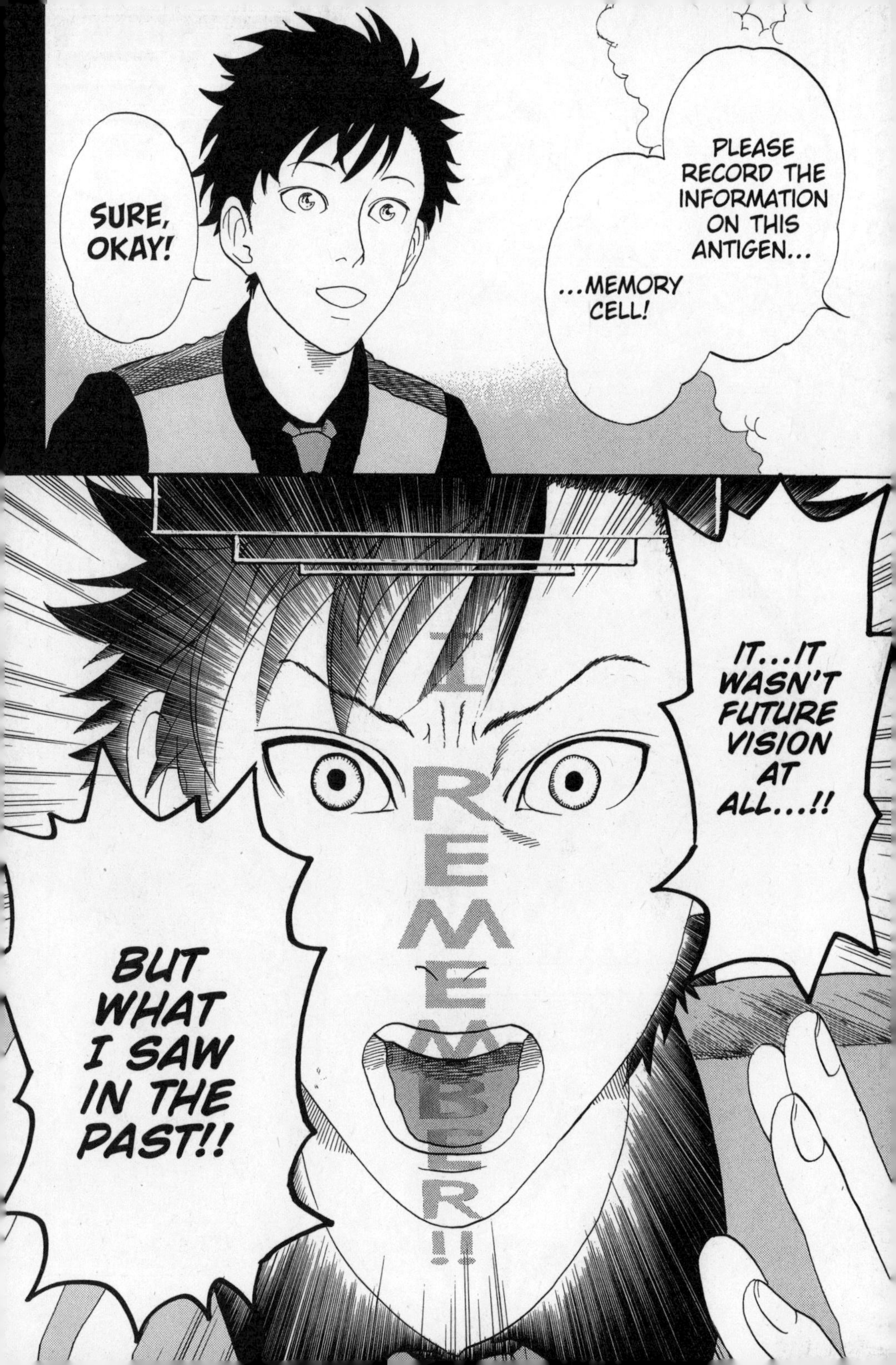
PLEASE RECORD THE INFORMATION ON THIS ANTIGEN... ...MEMORY CELL!
SURE, OKAY!
IT...IT WASN'T FUTURE VISION AT ALL...!!
I REMEMBER!!
BUT WHAT I SAW IN THE PAST!!

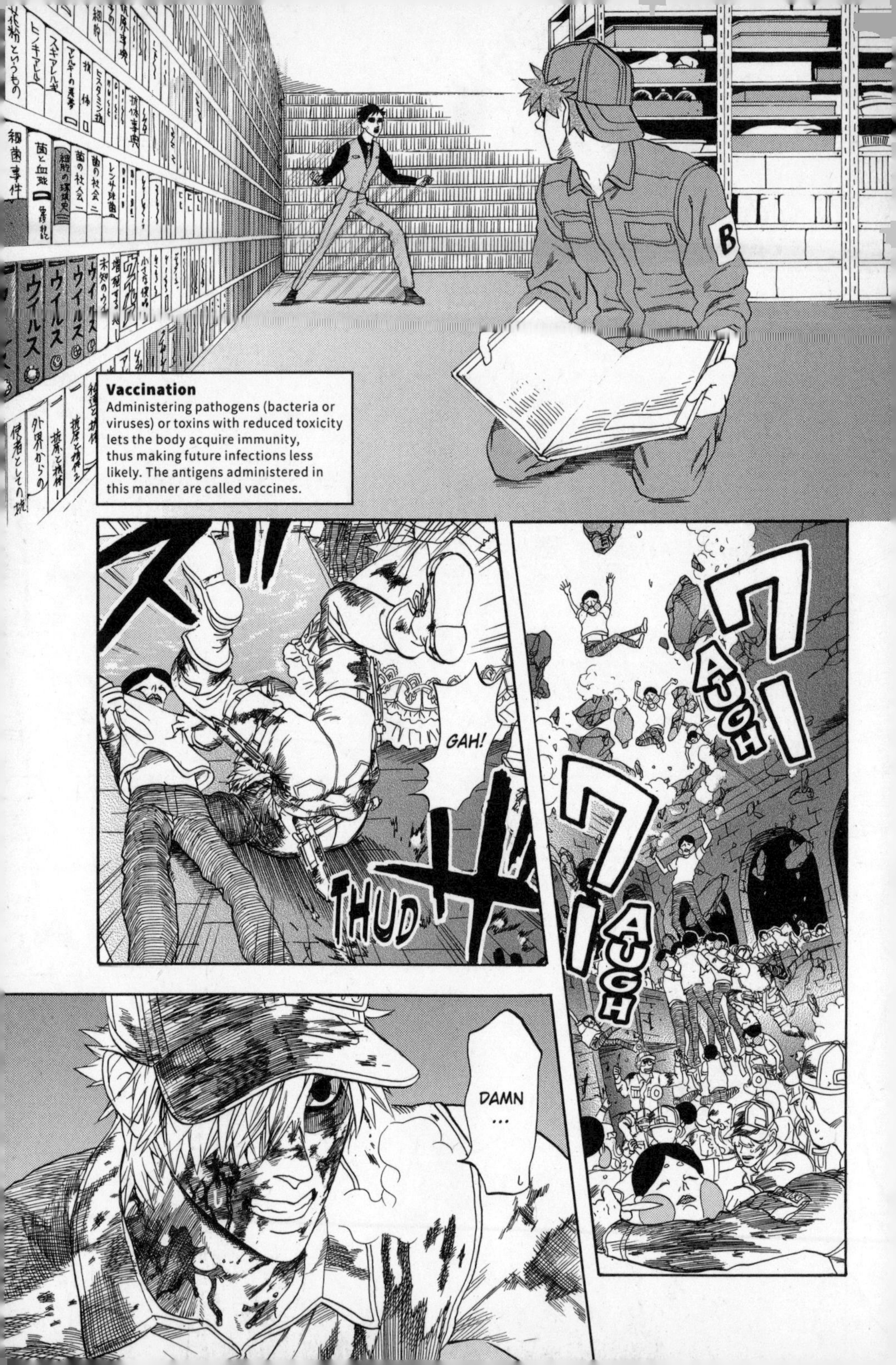
Vaccination
Administering pathogens (bacteria or viruses) or toxins with reduced toxicity lets the body acquire immunity, thus making future infections less likely. The antigens administered in this manner are called vaccines.
AUGH
AUGH
GAH!
THUD
DAMN ...

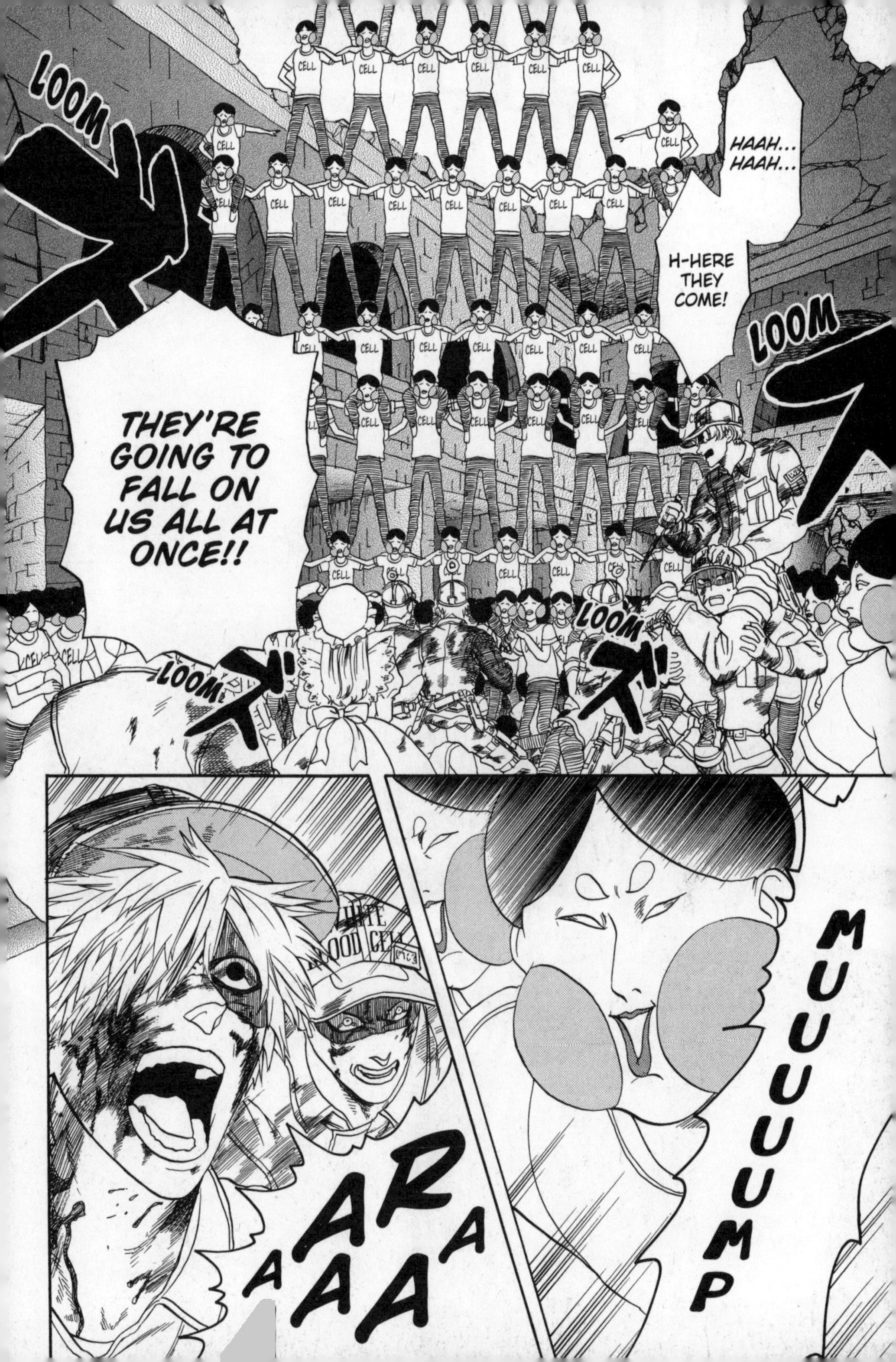
HAAH... HAAH...
H-HERE THEY COME!
LOOM
LOOM
THEY'RE GOING TO FALL ON US ALL AT ONCE!!
LOOM
LOOM
MUUUUUUMP
AAAARAAA

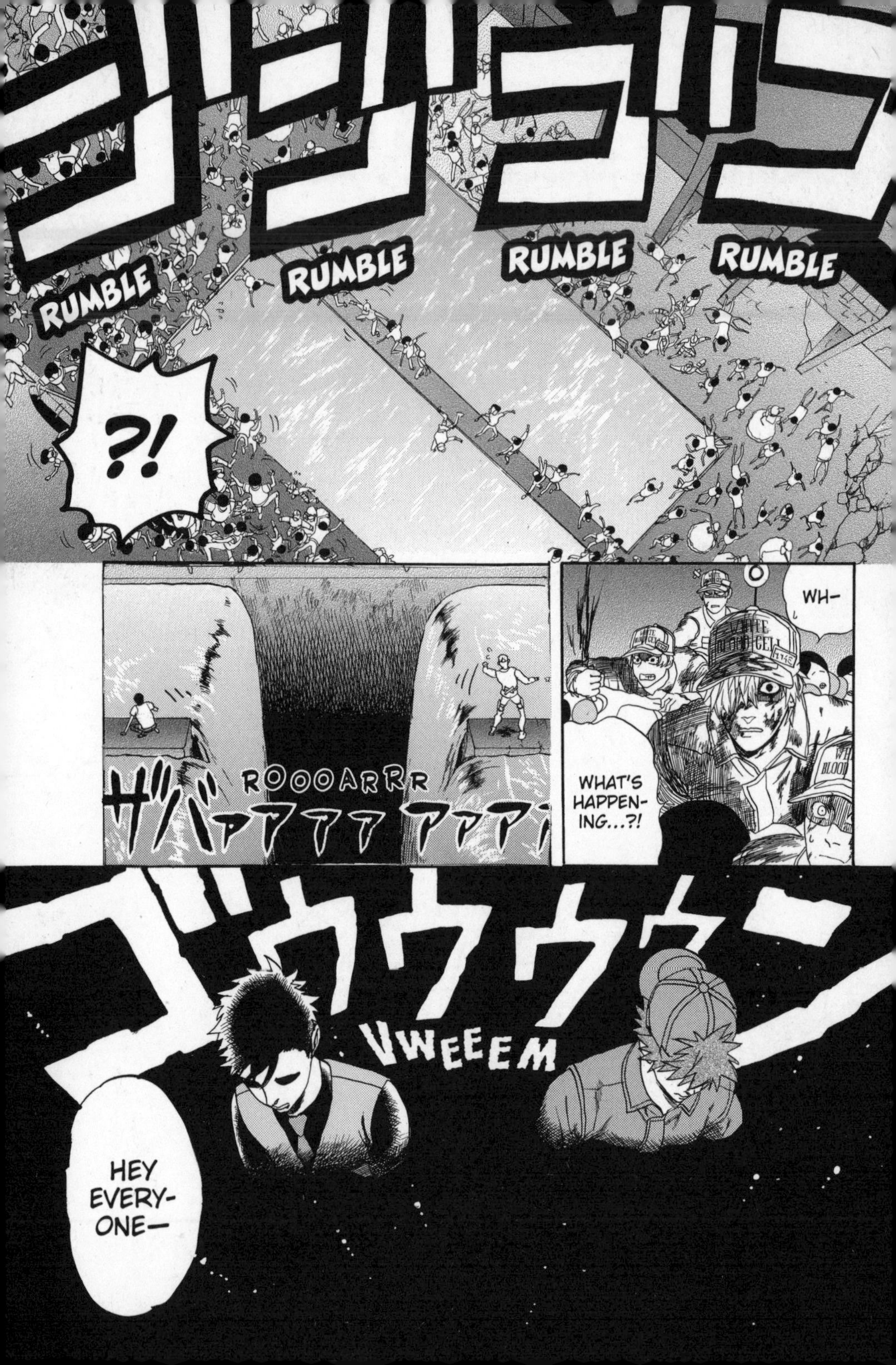
RUMBLE
RUMBLE
RUMBLE
RUMBLE
?!
WH-
WHAT'S HAPPEN-ING...?!
ROOOARRR
VWEEEM
HEY EVERY-ONE—

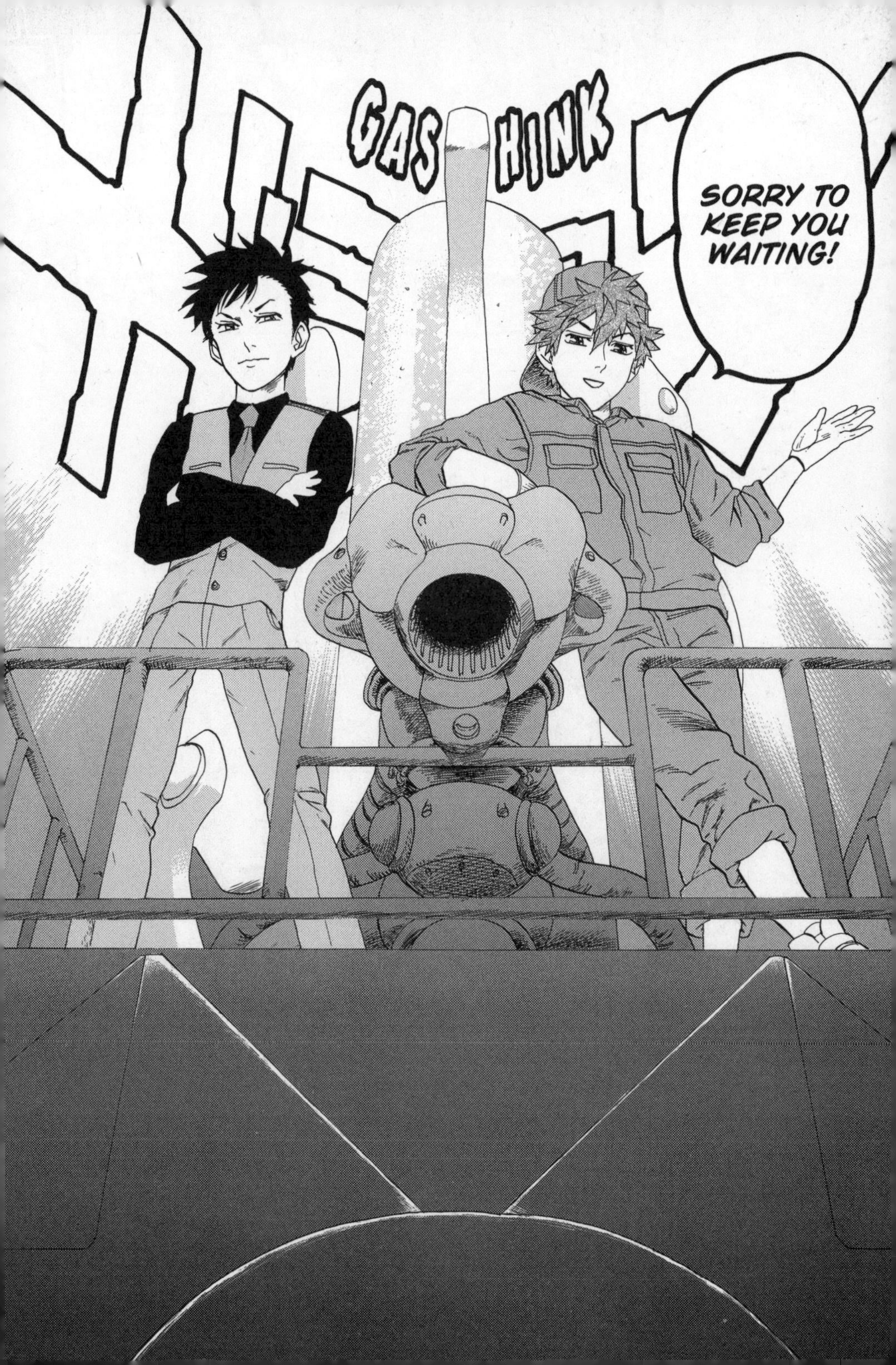
GASHINK
SORRY TO KEEP YOU WAITING!

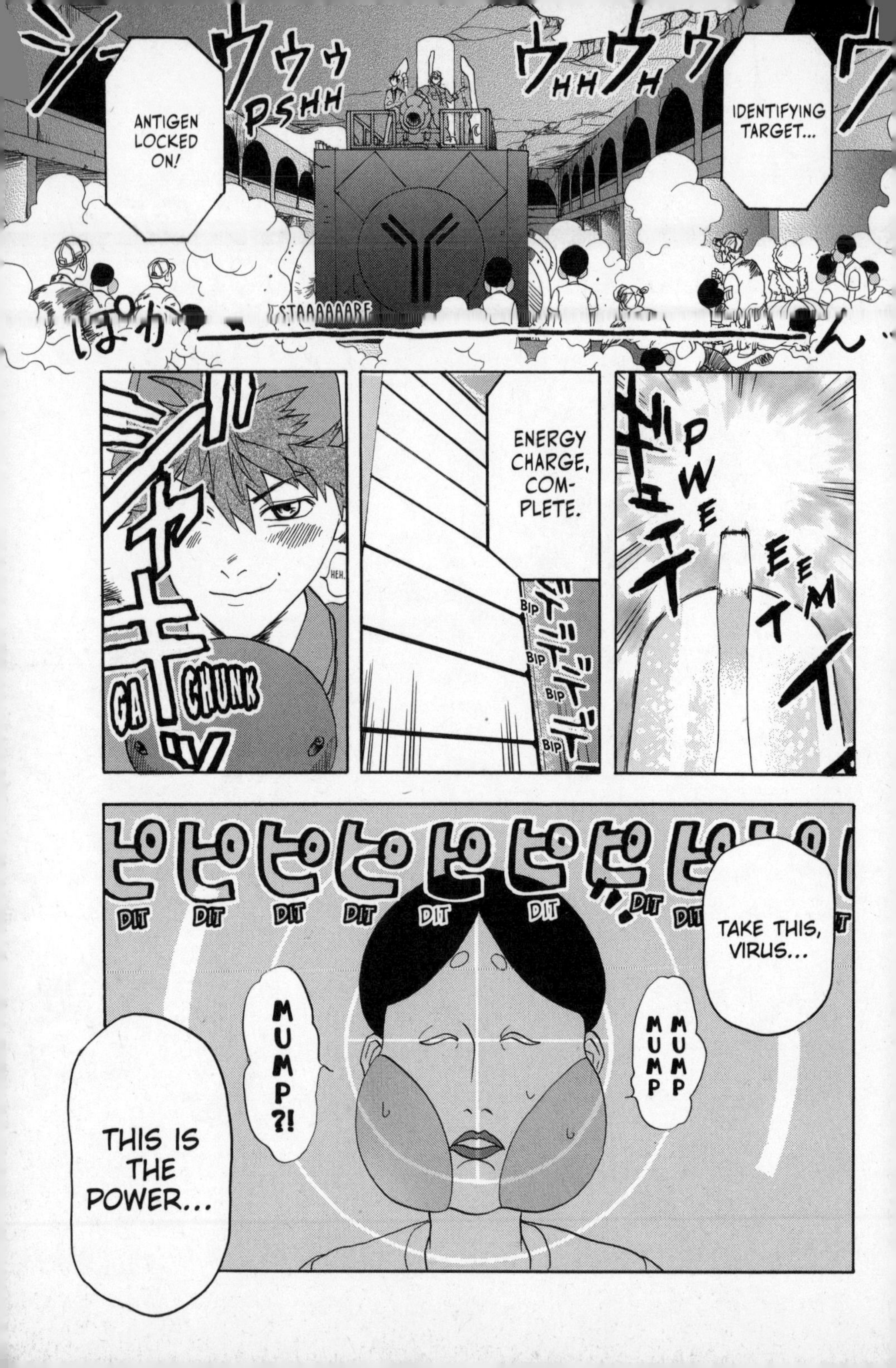
IDENTIFYING TARGET...
HH H
ANTIGEN LOCKED ON!
PSHH
STAAAAAARE
PWEEEM
ENERGY CHARGE, COM-PLETE.
BIP
BIP
BIP
BIP
HEH.
GA CHUNK
DIT DIT DIT DIT DIT DIT DIT DIT
TAKE THIS, VIRUS...
MUMP MUMP
MUMP MUMP
MUMP?!
THIS IS THE POWER...

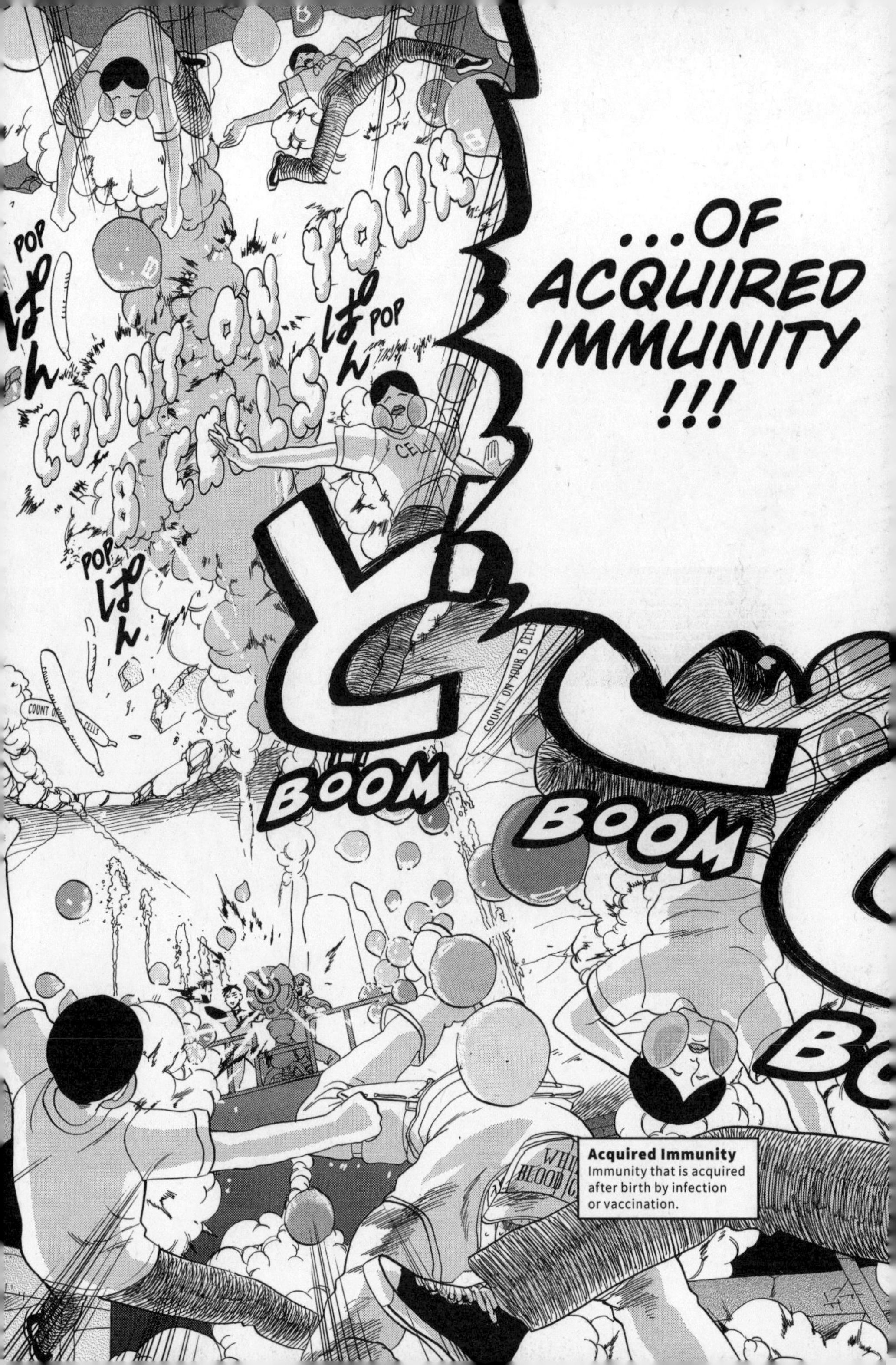
...OF ACQUIRED IMMUNITY !!!
COUNT ON YOUR B CELLS
POP ぱん
POP ぱん
POP ぱん
BOOM
BOOM
BO
CELL
COUNT ON YOUR B CELLS
COUNT ON YOUR B CELLS

Acquired Immunity
Immunity that is acquired after birth by infection or vaccination.

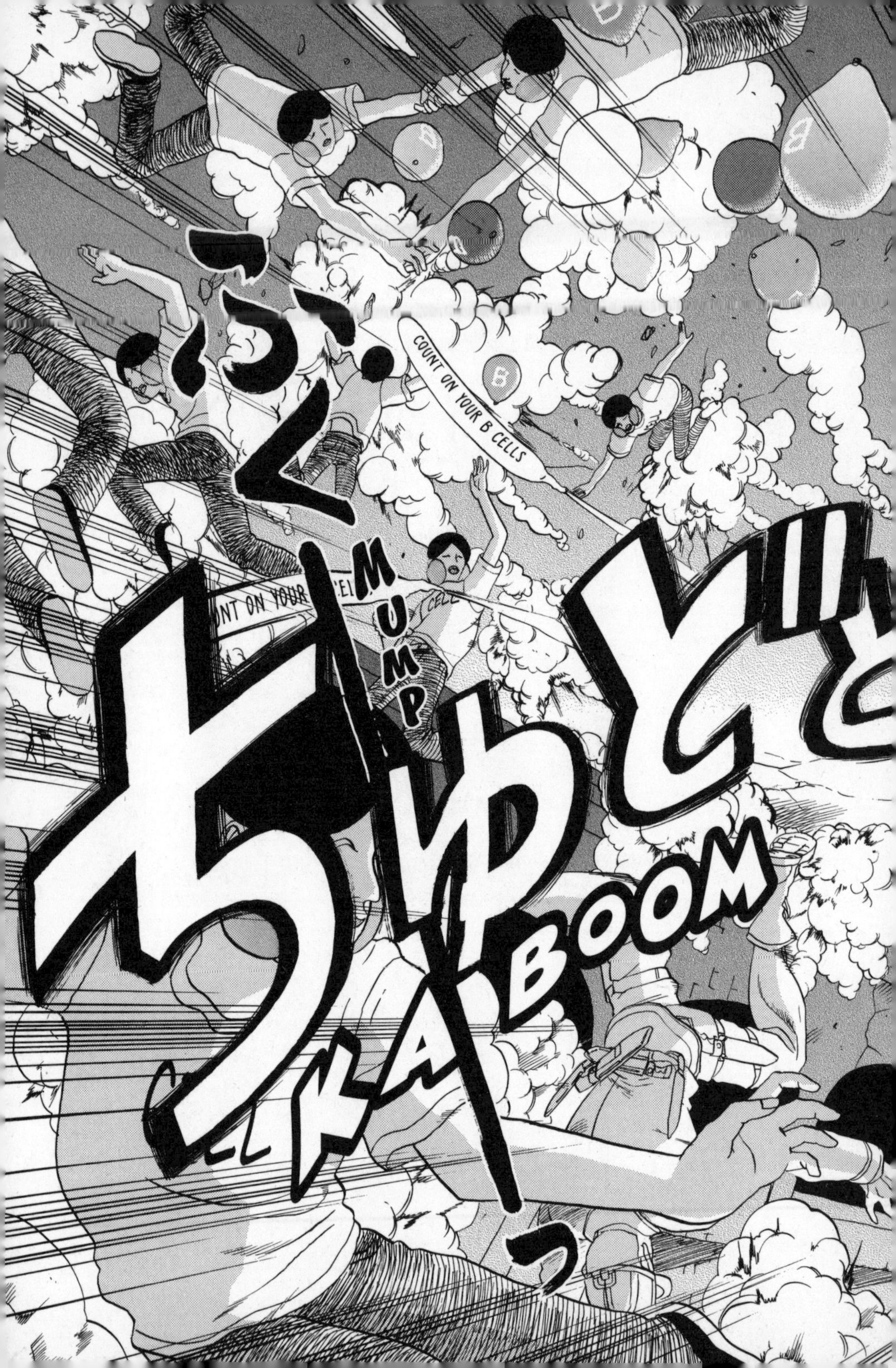
COUNT ON YOUR B CELLS
THUMP
NT ON YOUR CELL
KABOOM

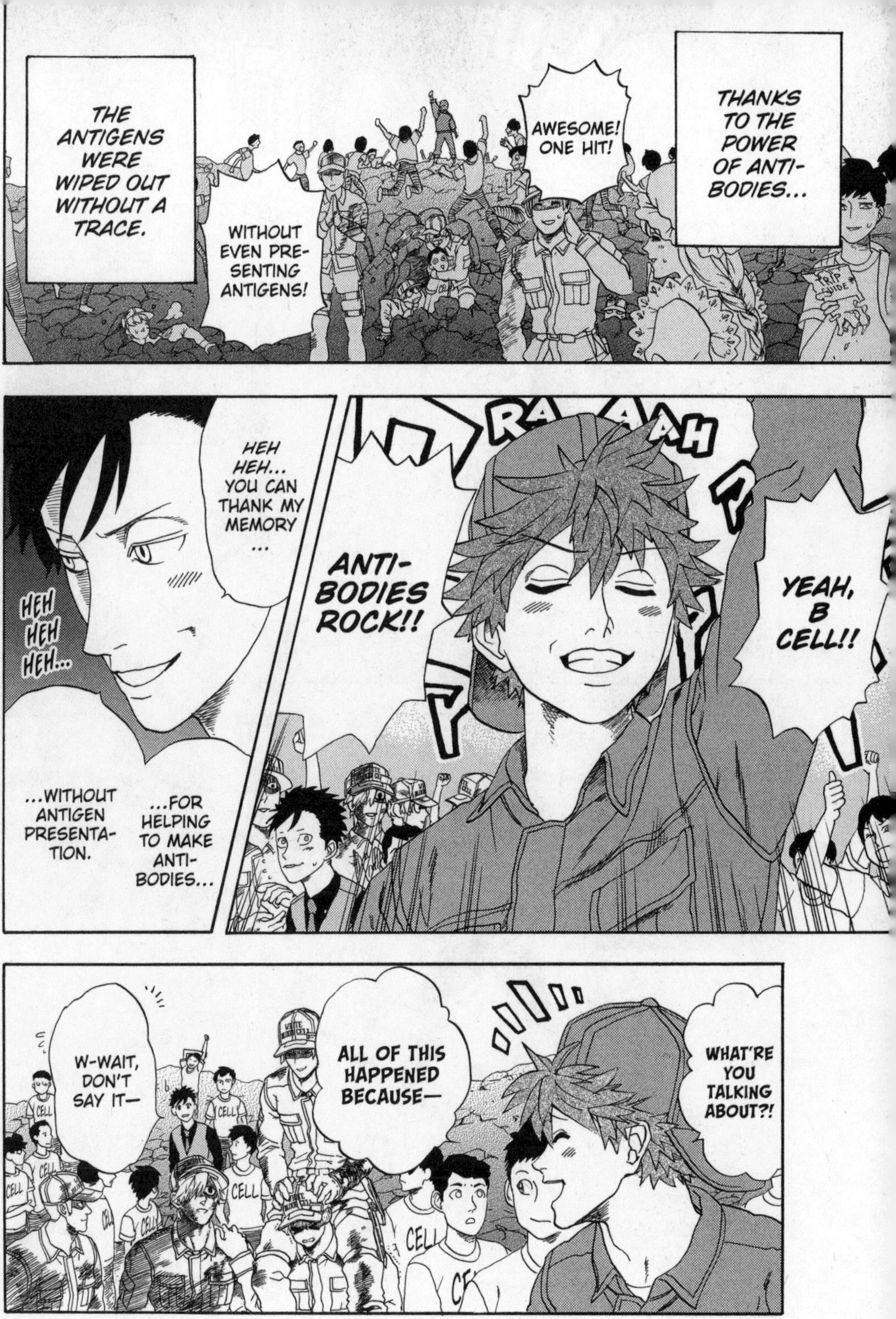
THANKS TO THE POWER OF ANTI-BODIES...
AWESOME! ONE HIT!
WITHOUT EVEN PRE-SENTING ANTIGENS!
THE ANTIGENS WERE WIPED OUT WITHOUT A TRACE.
YEAH, B CELL!!
RAAAAH
ANTI-BODIES ROCK!!
HEH HEH... YOU CAN THANK MY MEMORY ...
HEH HEH HEH...
...FOR HELPING TO MAKE ANTI-BODIES...
...WITHOUT ANTIGEN PRESENTA-TION.
WHAT'RE YOU TALKING ABOUT?!
ALL OF THIS HAPPENED BECAUSE—
W-WAIT, DON'T SAY IT—

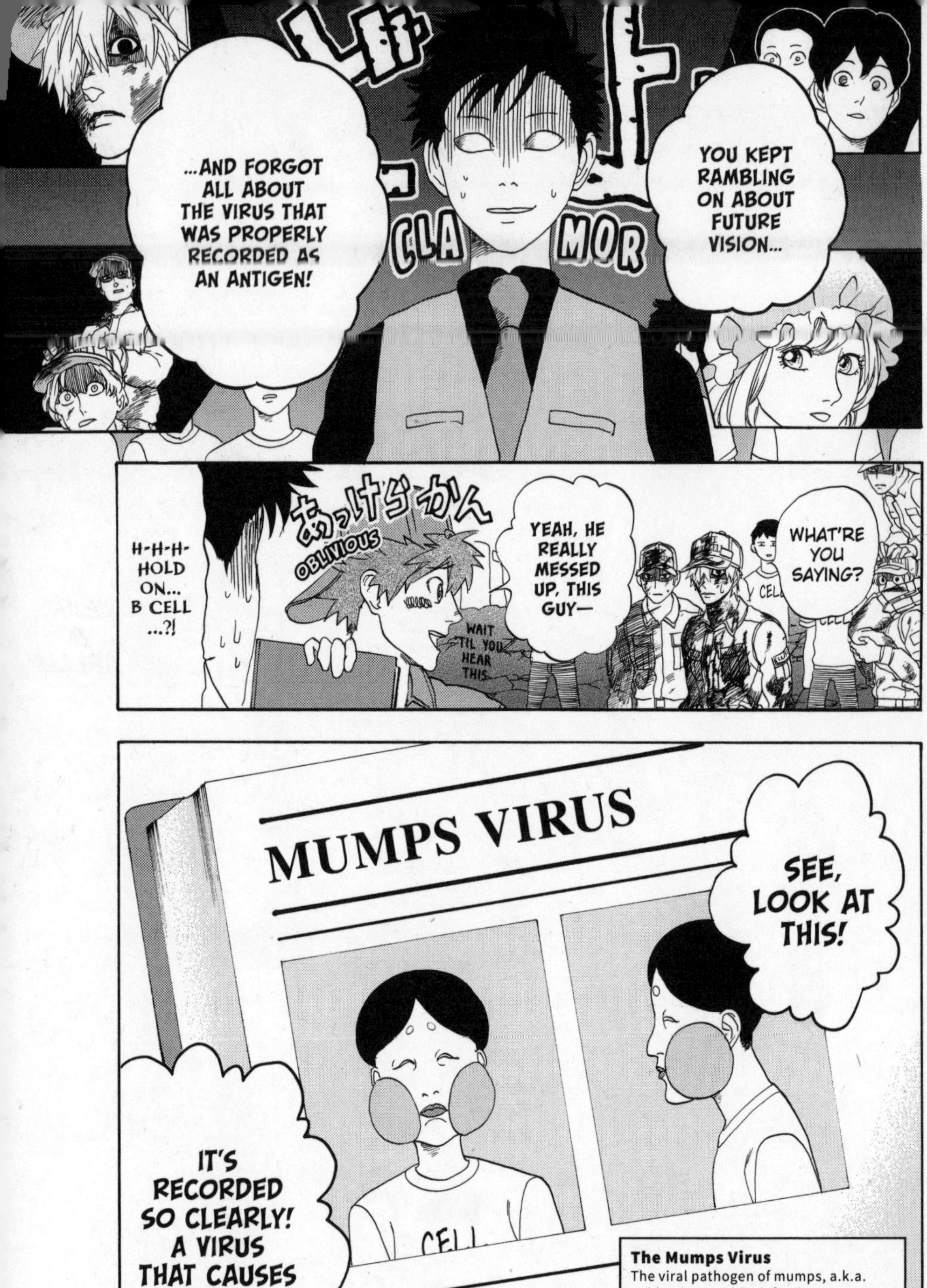

YOU KEPT RAMBLING ON ABOUT FUTURE VISION...
CLAMOR
...AND FORGOT ALL ABOUT THE VIRUS THAT WAS PROPERLY RECORDED AS AN ANTIGEN!
WHAT'RE YOU SAYING?
YEAH, HE REALLY MESSED UP, THIS GUY—
WAIT 'TIL YOU HEAR THIS
あっけらかん
OBLIVIOUS
H-H-H-HOLD ON... B CELL ...?!
MUMPS VIRUS
SEE, LOOK AT THIS!
IT'S RECORDED SO CLEARLY! A VIRUS THAT CAUSES MUMPS!
The Mumps Virus
The viral pathogen of mumps, a.k.a. epidemic parotitis. Infection causes one or both parotid glands (one of the large salivary glands) under the ear to swell.

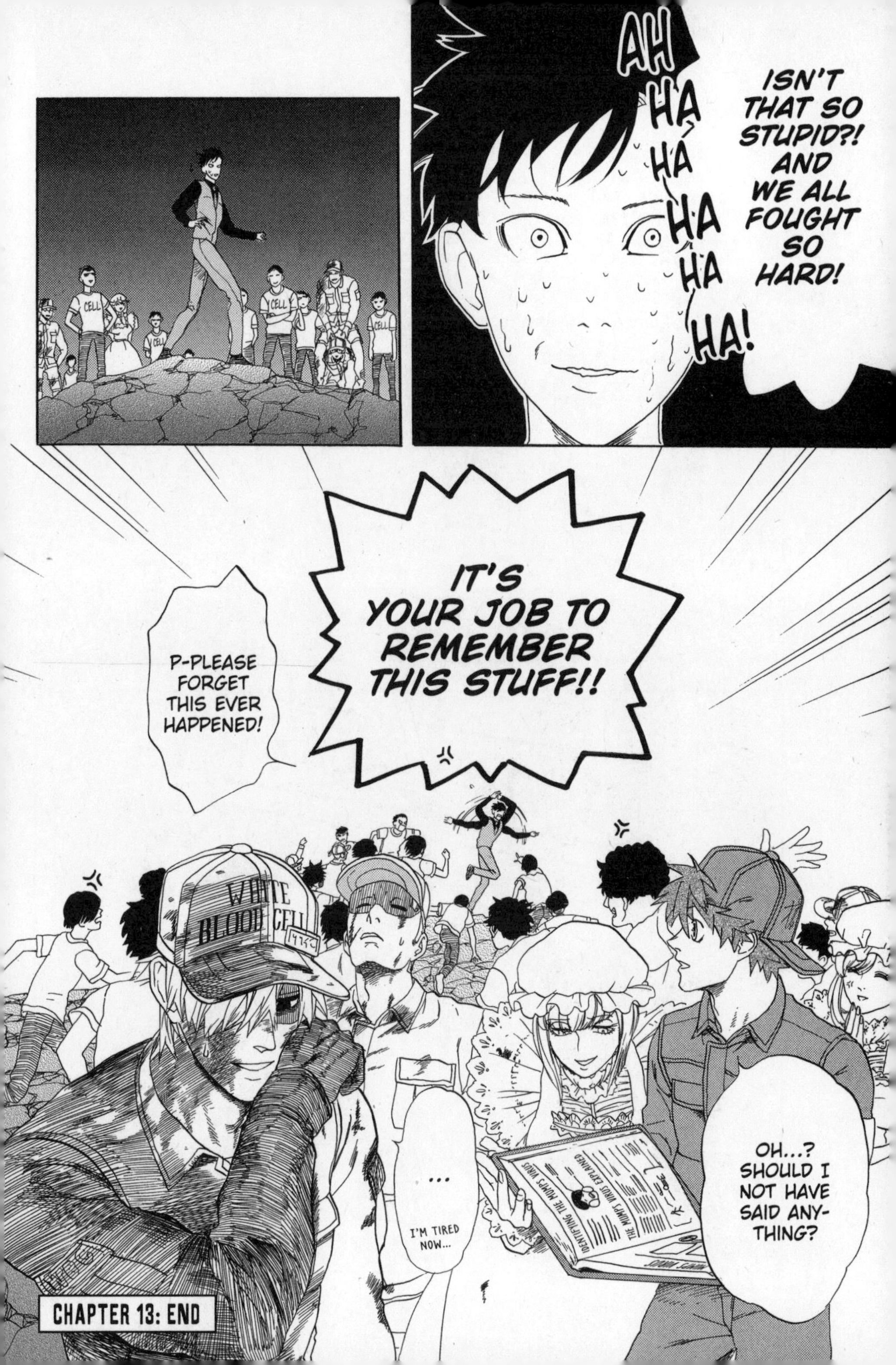
ISN'T THAT SO STUPID?! AND WE ALL FOUGHT SO HARD!
AH HA HA HA HA HA!
IT'S YOUR JOB TO REMEMBER THIS STUFF!!
P-PLEASE FORGET THIS EVER HAPPENED!
OH...? SHOULD I NOT HAVE SAID ANYTHING?
...
I'M TIRED NOW...
CHAPTER 13: END

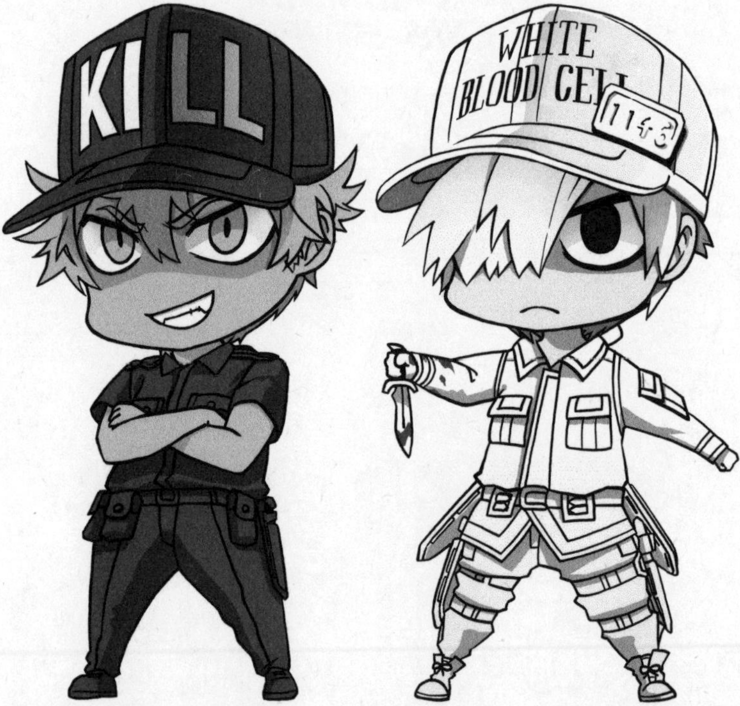
KILL
WHITE
BLOOD CELL
1146

Cells at Work!

はたらく細胞

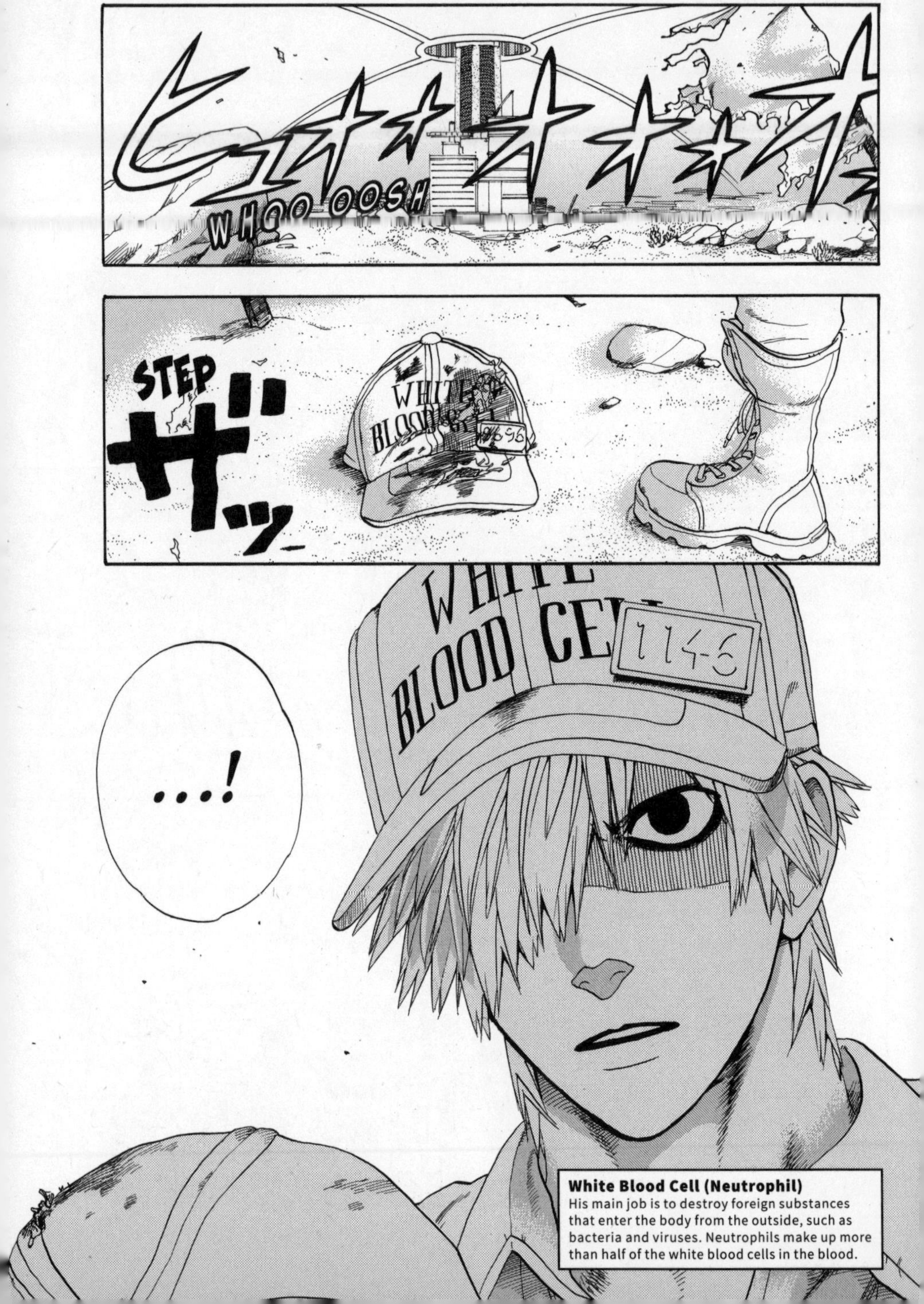
WHOO OOSH
STEP
ザッ
...!
White Blood Cell (Neutrophil)
His main job is to destroy foreign substances that enter the body from the outside, such as bacteria and viruses. Neutrophils make up more than half of the white blood cells in the blood.

CHAPTER 14: PIMPLE

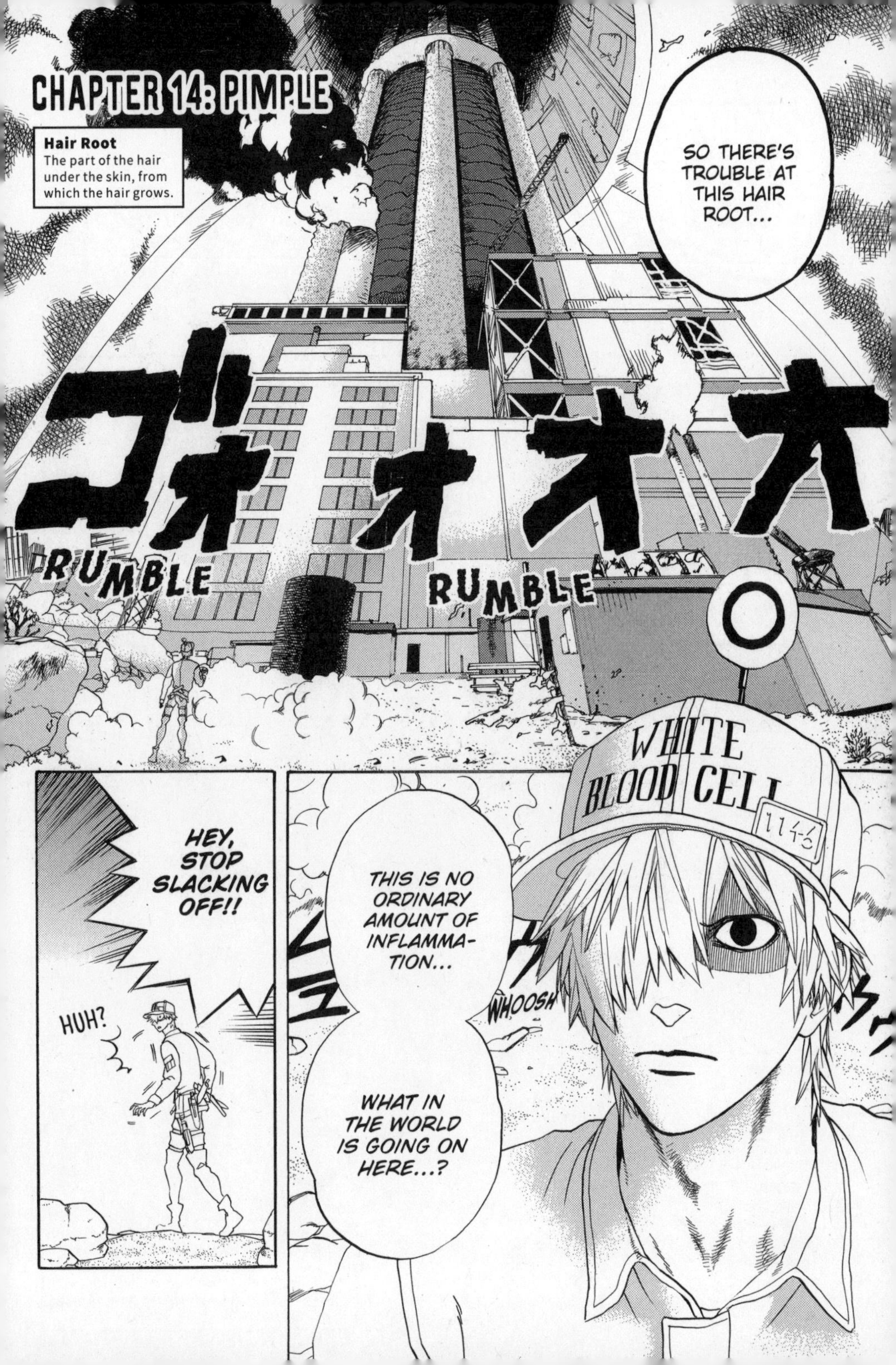
SO THERE'S TROUBLE AT THIS HAIR ROOT...
Hair Root
The part of the hair under the skin, from which the hair grows.
RUMBLE
RUMBLE
WHITE BLOOD CELL
1146
THIS IS NO ORDINARY AMOUNT OF INFLAMMATION...
WHOOSH
WHAT IN THE WORLD IS GOING ON HERE...?
HEY, STOP SLACKING OFF!!
HUH?

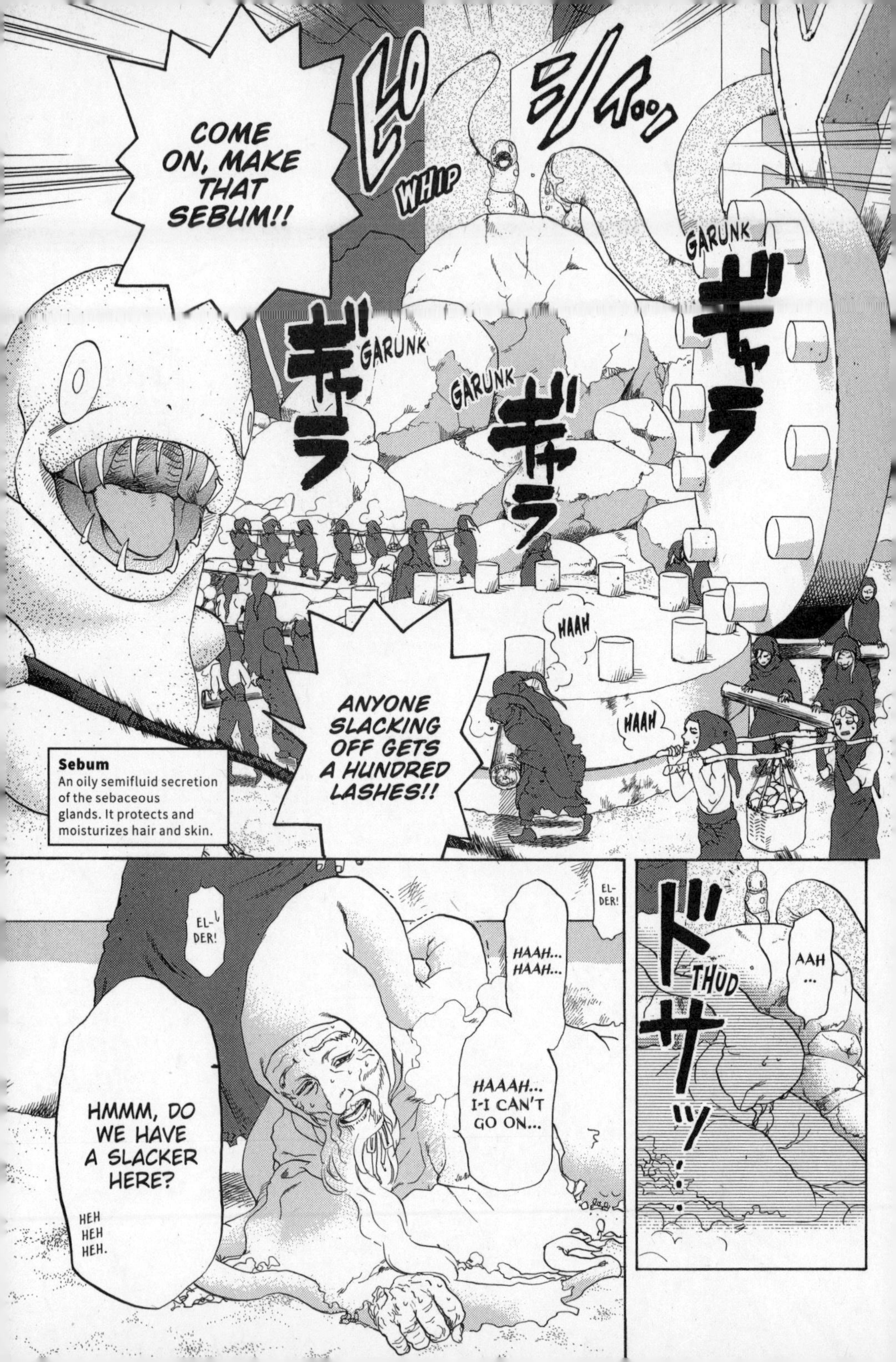
WHIP
GARUNK
ギャラ
COME ON, MAKE THAT SEBUM!!
GARUNK
ギャラ
GARUNK
ギャラ
HAAH
HAAH
ANYONE SLACKING OFF GETS A HUNDRED LASHES!!
Sebum
An oily semifluid secretion of the sebaceous glands. It protects and moisturizes hair and skin.
ドサッ
THUD
AAH...
EL-DER!
HAAH... HAAH...
HAAAH... I-I CAN'T GO ON...
EL-DER!
HMMM, DO WE HAVE A SLACKER HERE?
HEH HEH HEH.

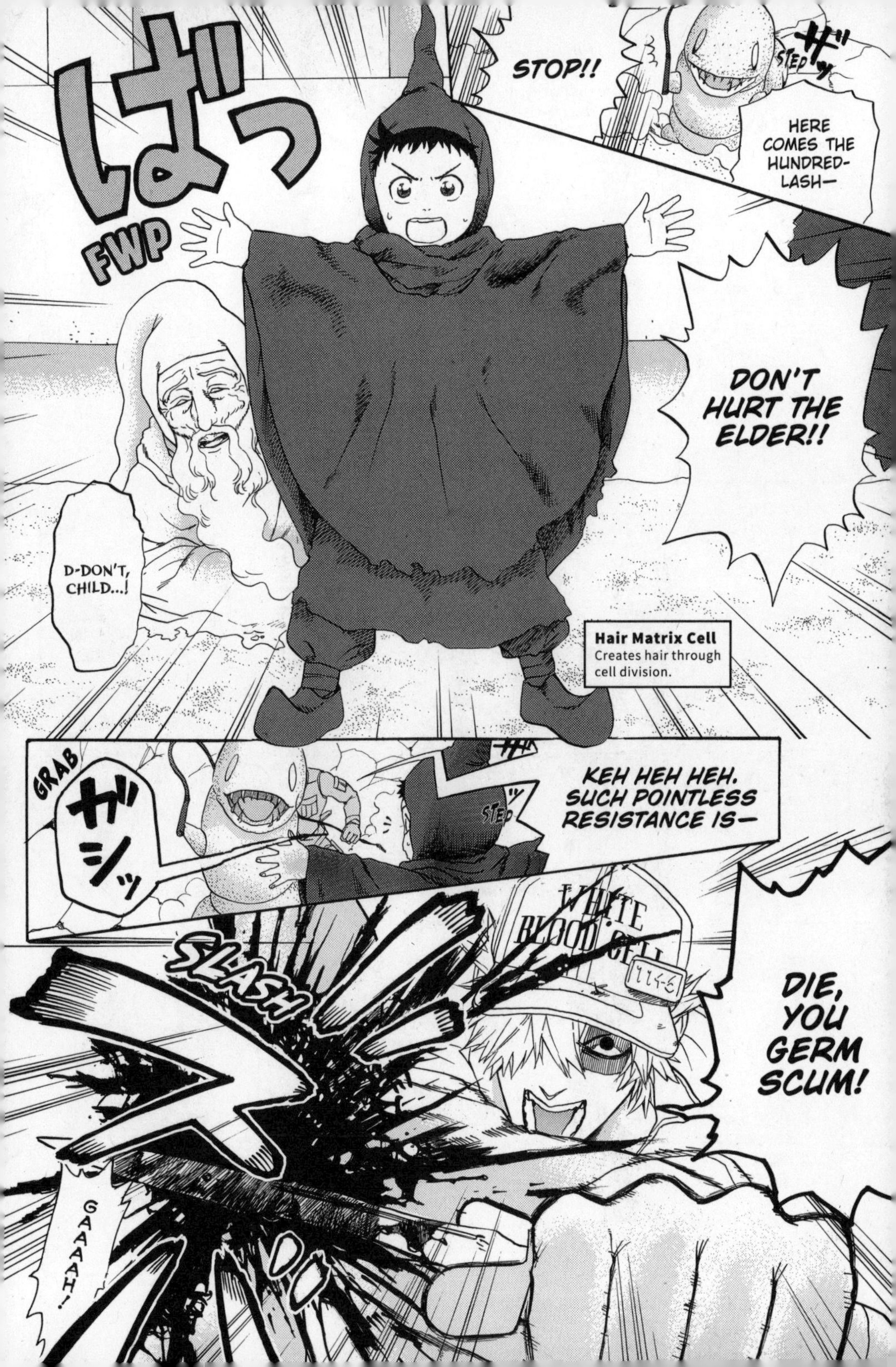

ザッ
STEP
HERE COMES THE HUNDRED-LASH—
STOP!!
DON'T HURT THE ELDER!!
ばっ
FWP
D-DON'T, CHILD...!
Hair Matrix Cell
Creates hair through cell division.
KEH HEH HEH. SUCH POINTLESS RESISTANCE IS—
STEP
ガシッ
GRAB
WHITE BLOOD CELL
1146
DIE, YOU GERM SCUM!
SLASH
GAAAAH!

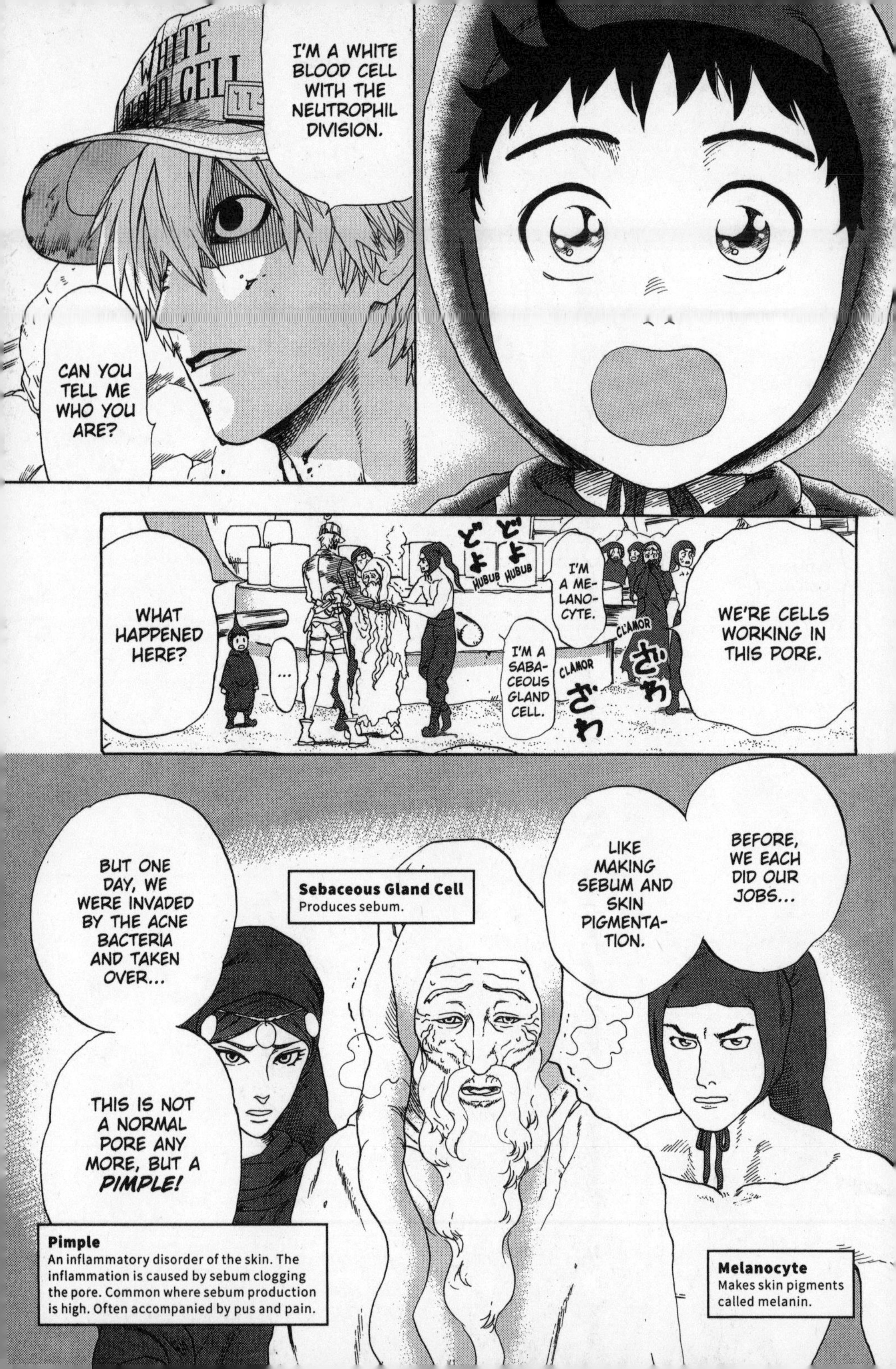

I'M A WHITE BLOOD CELL WITH THE NEUTROPHIL DIVISION.
CAN YOU TELL ME WHO YOU ARE?
WE'RE CELLS WORKING IN THIS PORE.
ざわ CLAMOR
ざわ CLAMOR
I'M A MELANOCYTE.
I'M A SABACEOUS GLAND CELL.
どよ HUBUB
どよ HUBUB
...
WHAT HAPPENED HERE?
BEFORE, WE EACH DID OUR JOBS...
LIKE MAKING SEBUM AND SKIN PIGMENTATION.
Melanocyte
Makes skin pigments called melanin.
Sebaceous Gland Cell
Produces sebum.
BUT ONE DAY, WE WERE INVADED BY THE ACNE BACTERIA AND TAKEN OVER...
THIS IS NOT A NORMAL PORE ANY MORE, BUT A PIMPLE!
Pimple
An inflammatory disorder of the skin. The inflammation is caused by sebum clogging the pore. Common where sebum production is high. Often accompanied by pus and pain.

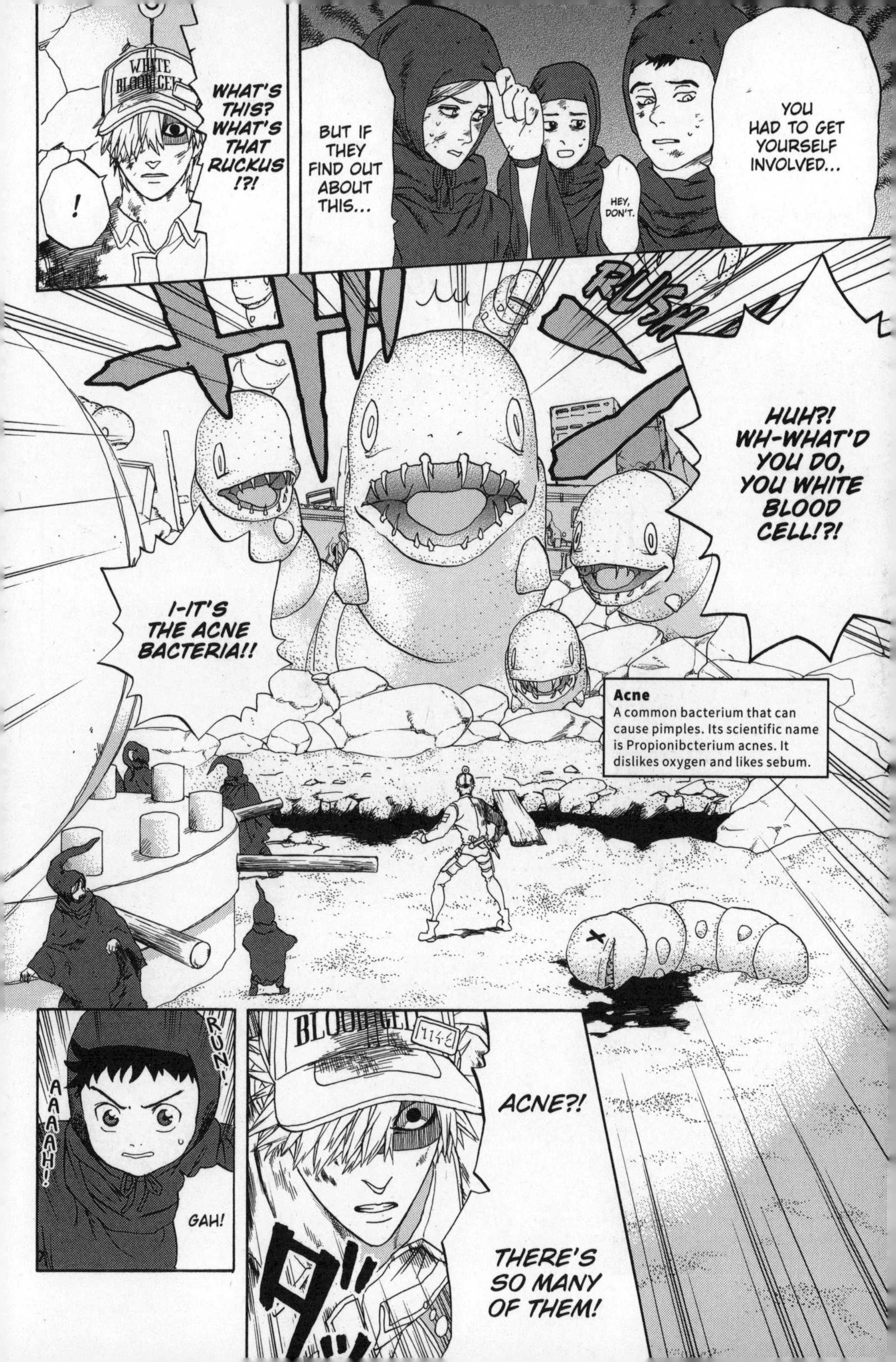
YOU HAD TO GET YOURSELF INVOLVED...
HEY, DON'T.
BUT IF THEY FIND OUT ABOUT THIS...
WHAT'S THIS? WHAT'S THAT RUCKUS!?!
!
RUSH
HUH?! WH-WHAT'D YOU DO, YOU WHITE BLOOD CELL!?!
I-IT'S THE ACNE BACTERIA!!
Acne
A common bacterium that can cause pimples. Its scientific name is Propionibcterium acnes. It dislikes oxygen and likes sebum.
ACNE?!
THERE'S SO MANY OF THEM!
RUN!
AAAAAH!
GAH!

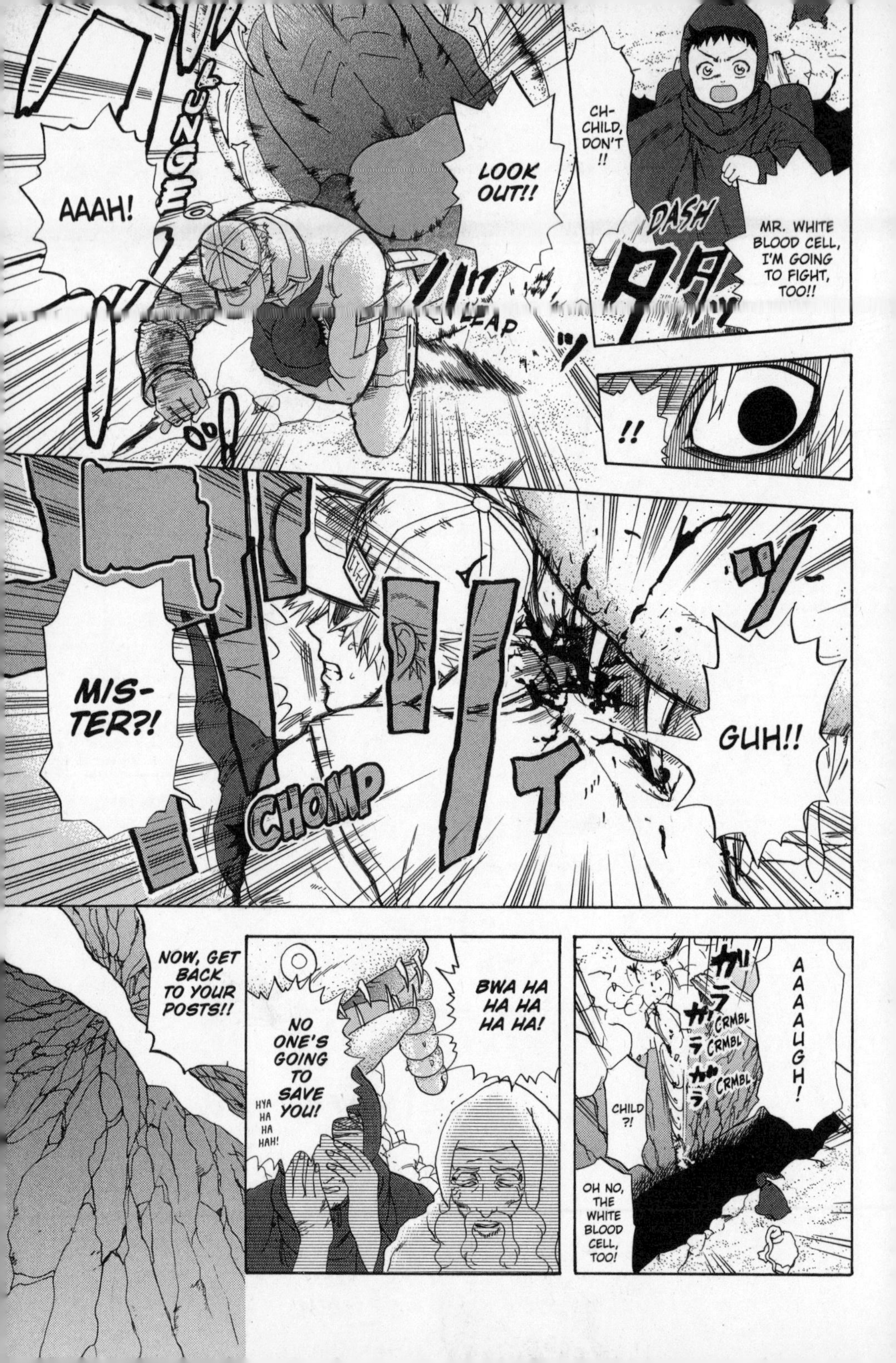
CH-CHILD, DON'T!!
MR. WHITE BLOOD CELL, I'M GOING TO FIGHT, TOO!!
DASH
!!
LOOK OUT!!
LUNGE
AAAH!
LEAP
GUH!!
MIS-TER?!
CHOMP
AAAAUGH!
CRMBL
CRMBL
CRMBL
CHILD?!
OH NO, THE WHITE BLOOD CELL, TOO!
BWA HA HA HA HA HA!
NO ONE'S GOING TO SAVE YOU!
HYA HA HA HAH!
NOW, GET BACK TO YOUR POSTS!!

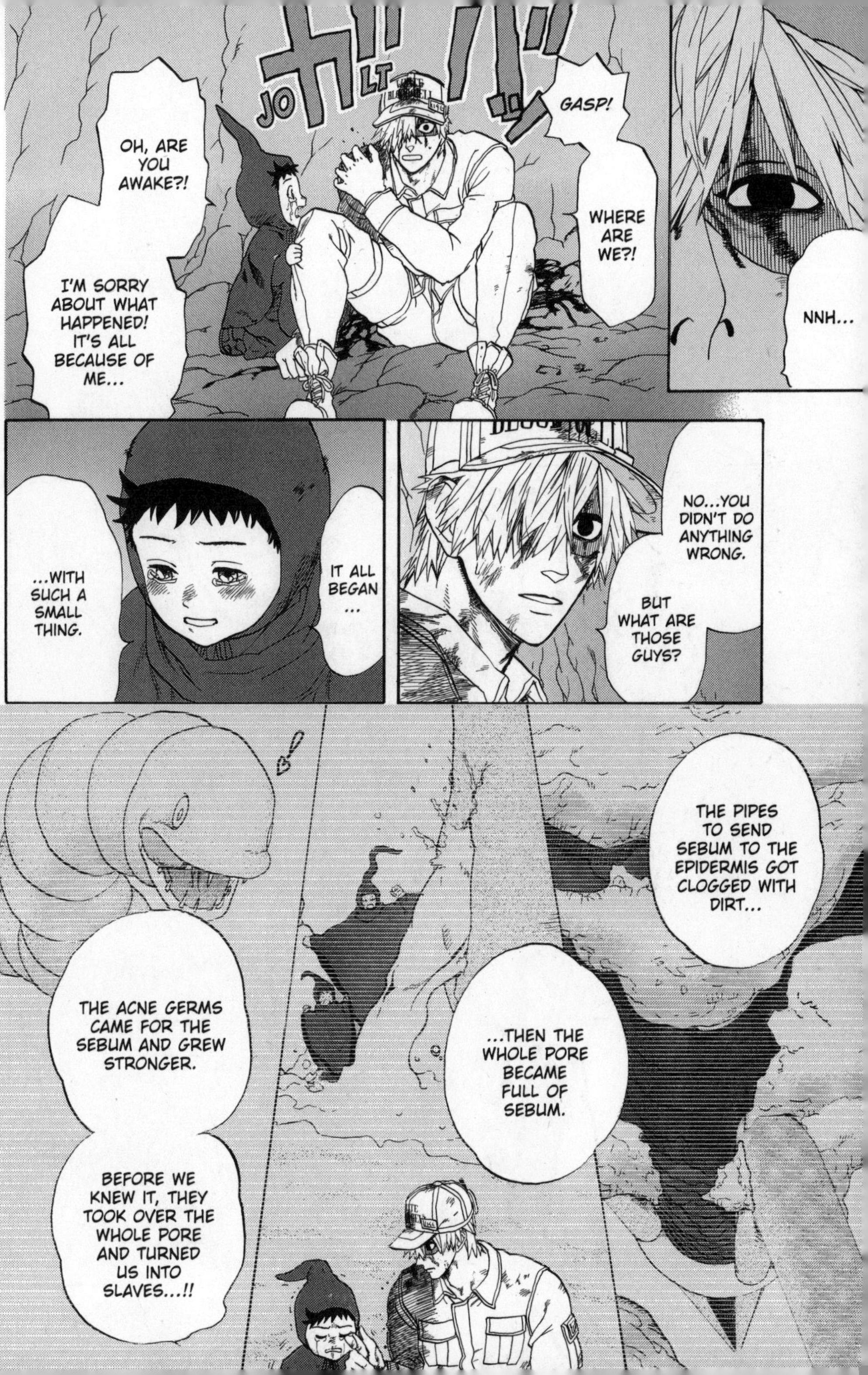
NNH...
JOLT
GASP!
WHERE ARE WE?!
OH, ARE YOU AWAKE?!
I'M SORRY ABOUT WHAT HAPPENED! IT'S ALL BECAUSE OF ME...
NO...YOU DIDN'T DO ANYTHING WRONG.
BUT WHAT ARE THOSE GUYS?
IT ALL BEGAN...
...WITH SUCH A SMALL THING.
THE PIPES TO SEND SEBUM TO THE EPIDERMIS GOT CLOGGED WITH DIRT...
...THEN THE WHOLE PORE BECAME FULL OF SEBUM.
THE ACNE GERMS CAME FOR THE SEBUM AND GREW STRONGER.
BEFORE WE KNEW IT, THEY TOOK OVER THE WHOLE PORE AND TURNED US INTO SLAVES...!!

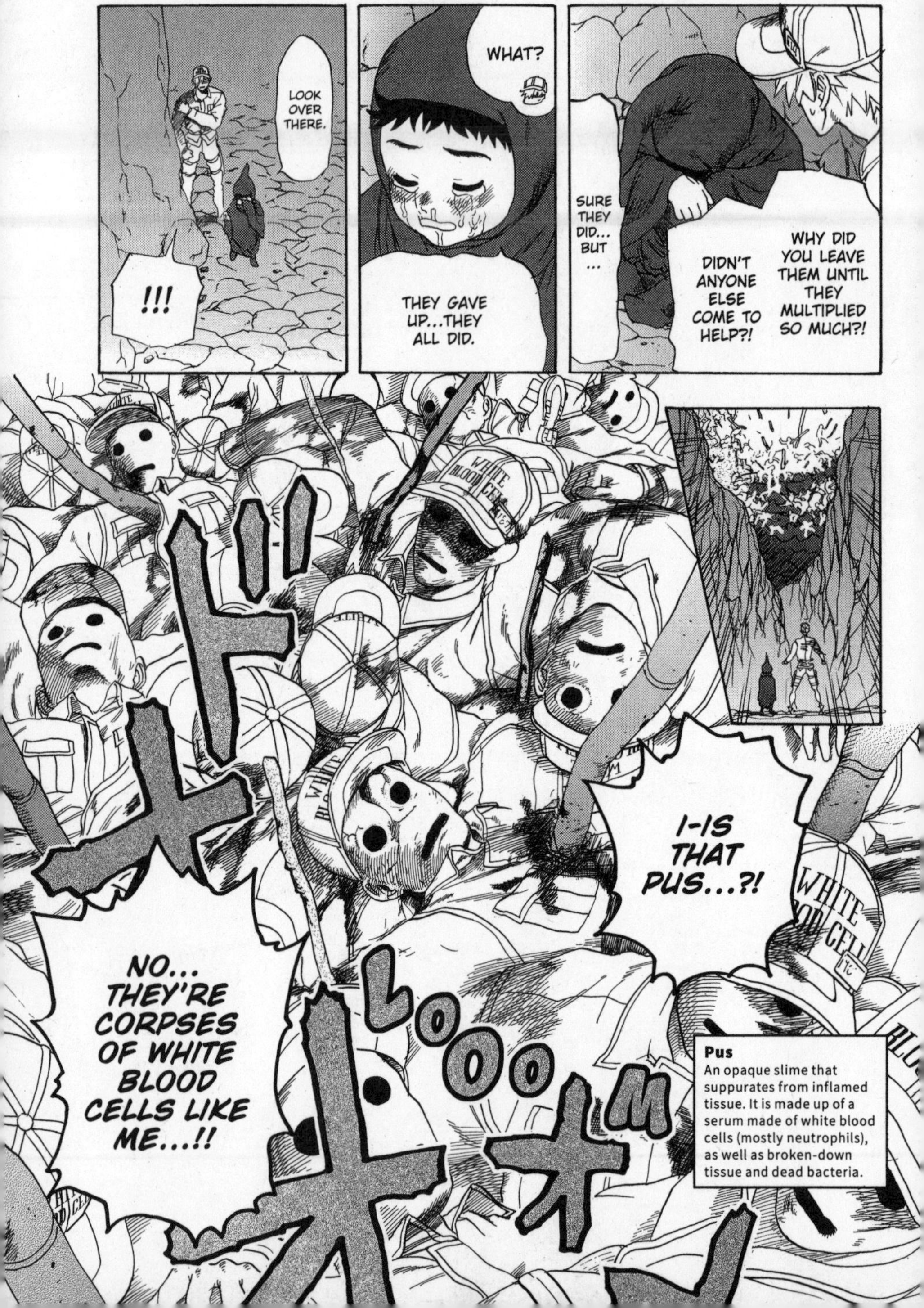

WHY DID YOU LEAVE THEM UNTIL THEY MULTIPLIED SO MUCH?!
DIDN'T ANYONE ELSE COME TO HELP?!
SURE THEY DID... BUT ...
WHAT?
THEY GAVE UP...THEY ALL DID.
LOOK OVER THERE.
!!!
I-IS THAT PUS...?!
NO... THEY'RE CORPSES OF WHITE BLOOD CELLS LIKE ME...!!
LOOOM
Pus
An opaque slime that suppurates from inflamed tissue. It is made up of a serum made of white blood cells (mostly neutrophils), as well as broken-down tissue and dead bacteria.

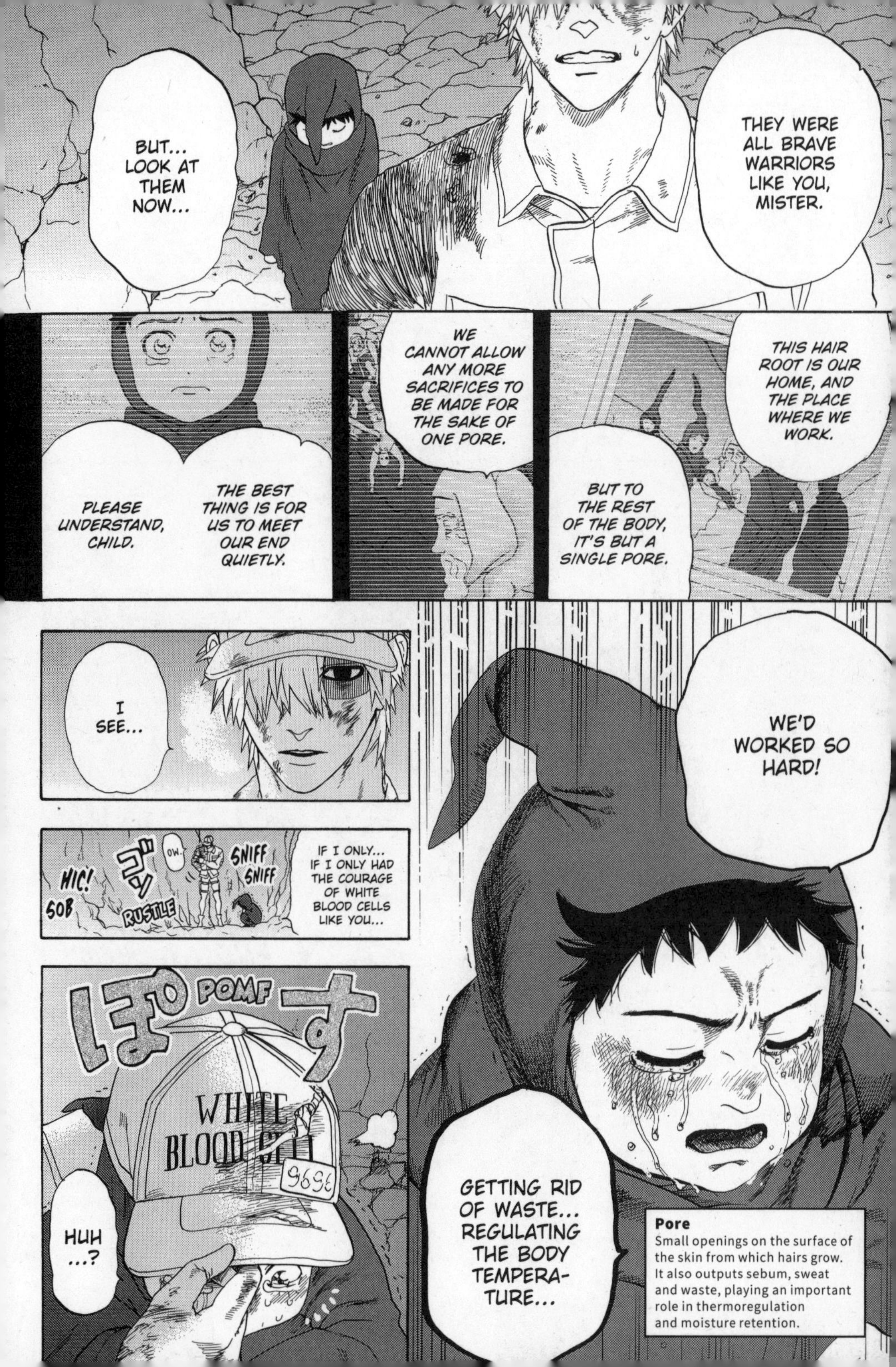
THEY WERE ALL BRAVE WARRIORS LIKE YOU, MISTER.
BUT... LOOK AT THEM NOW...
THIS HAIR ROOT IS OUR HOME, AND THE PLACE WHERE WE WORK.
BUT TO THE REST OF THE BODY, IT'S BUT A SINGLE PORE.
WE CANNOT ALLOW ANY MORE SACRIFICES TO BE MADE FOR THE SAKE OF ONE PORE.
THE BEST THING IS FOR US TO MEET OUR END QUIETLY.
PLEASE UNDERSTAND, CHILD.
WE'D WORKED SO HARD!
GETTING RID OF WASTE... REGULATING THE BODY TEMPERA-TURE...
Pore
Small openings on the surface of the skin from which hairs grow. It also outputs sebum, sweat and waste, playing an important role in thermoregulation and moisture retention.
I SEE...
IF I ONLY... IF I ONLY HAD THE COURAGE OF WHITE BLOOD CELLS LIKE YOU...
SNIFF
SNIFF
OW.
RUSTLE
HIC!
SOB
POMF
HUH ...?

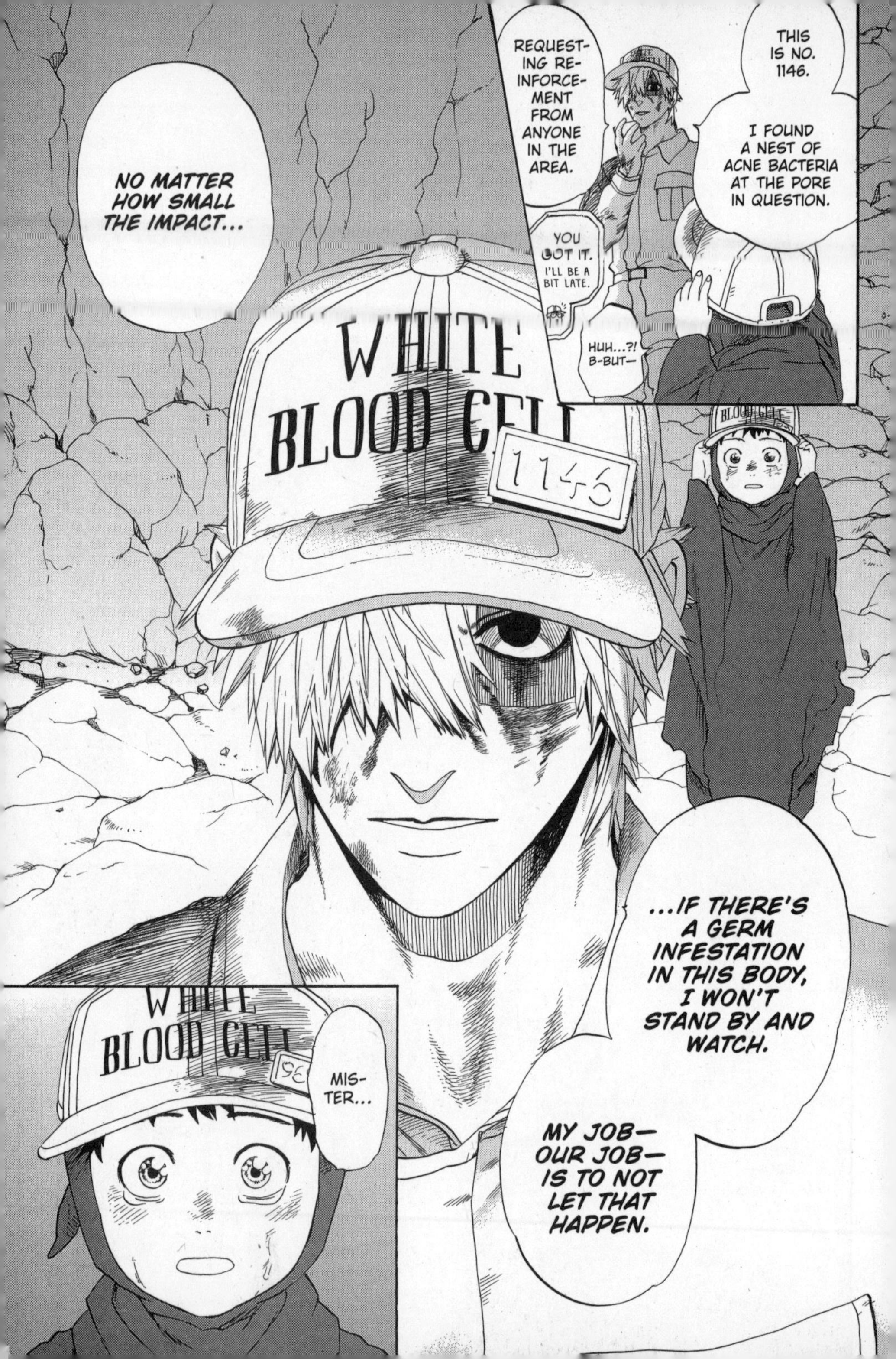
THIS IS NO. 1146.
I FOUND A NEST OF ACNE BACTERIA AT THE PORE IN QUESTION.
REQUESTING REINFORCEMENT FROM ANYONE IN THE AREA.
YOU GOT IT. I'LL BE A BIT LATE.
HUH...?! B-BUT—
WHITE BLOOD CELL
1146
NO MATTER HOW SMALL THE IMPACT...
...IF THERE'S A GERM INFESTATION IN THIS BODY, I WON'T STAND BY AND WATCH.
MY JOB—OUR JOB—IS TO NOT LET THAT HAPPEN.
BLOOD CELL
MIS-TER...

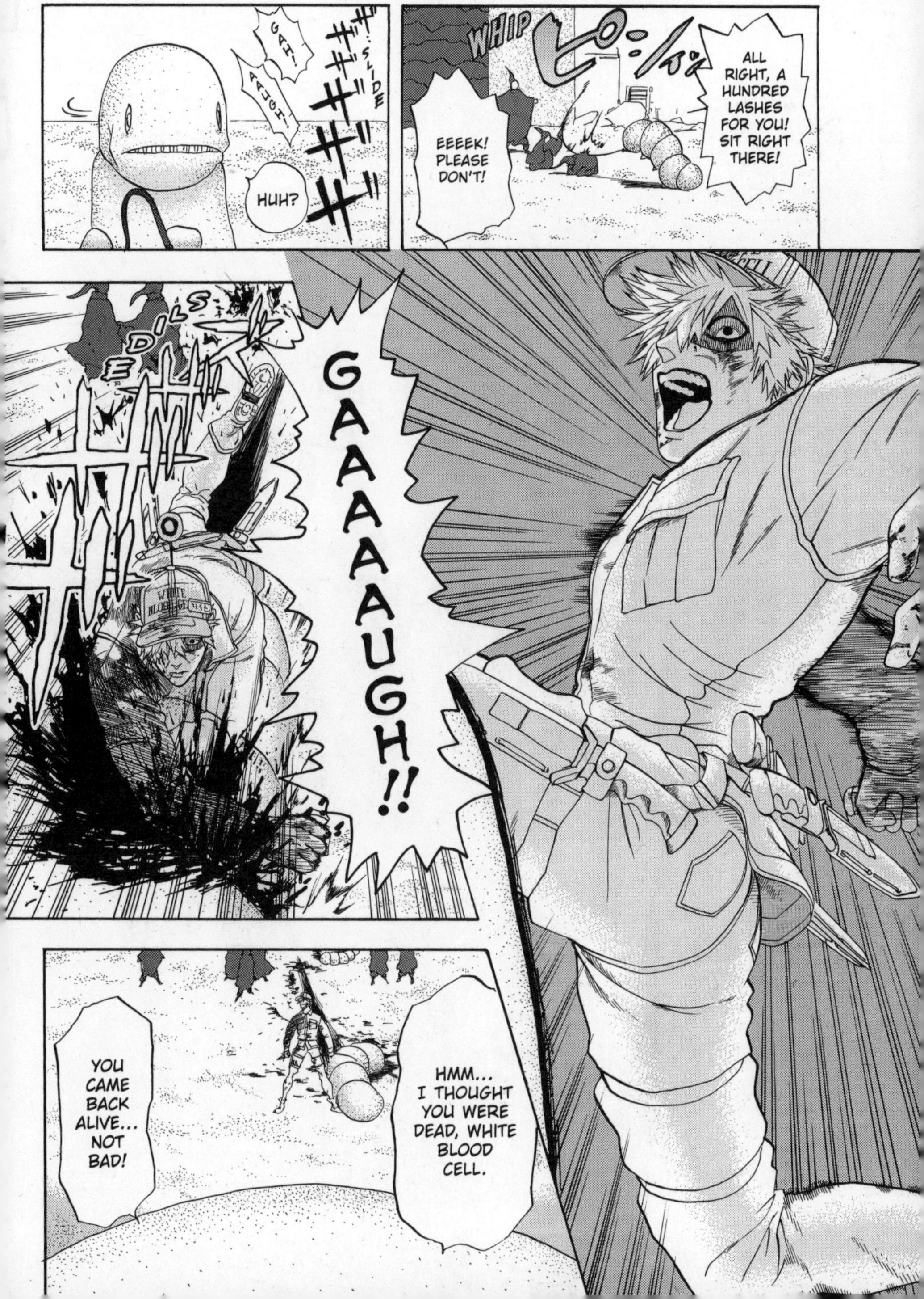
WHIP
ALL RIGHT, A HUNDRED LASHES FOR YOU! SIT RIGHT THERE!
EEEEK! PLEASE DON'T!
SLIDE
GAH!
AAUGH!
HUH?
GAAAAAUGH!!
SLIDE
HMM... I THOUGHT YOU WERE DEAD, WHITE BLOOD CELL.
YOU CAME BACK ALIVE... NOT BAD!

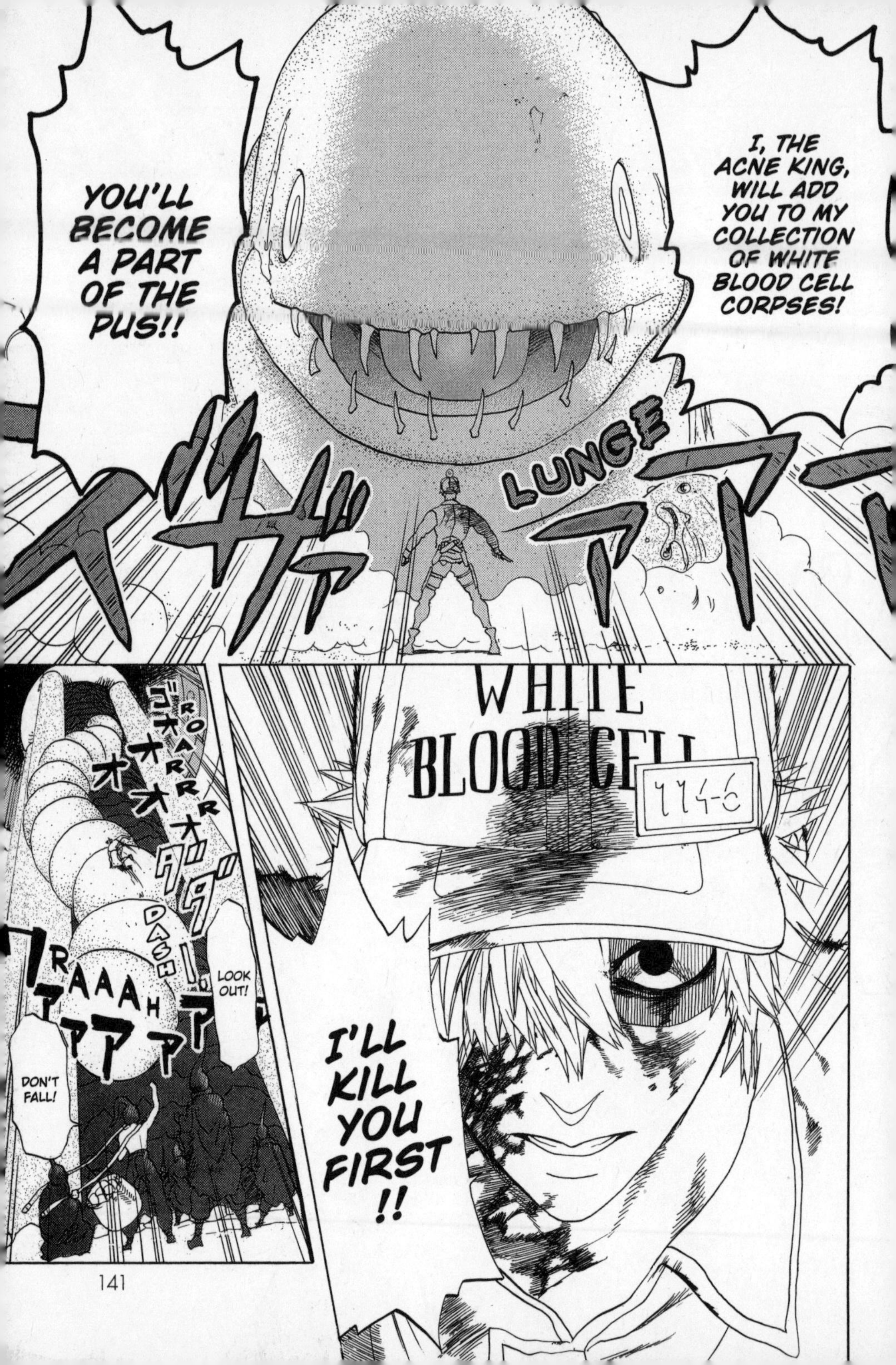

I, THE ACNE KING, WILL ADD YOU TO MY COLLECTION OF WHITE BLOOD CELL CORPSES!
YOU'LL BECOME A PART OF THE PUS!!
LUNGE
WHITE BLOOD CELL
I'LL KILL YOU FIRST!!
ROARRR
DASH
LOOK OUT!
RAAAH
DON'T FALL!

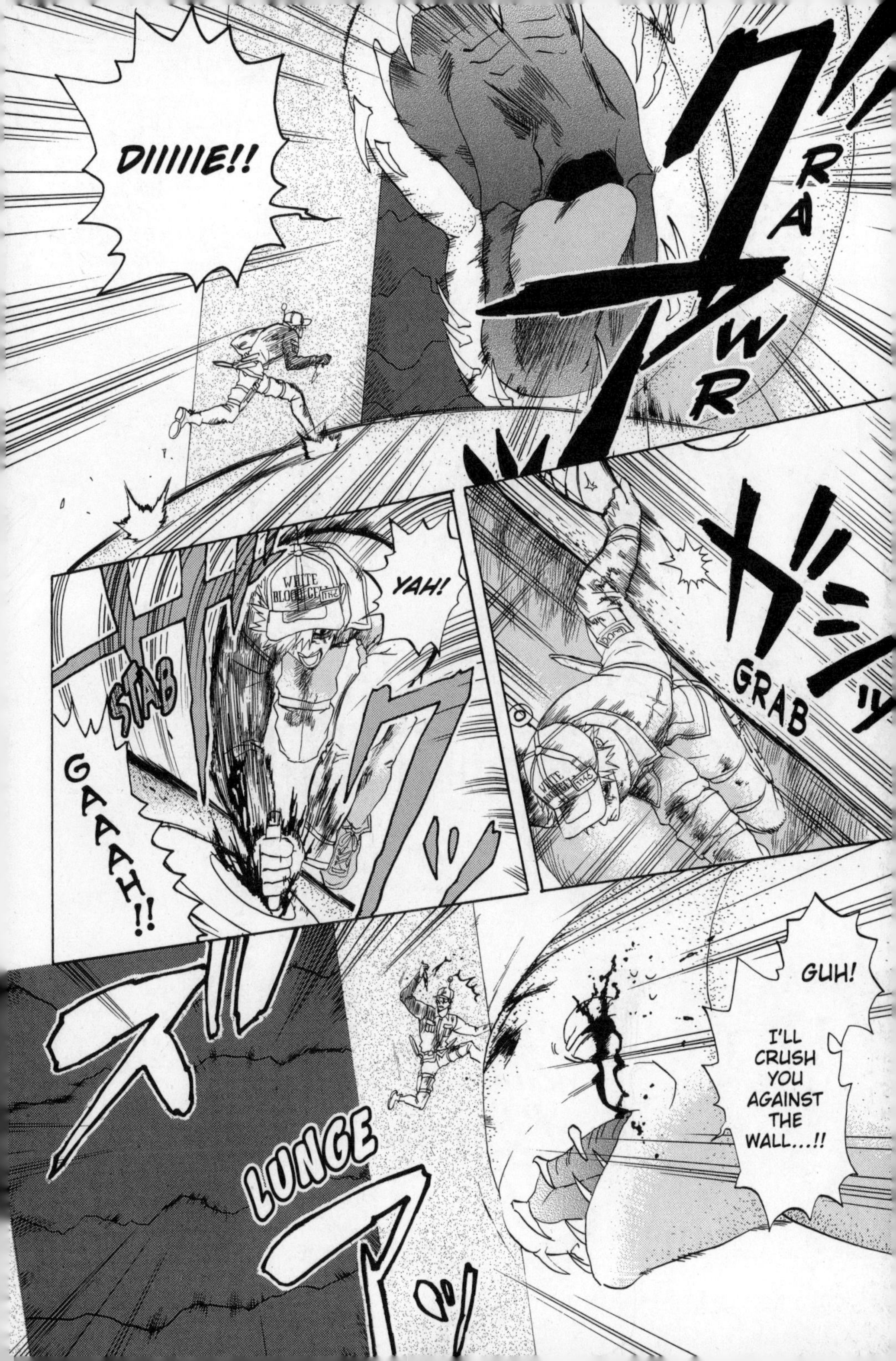
RAWR
DIIIIE!!
GRAB
YAH!
STAB
GAAAH!!
GUH!
I'LL CRUSH YOU AGAINST THE WALL...!!
LUNGE

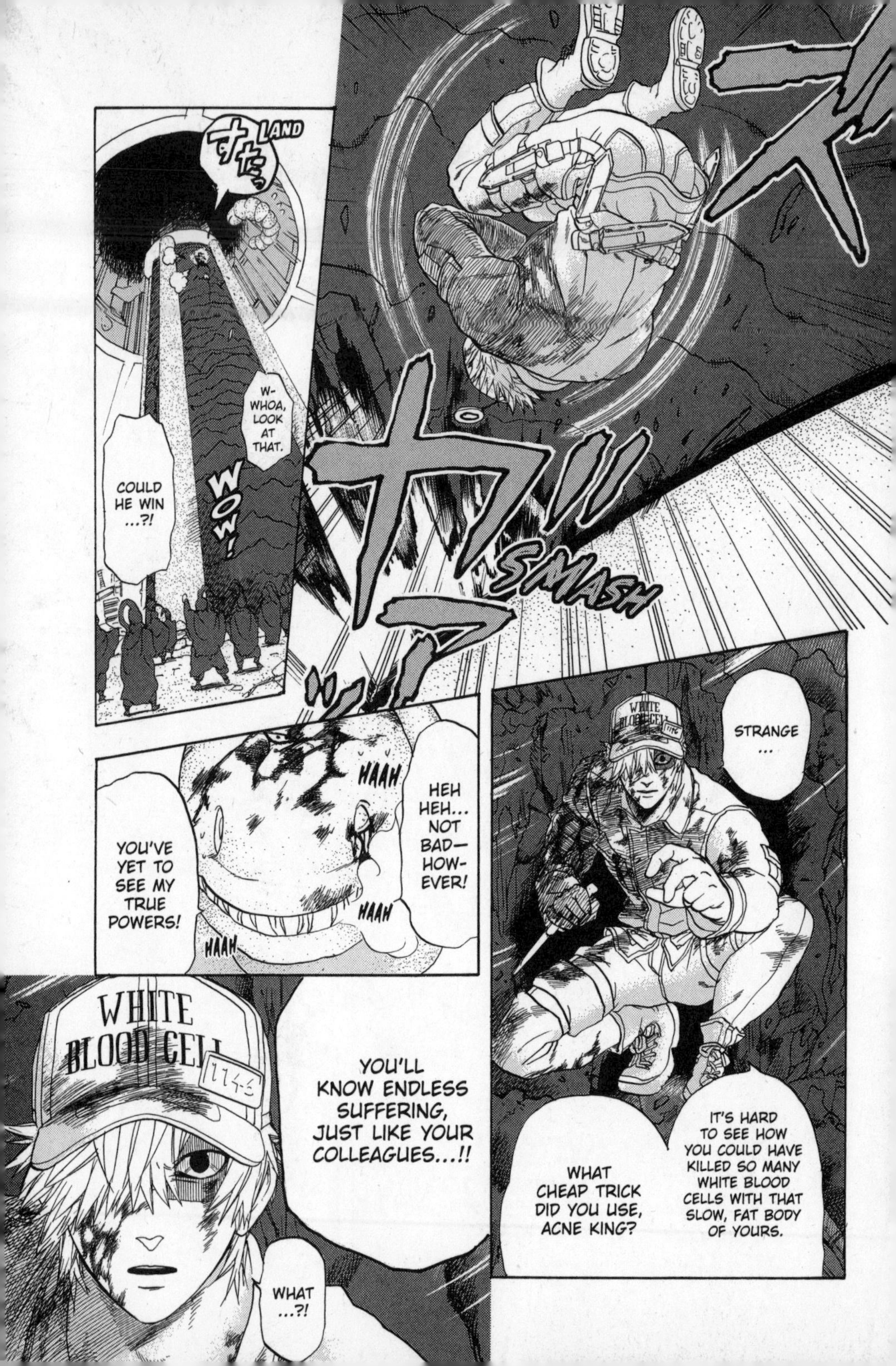
SMASH
すたっ LAND
W-WHOA, LOOK AT THAT.
WOW!
COULD HE WIN ...?!
STRANGE ...
IT'S HARD TO SEE HOW YOU COULD HAVE KILLED SO MANY WHITE BLOOD CELLS WITH THAT SLOW, FAT BODY OF YOURS.
WHAT CHEAP TRICK DID YOU USE, ACNE KING?
HAAH
HEH HEH... NOT BAD—HOWEVER!
HAAH
HAAH
YOU'VE YET TO SEE MY TRUE POWERS!
WHITE BLOOD CELL
YOU'LL KNOW ENDLESS SUFFERING, JUST LIKE YOUR COLLEAGUES...!!
WHAT ...?!

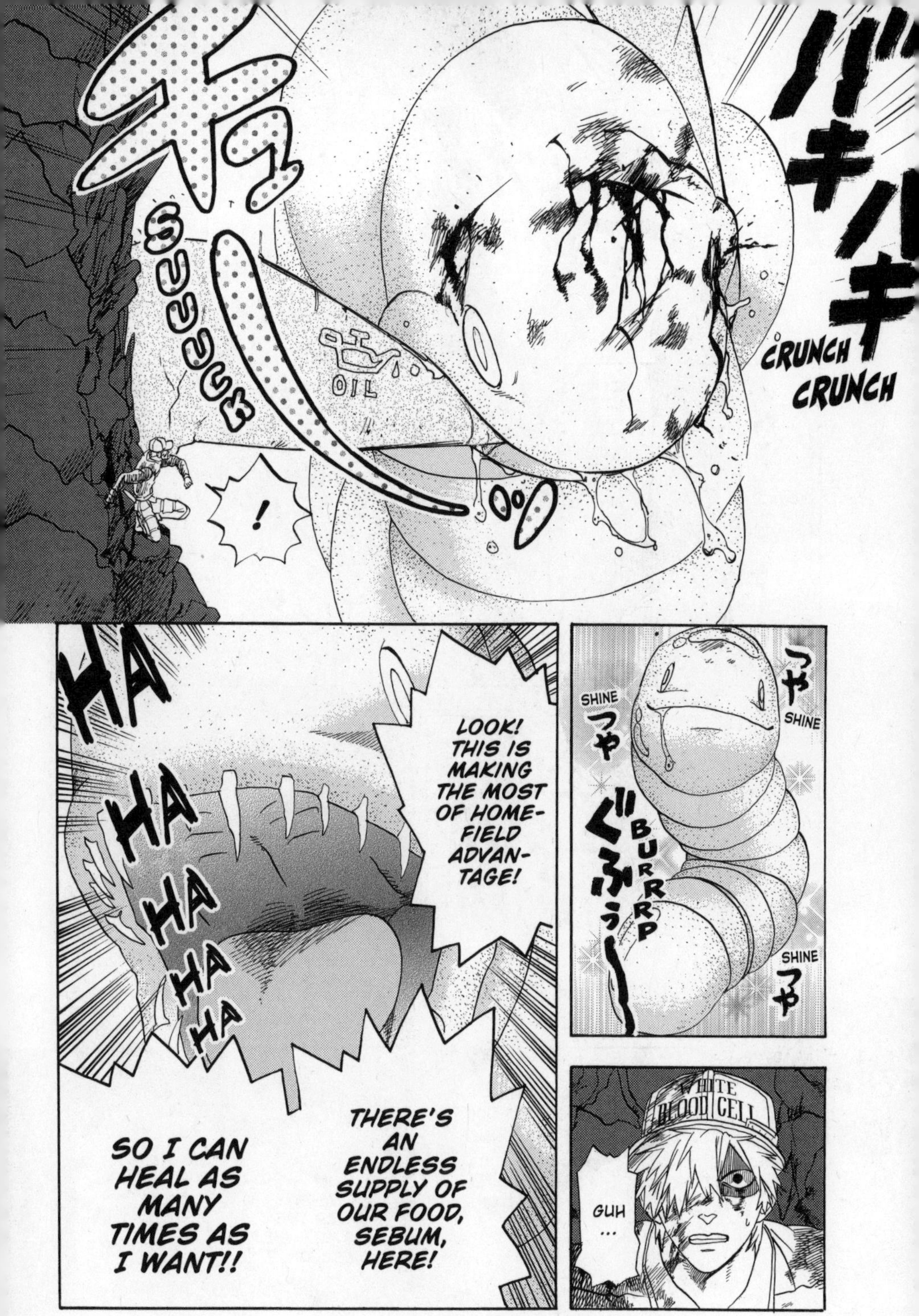

バキバキ
CRUNCH CRUNCH
ズズ
SUUUCK
OIL
0%
!
つや
SHINE
つや
SHINE
つや
SHINE
ぐふぅー
BURRP
WHITE BLOOD CELL
GUH...
LOOK! THIS IS MAKING THE MOST OF HOME-FIELD ADVAN-TAGE!
HA HA HA HA HA HA
THERE'S AN ENDLESS SUPPLY OF OUR FOOD, SEBUM, HERE!
SO I CAN HEAL AS MANY TIMES AS I WANT!!

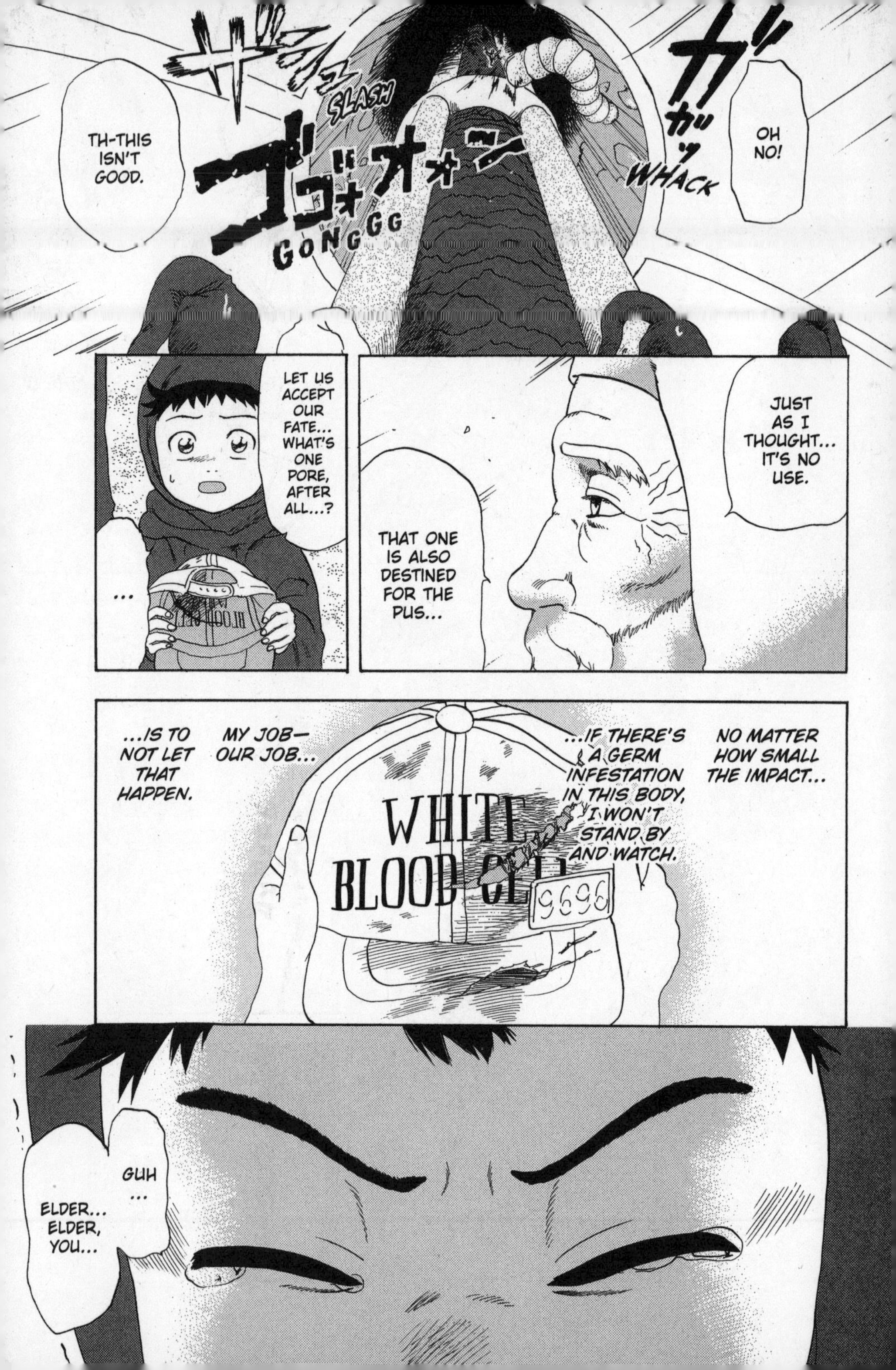

OH NO!
WHACK
GONGGG
SLASH
TH-THIS ISN'T GOOD.
JUST AS I THOUGHT... IT'S NO USE.
THAT ONE IS ALSO DESTINED FOR THE PUS...
LET US ACCEPT OUR FATE... WHAT'S ONE PORE, AFTER ALL...?
...
NO MATTER HOW SMALL THE IMPACT...
...IF THERE'S A GERM INFESTATION IN THIS BODY, I WON'T STAND BY AND WATCH.
MY JOB— OUR JOB...
...IS TO NOT LET THAT HAPPEN.
GUH ...
ELDER... ELDER, YOU...

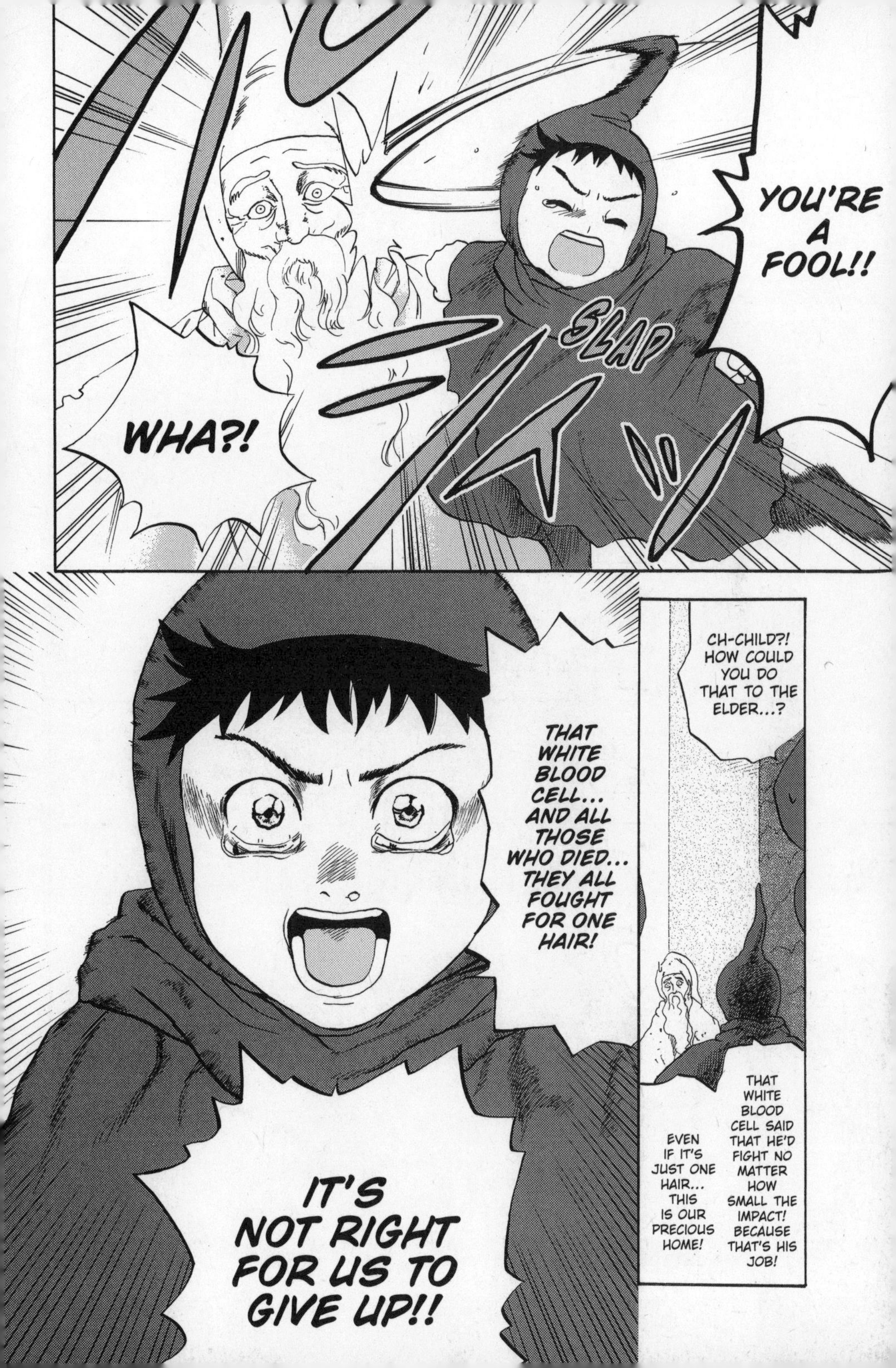
YOU'RE A FOOL!!
SLAP
WHA?!
CH-CHILD?! HOW COULD YOU DO THAT TO THE ELDER...?
THAT WHITE BLOOD CELL SAID THAT HE'D FIGHT NO MATTER HOW SMALL THE IMPACT! BECAUSE THAT'S HIS JOB!
EVEN IF IT'S JUST ONE HAIR... THIS IS OUR PRECIOUS HOME!
THAT WHITE BLOOD CELL... AND ALL THOSE WHO DIED... THEY ALL FOUGHT FOR ONE HAIR!
IT'S NOT RIGHT FOR US TO GIVE UP!!

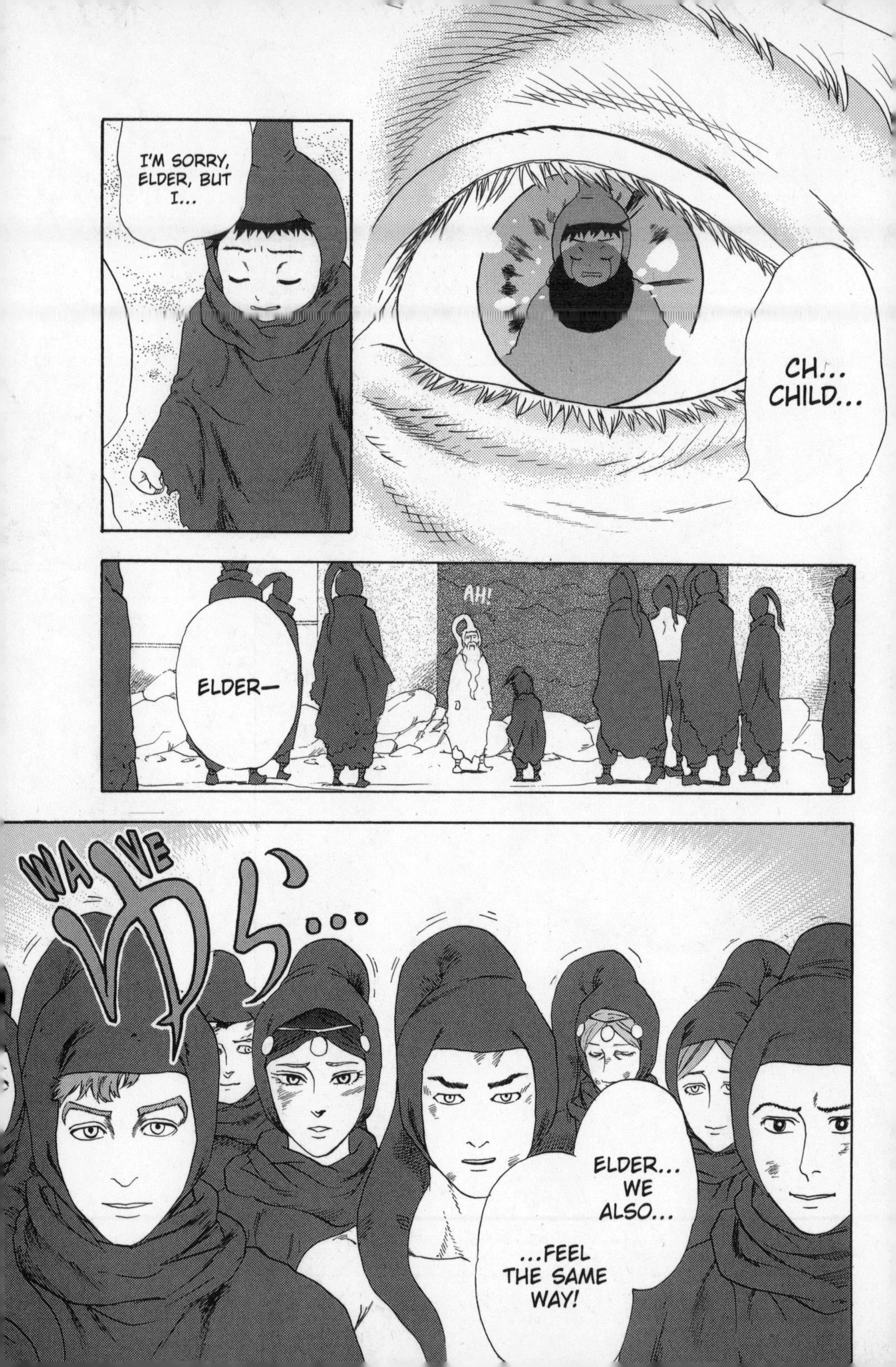
CH... CHILD...
I'M SORRY, ELDER, BUT I...
AH!
ELDER—
WAVE
ELDER... WE ALSO...
...FEEL THE SAME WAY!

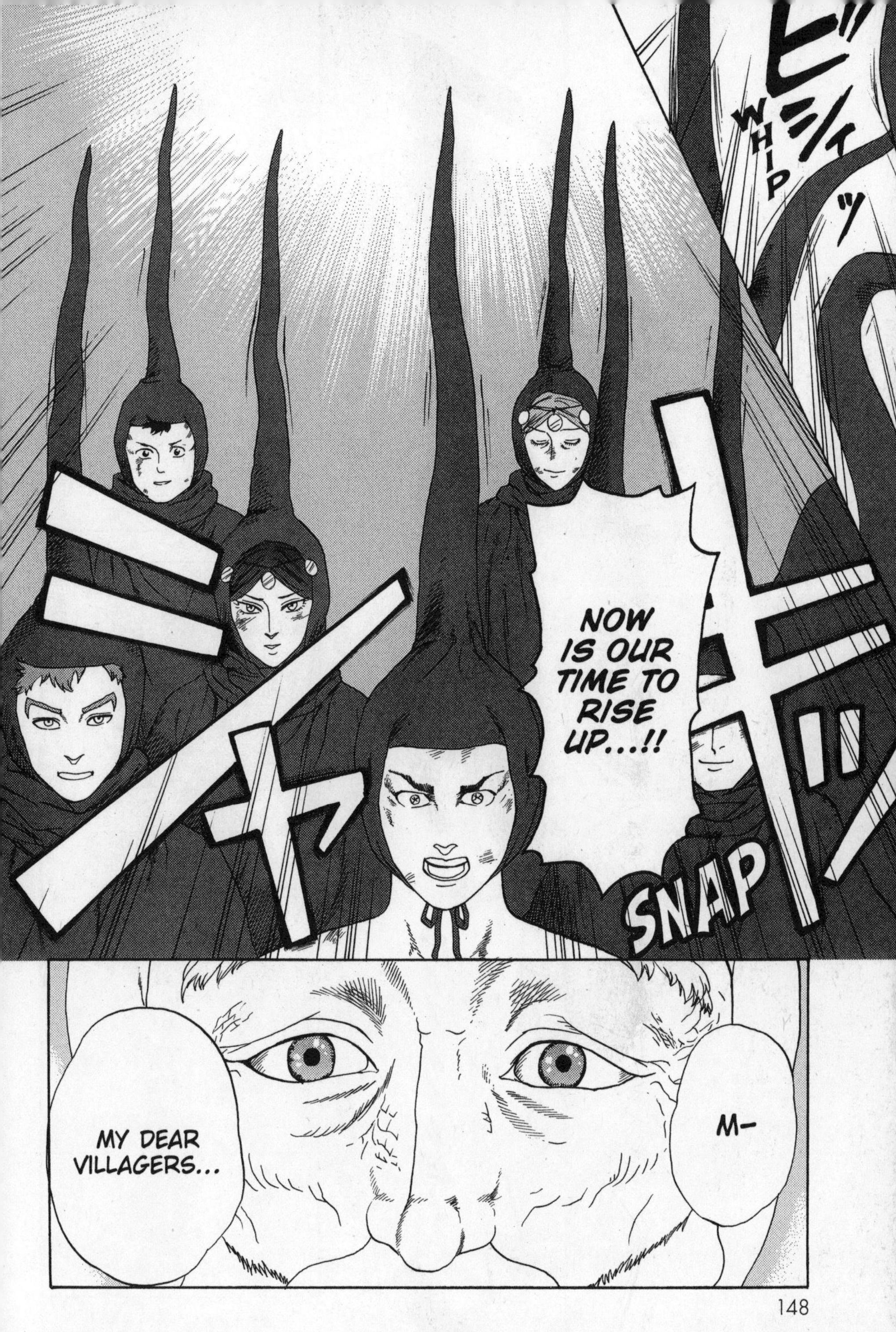
ビシィッ
WHIP
NOW IS OUR TIME TO RISE UP...!!
SNAP
M-
MY DEAR VILLAGERS...

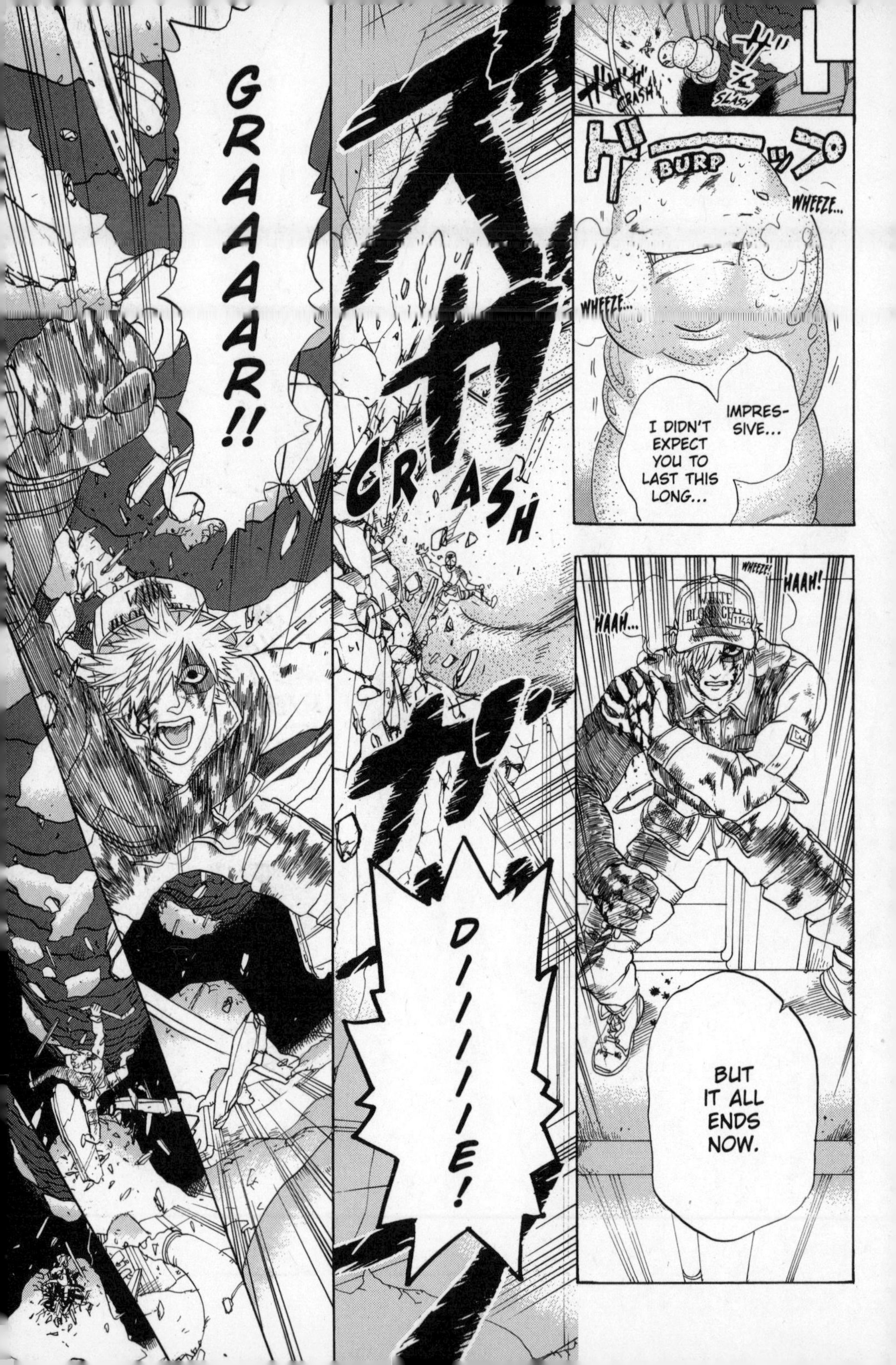

CRASH
SLASH
BURP
WHEEZE...
WHEEZE...
IMPRES-SIVE...
I DIDN'T EXPECT YOU TO LAST THIS LONG...
WHEEZE!
HAAH!
HAAH...
BUT IT ALL ENDS NOW.
CRASH
DIIIIE!
GRAAAAAR!!

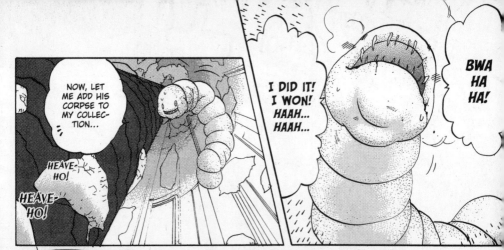

BWA HA HA!
I DID IT! I WON! HAAH... HAAH...
NOW, LET ME ADD HIS CORPSE TO MY COLLECTION...
HEAVE-HO!
HEAVE-HO!
HMM?
HEAVE-HO!
HEAVE-HO!
HEAVE-HO!
HEAVE-HO!
RRRUMBLE
WHAT'S THAT YELLING...?
BASHOONT
HEAVE-HO!
HEAVE-HO!

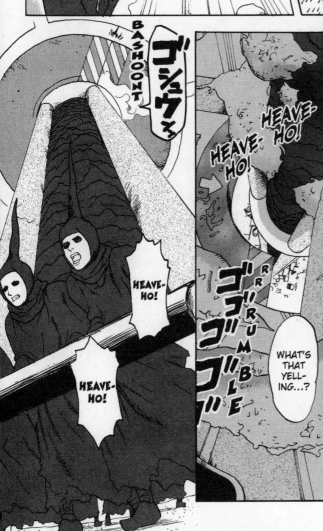

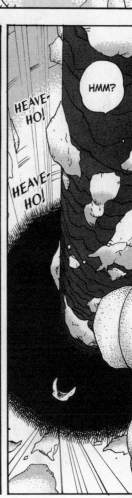

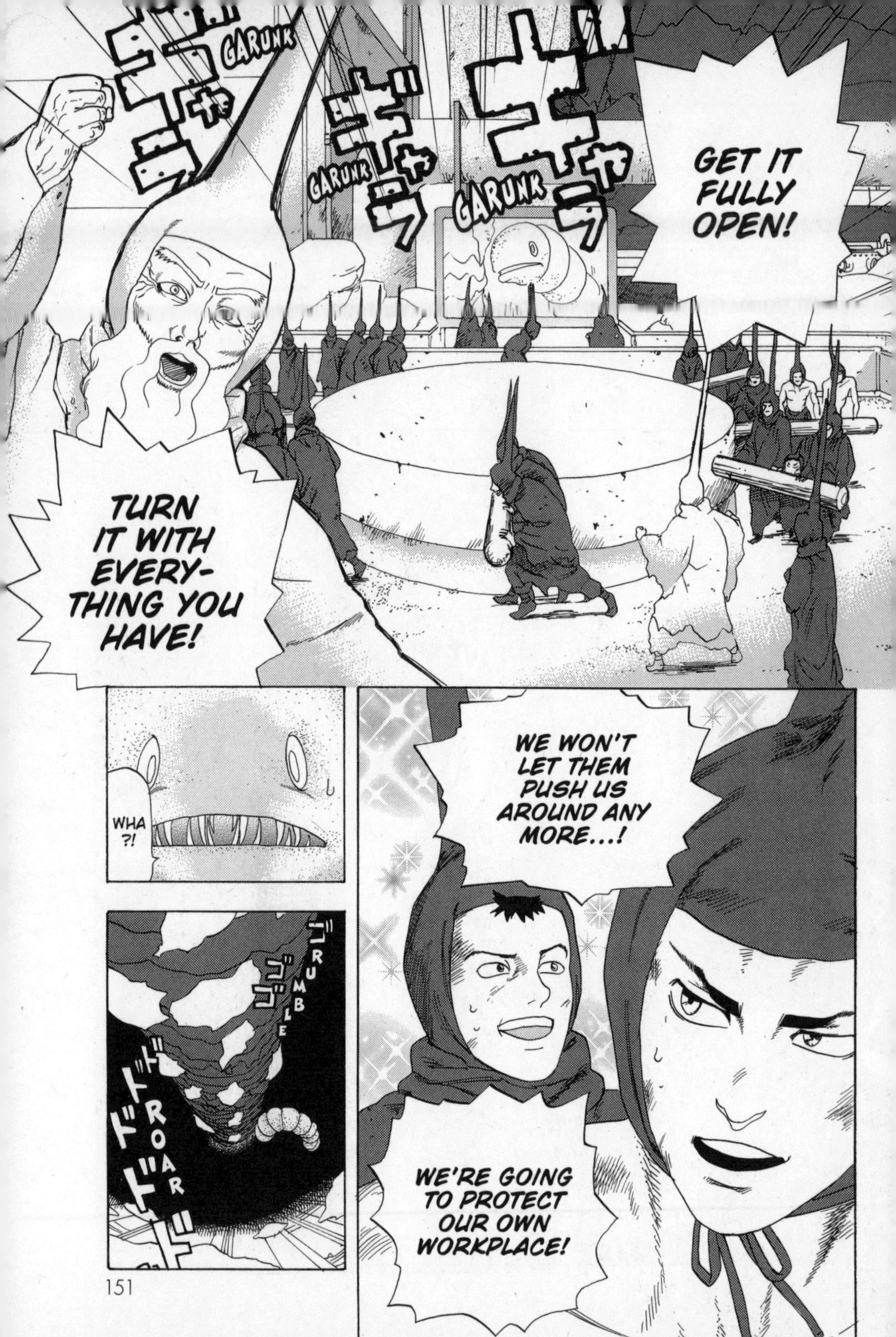
GET IT FULLY OPEN!
GARUNK
GARUNK
GARUNK
TURN IT WITH EVERY-THING YOU HAVE!
WE WON'T LET THEM PUSH US AROUND ANY MORE...!
WE'RE GOING TO PROTECT OUR OWN WORKPLACE!
WHA?!
RUMBLE
ROAR

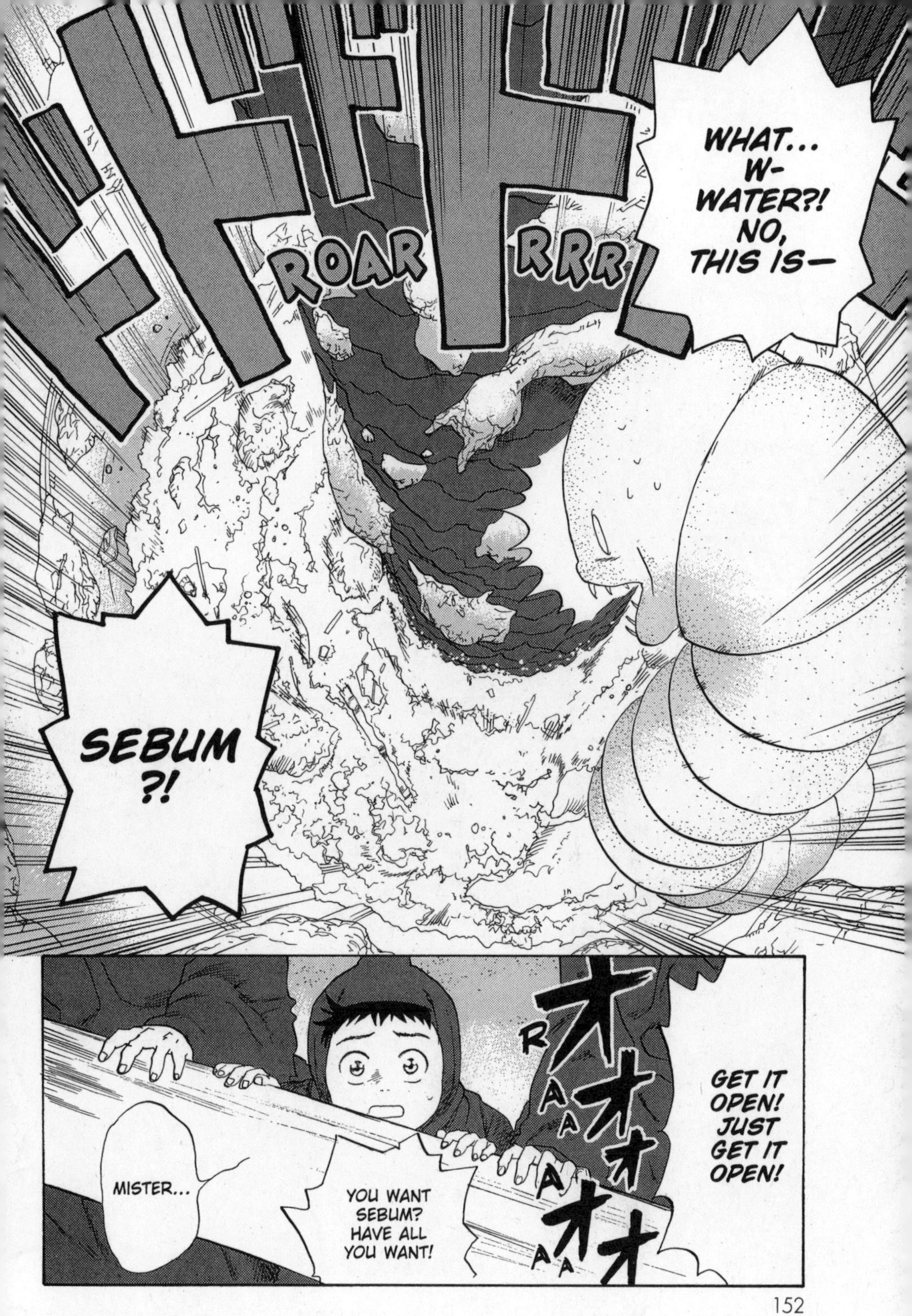
WHAT... W- WATER?! NO, THIS IS—
ROAR RRR
SEBUM ?!
GET IT OPEN! JUST GET IT OPEN!
RAAAA
YOU WANT SEBUM? HAVE ALL YOU WANT!
MISTER...

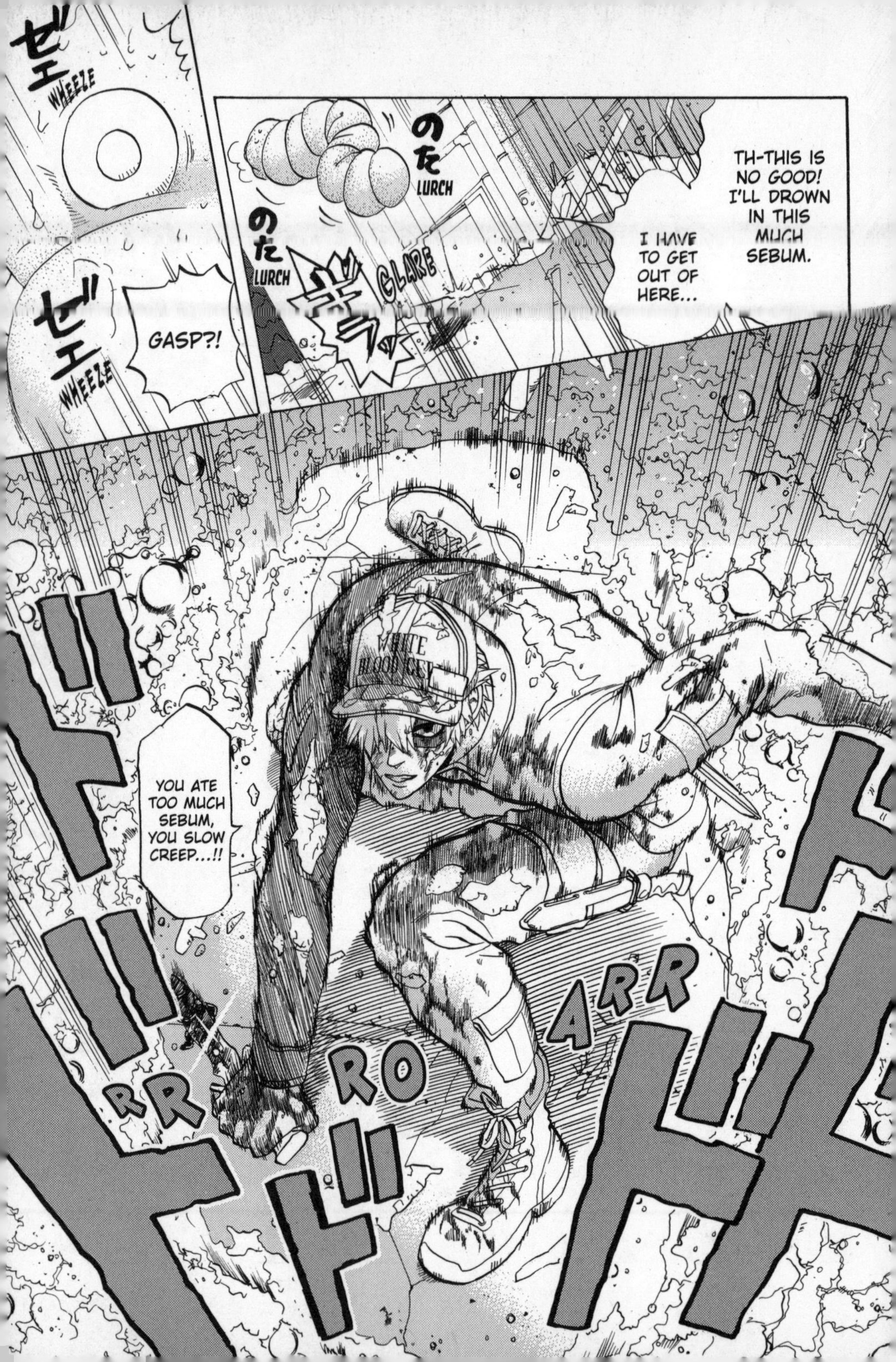
TH-THIS IS NO GOOD! I'LL DROWN IN THIS MUCH SEBUM.
I HAVE TO GET OUT OF HERE...
のた
LURCH
のた
LURCH
ギラッ
GLARE
ゼェ
WHEEZE
GASP?!
ゼェ
WHEEZE
YOU ATE TOO MUCH SEBUM, YOU SLOW CREEP...!!
RRROARR
ドドド

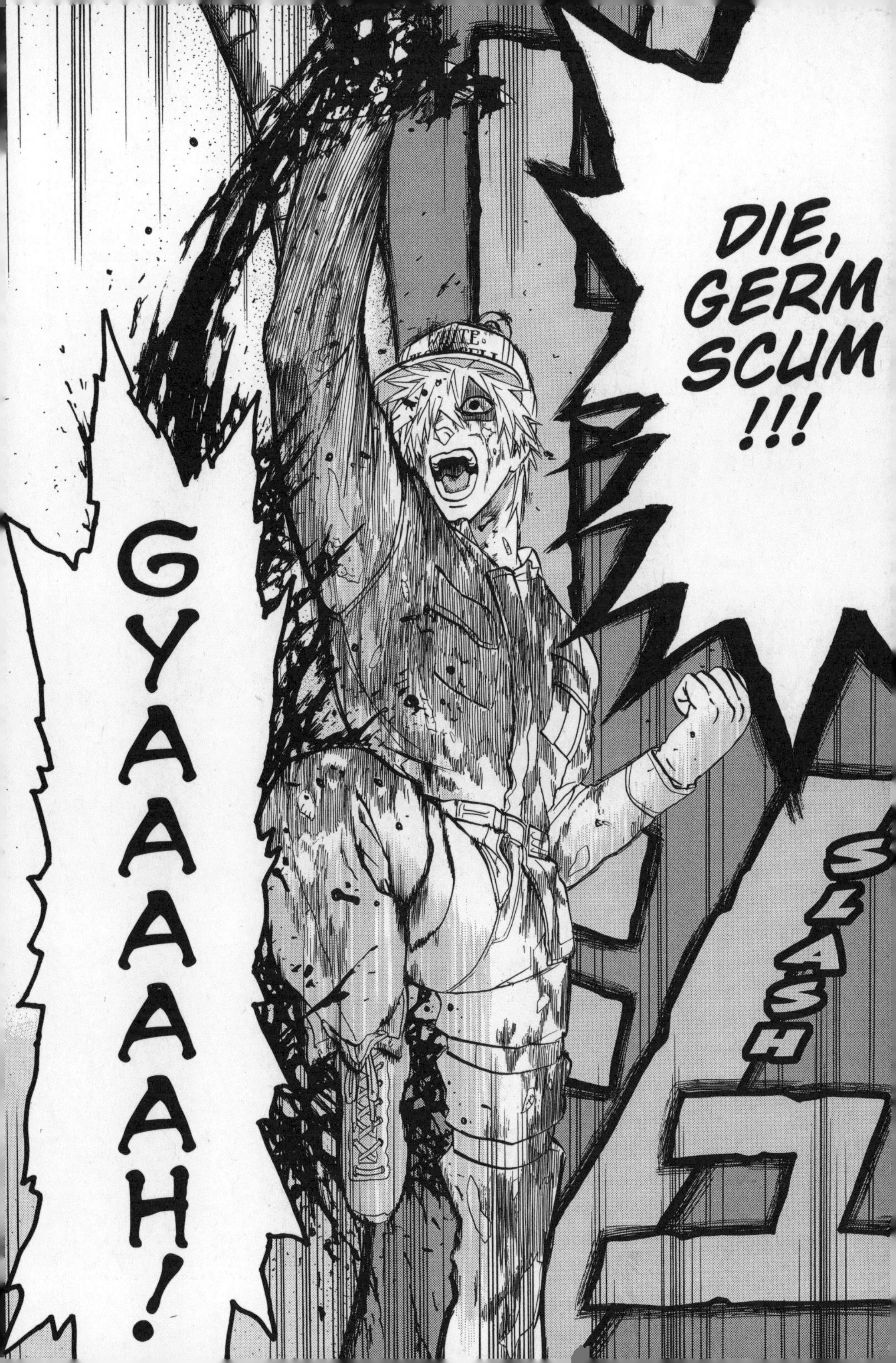
DIE, GERM SCUM!!!
SLASH
GYAAAAAH!

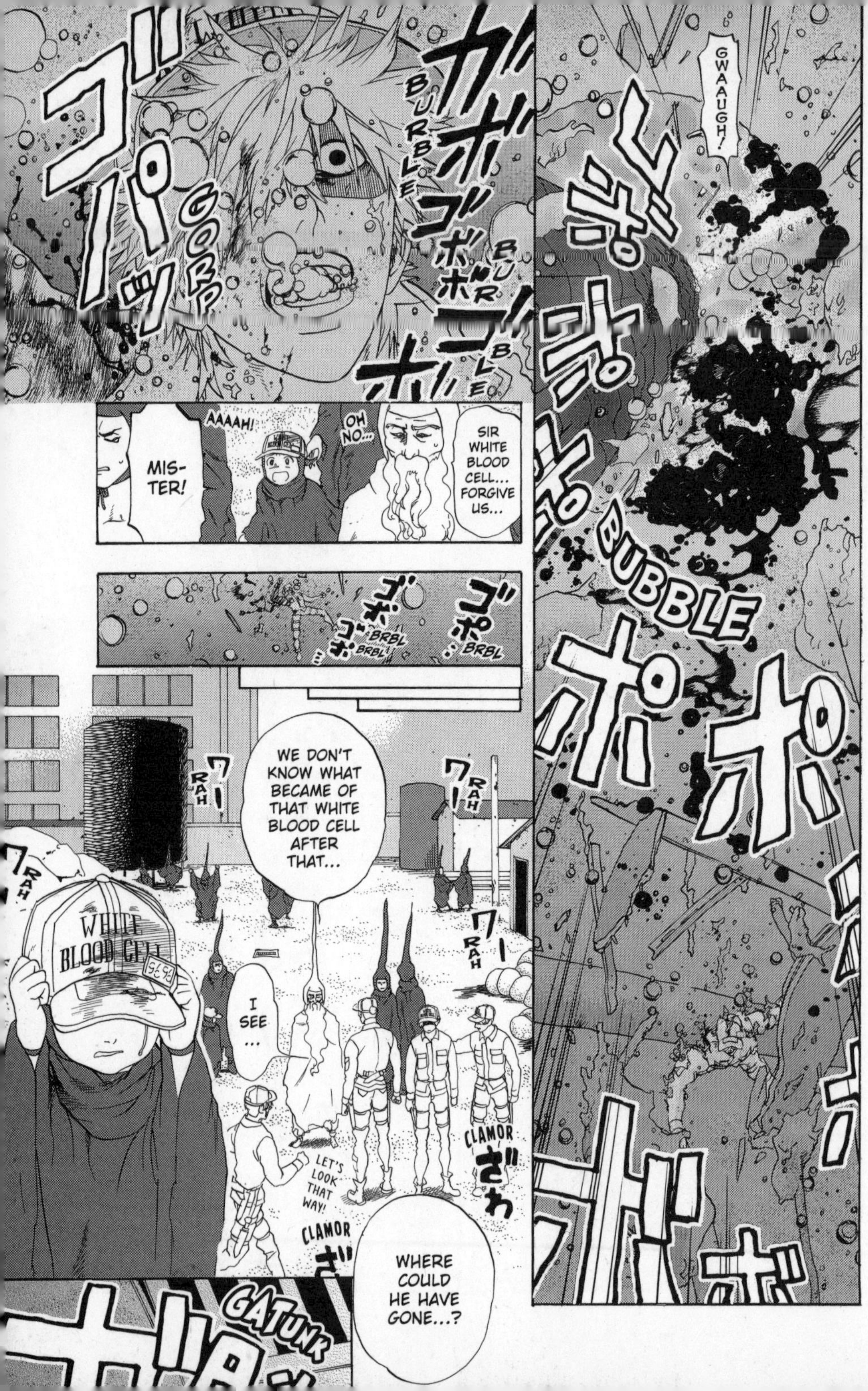
GWAAUGH!
BUBBLE
BURBLE
GORP
BURBLE
OH NO...
SIR WHITE BLOOD CELL... FORGIVE US...
AAAAH!
MIS-TER!
BRBL
BRBL BRBL
RAH
WE DON'T KNOW WHAT BECAME OF THAT WHITE BLOOD CELL AFTER THAT...
RAH
RAH
RAH
WHITE BLOOD CELL
I SEE...
CLAMOR
LET'S LOOK THAT WAY!
CLAMOR
WHERE COULD HE HAVE GONE...?
GATUNK

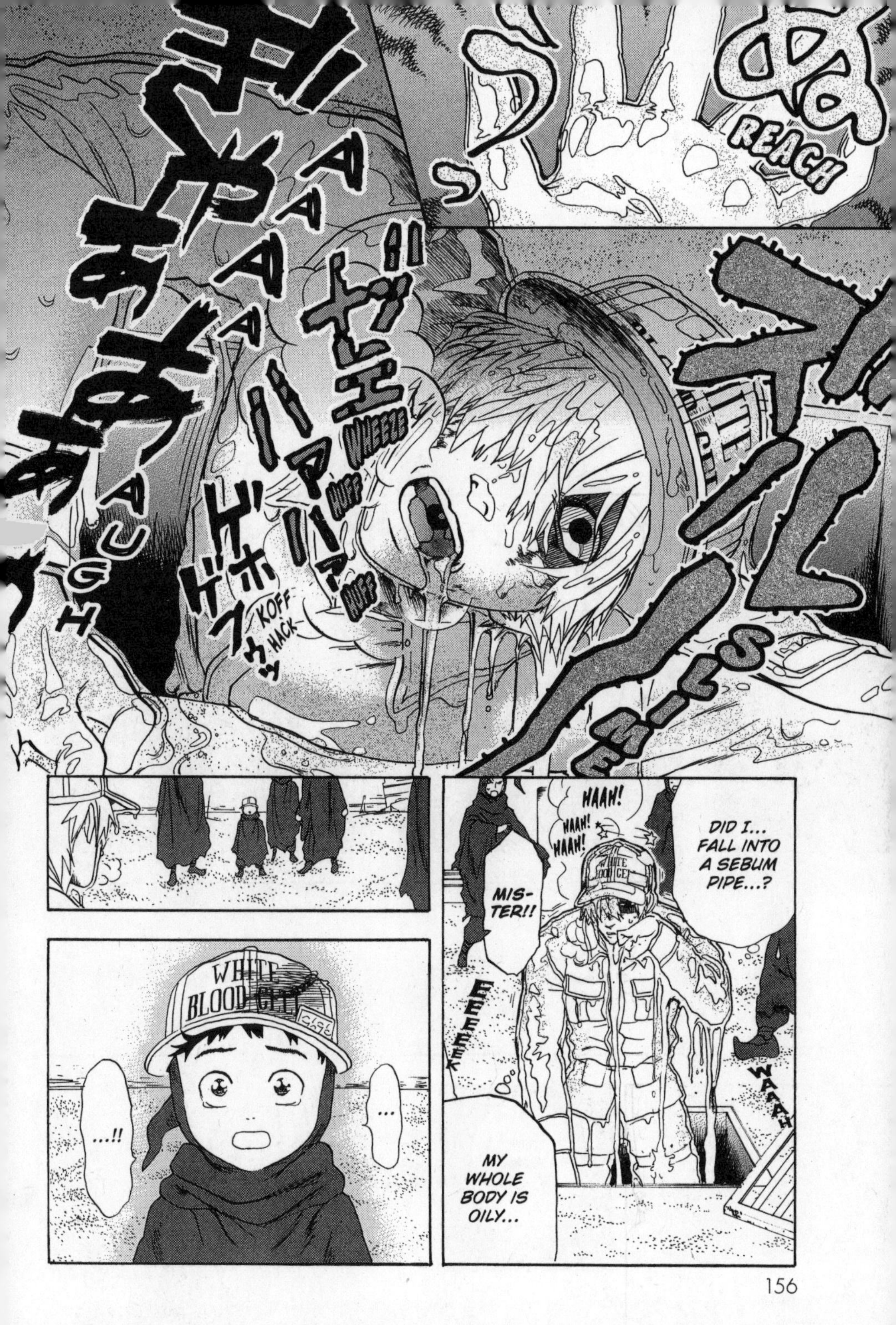

REACH
SLIME
WHEEZE
HUFF
HUFF
KOFF
HACK
AAAAA
AUGH
HAAH!
HAAH!
HAAH!
DID I... FALL INTO A SEBUM PIPE...?
MISTER!!
EEEEEEK
WAAAH
MY WHOLE BODY IS OILY...
WHITE BLOOD CELL
...
...!!

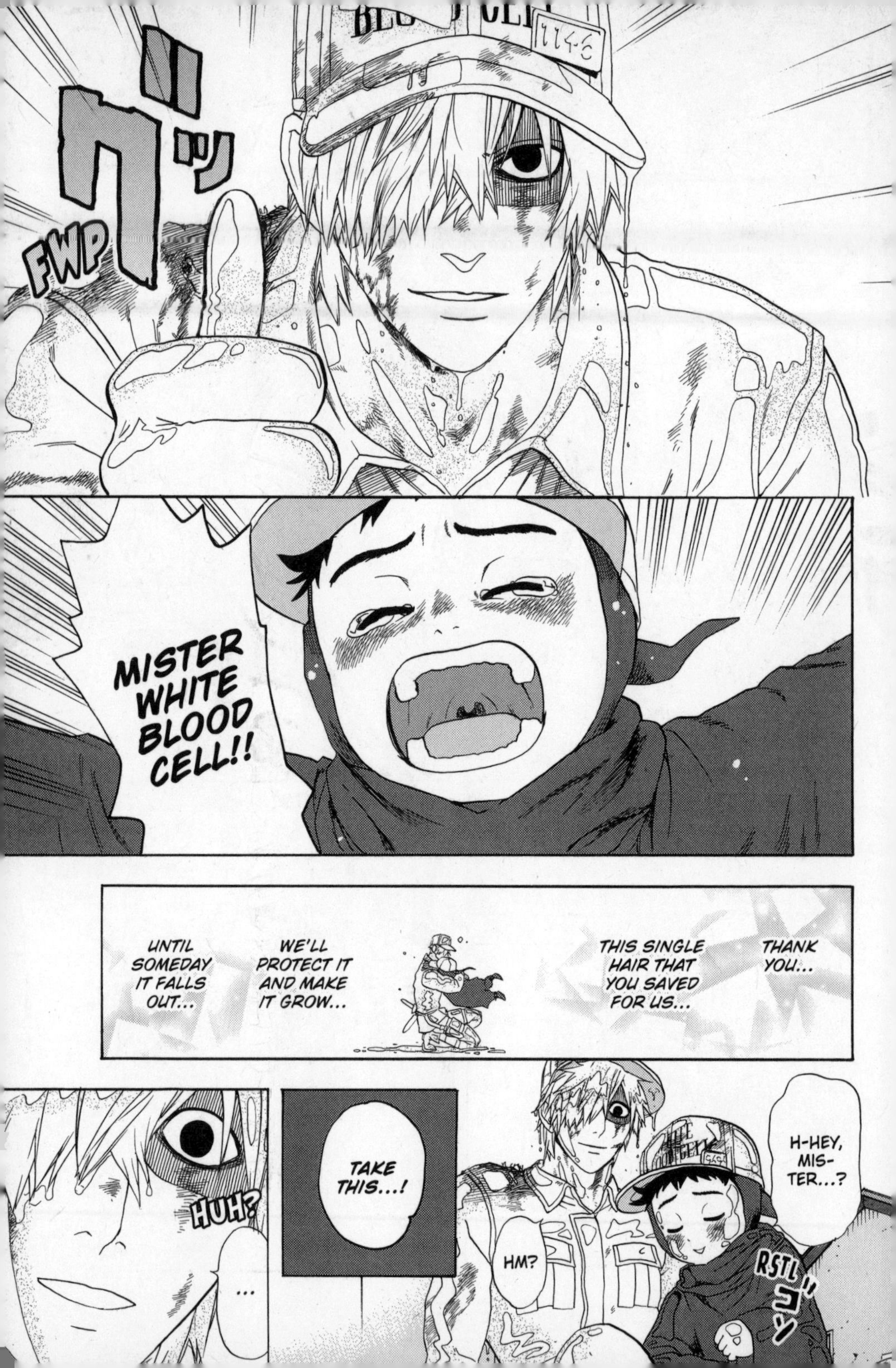
グッ
FWP
MISTER WHITE BLOOD CELL!!
THANK YOU...
THIS SINGLE HAIR THAT YOU SAVED FOR US...
WE'LL PROTECT IT AND MAKE IT GROW...
UNTIL SOMEDAY IT FALLS OUT...
H-HEY, MISTER...?
RSTL
HM?
TAKE THIS...!
HUH?
...

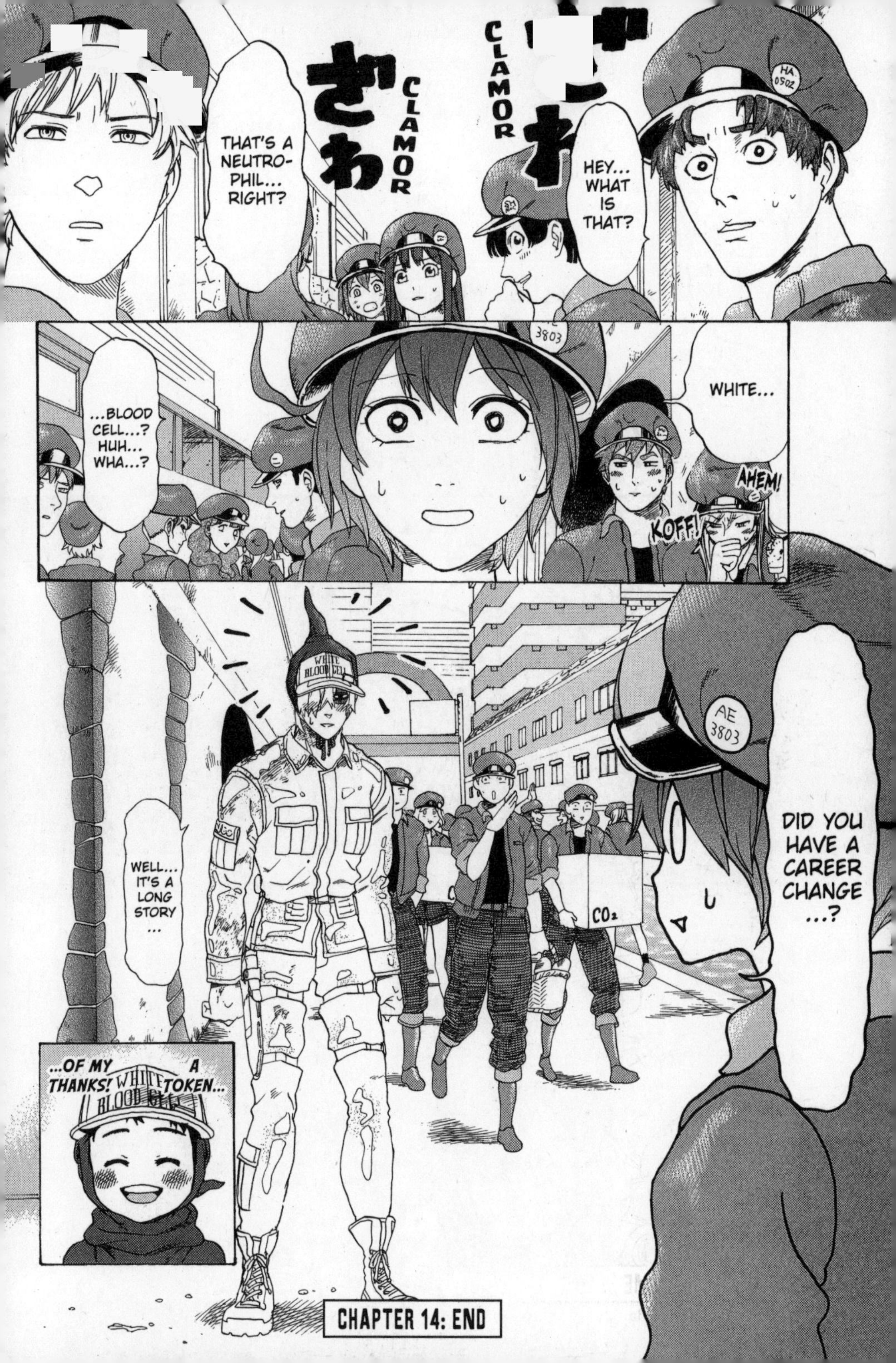
CLAMOR
HEY... WHAT IS THAT?
ざわ
CLAMOR
THAT'S A NEUTROPHIL... RIGHT?
WHITE...
AHEM!
KOFF!
...BLOOD CELL...? HUH... WHA...?
DID YOU HAVE A CAREER CHANGE ...?
WELL... IT'S A LONG STORY ...
A TOKEN... ...OF MY THANKS!
CHAPTER 14: END

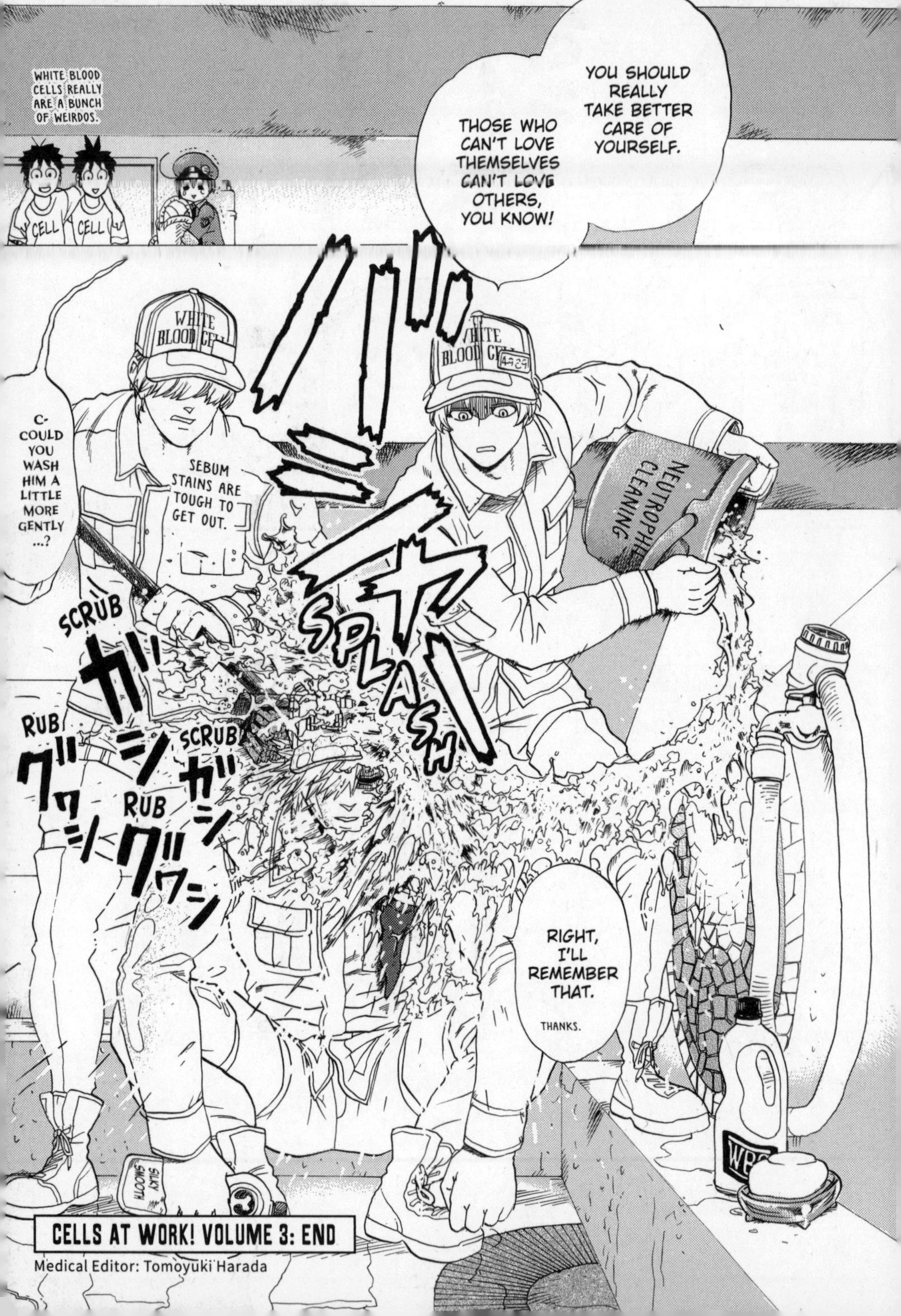
YOU SHOULD REALLY TAKE BETTER CARE OF YOURSELF.
THOSE WHO CAN'T LOVE THEMSELVES CAN'T LOVE OTHERS, YOU KNOW!
WHITE BLOOD CELLS REALLY ARE A BUNCH OF WEIRDOS.
CELL
CELL
WHITE BLOOD CELL
4989
NEUTROPHIL CLEANING
SPLASH
RIGHT, I'LL REMEMBER THAT.
THANKS.
WHITE BLOOD CELL
SEBUM STAINS ARE TOUGH TO GET OUT.
C-COULD YOU WASH HIM A LITTLE MORE GENTLY ...?
SCRUB
RUB
SCRUB
RUB
SILKY SMOOTH
WBC

CELLS AT WORK! VOLUME 3: END

Medical Editor: Tomoyuki Harada

Knives (two types)

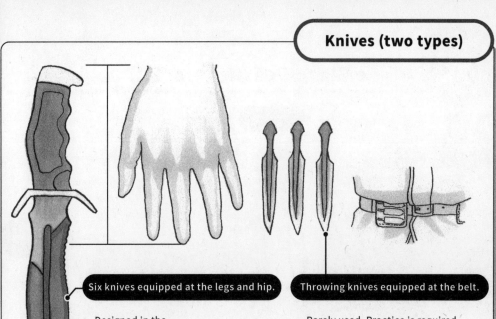

Six knives equipped at the legs and hip.

Designed in the style of a Russian "antiterror" knife.

Throwing knives equipped at the belt.

Rarely used. Practice is required so as to not hit allies when they have to be used.

White Blood Cells and Their Friends

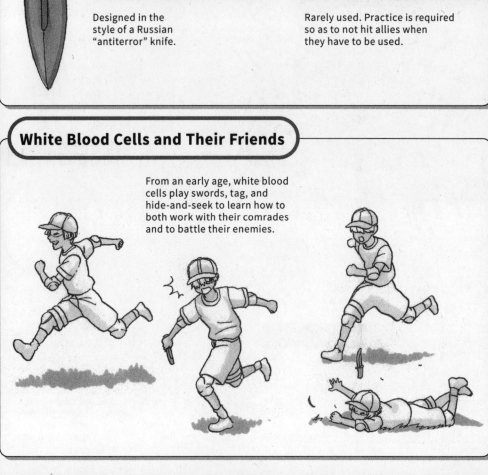

From an early age, white blood cells play swords, tag, and hide-and-seek to learn how to both work with their comrades and to battle their enemies.

*This is a fictitious setting for this manga, and does not reflect scientific fact.

White Blood Cell (Neutrophil) [schematic illustration]

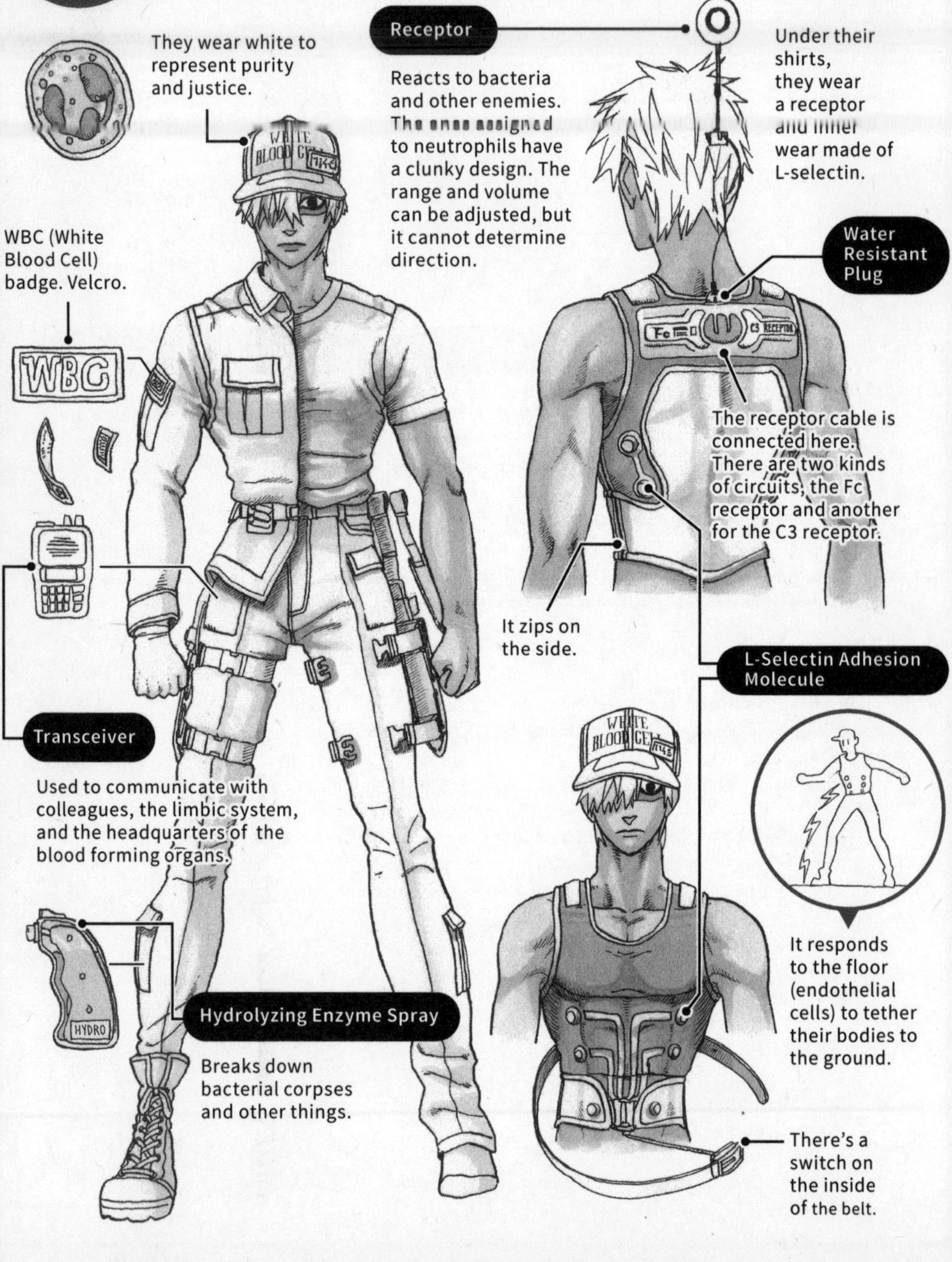

They wear white to represent purity and justice.
WHITE BLOOD CELL 1146
Receptor
Reacts to bacteria and other enemies. The ones assigned to neutrophils have a clunky design. The range and volume can be adjusted, but it cannot determine direction.
Under their shirts, they wear a receptor and inner wear made of L-selectin.
WBC (White Blood Cell) badge. Velcro.
WBC
Water Resistant Plug
Fc
C3 RECEPTOR
The receptor cable is connected here. There are two kinds of circuits, the Fc receptor and another for the C3 receptor.
It zips on the side.
L-Selectin Adhesion Molecule
Transceiver
Used to communicate with colleagues, the limbic system, and the headquarters of the blood forming organs.
WHITE BLOOD CELL 1146
Hydrolyzing Enzyme Spray
HYDRO
Breaks down bacterial corpses and other things.
It responds to the floor (endothelial cells) to tether their bodies to the ground.
There's a switch on the inside of the belt.

Cells at Work! volume 3 is a work of fiction. Names, characters, places, and incidents are the products of the author's imagination or are used fictitiously. Any resemblance to actual events, locales, or persons, living or dead, is entirely coincidental.

A Kodansha Comics Trade Paperback Original.

Published in the United States by Kodansha Comics,
an imprint of Kodansha USA Publishing, LLC, New York.

Publication rights for this English edition arranged through Kodansha Ltd., Tokyo.

First published in Japan in 2016 by Kodansha Ltd., Tokyo, as *Hataraku Saibou* volume 3.

ISBN 978-1-63236-390-9

Printed in the United States of America.

www.kodanshacomics.com

9 8 7 6 5 4 3 2

Translation: Yamato Tanaka
Lettering: Abigail Blackman
Editing: Paul Starr
Kodansha Comics edition cover design: Phil Balsman